The Muslim
Discovery of Europe

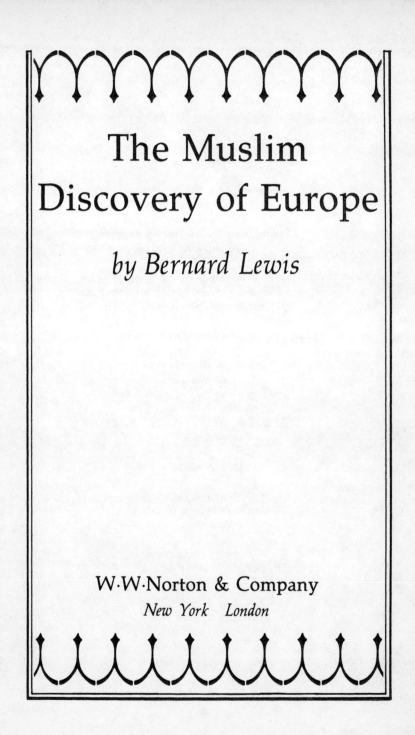

The Muslim
Discovery of Europe

by Bernard Lewis

W·W·Norton & Company
New York   London

For information about permission to reproduce selections from this book,
write to Permissions, W. W. Norton & Company, Inc.,
500 Fifth Avenue, New York, NY 10110

Library of Congress Cataloging in Publication Data
Lewis, Bernard.
The Muslim discovery of Europe.
Includes index.
1. Near East—Relations—Europe. 2. Europe—
Relations—Near East. I. Title.
DS63.2E8L48 1982   303.4'82   81–19009
AACR2

ISBN 0-393-32165-7 pbk.

W. W. Norton & Company, Inc.
500 Fifth Avenue, New York, N.Y. 10110
www.wwnorton.com

W. W. Norton & Company Ltd.
Castle House, 75/76 Wells Street, London W1T 3QT

6 7 8 9 0

To the cherished memory
of
Abdülhak Adnan Adivar
Aziz Ahmad
Mujtaba Minovi
Muhammad al-Nuwaihi
Discoverers, Teachers, Friends

Contents

Note on Transcription

Arabic and Persian are transcribed in accordance with the system most commonly used by Islamicists. For Ottoman I have followed the standard orthography of modern Turkish, in which c = j as in jest, ç = ch as in church, ş = sh as in sheet and ı represents a sound somewhere between i as in will and u as in radium. In the text, but not in the notes and references, I have used j instead of the unfamiliar c for Turkish names.

Preface to the 2001 Paperback Edition

In 1733 Samuel Johnson, then a young man of twenty-four, noted in his first published prose work that "a generous and elevated mind is distinguished by nothing more certainly than an eminent degree of curiosity; nor is that curiosity ever more agreeably or usefully employed, than in examining the laws and customs of foreign nations." Almost half a century later, in a conversation with his friend and biographer James Boswell, Johnson returned to the subject. Boswell had remarked: "I should wish to go and see some country totally different from what I have been used to; such as Turkey, where religion and everything else are different." To which Johnson replied: "Yes, Sir; there are two objects of curiosity,—the Christian world, and the Mahometan world. All the rest may be considered as barbarous."[1]

Johnson's dismissal of the great Asian and other civilizations as "barbarous" is of course absurd but not untypical of the ignorance and prejudice of the time. More interesting is his recognition of Islam as a religiously defined civilization comparable with Christendom, and therefore worthy of study.

Because of the long struggle between the two, fought over centuries and indeed millennia, their essential kinship has often been overlooked on both sides. Yet the two have much in common, and certainly far more in common with each other than either has with those remoter civilizations that Johnson so cavalierly dismissed as "barbarous." They share the same roots in the Judaic and Hellenistic traditions and the more ancient civilizations of the Middle East. And to Hellenistic philosophy and science and Judaic prophecy and revelation, they added a further element alien to both: the firm belief, held by the followers of both religions, that they are the exclusive possessors of God's final truth, which it is their duty to bring, by whatever means, to all humanity.

Between two such claimants, historically consecutive, theologically akin, geographically adjacent, conflict was inevitable.

Christian awareness of the new competing faith began almost immediately after its advent, with the triumphant emergence of the new religion from its Arabian homeland and its spread eastward to the borders of India and China, westward across North Africa and the Mediterranean islands into Europe. The vast majority of converts to the new religion, west of Iran, were converts from Christianity. The lands on the eastern and southern shores of the Mediterranean had been part of the Christian Roman Empire; they became and remained part of the realm of Islam. The advance went even further, including Sicily, which was restored to Christian rule at the end of the eleventh century, and the Iberian peninsula, where eight centuries of Christian-Muslim struggle ended in 1492 with the Christian conquest of Granada, the last center of Muslim power in Spain. For a while it seemed that all Europe was about to be absorbed, as Muslim armies from Spain crossed the Pyrenees and advanced into France, while others moved from conquered Sicily into the Italian mainland. In the year 846 an Arab fleet from Sicily even entered the Tiber, and raiders sacked Ostia and Rome. The Muslim advance on western Europe was eventually held and repelled, but other threats came from the East—the Islamized Tatars in Russia and, of far greater importance, the Turks, who conquered all of Greece and the Balkans twice, in 1529 and again in 1683, laid siege to Vienna, in the very heart of Christian Europe.

It is therefore not surprising that medieval Christian Europeans were keenly aware of what they saw as the Muslim threat—a double threat of both conquest and conversion. Rudimentary prudence dictated that they should learn something about their attackers, and about the religion they professed. Here and there, scholars in Europe, mostly Christian priests, tried to learn something about Islam, and equip themselves to refute its doctrines. A landmark was the completion, in July 1143, of a Latin translation of the Qur'ān, produced by the English scholar Robert of Ketton under the auspices of the famous Abbot of Cluny, Peter the Venerable.

But the study of Arabic in European Christendom was not restricted to such polemical purposes, which in any case were beginning to lose their urgency. There was another and, in the long run, more compelling motive. The civilization of the Arab Islamic world in the Middle Ages was in every sense on a higher level than that of Christian Europe. In mathematics, medicine and more generally in the sciences, a command of Arabic gave access to the most advanced knowledge existing at the time, specifically to translations of ancient originals, lost and forgotten in Europe, as well as the new material arising from the studies and experiments conducted by scientists in the Islamic world.

By the end of the Middle Ages both motives had lost their force. European scientists had caught up with and were beginning to surpass their colleagues in the Islamic world, and, in Western Europe at least, Christendom no longer felt threatened by either the weight of Muslim arms or the seduction of Muslim teachings. But the study of Arabic and of the culture enshrined in it did not diminish. On the contrary, it increased, but this time with a new motivation—the intellectual curiosity of the Renaissance and, nourishing it, the philological scholarship of the rapidly evolving humanist tradition. Centers of Arabic and related studies developed in most Western countries, and in the course of the sixteenth and early seventeenth centuries became part of the university curriculum.

A modern observer may wonder why so much attention was given to Arabic and so little to Turkish, at that time the language of government and commerce in the Middle East and even to some extent in North Africa. Thus, letters from the rulers of Algiers and Tunis preserved in Western archives are mostly in Turkish, the language of rulers, not Arabic, the language of their subjects.

The answer is clear. There were no chairs of Turkish in European universities for the same reason that there were no chairs of English or French or German. Modern languages were not a fit subject for scholarly teaching and research. Arabic, in contrast, was a classical and scriptural language, worthy to take its place with Latin, Greek and Biblical Hebrew.

Christian Europe had compelling reasons to interest itself in the languages and culture of the Middle East. In addition to the obvious appeal of an older and richer civilization and the even more obvious threat of a powerful and invading enemy, there was the call of religion. For the Christian, even in the far north, the very heart of his religion was in the Holy Land, since the seventh century under Muslim rule. His Bible and the faith that it enshrined had come to him from the Middle East, much of it written in Middle Eastern languages, and recording events in Middle Eastern lands. His places of pilgrimage—Jerusalem, Bethlehem, Nazareth—were all under Muslim rule, and except for the brief interval of the Crusades it was only by Muslim permission that he could visit them as a pilgrim.

The Muslim had no comparable concern with Christian Europe. His religion was born in Arabia; his prophet was an Arab; his scriptures were in Arabic; and his places of pilgrimage, Mecca and Medina, were safely in Muslim lands. Nor was there much else to attract Muslims to Europe. Its primary export to the Islamic world was its own people, as slaves; indeed, until the beginning of the modern age, there was little else in Europe to arouse their interest or curiosity. True, they were very interested in certain parts of the heritage of ancient Greece, but their concern was limited to what was useful: medicine, chemistry, mathematics, geography, astronomy, and also philosophy, in those days still numbered among the useful sciences. The medieval Muslims translated—or, to be precise, procured translations of—a large part of the philosophical and scientific literature of Greek antiquity; they did not, however, show any interest in the Greek poets, dramatists or historians.

Nor did they find anything of intellectual value in the Europe of their own day. During the centuries of the Arab presence in Spain and Sicily, the Tatar presence in Russia and, a little later, the Turkish presence in the Balkans, there is virtually no sign of any interest in either the classical languages of Europe or the vernaculars. Where translators were needed for practical purposes, Muslim rulers could always find them among their Christian or Jewish subjects, or among converts from those religions. One might put it this way: they were aware of belonging to the most advanced and enlightened civilization in the world, and of being the fortunate possessors of the richest and most advanced of languages. Everything worth reading or knowing was available in their language, or could be made available by immigrants or foreigners. It is an attitude that many of us today will easily recognize.

By the beginning of the nineteenth century, Muslims, first in Turkey and then elsewhere, were becoming aware of the changed balance, not only of power but also of knowledge, between Christendom and Islam, and, for the first time, they thought it worth the effort to learn European languages. The Ottoman historian Asim, writing in about 1808, observes: "Certain sensualists, naked of the garment of loyalty, from time to time learned politics from them; some, desirous of learning their language, took French teachers, acquired their idiom, and prided themselves . . . on their uncouth talk."[2] It is not until well into the nineteenth century that we find any attempt in any of the languages of the Middle East to produce grammars of dictionaries that would enable speakers of those languages to learn a Western language. And when it did happen, it was due largely to the initiative of those two detested intruders, the imperialist and the missionary. This is surely a striking contrast and it has prompted many to ask the question: why were the Muslims so uninterested?

This, I would suggest, is the wrong question. It was the Muslims who were being normal, not the Europeans. Not being interested in other cultures is the normal state of mankind. It was a peculiarity of the European and one can, indeed, be more specific, of the Western European during a certain period in his history, to exhibit this kind of interest in alien cultures to which he has no visible or ascertainable relationship. This kind of intellectual curiosity has evoked puzzlement and sometimes suspicion, especially among those who do not share it.

For most of the Middle Ages, statesmen and scholars in the great cities of the Islamic world looked on Europe as an outer darkness of barbarism and unbelief, offering nothing of interest and little of value. From time to time Muslim diplomats, traders or captives visited these people and, on their return, offered to their mainly uninterested compatriots some brief accounts of their quaint and primitive ways. Only a radical change of the relative positions of the two societies, and a dawning Muslim awareness of that change, evoked a new interest or rather, more specifically, a new concern.

Preface

In the Western tradition of history, the term discovery is commonly used to describe the process by which, from the fifteenth century onwards, Europe and more especially Western Europe set about discovering the rest of the world. The theme of this book is another and parallel discovery, similar in some ways, different in others, beginning earlier and continuing later, in which the European is not the explorer discovering barbaric peoples in strange and remote places, but is himself an exotic barbarian discovered and observed by enquirers from the lands of Islam. In the following pages an attempt is made to examine the sources and nature of Muslim knowledge concerning the West and the stages of its growth. The story begins with the first Muslim incursions into Europe. It continues with the great counteroffensive of Western Christendom against Islam and the resumption of the Muslim Holy War which that evoked; with the renewal and extension of commercial and diplomatic relations between the Muslim and Christian shores of the Mediterranean; and with the rise, after the end of the Middle Ages, of new Muslim monarchies in Turkey, Iran, and Morocco and their tentative explorations of Europe. It concludes with the first stages of the massive European impact, from the late eighteenth century onwards, on the Middle Eastern heartlands of Islam, and the beginnings of a new era in which the Muslim discovery of Europe was forced, massive, and, for the most part, painful.

The book falls into three parts. The first surveys the course of relations between Islam and western Europe, dealing with familiar events from an unfamiliar angle—that of the adversary. I have tried to see the battles of Tours and Poitiers through the eyes not of Charles Martel but of his Arab opponents; Lepanto from the perspective of the Turks; and the siege of Vienna from the camp of the besiegers. This narrative is characterized by the emphasis it gives to the Muslim view of the world and Islam's place in it.

The second part is concerned with media and intermediaries; with the languages used for communication between Muslims and Europeans, including questions of translation and interpretation, and with travelers—merchants, diplomats, spies, and others—who journeyed from Islamic lands to Europe. Some attention is also given to the role, as intermediaries, of refugees, of the non-Muslim subjects of the Muslim states, and of the new recruits to Islam from Europe. This section concludes with a look at the image of Western Europe as reflected in Islamic scholarship, more particularly in historical and geographical writings.

The third section of the book is devoted to specific topics—to economic matters, government and justice, science and technology, literature and the arts, people and society.

Much has been written in recent years about the discovery of Islam by Europe. In most of these discussions, however, the Muslim has appeared as the silent and passive victim. But the relationship between Islam and Europe, whether in war or in peace, has always been a dialogue, not a monologue: the process of discovery was mutual. Muslim perceptions of the West are no less deserving of study than Western perceptions of Islam, and have received less attention.

This book has been a long time in the making. I became interested in the subject more than twenty-five years ago, and presented a first paper to the International Congress of Historical Sciences in Rome in 1955. It was followed by other articles dealing with aspects of the discovery, and lectures delivered at universities and learned societies in North Africa, the Middle East and elsewhere, including several American universities. The material was first presented at greater length in a series of broadcasts in the Third Programme of the B.B.C. in 1957 and, most recently, in five public lectures delivered at the Collège de France in May 1980. To my hosts and audiences in all those places I am greatly indebted for the opportunities they offered to present and sometimes improve my exposition.

Preface ◆ 13

There remains the pleasant duty of thanking those who have in various ways contributed to the completion and publication of this work. I would like to express particular appreciation to Ms. Dorothy Rothbard of Princeton University and Ms. Peggy Clarke of the Institute for Advanced Study for their care and skill in typing and retyping my manuscript, sometimes under rather adverse conditions; to Ms. Cathy Kornovich of W. W. Norton for her meticulous and invaluable editorial work with the final typescript; to four graduate students at Princeton, Ms. Shaun Marmon and Mr. Alan Makovsky, for much valuable help, particularly in the final preparation, to Mr. David Eisenberg for reading and correcting a set of proofs, and to Mr. James L. Yarrison for some helpful suggestions; to Miss Norah Titley of the British Library, London, and Professor Glyn Meredith Owens of the University of Toronto for help and advice in finding suitable pictorial material to illustrate this volume; and to my friend and colleague Professor Charles Issawi for reading the final manuscript and offering a number of useful comments.

Princeton
April 20, 1981

The Muslim
Discovery of Europe

I

Contact and Impact

In the early years of the seventh century, when the Prophet Muhammad began his mission in Arabia, the whole of the Mediterranean world was still part of Christendom. On the European, Asian, and African shores alike, almost all the inhabitants were Christians of various denominations. Of the other religions of the Greco-Roman world, only two, Judaism and Manichaeism, had survived and were professed by minorities in these lands. In the eastern Mediterranean, the East Roman Empire, known to scholarship as the Byzantine Empire, continued to flourish, and with Constantinople as its capital ruled over Syria, Palestine, Egypt, and part of North Africa as well as Asia Minor and southeastern Europe. In the western Mediterranean, the Roman state had fallen, but the barbarian peoples, and the kingdoms they raised on the ruins of Rome, had adopted the Christian religion and tried with intermittent success to maintain at least the forms of the Roman state and the Christian church. Nor was the realm of Christendom limited to the Mediterranean lands. Beyond the eastern border of Byzantium, Mesopotamia, the metropolitan and westernmost province of the Persian Empire, was by the early seventh century predominantly Christian and thus part of the Christian though not the Roman world. Even in Arabia, beyond the imperial frontiers of both

Rome and Persia, Christian and Jewish minorities lived among the pagan majority.

Within a few decades of the death of Muḥammad in 632, his Arab followers had burst out of the Arabian Peninsula, attacked Byzantium and Persia, the two great empires that had divided the Middle East between them, and wrested vast territories from both. The Empire of Persia was conquered and absorbed in its entirety. From the Roman world the Arabs took Syria, Palestine, Egypt, and the rest of North Africa which, in turn, became their springboard for the invasion of Spain and the Mediterranean islands, notably Sicily. Defeating both the Byzantine and the barbarian armies, they were able to incorporate these countries in the new Islamic Empire and to threaten Christendom from both ends. In the east, Arab armies from Syria and Iraq pressed against Anatolia, then a Greek and Christian land and the heartland of the Byzantine Empire, while other Arab and Berber armies in the west swept from conquered Spain across the Pyrenees and threatened to engulf all of Western Europe. For a while, Muslim armies occupied Sicily, parts of southern Italy, and seemed to menace even Rome itself.

In the historical tradition of the West, the decisive battle which halted the Muslim advance and saved Western Europe for Christianity was the Battle of Tours and Poitiers, where, in the year 732, the Franks, commanded by Charles Martel, inflicted a decisive defeat on the armies of Islam. It was indeed on this occasion that the very notion of Europe as an entity which could be threatened or saved appeared for the first time. A famous passage from Gibbon's *Decline and Fall of the Roman Empire* may serve to illustrate the Western perception of this battle and of the fate which it averted:

> A victorious line of march had been prolonged above a thousand miles from the Rock of Gibraltar to the banks of the Loire; the repetition of an equal space would have carried the Saracens to the confines of Poland and the Highlands of Scotland; the Rhine is not more impassable than the Nile or the Euphrates, and the Arabian fleet might have sailed without a naval combat into the mouth of the Thames. Perhaps the interpretation of the Koran would now be taught in the schools of Oxford, and her pulpits might demonstrate to a circumcised people the sanctity and truth of the Revelation of Mahomet.[1]

"From such calamities," Gibbon continues, "was Christendom delivered by the genius and fortune of one man."

The Muslim tradition reflects a different view of the achievement of Charles Martel and the results of the Battle of Tours and Poitiers. The Arabs have a rich historiographic literature, celebrating in loving detail the successive phases of the jihād, the holy struggle for the faith against the unbelievers, and recording with meticulous honesty the setbacks as well as the victories of the conquerors.

They were, of course, well aware that in France they had reached the limits of their westward expansion, and some authors speak of Narbonne, a city which the Arabs held until 759 A.D., as "the last of the Muslim conquests in the land of the Franks." A later writer, interested in wonders and marvels, even tells of a statue in Narbonne with an inscription which read: "Turn back, sons of Ishmael, this is as far as you go. If you question me, I shall answer you, and if you do not go back, you will smite each other until the Day of Resurrection."[2] But the Arab historians of the Middle Ages mention the names neither of Tours nor of Poitiers, and know nothing of Charles Martel. The battle is mentioned under the name of Balāṭ al-Shuhadā', the Highway of the Martyrs, and is presented as a comparatively minor engagement. The name is not attested until the eleventh century and then only in the writings of Spanish Arab historians. In the Arabic historiography of the East, the event receives at most a passing mention. Ibn ʿAbd al-Ḥakam (803–871), author of the most important Arabic account of the conquest of North Africa and Spain, has only this to say:

> ʿUbayda [the governor of North Africa] had given authority over Spain to ʿAbd al-Raḥmān ibn ʿAbdallah al-ʿAkki. ʿAbd al-Raḥmān was a worthy man who made expeditions against the Franks. They are the remotest of the enemies of Spain. He gained much booty and overcame them. . . . Then he went on another excursion and he and all his companions suffered martyrdom for Islam. His death . . . took place in the year 115 [733–34]."[3]

Other historians are equally brief. It is noteworthy that Ṭabarī (d. 923), the most important Arabic historian of the East, and Ibn al-Qūṭiyya (d. 977), the first major historian of Muslim Spain, make no mention at all of the Battle of Tours and Poitiers.

If, however, the Muslim historiographic tradition either omits the Battle of Tours and Poitiers, or mentions it only as a minor episode, it has in contrast a great deal to say about the contemporaneous Arab attempts to conquer Constantinople. These unsuccessful sieges and assaults are celebrated both in history and in legend, and some episodes in the battle have even found their way into the eschatological details of the events that will presage the coming of the Messianic Age.

There can be little doubt that in disregarding Poitiers and stressing Constantinople, the Muslim historians saw events in a truer perspective than the later Western historians. The Frankish victors at Poitiers encountered little more than a band of raiders operating beyond their most distant frontiers, thousands of miles from home. They overcame a force that had already reached its limits and was spent. The Greek defenders of Constantinople, in contrast, met the flower of the caliph's armies, launched from home bases in a major attack on the enemy capital. The Greeks met and halted the force of Islam while it was still fresh and strong. From the Rock of Gibraltar to the banks of the Loire, as Gibbon remarks, is more than a thousand miles. But the Rock of Gibraltar lay many thousands of miles from Arabia. For the Arabs, the way to the Rhine through eastern Europe was shorter and easier—far less arduous than the road which they had taken to the Oxus and the borders of China. It was the failure of the Arab army to conquer Constantinople, not the defeat of an Arab raiding party at Tours and Poitiers, which enabled both Eastern and Western Christendom to survive.

The Arabs were well aware of the difference between the two Christendoms. For the Byzantines they commonly used the term Rūm, the Arabic and, later, also the Persian and Turkish form of Rome. Byzantium called itself the Roman Empire and its people called themselves Romans. To this day, the common term for Greeks in the languages of Islam is Rūm, the territories of the former Byzantine Empire are known as the lands of Rūm, and the Greek language is called Rūmī. Incidentally, even among the Greeks themselves, the Christian form of their language, both Byzantine and modern, is often known as *Romaike.* Arab geographers were not unaware that in Italy, too, there was a city bearing the name of Rome. This, however, was not widely known, and was seen as far less important than the other Rome by the Bosporus.

Despite the defeat at Constantinople, Muslim armies continued to advance both on the eastern and western borders of their empire. But they were reaching the limits of their expansion. In the west, the conquest of Sicily between 827 and 902 was the only significant territorial gain. In the east, the Muslims were halted at the borders of India and China. In the center, the Byzantine frontier remained relatively calm, and the capture of Constantinople was postponed to a remote future.

The holy war in its first great phase had virtually come to an end. The fire and passion of the early conquerors were long since spent; their hunger, whether for booty or martyrdom, satisfied. The new caliphal dynasty, the Abbasids, who had succeeded the Umayyads in the mid–eighth century, had shifted the capital eastwards from Syria to Iraq. In doing so they transformed the caliphate into an Asian rather than a Mediterranean empire. Their interest in the holy war was perfunctory, their concern with their western borders minimal.

For a while new Muslim states, based on Mediterranean countries, continued the struggle against the European Christians. But before long their attention was deflected from the holy war against the infidel to pressing internal problems. Since early times there had been sectarian differences within the Islamic world, between the mainstream Sunni form of Islam of which the Abbasid caliph in Baghdad was the legitimate chief, and the various sects, most of them loosely grouped under the heading of Shīʿa, who challenged both the consensus of the Sunnis and the legitimacy of the Sunni caliph. During the tenth century, a sectarian rival caliphate, that of the Fatimids, emerged, first in Tunisia and then in Egypt, and challenged the Abbasids for the headship of the whole Islamic world. There had been other autonomous and even independent rulers in Muslim states before the Fatimids, but most of them had been willing to pay at least lip service to the suzerainty of the Sunni Abbasid caliph. The Fatimids denied even this, and, on the contrary, claimed themselves to be the sole legitimate caliphs of Islam, who had come to oust the Abbasid usurpers. Instead of one there were now two caliphs in Islam and they soon became three when the Umayyad Emir of Cordova in Spain, threatened by Fatimid expansionism and subversion, proclaimed himself caliph in his own dominions. The religious schism and the clash of rival caliphates now became the main concern of the Muslim world, and the old conflict on the borders was all but forgotten. Both the Sunnis and Shīʿa came to share the general feeling that the heroic age was over, that the boundaries between Islam and Christendom were more or less permanent, and that some form of recognition and even relationship with non-Muslim states was unavoidable.

But if the Muslim holy war had for the time being come to an end, that of the Christians was just beginning. They had not forgotten that the greater part of the Muslim Empire consisted of lands that had once belonged to Christendom, including the Holy Land itself, where the Christian religion had been born. The Christian counteroffensive against Islam was encouraged by the obvious weakness and disunity that had meanwhile overtaken the Muslim world. Others took advantage of this disarray as well. The first serious inroads on Muslim territory were made by peoples who were neither Christian nor Muslim but heathen—the Khazar Turks in the east, the Vikings in the west. But these were no more than short episodes and soon ended. Far more important was the recovery of Christian power and the growing determination to reconquer the lost lands of Christendom.

The Christian reconquest began at the extremities. In Spain, the small Christian principalities, which had managed to maintain a pre-

carious existence in the far north of the Iberian Peninsula, started to
consolidate and extend their territories, helped in this by Frankish and,
later also, by Norman attacks on the Muslim lands. In the east, other
Christian peoples, the Georgians and the Armenians from the Cauca-
sus, began to rebel against their Muslim overlords. By the second half
of the tenth century even the Byzantines were able to launch powerful
military offensives against the Muslims in Mesopotamia, Syria, and
the Greek islands, and to recover many of the territories which they
had lost.

During the eleventh century the forces of Christendom gained
major victories against Islam. In the east the Christian Kingdom of
Georgia resisted Muslim attempts to subdue it and entered on a great
age of expansion, during which it dominated the whole Transcauca-
sian bridge between the Black Sea and the Caspian. In the central
Mediterranean, Christian invaders landed in Sardinia and Sicily and
recaptured them from their Muslim rulers. In the Iberian Peninsula,
the Reconquista, advancing steadily southwards, brought Toledo in
Spain and Coimbra in Portugal back into Christian hands.

Finally, beginning in 1098, groups of Christians from western
Europe conquered and, for a while, held the coastal plains of Syria and
Palestine through a series of campaigns which came to be known in
the history of Christendom as the Crusades.

They were not so known among the Muslims. The words "Crusade" and "Crusader" are unknown in contemporary Muslim writings
and, indeed, appear to have had no equivalents in Arabic or other
Islamic languages until terms were coined in Christian Arabic writings
at a somewhat later date. To contemporary Muslim observers, the
Crusaders were simply the Franks or the infidels—one more group
among the many unbelievers and barbarians who were attacking the
world of Islam, distinguished from the others only by their warlike
ferocity and the successes which it brought them. In this the Muslims
did not differ greatly from the Christian Europeans, who for long
refused to recognize Islam as a rival religion and referred to Muslims
as infidels, paynims, or, more politely, called them by ethnic names
like Saracen or Moor, Turk or Tatar.

Crusader successes were due in no small part to Muslim weakness.
By the middle of the eleventh century the civilization of Islam was
already showing signs of decay. As a result of its growing inner problems and political fragmentation, its territories were subjected to a
series of successful attacks by what were perceived by Muslims as
both external and internal barbarians, continuing for nearly three centuries. In Africa, a new religious movement united the Berber tribes of
Southern Morocco and the Senegal-Niger area. It launched them on a

movement of expansion that culminated in the creation of a new Berber empire comprising the greater part of northwest Africa and Muslim Spain. From the east, from Central Asia and beyond, the lands of Islam were invaded by the Steppe peoples—first Turks and then Mongols—whose migrations and conquests changed the whole ethnic, social, and cultural pattern of Middle Eastern society. Even inside the empire, the breakdown of civil administration allowed the Bedouin and other nomads to range freely in what had once been irrigated and cultivated lands.

But it was none of these forces that inflicted the greatest and most permanent damage on the world of Islam. The Berbers and Bedouin were, after all, Muslims, and the Turks were soon converted to become the most valiant champions that Islam has ever known. The first vital threat to Islam came from the infidel barbarians in the north—that is, from Europe.

The contemporary Damascene chronicler Ibn al-Qalānisi records the arrival of the Crusaders in the year of the Hijra 490, corresponding to 1096–1097, in these terms:

> And in this year a series of reports began to come in concerning the appearance of the armies of the Franks from the direction of the Sea of Constantinople, with forces so numerous that their numbers cannot be reckoned. These reports followed one another, and as they were spread and made known, people became anxious and disquieted. . . .[4]

Over a century later in faraway Mosul, the great historian Ibn al-Athīr saw these events in a larger perspective:

> The first appearance of the Empire of the Franks, the rise of their power, their invasion of the lands of Islam and occupation of some of them occurred in the year 478 [1085–86], when they took the city of Toledo and others in the land of Andalus, as has already been set forth. Then in the year 484 [1091–92] they attacked the island of Sicily, and conquered it, and this too I have related before. Then they forced their way even to the shore of Africa, where they seized a few places, which were however recovered from them. Then they conquered other places, as you will now see. When the year 490 [1096–97] came, they invaded the land of Syria. . . .[5]

And there, sweeping all before them, the Crusaders were able to set up a string of Frankish, Christian, feudal states stretching along the Syrian and Palestinian coasts from the foothills of Taurus to the approaches to Sinai. It was more than two centuries before the last vestiges of these Christian principalities on Muslim soil were swept away by the Muslim holy war.

At first the incursion of these newcomers was received by the princes of Islam with indifference, and before long the Latin states found their place in the crisscross pattern of Syro-Palestinian politics. The original jihād had long since ended and even the spirit of the jihād seemed lost and forgotten. This was an age of violence and of change, when the lands of Islam were being attacked on every side, from Central Asia and Berber Africa as well as from Christendom. Even in Aleppo, Damascus, and Cairo, the loss of Palestine and of the Syrian coast at first evoked little interest. Elsewhere, it passed virtually unnoticed. Ibn al-Athīr, writing in the early thirteenth century, describes how the first refugees from Crusader-occupied Palestine arrived in Baghdad, spoke of their troubles, and appealed for help. None was forthcoming. The lack even of correct information is shown by an Iraqi poet of the time who, lamenting the fall of Jerusalem and the failure of the Muslims to rally to its defense, speaks of the conquerors as Rūm, that is to say Byzantines.[6] In both west and east, Muslim rulers were willing to deal with their new neighbors and even, on occasion, to make alliances with them against fellow Muslims. For over two hundred years Franks and Muslims were in close and daily contact with one another in Syria and Palestine, often in battle but often, also, in trade and diplomacy, and even in alliance. For centuries after the end of the Crusades, Western merchants and pilgrims traveled in Egypt and the Levant while Muslim rulers signed commercial treaties with one after another of the Western trading states.

In the far west, the Christian reconquest gained complete and final victory. Muslim rulers and then even Muslim subjects were driven from Spain and Portugal, and before long the triumphant Spaniards and Portuguese were pursuing their former masters into Africa. In the east, the Crusaders were able to maintain themselves for a while thanks to repeated reinforcements from Europe, but they were weakened by successive Muslim attacks until the last bastion of Latin power in Palestine, the port of Acre, fell to the Mamluk sultan in 1291.

Some faint remnants of the spirit of the Crusades lingered on in Europe for a while and helped to inspire some rather futile expeditions against the Mamluks in Egypt and against the new and rising power of the Ottoman Turks. But by the later Middle Ages Christian Europe had lost interest and was busy with other matters. While Christians forgot the Crusade, Muslims remembered the jihād and once again launched a holy war for the faith, first to restore and defend what had been lost to Christian invaders and then, in the flood of victory, to bring the message and the power of Islam to new lands and new peoples that had never known them before.

The impact of the Crusaders on the countries which they had ruled for up to two centuries was in most ways remarkably slight. In these states, they had never formed more than a dominant minority of western European Catholics—barons, clergy, and merchants with their various retainers and subordinates. The great mass of the population was native, consisting of Muslims, Christians of various Eastern churches, and some Jews. With the departure of the Crusaders, these lands were easily reincorporated into the Islamic society and policy.

But in two respects the Crusades left a permanent mark. One was the worsening of the position of the non-Muslim subjects of the Muslim state. The embitterment resulting from the long struggle between Islam and Christendom, the needs of security in areas of mixed Muslim and Christian population at a time when religious loyalty was primary, and, perhaps one should add, the example of persecution set by Christian kings and prelates, all combined eventually to bring about a harsher attitude on the part of the Muslims. From this period onwards, relations between the Muslims and their Christian and Jewish subjects became more distant and, often, more difficult.[7]

The other permanent change was in relations between the Middle East and Europe. Before the eleventh century these were very limited. The Crusader states initiated a new structure of relationships which on the whole their Muslim successors found it expedient to retain. Under Crusader rule European merchants, mostly Italians, had established themselves in the Levant ports where they formed organized communities subject to their own chiefs and governed by their own laws. The Muslim reconquest of these ports did not end the activities of the European merchants. On the contrary, Muslim rulers were careful not to disturb them and preferred to encourage this trade, which was a source of advantage to them as well as to those engaged in it. European merchants continued to flourish in the former Crusader strongholds and now appeared even in Egypt and other places which the Crusaders had never conquered.

These new links with Europe also affected the Christian minorities living in the Middle East under Muslim rule. From this time onwards they were increasingly in touch with the West, partly through dealings with European traders, partly also through religious connections between various groups of Arabic-speaking Christians who had broken away from the Eastern churches to form Uniate communities in communion with the Church of Rome. These commercial and ecclesiastical contacts helped to create a small nucleus of native Arabic speakers who had some knowledge of a European language and some contact with Europeans. In later times these westward-looking Middle Eastern Christians were to play a role of great importance. For long, however,

their role and that of the resident Western merchants in Middle Eastern cities was severely circumscribed. The social segregation that from
Crusading times onwards separated the local non-Muslims from the
Muslim majority of the population also affected the resident communities of Western merchants, and reduced contacts between them
and the Muslim population to the bare minimum necessary for commercial and, occasionally, political communications.

In 1174, Saladin wrote a letter to the caliph in Baghdad justifying
his policy of encouraging Christian traders in the territories which he
had reconquered from the Crusaders. He had, he said, made arrangements with them and thereby changed the conditions of trade to
Muslim advantage:

> . . . the Venetians, the Pisans, and the Genoese all used to come, some-
> times as raiders, the voracity of whose harm could not be contained and
> the fire of whose evil could not be quenched, sometimes as travelers
> trying to prevail over Islam with the goods they bring, and our fearsome
> decrees could not cope with them . . . and now there is not one of them
> but brings to our lands his weapons of war and battle and bestows upon
> us the choicest of what he makes and inherits . . .[8]

And this desirable result, Saladin explains, had been brought about by
establishing communications and arranging terms with them, "such
that we desire and they deplore, such as we prefer and they do not."

The Christian church was of the same opinion, but its thunder and
its decrees of excommunication were powerless to prevent the resumption and extension of trade between the Christian and Muslim worlds.
It is ironic that, apart from a few castles, this renewal of trade with the
West was probably the only permanent effect of any importance left
by the Crusaders in the East.

While Western commerce grew and flourished, Western arms suffered a series of crushing defeats. The Crusaders were evicted from all
their conquests, and for the second time great areas of hitherto Christian territory were lost to Muslim attackers. Once again, as in the early
days of Islam, the Muslims launched a holy war against Christendom.
This time their armies reached to the very heart of Europe.

The holy war which defeated and finally dislodged the Crusaders
did not emerge from the countries which they occupied nor from the
peoples whom they had conquered or threatened. The new impetus
came from further east and from a new power in Islam, that of the
Turks, a people of East Asian origin who had entered the lands of the
caliphate between the ninth and eleventh centuries and had become
the military and political leaders of Islam. Their coming had preceded

the Crusades. Their conquest of Syria had even, in a sense, provoked them.

During the age of Turkish hegemony, the Muslim world recovered a new militancy and embarked on new jihāds which brought important territorial gains, some of them permanent. The first major Turkish conquest at the expense of Christendom was that of eastern and central Anatolia, the great bastion of the Byzantine Empire, which had for long formed the main barrier to Muslim advance. In the late eleventh and twelfth centuries, the Seljuk Turks transformed Anatolia, by conquest and settlement, into a Turkish and Muslim land that later became the launching pad for a second and far more dangerous Islamic invasion of Europe.

But in the meantime the Muslims themselves were invaded and conquered by a new and deadly enemy from the east. In the early years of the thirteenth century, a Mongol chieftain later known by the title of Jenghiz Khan succeeded after bitter struggles in uniting the warring nomadic tribes of Mongolia and launching them on a vast campaign of conquest. By 1220 all of central Asia was in his hands, and in the following year the Mongols crossed the Oxus River and embarked on the conquest of Iran. The death of Jenghiz Khan in 1227 brought only a brief respite, and soon his successor, the new khan, was ready to resume the attack. By 1240, the Mongols had conquered western Iran and invaded Georgia, Armenia, and northern Mesopotamia; in 1243 they met and overwhelmed the forces of the Seljuk Turkish sultan of Anatolia.

In the middle of the thirteenth century, a new move westward was planned and executed by the Mongols. Prince Hülegü, a grandson of Jenghiz Khan, crossed the Oxus with orders from the great khan to conquer all the lands of Islam as far as Egypt. Within a few months, the long-haired Mongol horsemen thundered across Persia, overcoming all resistance, and in January 1258 converged on the city of Baghdad. They stormed, looted, and burned the old caliphal capital, and on the 20th February 1258 the last caliph, with as many members of his family as could be found, was put to death. For the first time since the days of the Prophet, a non-Muslim people had invaded the heartlands of Islam, destroyed the great historic institution of the caliphate and established a pagan domination over the believers. Only in Egypt did the Mamluk Sultans hold firm and block the entry of the Mongols into the continent of Africa.

To the north, the Mongol advance continued. Moving westward from central Asia, their horsemen rode north as well as south of the Caspian and Black seas, and conquered the greater part of what is now

Russia, reaching into the borderlands of Poland, Hungary, and even Silesia. In the lands north of the Black Sea, the Mongol conquerors created, for the first time, a political framework for the steppe peoples —mostly Turkish—who ranged over that area. Relatively few in number, the Mongol rulers relied heavily on their more numerous Turkish subjects, who had preceded them in this westward migration. In time, abandoning their own Mongol language, they began to speak Turkish and were merged with the Turks. This was especially important in the steppes of eastern Europe, where Turkish tribes formed an important part of the population. The resulting Turko-Mongol inhabitants are often known as Tatars, a term that, strictly speaking, refers only to certain groups among the Turko-Mongols but is often used loosely to designate them all. The period of their predominance is known in Russian history as "the Tatar yoke." After the breakup of the empire of the great khans, their dominions were divided into a number of smaller states, each ruled by a line of khans claiming descent from Jenghiz Khan. The Mongol state in eastern Europe is known in Russian and, hence, also in European usage as the Khanate of the Golden Horde. With the Turkification of the Mongols and the conversion of the Golden Horde to Islam in the late thirteenth and early fourteenth centuries, a Muslim-Turkish state dominated the whole of eastern Europe from the Baltic to the Black Sea and exacted tribute from the princes of Muscovy and other Slavic rulers. In the fifteenth century, the Khanate of the Golden Horde grew weak; it was finally overthrown in 1502, giving way to smaller khanates based on Kazan, Astrakhan, and the Crimea. This marked the end of Muslim hegemony in eastern Europe and opened the way for the rise and eventually the domination of Muscovy.

Further south the Mongols were able to establish themselves in Iran and Iraq and to gain supremacy over the Seljuk state in Anatolia. They were, however, unable to overcome the surviving Islamic Empire based in Egypt, that of the Mamluk sultans. Locked in a life and death struggle with Egypt, the Mongol rulers of Iran, not unnaturally, began to look westward for allies against the common enemy. In Europe, the princes of Christendom responded with lively, if cautious, enthusiasm to the idea of a new Crusade, this time in alliance with a great non-Muslim power beyond the empire of Islam, which was thus to be subjected to a war on two fronts. For a while there was vigorous diplomatic activity between the courts of the Mongol khans and those of Christian Europe. Mongol emissaries—most of them eastern Christians—came to Rome, to France, and even to England where King Edward I showed some interest in the project of a Mongol alliance. At the same time, European Christian travelers—merchants, diplomats, and missionaries—visited the Persian dominions of the great khan. Some of them, like the famous Marco Polo, profited from the *pax Mongolica* and traveled by the land route across Asia to Mongolia and China.

The westward jihād of the Seljuk Turks was halted with the breakup of the Seljuk Sultanate of Anatolia, known as the Sultanate of Rūm. It was resumed by their heirs, the Ottomans. The Ottoman state began as a principality of frontier fighters, one of several successor states to the Seljuk Sultanate in Anatolia. The name Ottoman is a corruption of the name of its first ruler Osman who, according to tradition, reigned from 1299 to 1326.

The first Ottoman state came into being on the border between Islam and Christendom in Anatolia. Its ruler used the title of Border Chief or, sometimes, Leader of the Gazis, the frontier-fighters in the holy war. A fourteenth-century Turkish poet whose Ottoman saga is the earliest written Ottoman historical source defines the gazi as "the instrument of God's religion . . . God's sweeper who cleanses the earth from the filth of polytheism . . . God's sure sword."[9] In time, with the advance of Ottoman arms and the vast extension of Ottoman power, the principality grew into a state and the state into an empire. But the Ottoman Empire remained a polity penetrated from its very origins with a sense of mission in the holy war.

In this holy war, Europe was a frontier to which the Ottomans, and indeed many other Muslims, looked in much the same way as Europeans were to view the Americas from the sixteenth to the eighteenth century. Beyond the northern and western frontiers lay rich and barbarous lands to which it was their sacred mission to bring religion and civilization, order and peace—while reaping the customary rewards of the pioneer and the frontiersman. The ending of Ottoman expansion —the closing of the frontier—brought profound changes both inside the Ottoman Empire and in Ottoman perceptions of what lay beyond the frontier.

In their imperial phase, the Ottoman sultans saw themselves as the legitimate successors of the Byzantine emperors, a claim manifested even in the title that they commonly used, Sulṭan-i Rūm—Sultan of Rome. With the capture of Constantinople in 1453, Sultan Mehmed II, known henceforth as the Conqueror, added the coping stone to his arch of conquest. The two parts of the old empire, Asia and Europe, were in his hands; the old imperial capital was now the seat of his government.

The Turkish chroniclers, not surprisingly, offer many accounts of the conquest of Constantinople. The earliest—the narratives of the gazis and their spokesmen—are simple and direct. The gazi historian Oruç describes it as follows:

> In Edirne guns as big as dragons were cast and muskets made ready. Sultan Mehmed left Edirne for Istanbul, bringing these guns with him. When the guns were set up and began to shoot from every side, they destroyed the towers and walls of the fortifications of Istanbul and the infidels inside could not attain the victory for which they fought. The ruler of Istanbul was brave and asked for no quarter. The priests said that according to what was written in the gospels the city could not be captured. Believing in their words, he set up guns and muskets on every side to defend the towers. While his men went into the body of the tower, they talked all kinds of nonsense. God forfend, they blasphemed against the reverence of the Prophet and spoke nonsensical words. Because of their pride, almighty God visited this disaster upon them. Sultan Mehmed, the son of Sultan Murad, inspired by zeal, said "in the cause of God" and commanded plunder. The gazis, entering by force on every side, found a way in through the breaches in the fortress made by the guns and put the infidels in the fortress to the sword. The way was opened to the rest of the soldiers. They came through the trenches and set up ladders. They threw these against the walls of the towers and climbed up them. Mounting on the tower they destroyed the infidels who were inside and entered the city. They looted and plundered. They seized their money and possessions and made their sons and daughters slaves. Sultan Mehmed also gave orders to plunder the houses. In this way what could be taken was taken. The Muslims took so much booty that the wealth gathered in Istanbul since it was built 2400 years before became the portion of the gazis. They plundered for three days, and after three days plunder was forbidden. Istanbul was taken on Tuesday the 21st of Rebi ül-evvel of the year 857 [corresponding to 29th May 1453].[10]

This kind of narrative, written in plain Turkish for plain men, reflects the outlook of the gazis on the frontier. The more sophisticated Ottoman historiography of the sixteenth century presents a somewhat different picture.

> That wide region, that strong and lofty city . . . from being the nest of the owl of error, was turned into the capital of glory and honor. Through the noble efforts of the Muhammadan sultan, for the evil-voiced clash of the bells of the shameless misbelievers was substituted the Muslim call to prayer, the sweet five times repeated chant of the Faith of glorious rites, and the ears of the people of the Holy War were filled with the melody of the call to prayer. Churches which were within the city were emptied of their vile idols, and cleansed from their filthy and idolatrous impurities; and by the defacement of their images, and the erection of

the Islamic prayer-niches and pulpits, many monasteries and chapels became the envy of the Gardens of Paradise. The temples of the mis-believers were turned into the mosques of the pious, and the rays of the light of Islam drove away the hosts of darkness from that place so long the abode of the despicable infidels, and the streaks of the dawn of the Faith dispelled the lurid blackness of oppression, for the word, irresistible as destiny, of the fortunate sultan became supreme in the governance of this new dominion. . . .[11]

With Constantinople as his capital, it was natural for the Muslim heir to pagan and Christian Rome to look westward for the next step. Ottoman forces were advancing at both ends of the Adriatic. At the northern end the Ottoman cavalry was raiding within reach of Venice. At the southern end they consolidated their position on the Albanian coast and seized the adjoining islands. In August 1480 an Ottoman naval expedition commanded by Gedik Ahmed Pasha, the Kapudan (Grand Admiral) of the Ottoman fleet, set sail from Valona in Albania and captured the Italian port of Otranto. The following spring the pasha assembled a new expeditionary force for the purpose of reinforcing his bridgehead and expanding the Ottoman conquests in Italy.

In the year 884, [says the chronicler,] Gedik Ahmad Pasha sailed with a mighty fleet to the peninsula of Apulia. Arriving there, with the help of God and the concern of the sultan, the shadow of God, he stormed the fortress of Apulia which resembles the fortress of Constantinople. He conquered much territory. The temples of idols became mosques of Islam and the five-fold prayer which is the watch call of Muhammad, upon him be peace, was sounded.[12]

But Sultan Mehmed the Conqueror was already dying, and his death interrupted the pasha's promising plans. In the words of a slightly later Turkish historian:

Until the sultan transferred to another world he (Gedik Ahmed) remained in Apulia and started on immense conquests. After the death of Sultan Mehmed, Gedik Ahmed went to greet Sultan Bayezid, and the infidels who were there caused much trouble to the Muslims. The end of the matter was that the infidels recaptured Apulia and of the Muslims who were there, some died and some, after a thousand tribulations, escaped. . . .[13]

In the course of the struggle for the succession between the new Sultan Bayezid II and his brother Jem, the Ottoman troops were withdrawn from Otranto, and the plan to conquer Italy was postponed and eventually abandoned. The ease with which, a few years later in 1494–

1495, the French were able to conquer the Italian states one after another, almost without resistance, suggests that had the Turks persisted in their plans they would have conquered most or all of Italy without undue difficulty. A Turkish conquest of Italy in 1480, when the Renaissance was just beginning, would have transformed the history of the world. But though Italy was left unconquered, the Ottoman sense of imperial mission remained strong, and the Ottoman armies advanced far into Europe.

Their aim was to reach even farther. From the sixteenth century onwards there are frequent references in Turkish sources to a remote and legendary city called Kızıl-elma or Red Apple. The name was allegedly derived from the appearance of the golden dome on a large church standing in this city. The city of the red apple is the final goal of Turkish-Muslim conquest, and its capture will seal the end of the jihād and the final victory of Islam. It was identified with various Christian capitals that were objectives of Turkish arms, first Constantinople, then Budapest, and then at different times Vienna and Rome. Indeed, the Turks made Constantinople their own, held Budapest for a century and a half, twice laid siege to Vienna, and for a while seemed to threaten even Rome.

By the reign of Sultan Süleyman the Magnificent (1520–1566), the empire was at the peak of its power. In Europe the Ottoman armies, already masters of Greece and the Balkans, advanced across Hungary to besiege Vienna in 1529. In the East, Ottoman warships challenged the Portuguese in the Indian Ocean while in the West the Muslim rulers of North Africa except Morocco submitted to Ottoman suzerainty and thus brought Muslim naval power into western seas and even to the Atlantic where corsairs from North Africa raided as far away as the British Isles.

Once again, as in early days, the advance of Islam seemed to pose a mortal threat to Christendom. The Crusade was dead, the jihād had taken its place. Richard Knolles, the Elizabethan historian of the Turks, was expressing the common feeling of Europe when he spoke of the Turkish Empire as "the present terror of the world."[14] Even in faraway Iceland the Lutheran Book of Common Prayer in use in the churches besought God to save them from "the cunning of the Pope and the terror of the Turk." That the latter was no idle fear is shown by the appearance in 1627 of Barbary Corsairs in Iceland whence they carried several hundred captives to the slave markets of Algiers.

The victories of Süleyman the Magnificent were the high watermark of the Turkish tide, and the beginning of the ebb. The Ottoman armies withdrew from Vienna, the Ottoman fleet from the Indian

Ocean. For a while the still-imposing facade of Ottoman military power concealed the real decline of the Ottoman state and society. In Hungary, Turks and Christians continued to fight inconclusive battles, and as late as 1683 the Turks were able to make a second attempt to capture Vienna. But it was too late, and this time their defeat was final. In some parts of the world, notably tropical Africa and southeast Asia, Islam was continuing its advance. In Europe, however, Islam suffered a decisive reverse, which the Ottoman victories had for a while obscured and delayed but did not prevent.

The response of European Christendom to the first great jihād had been the Reconquest and the Crusades. The response to the second wave of Islamic advance culminated in the expansion of Europe which has come to be known as imperialism. It began, not surprisingly, at the two extremities of Europe, in countries which had themselves been subject to Muslim rule—in the Iberian Peninsula and in Russia. It subsequently spread until it engulfed almost the whole world of Islam.

In 1492, the last Muslim stronghold in Spain was conquered by the armies of Ferdinand and Isabella. By then the European counterstroke was well under way. The reconquest of Portugal had been completed in 1267, almost two and a half centuries before that of Spain. In 1415, the Portuguese captured Ceuta on the north coast of Morocco, thus carrying the war into enemy camp. During the sixteenth century the Portuguese made a determined effort to establish themselves in Morocco. They briefly occupied Tangier, and retained a few bases in the south for rather longer. But the main Portuguese enterprise in North Africa ended with their defeat at the hands of the Moroccans at the Battle of al-Qaṣr al-Kabīr in 1578.

The Spaniards, too, in a similar impetus of reconquest, followed their defeated former masters from Europe to Africa, and between 1497 and 1510 captured a number of places on the North African coast from Melilla in Morocco as far east as Tripoli. This enterprise, like that of the Portuguese, came to nothing. Their purpose, in any case, was limited—to prevent at source all attempts at a Muslim recovery and return, and to protect their shores and their ships from Muslim corsairs. As Ottoman naval power began to dominate the Mediterranean, the Spaniards abandoned any serious attempt to invade North Africa and, like the Portuguese, were content to hold a few strong points with small garrisons.

The real counterblow by western Europe against the East came in quite another quarter. When Vasco da Gama arrived in Calicut he explained that he had come "in search of Christians and spices." It was a fair summary of the motives that had sent the Portuguese to Asia, as perhaps also, with appropriate adjustments, of the jihād to which, in a sense, the Portuguese voyages were a long-delayed reply. The sentiment of Christian struggle was strong among the Portuguese who sailed to the East. The great voyages of discovery were seen as a religious war, a continuation of the Crusades and of the Reconquest, and against the same enemy. In eastern waters, it was Muslim rulers —in Egypt, Turkey, Iran, and India—who were the chief opponents of the Portuguese and whose domination they ended. After the Portuguese came the other maritime peoples of the West, who together established a west European ascendancy in Africa and southern Asia that lasted until the twentieth century.

So secure was their domination that the Europeans were even able to fight each other on eastern battlefields, to the occasional advantage of the local powers. One such incident became famous. In 1622 the Portuguese, who had seized the port of Hormūz in the Persian Gulf, were expelled by a Persian army with English assistance. The victory is celebrated in a Persian epic poem, and the temporary alliance justified by a Persian historian of the time:

> The situation had now changed, because a group of Englishmen had recently presented themselves at the Safavid court and had said that, whenever the Shah wished to recapture Hormūz, they were ready to help him with troops. They explained to the Shah that they were enemies of the Portuguese, and that their mutual hostility derived in part from sectarian differences. After Hormūz had been recaptured, they said, ships from other ports under English control would ensure that the Portuguese did not regain a foothold there. Shah ʿAbbās decided to accept the offer of help made by the English. As the saying goes:
>
> > "Although the water from the Christian well is impure,
> > It only washes a dead Jew, so what is there to fear?"[15]

In a book written in 1580, an Ottoman geographer warns the sultan of the dangers to the Islamic lands and the disturbance to Islamic trade resulting from the establishment of Europeans on the coasts of America, India, and the Persian Gulf; he advised the sultan:

> Let a channel be cut from the Mediterranean to Suez, and let a great fleet be prepared in the port of Suez; then with the capture of the ports of India and Sind, it will be easy to chase away the infidels and bring the precious wares of these places to our capital.[16]

Unfortunately for the Ottomans, his proposal, already made earlier by the Venetians, was not followed. Instead, the Ottoman sultan and his main Christian rival, the king of Spain, reached an armistice which left both monarchs free to fight against their own heretics—the sultan

1. *Portuguese repelling Persian attack on Hormūz*

2. *Setting the fortress of Hormūz on fire*

3. *Persian commander receiving a deputation of two Portuguese*

against the Shi'ites of Iran; the king against the Protestants of Northern Europe. The Suez Canal was not opened until centuries later and then served the needs of a different empire. The Ottoman naval expeditions to the Indian Ocean in the sixteenth century failed against the superior ships and armament of the Portuguese.

The same pattern of recovery, reconquest, and counterattack may be discerned in the other European country that was conquered and ruled by Muslims in the Middle Ages—that is, in Russia. Compared with Moorish rule in Spain, the domination of Russia by the Golden Horde was of brief duration and limited effect. Nevertheless, the "Tatar Yoke" left a profound mark on the Russian memory.

The Russian reconquest began somewhat later than the Iberian, when, in 1380, Dmitri Donskoy, Grand Prince of Moscow, defeated the Tatars in a pitched battle at Kulikovo Field. Though celebrated in Russian history and legend, this victory was not decisive, since two years later the Tatars rode north again, devastated the Russian lands, and captured Moscow, where they reimposed the tribute. It was not until 1480 that divisions among the Muslims allowed Ivan the Great of Moscow to free himself from all tribute and dependence.

Like the Spaniards and the Portuguese but with incomparably greater success, the Russians, having thrown off the yoke, set out to pursue their former masters. A long and bitter struggle with the Volga Tatars ended with the Russian capture of Kazan in 1552. After this decisive victory they were able, without undue difficulty, to advance all the way down the Volga and seize the port city of Astrakhan in 1556. The Russians now controlled the Volga and had reached the Caspian. They had overcome most of their Muslim adversaries on their route towards the south and were now raiding directly against Ottoman and Crimean Tatar territory.

The Ottomans, aware of the danger, tried to counter it. A major expedition was launched against Astrakhan with the aim of capturing it and using it as the base of an Islamic defensive system. Part of the plan was to dig a canal linking the Don and Volga Rivers through which Ottoman fleets could move between the Black Sea and the Caspian. This would have enabled the Ottomans to establish regular communications with the Muslim rulers of Central Asia and thus form a solid barrier against any further Russian advances to the south or to the east.[17]

The project failed and came to nothing. The Tatar Khans of the Crimea were able for some time to fend off the Russian attack and retain their links with the Ottoman sultans, whom they accepted as their suzerains. The Black Sea remained for the time being under

Turkish-Muslim control, and between the Crimea and Istanbul there was an important trade, especially in foodstuffs and in slaves of east European origin. But the way was now open for the great Russian advance into Asia.

While the seafaring merchants of western Europe sailed around Africa and ensconced themselves in the coastal cities of southern and southeast Asia, Russian soldiers and administrators, followed by Russian traders and peasants, advanced overland to the Black Sea, to the Caspian, to the Pamir Mountains, and on to the Pacific Ocean. East and west Europeans alike were helped in their expansion into Asia and Africa by military and technological superiority. The Russians encountered no major power in their advance eastwards; the west European empires, with ships built to withstand the Atlantic gales, had an advantage in navigational skills and naval armament which no Asian country could match.

Only in one place, on the continent of Europe, did a Muslim state, the Ottoman Empire, still in its decline the most powerful in all Islam, stubbornly resist the advance of Christian Europe towards the Balkans, the Aegean, and Constantinople. But even while resisting Europe, the Ottomans found themselves slipping more and more under European influence and even obliged, in order to defend themselves, to adopt a number of European practices and ways.

These changes compelled the Muslims to make a painful readjustment. Accustomed to look down on the rest of the world from a comfortable altitude of true religion and superior power, they now found themselves in a situation where the hitherto despised infidels were steadily gaining strength. In their own view of history, the Muslims were the bearers of God's truth with the sacred duty of bringing it to the rest of mankind. The House of Islam, of which they were a part, embodied God's purpose on earth. Their sovereigns were the heirs of the Prophet and the custodians of the message which he had brought from God. The Islamic state was the only truly legitimate power on earth and the Islamic community the sole repository of truth and enlightenment, surrounded on all sides by an outer darkness of barbarism and unbelief. God's favor to his own community was demonstrated by their power and their victories in this world. So it was and so it had always been since the days of the Prophet himself.

These beliefs, inherited from early Muslim times, had been convincingly reinforced by the great Ottoman successes of the fifteenth and sixteenth centuries and revived by the transient but important victories sometimes won by Muslim arms as late as the eighteenth century. It was hard for Muslims to adapt themselves to a world in which the course of events was determined not by the power of Islam but by the Christian adversary and in which the very survival of the Muslim state might at times depend on the help or even the good will of some of the Christian rulers.

While the Cossacks of Russia and the caravels of the Portuguese were menacing the lands of Islam from both north and south, the heartlands from Central Asia across the Middle East to North Africa still retained their independence. In the period of European expansion from both ends, from the sixteenth to the nineteenth centuries, five political centers of power had emerged in the Islamic world: in India, Central Asia, Iran, the Ottoman Empire, and North Africa. In India, the Muslims, though forming a minority of the population, had for some time past maintained political supremacy. In the sixteenth century an intruder from Central Asia, the great Babar, founded a new dynasty. Under his rule and that of his successors, the so-called Mogul Emperors, Islamic dominance in India entered on its final and greatest phase. It ended with their ultimately fatal encounter with the west Europeans.

Further north in Central Asia, the breakup of the Islamized Mongol Khanate which had ruled these lands left a series of smaller Muslim states in the vast area between the Caspian Sea and China. These too encountered the advancing European, this time in the guise of the Russian, and were, in due course, conquered by him and incorporated in the Russian empire.

At the opposite end of the Islamic world, in North Africa, Morocco survived for some centuries as an independent monarchy while Algeria, Tunisia, and Libya submitted to Ottoman suzerainty but were governed by local rulers. All of these were, in the course of the nineteenth and early twentieth centuries, incorporated in the French, Spanish, and Italian empires.

Only two states succeeded in surviving the universal debacle— Turkey and Iran. Though the independence of both was at times threatened and often infringed, it was never entirely lost.

After the initial Portuguese impetus, the activities of the western Europeans in Asia were mainly commercial and maritime and only gradually led to the establishment of political domination. Even then this was confined, in the main, to southern and southeastern Asia and eastern Africa and thus affected the Middle East only indirectly. In the central lands the political and strategic interests of the Western powers were for a long time of far less concern than those of the central and east European powers.

However, the consolidation of Portuguese and, later, English and

Dutch power in Asia and Africa meant that the Middle East, both Iran and the Ottoman Empire, was effectively encircled, with Russians along the northern boundaries and west Europeans on both sides. It was this encirclement rather than, as was once thought, the earlier circumnavigation of Africa by the Portuguese, that in time led to the reduction and diversion of the spice trade. This trade, which for centuries had passed through the Red Sea and Persian Gulf to the Mediterranean and Europe, enriching the Middle East on its way, was now transferred to the oceanic routes, controlled by westerners at both ends.

These changes were slow and their effect was not quickly understood. As perceptive an observer as the imperial ambassador in Istanbul, Ogier Ghiselin de Busbecq, in a letter dated 1555, complained that Europeans were squandering their efforts seeking for spoil and gold in "the Indies and the Antipodes over vast fields of oceans," while the very existence of European Christendom was threatened by the Turk.[18]

Even in the late seventeenth century, the threat had not vanished. In 1683, the Turks made their second and last attempt to capture Vienna. After many weeks, the Ottoman armies were finally compelled to abandon the siege and before long were driven into headlong retreat. A contemporary Ottoman chronicler tells the story with characteristic brevity and frankness:

> A prisoner was captured and questioned. He said that the Austrian emperor had sent letters to every side appealing for help to all the kings of Christendom, and that only the king of Poland, the accursed traitor called Sobieski, had come to his aid in person and with troops and with the soldiers and hetmans of Lithuania and with 35,000 cavalry and infantry of the Polish infidels. The Austrian emperor had also sent his own men together with such reinforcements as he had been able to get from the rest of Christendom with cavalry and infantry gathered together making 85,000 chosen Germans with 40,000 horsemen and 80,000 footmen altogether 120,000 infidels. All these gathered together in this place and, it was reported, were intending to attack the soldiers of Islam who were in the trenches around Vienna. . . .[19]

The Ottoman chronicler makes no attempt to conceal the disaster that followed:

> . . . everything that was in the imperial [Ottoman] camp, money and equipment and precious things, was left behind and fell into the hands of the people of hell. The accursed infidels in their battalion (may it be crushed) came in two columns. One of them advancing along the bank

of the Danube entered the fortress and stormed the trenches. The other captured the imperial army camp. Of the disabled men whom they found in the trenches they killed some and took others prisoner. The men remaining in the trenches, some 10,000 of them, were incapable of fighting, having been wounded by guns, muskets, cannon, mines, stones, and other weapons, some of them lacking an arm or a leg. These they at once put to the sword and, finding some thousands of their own prisoners, freed them from their bonds and released them. They succeeded in capturing such quantities of money and supplies as cannot be described. They therefore did not even think of pursuing the soldiers of Islam and had they done so it would have gone hard. May God preserve us. This was a calamitous defeat of such magnitude that there has never been its like since the first appearance of the Ottoman state.[20]

The first Turkish attempt to capture Vienna in 1529, though not successful, had ended in a stalemate which still left the Ottomans as a major threat to the heart of Europe. The second siege and second withdrawal in 1683 were quite a different matter. This time the failure was clear and unequivocal, the withdrawal followed by crushing defeats in the field and the loss of lands and cities. The Ottoman sentiment of these changes is expressed in a popular song of the time, a dirge for the loss of Buda, recaptured by the Christians in 1686.

> In the mosques there is no more prayer
> In the fountains no more ablution
> The populous places have become desolate
> The Austrian has taken our beautiful Buda.[21]

More prosaically, an Ottoman officer who visited Belgrade during its occupation by the Austrians noted that the new masters had made some changes in the city: they had turned some mosques into barracks, others into munitions depots. The minarets were still standing, but in one of them the top had been removed and the minaret made into a clock tower. The baths were also left standing but had been converted into dwellings. Only one bathhouse was still functioning. The houses and shops along the Danube River bank had all been made into wine taverns. The poor among the subjects, he said, were weakened and oppressed by the Germans.[22]

The Peace Treaty of Carlowitz, signed 26th January 1699, marked a crucial turning point not only in the relations between the Ottoman and Hapsburg Empires but, more profoundly, between Christendom and Islam. For some centuries past the Ottoman Empire had been the leading power of Islam, representing it in the millennial conflict with its western Christian neighbors. While the real power of Islam in relation to Europe had in many respects declined, the change was for

a while hidden from Christians and Muslims alike. After the withdrawal from Vienna and the military and political defeats that followed it, however, the new relationship became clear to both sides.
Europe still had a Turkish problem, but it was now the problem of the
uncertainties arising from Turkish weakness, not the menace of Turkish power. Islam, which had long ceased to be regarded by the
churches as a serious religious adversary, now ceased to be even a
military threat. On the Turkish side, too, we find signs of a new
awareness that the lands beyond the frontier were no longer a wilder-
ness of ignorant and infidel barbarians to be conquered and then
converted or subjugated at leisure, but a dangerous enemy, a threat to
the whole future of the empire.

The menace of Western naval power was already clear by the early
sixteenth century. Lûtfi Pasha, the grand vizier of Süleyman the Magnificent, relates that one day Sultan Selim I (1512–1520), conqueror of
Syria and Egypt, told his chief advisor "my purpose is the conquest of
the land of the Franks." To this the advisor replied: "My sultan, you
live in a city whose benefactor is the sea. When the sea is unsafe no
ship comes; when no ship comes Istanbul's prosperity is gone." Sultan
Selim was already dying when this conversation took place and he did
nothing about it. Lûtfi Pasha raised the matter again with Süleyman
and told him: "Under the previous sultans there were many who ruled
the land but few who ruled the sea. In the conduct of war at sea, the
infidels are superior to us. We must overcome them."[23] The Turks did
not overcome them, and the lesson was driven home in the catas-
trophic Ottoman defeat in the great naval battle of Lepanto in 1571.

The blow was a heavy one and the Ottomans characteristically
made no attempt to disguise it. A contemporary Turkish document
citing the report of the Beylerbey of Algiers describes the result with
classic terseness:

> The Imperial fleet encountered the fleet of the wretched infidels and the
> will of God turned another way.[24]

Significantly, while the battle is known in European annals by the
name of the Greek seaport near which it was fought, in the Turkish
chronicles it is known simply as *singin*—a Turkish word meaning a
crushing defeat or rout. But the battle was less decisive than had at first
appeared, and the Ottomans were able to recover a large part of their
naval strength in the Mediterranean and to maintain all their possessions against attack. A Turkish chronicler tells us that when the Sultan
Selim II (1566–1574) asked the grand vizier Sokollu Mehmed Pasha
about the cost of building a new fleet to replace the ships destroyed

at Lepanto, the grand vizier replied: "The might of the empire is such that if it were desired to equip the entire fleet with silver anchors, silken rigging and satin sails, we could do it."[25]

The defeat of the Ottoman armies in Europe was far more serious and far more readily understood. It resulted in the loss of major provinces and the emergence of a new threat to the remainder and, most important of all, in a basic change in the relationship between the empire and its neighbors and enemies.

In seeking to mitigate the consequences of this defeat, the Turks had recourse for the first time to a new device, diplomacy, and adopted a new tactic—that of seeking the help of west European countries, in this case England and Holland, to mediate on their behalf and to counterbalance the hostile power of their nearest neighbors.

There had been earlier attempts at such negotiations with Western powers. Süleyman had entered into some kind of agreement with Francis I of France against the Hapsburg powers, which the French— and also their European adversaries—saw as an alliance.

The Turks saw it somewhat differently. A sixteenth-century Turkish author writes:

> The Bey of France [a title which reduced that monarch to the level of an Ottoman provincial governor] had always declared his adherence [the Turkish word is *intisab,* normally used in the context of client-patron relations] to the Threshold of the Nest of Felicity and manifested his devotion to the Porte which is the abode of power . . . finding himself under siege and after consulting his viziers and his counsellors, he found them all agreed that their wisest and best course was to take refuge and seek contact with the world-encompassing throne of the sultan.

The Bey of France, therefore, sent an ambassador to Istanbul to ask for help and to deliver this message:

> A relentless enemy has conquered and overwhelmed us with the help and aid of the evildoing king of the ill-omened Hungarians. If the sultan of the world would generously condescend to repel this accursed helper of our foes we would then be able to meet and fight him and have the power to frustrate their evil purposes. Slaves of gratitude to the Lord of Majesty, we would eagerly bend our necks and bow our heads to the yoke of his obedience.[26]

The glorious and magnanimous sultan, says the historian, moved by pity for the misfortunes of the unhappy Frenchman, decided to help him, and the Ottoman armies accordingly set forth to chastise the accursed and unavailing Hungarians.

In 1552, there were even joint French and Turkish operations against Spanish ports, which receive a passing mention in some but not all of the Ottoman histories.

Towards the end of the sixteenth century, there was some correspondence with Queen Elizabeth I of England about a variety of subjects, including an occasional reference to a possible united front against the common Spanish enemy. But these were desultory negotiations, the initiative coming mainly from the Western side. For the Turks, they lacked urgency and produced no results. In the aftermath of the second defeat at Vienna, however, a new diplomacy emerged which set the pattern for a long time to come. In the course of the eighteenth century, there is a dawning awareness among the Ottomans that they are no longer the Empire of Islam confronting Christendom but one state among several, among whom there might be allies as well as enemies. The idea was not an easy one to accept, and even at the end of the eighteenth century still encountered resistance. Turkey was at war with both Russia and Austria. A suggestion was made, with some cogency, that it might be useful to conclude treaties with Sweden, which was also at war with Austria, and with Prussia, which could distract Austria from the rear. Treaties were accordingly signed with both countries, in 1789 and 1790, respectively, which amounted to a military alliance. The Turks had long since become accustomed to co-existence with European powers, and even to a relationship for which they commonly used such words as "friendly" and "friendship." Europeans occasionally saw such relationships as alliances; the Turks never did, and the idea of an alliance with Christian powers, even against other Christian powers, was strange and, to some, abhorrent. The army judge, Şanizade, denounced such an alliance as contrary to the holy law, citing as his authority a verse in the Qur'ān: "O you who believe! Do not take My enemies and your enemies as friends."[27] The army judge was overruled by the chief Mufti, Hamidizade Mustafa Efendi, who cited the saying of the Prophet that "God will help the cause of Islam with men who are not of Islam" as well as with other texts and arguments.[28] This opinion prevailed, though there have been many who have found it unacceptable.

Only in one area did the old style jihād still continue—in the western Mediterranean. In the Barbary States, the independent kingdom of Morocco and the three principalities of Algeria, Tunisia, and Tripolitania under nominal Ottoman suzerainty, a state of perpetual holy war against Christendom remained at least theoretically in force. The holy war was waged by naval rather than military means and remained a continuing problem for the states of Christendom. To the Europeans, the sea rovers of the North African states were pirates. For themselves they were fighters in the holy war, and might at worst be described as privateers. What for Europeans was piracy on the high seas, for the North African states was maritime jihād against the enemies of the faith. It brought rich rewards in prize money for captured ships and their cargoes, and an additional advantage not open to European privateers. Under Sharīʿa law, infidels captured in a jihād were lawfully sold into slavery. If they could arrange to ransom themselves, at their market price, so much the better for them. If not, they remained slaves in the possession of their new masters.

The privateering of the North African states, tolerated and at times even encouraged because of the rivalries of the European powers, continued right through the eighteenth century. The Revolutionary and Napoleonic Wars gave a new importance to the North African states and the anxious competition of the European belligerents for their goodwill and for the use of their facilities enormously strengthened their position. After 1815, however, they were no longer needed, and the Western powers, including by now the United States, took determined action to end this menace to Western communications and transport.

An interesting contemporary picture of some aspects of the relations between Western governments and the Barbary Corsairs may be gathered from the report of an Ottoman ambassador in Madrid in 1787–1788. As representative of the sultan, the nominal suzerain of the Bey of Algiers, he was much concerned about an agreement newly signed between the bey and the king of Spain and found an opportunity to discuss the matter with the bey's emissary in Madrid, who gave him some reassurance:

> The armistice agreement *(musalaha)* which the Algerians have made with Spain is entirely to their advantage. According to this agreement, the Spaniards were to ransom their 1250 captives in Algiers at a price of 1000 reals each. The amusing part of this is that when, after the agreement, the money reached Algiers, the Algerians took the whole of it as the price of the captives who had died in captivity and the Spaniards could do nothing against this. The documents also provide that the king of Spain, in addition to sending, as gifts to the ruler of Algiers, five hundred purses, jewels, and other goods, will pay a substantial sum in cash for peace, and give them materials needed for the navy and the arsenals. . . . There were also over a hundred Algerian captives in Spain, whom, according to the agreement, the Algerians were supposed to ransom for money. Instead, they said: "We have no need of these traitors and cowards—had they not been such they would not have been captured." The Spaniards, bewildered by this, hid it from the other

states. To end the matter, they wrote a private letter to the ruler of Morocco saying: "If you want them, we will release them for your sake." The latter, inspired by Islamic solidarity, agreed, and the prisoners were released to him. He gave each of them some expense money and clothing and sent them back to Algiers. The Spaniards sought to save face by spreading a report that they had acted in response to a request from the ruler of Morocco. In sum, the religious steadfastness of Algiers has impressed the infidels and compelled the Spaniards to submit. One day in Madrid, in conversation with an important Algerian personage, I asked him: "Why do you make peace with them when you are profiting from them so much?" He replied: "Our profits are indeed enormous. This peace will last at most three years, during which we retain our previous gains. As for now, we are collecting enough for two or three years, and we suffer no loss." He meant by this that the peace is no more than writing on water.[29]

Despite some occasional successes, the eighteenth century was on the whole a bad time for the Islamic states and the awareness among Muslims of their changed position is indicated in a number of ways. Several factors combined to bring about this change. In their dealings with Europe, the Middle Eastern powers were affected by the increasing complexity and resulting higher cost of armament and war. Their trade and internal economies had been adversely affected by the great inflation of the sixteenth and seventeenth centuries. These processes were accelerated by technological backwardness, or rather, lack of progress, in agriculture, industry, and transport within the countries of the Middle East.

A major shift in prices seems to have begun in the latter part of the sixteenth century. This was the Middle Eastern reflection of a wider process resulting from the disruptive effects of the inflow of American gold and silver. The purchasing power of these precious metals was greater in the Ottoman Empire than in the West but less than in Iran and India. Persian goods, especially Persian silk, were in great demand both in the Ottoman lands and in Europe where, however, there was no demand of comparable magnitude and persistence for any Ottoman product. Grain and textiles were the two most important Ottoman exports to Europe. The latter had at one time consisted largely of manufactured goods, but this trade was gradually reduced, only cotton cloth remaining for a little longer as a significant item among the exports from the Middle East to the West. The composition of trade shifted overwhelmingly the other way, with Europe sending manufactured textiles, including Indian cloths, to the Middle East and importing raw materials such as cotton, mohair, and especially silk, much of it from Iran. Not surprisingly, despite the inflow of gold and silver from the West, Ottoman records reveal a chronic lack of precious metals, insufficient even to meet the needs of minting coins.

While agriculture derived some benefit from the introduction of two new crops, tobacco and maize, from the West, the general situation was one of technological and economic stagnation. The European agricultural and industrial revolutions found no parallel and had no influence on the countries of the Middle East. Middle Eastern industry continued to be in the form of handicrafts which flourished until the latter part of the eighteenth century but showed few if any signs of technological improvement.

These changes also affected the Ottoman capacity to maintain military supplies—to obtain the raw materials necessary to build ships, cast guns, and even to mix gunpowder. This was certainly one of the factors in the steady decline of Ottoman military effectiveness, itself part of a larger process in which the power of the Ottoman Empire was reduced and weakened in relation to that of its rivals. The discovery and colonization of the New World shifted the center of gravity of world trade to the Atlantic Ocean and to the open seas around South Africa and southern Asia. The Mediterranean and Middle Eastern worlds, though still in many ways significant, were losing a great deal of their economic importance and, in particular, those advantages provided by their intermediate position in respect to the three continents of Europe, Asia, and Africa. With the opening of the oceanic routes, the Mediterranean and Middle East no longer mattered as much as previously. The Ottoman Empire, a Mediterranean and Middle Eastern power, was correspondingly reduced in stature.

European economic domination in the Middle East was buttressed and maintained in a number of ways. While the import of Middle Eastern products by the West was restricted and sometimes excluded by protective tariffs, Western trade to the Middle East was sheltered by the capitulations system which amounted to a right of free and unrestricted entry. The term capitulations (Latin *capitula* "chapters"— i.e., an itemized document) was used in Ottoman times for the privileges granted by the Ottoman and other Muslim rulers to Christian states, allowing their citizens to reside and trade in the Muslim dominions without becoming liable to the fiscal and other disabilities imposed by those Muslim rulers on their own non-Muslim subjects. Originally, these privileges were granted as an act of grace and condescension, from a mighty monarch to a humble suppliant. This relationship is reflected in the language of the documents, in which such words as devotion, submission, and even servitude *(rıkkiyet)* are used to describe the proper response of the recipient.[30] With the progressive decline in the power of the Muslim states and the change in the effectual relationship between them and their Christian neighbors, the capitulations came to confer privileges greatly in excess of those originally intended. They included exemption from local jurisdiction and taxation, the citizens of the capitulatory powers being answerable only to their own consular courts. By the late eighteenth century, the protection of a European power conferred important commercial and fiscal advantages and the practice grew up whereby European diplomatic missions distributed *berats,* documents, or certificates of protection, in abusive extension of their capitulatory rights. Originally, these certificates were intended only to protect locally recruited officers and agents of the European consulates. They were, by abuse, sold or granted to increasing numbers of local merchants who thus acquired a privileged, protected status.

At first, the Turks saw the problem of their weakness and decline in purely military terms, and propounded military remedies. Christian armies had proved superior to Muslim armies in the field; there might therefore be some advantage in adopting the weapons, techniques, and methods of training of the victors.

Numerous memoranda were written by Ottoman officials and other writers urging this point. One of them, by Ibrahim Müteferrika, a Hungarian Unitarian converted to Islam, was printed in Istanbul in 1731—among the first books published from the first Turkish press, which Ibrahim himself had founded. Devoted ostensibly to administrative and tactical questions, the book is divided into three sections. The first draws attention to the importance of well-ordered systems of government and describes the various types existing in Europe. The second discusses the value of scientific geography, the key to the knowledge of one's own and one's neighbors' territories, as a necessary part of the military art and as an aid to administration. In the third part, the author reviews the different types of armed forces maintained by the European states, their methods of training, their command structure, their methods of combat and their military laws. Ibrahim is careful, in discussing the Frankish infidels and their ways, to express himself with the appropriate disgust. At the same time, however, he makes it clear that the Frankish armies were stronger and better, and that the Ottomans had to imitate them if they were to survive.[31]

The lesson was understood. In 1729 a French nobleman, the Count de Bonneval, arrived in Turkey where he embraced Islam, adopted the name Ahmed, and entered the Ottoman service. In 1731 he was charged with the task of reforming the bombardier corps. In 1734 a school of military engineering was established, and in the following year Bonneval was made a pasha and given the rank and title of "chief bombardier." This experiment petered out, but another began in 1773 with the opening of a school of naval engineering.

The importation of military instructors from the West, mostly from France but also from other European countries, to train Turkish officers in the new art of warfare brought a number of important consequences. It involved a new relationship between infidel teachers and Muslim students who now had to respect as mentors and guides those whom they had been accustomed to despise. They had to accept instruction, moreover, in barbarous languages which they had hitherto felt no need to learn. They had to learn them to understand their teachers, to read their drill books and their artillery manuals. But once they had learned French, they found other reading matter more interesting and more explosive.

The same period saw another innovation, of comparable importance—the introduction of printing, in which Ibrahim Müteferrika had played an important part. Printing presses had been introduced to Turkey from Europe by Jewish refugees before the end of the fifteenth century, and Jewish presses established in Istanbul, Salonika, and other cities. The Jews were followed by the Armenians and the Greeks, who also set up presses in their own languages in Ottoman cities. These were, however, authorized on the strict condition that they did not print any books in Turkish or Arabic. This ban remained in effect until the early eighteenth century when it was abandoned, thanks largely to the initiative of Said Çelebi, son of an ambassador who was sent to Paris in 1721. The first book appeared in February 1729. When the press was forcibly closed in 1742 it had printed seventeen books, most of them dealing with history, geography, and language. The press was reopened in 1784, since when printing has spread all over the Middle East.

All in all, however, Western influence for long remained slight, mainly because the penetration of European ideas reached only a very small group of the population; even this limited impact was contained and sometimes reversed by reactionary movements such as that which led to the destruction of the first Turkish printing press in 1742. If military defeat was the main stimulus to an increasing acceptance of Western ideas, its effect was somewhat weakened in the early eighteenth century, when for a while the Ottomans were able to hold their own and, at times, even to score some successes. But the stimulus was renewed with unmistakable force by the sequence of events at the end of the eighteenth century. The first blow was the Treaty of Küçük

Kaynarja of 1774, which ratified a crushing Ottoman defeat at Russian hands and conferred immense territorial, political, and commercial advantages on Russia. The second was the Russian annexation of the Crimea in 1783. Though this was not the first territorial loss, it marked an important change. The previous losses had been of conquered countries inhabited by Christian populations with only small groups of Turkish rulers and settlers. The Crimea was different. Its people were Turkish-speaking Muslims whose presence in the Crimea dated back to the Mongol conquests of the thirteenth century and perhaps earlier. This was the first cession of old Muslim territory inhabited by Muslim peoples, and it was a bitter blow to Muslim pride.

The third shock came from France where, for the first time since the Crusades, a military invasion was launched against the heartlands of Middle Eastern Islam. In 1798, a French expedition commanded by General Bonaparte landed in Egypt, then an Ottoman province, and occupied it with little difficulty. The French occupation was of brief duration and Egypt was subsequently restored to Muslim rule. The episode had, however, shown both the strategic importance and the military weakness of the Arab lands, hitherto sheltered by the power, and still more the authority, of the Ottoman Empire.

A much greater consequence of this third event was the penetration into the Islamic lands of the new ideas of the French Revolution. This was the first movement of ideas in Europe to break through the barrier that had separated the world of the unbelievers from the world of Islam and to exercise a profound influence on Muslim thought and action. One of the reasons for this success, when all previous movements had failed, is no doubt that the French Revolution was secular —the first great social and intellectual upheaval in Europe to find ideological expression in nonreligious terms. Such earlier European movements as the Renaissance, the Reformation, the scientific revolution, and the Enlightenment had passed without effect in the Islamic world, without even being noticed. Perhaps the main reason for this is that all of them were, more or less, Christian in their form of expression and therefore barred from entry by the intellectual defenses of Islam. Secularism as such had, of course, no special attraction for Muslims, quite the reverse; but an ideology that was non-Christian could be considered by Muslims with a detachment that was not possible for doctrines tainted with a rival religion. In such a secular or, rather, religiously neutral ideology, Muslims might even hope to find the talisman that would give them the secrets of Western knowledge and progress without endangering their own traditions and way of life.

At first, the governing elites of Turkey did not view events in this

light. As the revolution spread from France to other European countries, they still saw it as a domestic affair of France or, at most, of
Christendom. The Ottoman Empire, as a Muslim state, was untroubled by the chaos in Christendom and immune from the contagion of
this Christian sickness. Some even saw possible advantages. In January
1792, Ahmed Efendi, private secretary to the sultan, noted in his diary
that the revolution, by distracting the attention of the European powers and providing another bait for their greed, had made life easier for
Ottomans. He piously concluded: "May God cause the upheaval in
France to spread like syphilis [firengi] to the other enemies of the
empire, hurl them into prolonged conflict with one another, and thus
accomplish results beneficial to the Empire. Amen."[32]

It was no doubt this belief in their immunity that led the Turks to
reject Russian overtures for common action against France, and even
a more modest request, submitted jointly by the Austrian, Prussian,
and Russian envoys, that they stop Frenchmen in Turkey from wearing tricolor cockades. The Ottoman historian, Jevdet Pasha, cites a
conversation:

> One day the Austrian chief dragoman came to the chief secretary
> Raşid Efendi and said: "May God punish these Frenchmen as they
> deserve: They have caused us much sorrow. For heaven's sake—if only
> you would have these cockades stripped off their heads!" To this request
> Raşid Efendi replied: "My friend, we have told you several times that
> the Ottoman Empire is a Muslim state. No one among us pays any
> attention to these badges of theirs. We recognize the merchants of
> friendly states as guests. They wear what headgear they wish on their
> heads and attach what badges they please. And if they put baskets of
> grapes on their heads, it is not the business of the Sublime Porte to ask
> them why they do so. You are troubling yourself for nothing."[33]

In October 1797, by the Treaty of Campo Formio, the French liqui-
dated the Venetian state and empire, and shared its possessions with
Austria. They themselves annexed the Ionian Islands and some places
on the adjoining Albanian and Greek coasts. France and Turkey, for
centuries friends, now became neighbors—and ancient friendship
wilted under the strain. With Hellenic citizens of the French republic
immediately next door to the *rayahs* of Ottoman Greece, the contrast
could not be concealed nor contact avoided. Before long the Ottoman
governor of the Morea began to send disturbing reports to Istanbul.
The French, he said, despite their protestations of friendship for the
Sublime Porte, had serious designs against it. As heirs to the Venetians
they were even planning to demand the return of other former Venetian possessions, such as the island of Crete and the Morea itself. Nor
was that all. There were alarming reports of meetings and ceremonies

just beyond the borders of the empire, with speeches about liberty and equality and even about the restoration of the ancient glories of Hellas.[34] This time, when the new Russian ambassador spoke of these things and of the threat to all established regimes posed by the events in France, the Pashas were more attentive, and Ahmed Atıf Efendi, the Ottoman chief secretary, wrote a memorandum for the high council of state discussing the Austrian and Russian invitation to the Ottomans to join them in a coalition against France in order to prevent the Revolution from spreading. So novel a notion required some explanation, and Ahmed Atıf Efendi painstakingly supplied it:

> In view of the foregoing observations, the question under consideration is this: Is the empire subject to the same danger as the other states, or is it not? Though, since the beginning of this conflict, the empire has chosen the path of neutrality, it has not refrained from showing friendship and good will and conducting itself in such a way as virtually to give assistance to the French Republic, to such a degree as to occasion repeated protests of the other powers. At a time when France was in grave straits and afflicted by dearth and famine, the empire permitted the export of copious supplies from the God-guarded realms and their transportation to the ports of France, and thus saved them from the pangs of hunger. In recompense, the French Republic and its generals have not refrained from attempting, by word and deed, to subvert the subjects of the empire. In particular, at the time of the Partition of Venice, they seized the islands and four towns on the mainland near Arta called Butrinto, Parga, Preveza, and Vonitza; their action in recalling the form of government of the ancient Greeks and installing a regime of liberty in these places reveals beyond any need for comment or explanation the evil intentions in their minds.[35]

Here again, it was the Greek and other Christian subjects of the empire that were regarded as vulnerable, and not the Muslims themselves. But on 1st July 1798, Bonaparte's expedition to Egypt landed in Alexandria and inaugurated a new era in Islamic history.

The contemporary Muslim unawareness and incredulity are reflected in the account given by the Egyptian historian Jabarti in his day-by-day chronicle of these unprecedented events:

> On Sunday, the 19th of the holy month of Ramadan of this year (1213/1798) letters arrived [in Cairo] by the hand of messengers from the seaport of Alexandria. Their content was that on Thursday, the 8th of that month, ten English ships had arrived at the port and had halted offshore within sight of the townspeople, and after a short time fifteen other ships arrived. The people of the port waited to see what they wanted and a small boat came inshore in which were ten persons. They landed and met the notables of the city and the chief *(Ra'is)* holding

authority from the ruler, al-Sayyid Muḥammad Karīm. . . . They were asked concerning their purpose and they replied that they were Englishmen and that they had come seeking for Frenchmen who had set forth with a very large force bound for an unknown destination. "We do not know," they said, "what is their purpose and we fear that they may attack you and you will be unable to defend yourselves against them and prevent them from landing."

Al-Sayyid Muḥammad Karīm did not accept this statement and suspected that it was a trap. He replied to them harshly. To which the envoys of the English replied: "We shall wait in our ships at sea and watch the port. We shall ask nothing from you but help with water and provisions, for which we shall pay." But this was refused to them with the answer: "These are the lands of the sultan and neither the French nor any other have any business here. Therefore, go from us." Thereupon, the English envoys went back and set sail, so as to seek provisions in some place other than Alexandria and so that God might accomplish His ordained decree. . . . On Wednesday the 20th of the same month, messages arrived from the seaport of Alexandria and also from Rosetta and Damanhūr saying that on Monday the 18th the French ships had arrived in great numbers. . . . They went ashore with weapons of war and soldiers, unbeknown to the people of the seaport, and by next morning they had spread like locusts around the city.[36]

Jabartī and his contemporaries in Egypt, while discussing at some length the arrival and activities and, finally, the departure of Bonaparte's expedition in Egypt, show no interest or concern in the internal history of France, still less in that of the rest of Europe. The French had come, they stayed a while, they did various things, and they left. No one cared to ask, let alone ascertain, why they had come and why they went. The coming of the infidel was seen as a kind of natural disaster, as little subject to control, as little in need of explanation. Only one of them, a Lebanese Christian known as Nicola Turk, attempted a very brief account of the French Revolution—surely the first in Arabic—as an introduction to his history of Egypt from 1789 to 1804:

We begin with the history of the appearance of the French Republic in the world after they killed their king and this at the beginning of the year 1792 of the Christian era corresponding to the year 1207 of the Islamic *hijra*. In this year the people of the kingdom of France rose up in their entirety against the king and the princes and the nobles, demanding a new order and a fresh dispensation, against the existing order which had been in the time of the king. They claimed and confirmed that the exclusive power of the king had caused great destruction in this kingdom, and that the princes and the nobles were enjoying all the good things of this kingdom while the rest of its people were in misery and abasement. Because of this they all rose up with one voice and said: 'We shall have no rest save by the abdication of the king and the establishment of a Republic.' And there was a great day in the city of Paris and the king and the rest of the people of his government, princes and nobles, were afraid, and the people came to the king and informed him of their purpose. . . .[37]

Nicola continues with a reasonably accurate account of the events that followed in France and in the rest of Europe.

The penetration of the French to the heart of the Muslim Middle East and the appearance of the British as the only power strong enough to challenge them brought a rude shock to the Muslim complacency. It was not the only one. While the British and French were extending their operations to the Eastern Mediterranean, the Russians were continuing their overland advance southwards. A new phase had begun in 1783, with the annexation of the Crimea. From there the Russians advanced rapidly in both directions along the northern shores of the Black Sea, subjugating and settling lands previously ruled and inhabited by Turks, Tatars, and other Muslim peoples. This led to another war with Turkey at the end of which, in 1792, the Ottomans were compelled to recognize the Russian annexation of the Tatar Khanates and to accept the Kuban River in Circassia as the frontier between the Russian and Ottoman Empires. The Russians had ended the centuries-long Muslim domination of the Black Sea and were threatening the frontiers of the Ottoman Empire at both its eastern and western ends. They were also threatening Iran, where a newly established dynasty, the Qājārs, tried to recover the Caucasian lands which had been lost to Russia, and failed. Facing a Persian invasion, some of the inhabitants of the ancient Christian kingdom of Georgia appealed for Russian protection, and the czar responded by proclaiming, in January, 1801, the annexation of Georgia to the Russian empire. This was followed in 1802 by the reorganization of Daghistan, the lands between Georgia and the Caspian, as a Russian protectorate, and shortly after by the absorption of another small trans-Caucasian kingdom. The way was now clear for an attack on Iran, which began in 1804, and resulted in the Russian annexation of Armenia and northern Azerbaijan.

By this time the French had left Egypt, but there was widespread fear that they might return. The competing British presence gave scant comfort. Nicola's chronicle clearly reflects Muslim foreboding about this double threat from western and eastern Europe:

In this month (February 1804) reports came to this country from other parts that the French had sent a great force into the Mediterranean with many ships and numerous troops, bound for the East. . . . The people in the East were in great fear of this, and it was rumored that the English were also coming with ships and men to Alexandria . . . to guard the land of Egypt against the French. . . . These rumors multiplied, and the minds of the Egyptians were uneasy about these European states, because they had witnessed their warlike prowess and their valor. People said that one or other of the Frankish kings was bound to seize the land of Egypt because they saw the lack of strength of the men of Islam in warfare and in pitched battles and their lack of steadfastness. . . .

At this time there were also rumors about Sultan Constantine, the brother of Sultan Alexander, the sultan of Russia, known as al-Muskūb, that he had taken the kingdom of Georgia and seized the lands of the Persians and was hastening towards Baghdad. The Ottoman State was in great fear of this sultan, who was nicknamed the "Yellow Rock" or the "Yellow Barbarian." The Muscovite State had had many wars and battles with the Ottoman State, from the time of Sultan Ahmed, who succeeded in 1115 [1703] until the time of Sultan Selim, who succeeded in 1203 [1789]. This empire has been growing and expanding without pause, crushing peoples and seizing lands and winning battles until this year 1218 [1804]. It has become mighty—and how mighty! And the times are propitious for them and that State has seized the lands of the Tatars and of the Georgians and of the Persians. It has begun to expand and to grow and this will continue as long as God wishes.[38]

The French did not, in fact, return. By the peace of 1802 they had withdrawn from both Egypt and the Ionian Islands. No longer a neighbor of Turkey, France was better able to communicate her ideas to the Turks. The letters of Halet Efendi, Turkish ambassador in Paris from 1803 to 1806 are revealing:

> I ask you to pray for my safe return from this land of infidels, for I have come as far as Paris but I have not yet seen the Frankland that some people speak of and praise. In what Europe these wonderful things and these wise Franks are to be found I do not know. . . .
>
> Glory be to God, the minds and beliefs of these people! It is a strange thing that this Frankland, with the praises of which our ears have for so long been filled, we found to be not only unlike what was said but the reverse. . . .
>
> If anyone with the intention of either intimidating you or leading you astray praises Frankland, then ask him this question: "Have you been to Europe or have you not?" If he says: "Indeed I have been there and I enjoyed myself a while" then assuredly he is a partisan and a spy of the Franks. If he says, "No, I have not been, I know it from history books" then he is one of two things. Either he is an ass who takes heed of what the Franks write or else he praises the Franks out of religious fanaticism.[39]

The assumption in the final phrase is that anyone who does praise the Franks is himself a Christian—presumably an Ottoman Christian —praising his European coreligionists.

Halet Efendi was a convinced reactionary and hater of all things Western, but his letters reveal how strong French influence had become. The spread of French ideas, even in Istanbul, is confirmed by the imperial historiographer Ahmed Asim Efendi, who wrote a chronicle of the years 1791–1808, and has something to say about French activities in Turkey. The French had presented themselves as friends and had conducted intensive propaganda. They had confused the minds, not only of the great ones of the state but also of the common people. To spread their pernicious ideas they sought the company of Muslims, beguiling them with protestations of friendship and good will and, thus, through familiar and intimate social intercourse had found many victims.

> Certain sensualists, naked of the garment of loyalty, from time to time learned politics from them. Some, desirous of learning their language, took French teachers, acquired their idiom and prided themselves . . . on their uncouth talk. In this way the French were able to insinuate Frankish customs into the hearts and endear their modes of thought to the minds of some people of weak mind and shallow faith. The sober-minded and farsighted and the ambassadors of the other states all saw the danger of the situation. Full of alarm and disapproval, they reviled and condemned these things both implicitly and explicitly, and gave forewarning of the evil consequences to which their activities would give rise. This malicious crew and abominable band were full of cunning, first sowing the seed of their politics in the soil of the hearts of the great ones of the state, then by incitement and seduction to their ways of thought, undermining—God preserve us—the principles of the Holy Law.[40]

The impact of the West on the Middle East had entered a new and violent phase.

II

The Muslim View
of the World

The Western world has in the course of the centuries devised a number of ways of subdividing mankind. The Greeks divided the world into Greeks and barbarians, the Jews into Jews and Gentiles. Later the Greeks also invented a geographical classification in which the world was seen as consisting of continents—Europe, their own, and Asia, that which lay on the opposite side of the Aegean Sea. Eventually, when a larger and remoter Asia was seen to loom beyond the Aegean coast, that became Asia Minor and the name Asia given a wider extension. In time, Asia (i.e., non-Europe) was also subdivided, and that part of it which lay on the southern shore of the Mediterranean was given new names in Greek and Latin—first Libya, later Africa. The medieval world was, for Europeans, divided initially between Christendom and heathendom and, then, within Christendom by monarchies. The modern world has adopted the nation-state as its basic classification, the determinant of identity and loyalty.

The Muslim view of the world and its peoples was differently constructed. Until the nineteenth century, Muslim writers on history and geography knew nothing of the names which Europeans had given to the continents. Asia was unknown, an ill-defined Europe—spelled Urūfa—received no more than a passing mention, while Africa, Arabicized into Ifrīqiya, appeared only as the name of the eastern Maghrib, consisting of Tunisia and the adjoining areas. Muslim geographical writers divided the world into "climates" *(iqlīm)* deriving from the ancient Greek *clima,* but this is a purely geographical classification without any of the political or even cultural implications injected into the names of the continents in modern Western parlance. Muslim historical writings make virtually no reference to the *iqlīms* and they seem to have occupied no place in the corporate self-awareness of Muslim peoples.

The division of the world into countries and nations, so important in the Western world's perception of itself and definition of its loyalties, is of comparatively minor importance in the world of Islam. Territorial designations are of so little significance that many countries even lack a specific country name. A remarkably high proportion of the names borne by the modern states into which the Islamic world is divided are new creations. Some of them, like Syria, Palestine, or Libya, are exhumed from classical antiquity; some of them, like Iraq or Tunisia, the names of medieval provinces; some of them, like Pakistan, entirely new inventions. Arabia and Turkey, despite the antiquity of the countries and, for that matter, of the peoples which they designate, are modern introductions from the West. Arabic has no territorial term for Arabia but is compelled to make use of such locutions as the Land or the Peninsula of the Arabs. The name Turkey, although used for many centuries by Westerners, was adapted and adopted into Turkish only in the twentieth century to designate a country which had been previously called by dynastic or regional names. Often, the same name serves in classical usage for the country or province and its main city—usually the name of the city being applied to the country around it. At no time before the nineteenth century was any sovereignty defined in territorial terms. On the contrary, a territorial designation applied to a monarch was seen as belittling.

The same is true, though to a lesser extent, of ethnic terms. Such ethnic entities as the Arabs, the Persians, or the Turks figure prominently in Islamic literature, and membership of one or other of these groups defined by language, culture, and sometimes descent was an important part of the self-awareness of individual Muslims. But it was rarely of any political significance. Muslim monarchs did not normally define their sovereignties or formulate their titles in terms of nations, nor was the ethnic, linguistic, or territorial nation seen as a natural basis of statehood.

In the Muslim world view the basic division of mankind is into the House of Islam *(Dār al-Islām)* and the House of War *(Dār al-Ḥarb).* The one consists of all those countries where the law of Islam prevails, that is to say, broadly, the Muslim Empire; the latter is the rest of the world. Just as there is only one God in heaven, so there can be only one sovereign and one law on earth. Ideally, the House of Islam is conceived as a single community, governed by a single state, headed by a single sovereign. This state must tolerate and protect those unbelievers who are brought by conquest under its rule, provided, of course, that they are not polytheists but followers of one of the permitted religions. The logic of Islamic law, however, does not recognize the permanent existence of any other polity outside Islam. In time, in the Muslim view, all mankind will accept Islam or submit to Islamic rule. In the meantime, it is a religious duty of Muslims to struggle until this end is accomplished.

The name given by the Muslim jurists to this struggle is *jihād,* an Arabic word meaning effort or striving. One who performs this duty is called *mujāhid.* The word occurs several times in the Qur'ān in the sense of making war against the unbelievers. In the early centuries of Islamic expansion, this was its normal meaning. Between the House of Islam and the House of War there was, according to the *sharīʿa,* the Holy Law as formulated by the classical jurists, a state of war religiously and legally obligatory, which could end only with the conversion or subjugation of all mankind. A treaty of peace between the Muslim state and a non-Muslim state was thus in theory juridically impossible. The war, which would end only with the universal triumph of Islam, could not be terminated; it could only be interrupted for reasons of necessity or of expediency by a truce. Such a truce, according to the jurists, could only be provisional. It should not exceed ten years and could, at any time, be repudiated unilaterally by the Muslims who, however, were obliged by Muslim law to give the other side due notice before resuming hostilities.

Even during such periods of relative peace, traffic with the infidel was discouraged. Muslim law distinguishes between those actions which are actually forbidden *(harām)* and those which are regarded as reprehensible *(makrūh).* Travel to the House of War belonged to the latter category, and the jurists for the most part agreed that the only legitimate reason for a Muslim to travel to the House of War was to ransom captives. Even trade was not an acceptable purpose, though some authorities permitted the purchase of food supplies from Christian lands in case of dire necessity.[1]

The law relating to jihād, like the greater part of the *sharīʿa,* received its classical form during the first century and a half of the Islamic era, when the Arab armies were advancing on France, Byzantium, China, and India, and when there seemed no reason to doubt that the final and universal triumph of Islam was not only inevitable but imminent. Thereafter, in this as in other respects, a gap began to appear between legal doctrine and political fact—a gap which rulers and soldiers ignored and jurists did their best to hide. The single Islamic universal state, which had existed in reality as well as in principle in the first century or two, broke up into smaller states. The irresistible and perpetual jihād was brought to an end and, in time, a relationship of mutual tolerance was established between the world of Islam and the rest. The latter was still perceived and designated as the House of War, but its subjugation was postponed from historic to messianic time. In the meanwhile, more or less stable frontiers came into existence between Muslim and non-Muslim states on which peace rather than war was the normal condition. This peace might be infringed by raiding, the frontier might from time to time be displaced by war, but from the age of the Reconquest and the Crusades onwards such displacements of the frontier could mean the withdrawal as often as the advance of the boundaries of Muslim power.

These changes and the consequent development of diplomatic and commercial relations with the outside world posed new problems for the jurists. They responded in this as in other fields with skillful interpretations. The duty of holy war was qualified and reinterpreted. The cessation of hostilities with the House of War could indeed only be accomplished by a limited truce, but such a truce could be renewed as often as required and thus become, in effect, a legally regulated state of peace.

Some jurists even recognized an intermediate status, the House of Truce or House of Covenant (Dār al-Ṣulḥ or Dār al-ʿAhd) between the House of War and the House of Islam. This consisted of certain non-Muslim states which had entered into a contractual relationship with the Muslim state by which they recognized Muslim suzerainty and paid tribute but retained some autonomy in their own form of government. By choosing to regard gifts as tribute, Muslim rulers and their juridical counselors could extend the scope of the covenant (ʿAhd) and cover a wide variety of arrangements with non-Muslim powers concerning political, military, and commercial matters. A non-Muslim from the House of War, might even visit the Muslim lands and be given a safe conduct, called amān. According to the jurists, any free adult male Muslim could give an amān to one or several persons. The head of the Muslim state could give a collective amān to a larger entity such as a city, the subjects of a sovereign, or a commercial corporation. The practice of granting amān greatly facilitated the development of commercial and diplomatic relations between Muslim and Christian states and provided an Islamic legal framework for the rise of resident communities of European traders in Muslim cities. One of the determining differences between the two sides was that there was no *amān* for Muslim visitors, still less residents, in Christian Europe. *Amān* was a purely Muslim legal formula for peaceful contact. However, with the growing shift in the balance of real power, these relations were to an increasing extent regulated not by Islamic law but by European commercial and diplomatic practice.

In both ideal and legal terms the House of Islam was a *single* entity, and despite the many sectarian, regional, national, and other differences that arose between Muslims, there always was and still remains a strong sense of common identity. It was natural, therefore, that Muslims tended to attribute a similar unity to the House of War. According to a saying sometimes ascribed to the Prophet Muḥammad, "Unbelief is one nation." Both the attribution and the content of the statement are patently false, but it does express a common attitude reflected in Muslim writings and practice. The really significant division of mankind is between Muslims and unbelievers. If the divisions among Muslims were of secondary importance, the parochial subdivisions of the unbelievers and, particularly, of those who lived beyond the Islamic frontier, were of even less interest or significance.

In fact, of course, Muslims did recognize certain important divisions among the generalized mass of unbelievers. One of them was between those who possessed and those who did not possess revealed religions. For atheists or for polytheists the choice was clear—Islam or death. For Jews and Christians, possessors of what were regarded as revealed religions based on authentic though superseded revelations, the choice included a third term—Islam, death, or submission. Submission involved the payment of tribute and the acceptance of Muslim supremacy. Death might be commuted to slavery. Those who submitted, according to Muslim law and practice, could be accorded the tolerance and protection of the Muslim state. The resulting relationship was regulated by a pact called, in Arabic, the *dhimma.* Those benefiting from it were known as *ahl al-dhimma,* people of the pact, or more briefly as *dhimmīs.* This was the term commonly applied to Jews, Christians, and some others who became subjects of the Muslim state. Under the rules of the *dhimma* they were permitted to practice their own religions, maintain their own places of worship and, in many ways, run their own affairs, provided they gave unequivocal recognition to the primacy of Islam and the supremacy of the Muslims. This recognition was expressed through a series of restrictions imposed by the holy law on the *dhimmīs,* affecting the clothes they might wear, the beasts they might ride, the arms they might bear, and similar matters. Most of these disabilities had a social and symbolic rather than a tangible and practical character. The only real economic burden imposed on unbelievers was fiscal. They had to pay higher taxes, a system inherited from the previous empires of Iran and Byzantium. Above all, they had to pay the poll tax known as *jizya,* levied on every adult male non-Muslim.

The term *dhimmi* was used only for Jews and Christians living in Muslim territories and subject to the rule of the Muslim state. Christians remaining beyond the frontier were called *ḥarbī,* i.e., dwellers in the House of War. Those who came from the House of War to the House of Islam as visitors or temporary residents, with safe conduct, were known as *musta'min,* i.e., holder of *amān.* The information about non-Muslims available in the Muslim world was, not surprisingly, fullest and most accurate about *dhimmīs,* considerably less about *musta'-mins,* and limited and unreliable about the denizens of the House of War.

The broad outlines could, however, be seen. The main classification, as already indicated, was by religion. Jews and Christians were seen as religio-political communities, like Islam itself, but inferior. Indeed, it has been argued with perhaps some exaggeration that the notion of religion as a class or category, of which Judaism, Christianity, and Islam are individual examples, originated only with the advent of Islam and the ability of Muslims to perceive and recognize two distinct predecessors to their own form of religious revelation and polity.[2] No such awareness can be found among earlier Christians or Jews nor among any of the other cults of the ancient world. For a Muslim, the advent of Muḥammad and the revelation of the Qur'ān marks the last in a series of similar events through which God's purpose was revealed to mankind. There had been a number of prophets whom God had sent on a mission to mankind as bearers of a revealed book. Muḥammad was the seal of the prophets and the Qur'ān the final and perfect revelation. All that was of value in earlier revelations was contained in it. What was not contained in it was due to the corruption or distortion of earlier revealed texts.

Neither Jews nor Christians were strangers to Islam. Both religions were represented in pre-Islamic Arabia. Both were known to the Prophet and both figure in the Qur'ān and in the most ancient traditions. Islam, in a sense, defined itself against the previous beliefs—against Judaism and Christianity as much as against the pagan Arabian cults with which Muḥammad fought his main battles. When the

Qur'ān (Sura 112) proclaims that "He is God, unique, God alone, He does not beget and is not begotten, none is equal to Him,"[3] it is rejecting Christian theology. When it says (Sura 16:115) "Eat from among what God has assigned to you, what is permissible and good. Thank God for His Benefaction . . . ," it is discarding some Jewish dietary laws.[4] The principle of separateness and coexistence is usually justified by citing Sura 109. "Say: O Unbelievers! I shall not worship what you worship. You do not worship what I worship. I am not a worshiper of what you have worshiped and you are not worshipers of what I have worshiped. To you, your religion. To me, my religion."[5] This was a new notion, without antecedents in either Christian or Jewish belief and practice.

After the Islamic conquests the Muslims found themselves as a ruling minority among predominantly Christian populations all the way from Mesopotamia to Spain. They therefore had ample opportunity to observe large parts of the Christian world at work, at worship and at play. A certain amount of information concerning Christian beliefs and practices became part of the common knowledge of educated Muslims, and some aspects of Muslim doctrine and usage were even influenced by Christian example. An occasional Muslim scholar made some study of Christian and Jewish religion and scripture. Sometimes this was for purposes of refutation, though this motive is usually to be found only among new converts from these religions to Islam. Sometimes the interest is scholarly rather than polemical, and some discussion of Christian and Jewish scripture and belief was included in Muslim books on the classification of religions and doctrines—a subject and a literature which seem to have made their first appearance in medieval Islam.

As the Christians and Jews living under Islamic rule gradually adopted the Arabic language in place of their previous idioms, they began to produce their own literature in Arabic, including translations of the scriptures. Often these Christian and Jewish writings, though in Arabic, were in other scripts—Syriac for the Christians, Hebrew for the Jews—and thus inaccessible to Muslim readers. Even, however, when they were written in the Arabic script, they seemed to have attracted little attention from Muslim scholars. In general, while granting some measure of tolerance to Christians and Jews, they accorded them little respect. For the Muslim, convinced of the perfection of Islam and the supremacy of Muslim power, these were followers of superseded religions and members of conquered communities. They could, therefore, offer little of interest or value to him.

Some of the same considerations also determined Muslim attitudes towards the infidel living beyond the frontier. But in this respect other considerations were also at work. During the early centuries the Islamic Empire and community expanded principally eastward and westward. To the north and south of the Muslim lands, the empty plains of Eurasia and the jungles and deserts of Africa offered little attraction, and the advance of Islam in these regions was slow and late. The main effort of conquest and conversion was directed to more populous and more rewarding regions, westward to North Africa and thence into Europe; eastward across Iran to Central Asia and the approaches to India and China. On both sides the Muslims met formidable adversaries; in the east, first the great Empire of Persia, beyond that the warlike peoples of the steppes and forests and the great powers of India and China; in the west, the Byzantine Empire and beyond it the remoter kingdoms of Christendom.

From the Muslim point of view there was a major difference in quality between the war against the Christians and the wars on the other frontiers of Islam. Among the peoples of the steppes and the jungles, even in the great civilizations of China and India of which they had limited knowledge or understanding, they saw no recognizable alternative to Islam. A Muslim advance in these regions was part of the inevitable Islamization of the pagan peoples. It encountered no major military adversary and no serious religious alternative. The struggle in the west, in contrast, was against a rival religious and political system which denied the very basis of the universal mission of Islam and did so in terms which were both familiar and intelligible. The Muslim conviction of their own predestined final victory did not blind them to the significance and the uncertainty of this wide-ranging and long drawn-out conflict between two faiths and two societies. In Muslim writings, the Christian world becomes the House of War par excellence, and the war against Christendom is the very model and prototype of the jihād.

Between the eleventh and the fifteenth centuries, the retreat of Islam and the advance of the Christian reconquest in Italy, Portugal and Spain brought large and old-established Muslim populations under Christian rule. In all these countries the reconquest was followed—sometimes after an interval of tolerance—by a determined effort on the part of Christian rulers to convert or else evict their Muslim subjects. In these efforts they were, in the long run, successful.

In general, Christian unwillingness to tolerate Muslim subjects was matched by Muslim unwillingness to remain under Christian rule. Most Muslim jurists held that it was impossible for a Muslim to live under a non-Muslim government. If an infidel in the lands of the infidels was converted to Islam, it was his duty to leave his home and country and travel to a land where Muslims ruled and Muslim law prevailed. The scriptural authority for this doctrine was the migration *(hijra)* of the Prophet Muḥammad and his companions from Mecca to Medina—the event which marked the birth of the Muslim state and the beginning of the Muslim era. Where the Prophet had led, others were expected to follow.

The loss of Muslim lands to Christian conquerors raised the question in a new and acute form. This problem was first confronted by jurists of the Mālikī school, which predominated in North Africa and in Muslim Spain and Sicily. Mālikī jurists in their discussions of the legal questions posed by the loss of Muslim territory to infidels were divided. A few argued that if a Christian ruler allowed the free practice of the Muslim religion and permitted Muslims to live according to the prescriptions of the Holy Law, then Muslims might be permitted to stay. Some even went further and were willing to allow Muslims subject to intolerant infidels to conceal their own religion in order to survive. The prevailing view, however, was that at least some and preferably all of the Muslims of a country conquered by the infidels should do as their forebears in Mecca had done, and go on a *hijra* from heathendom to Islam. A classical formulation was given in a ruling by the Moroccan jurist al-Wansharīsī, who held that it was the duty of all Muslims to emigrate rather than to remain under infidel rule. If the infidels were tolerant, this made the need to depart more rather than less urgent, since the danger of apostasy was correspondingly greater. Even Muslim tyranny, says al-Wansharīsī, is better than Christian justice.[6]

In general, however, Christian justice was not on offer. There were exceptions. Muslims stayed for a while in reconquered Sicily, under the relatively tolerant rule of the Normans, and in those parts of Spain which had been reconquered by the Christians. But their survival depended on the continued presence of Muslim states in the south, which exacted mutual tolerance from the Christian north. After the final Christian victory in 1492, such tolerance was no longer needed, and the edict of expulsion followed very shortly afterwards.

The problem arose again in eastern Europe, with the Russian conquest of the Muslim lands north and east of the Black Sea, and with the loss of successive Ottoman provinces in the Balkans. New groups of Muslims came under Christian rule, and some of them found the same answer—emigration. But in the age of European imperial expansion this could no longer be a solution. With the rise of the Russian, British, French and Dutch empires, Christian rule was finally extended to the main centers of the Islamic world, where great Muslim populations perforce remained where they were, under infidel domination.

Despite its importance for them, Muslims showed remarkably little interest in the world of Christendom. The part which they knew best was, naturally enough, the Greek Christian Empire of Byzantium. In Muslim annals, this empire, known as the land of Rūm, was the chief adversary of the Muslim State. It is frequently mentioned in the history of the wars of Islam, and its provinces, particularly those immediately beyond the border, are discussed in some detail in Muslim geographical and historical writings.

In the year 1068—that is, two years after the Battle of Hastings and thirty years before the arrival of the Crusaders in Palestine—a certain Ṣāʿid ibn Aḥmad, Qadi of the Muslim city of Toledo in Spain, wrote a book in Arabic on the categories of nations. In his introduction he divides the nations of the human race into two kinds, those that have concerned themselves with science and learning and those that have not. The nations that have contributed to the advancement of knowledge are eight in number—the Indians, Persians, Chaldees, Greeks, Romans (a term which includes the Byzantines and eastern Christians generally), Egyptians, Arabs (including Muslims in general), and Jews. These nations form the subject of the rest of the book. Of the remainder of humanity he singles out the Chinese and the Turks as "the noblest of the unlearned peoples," who are worthy of respect for their achievements in other fields, the Chinese for their skill in handicrafts and in the pictorial arts, and for their endurance; the Turks for their courage, their skill in the arts of war, their horsemanship, and their proficiency in the use of the lance, the sword, and the bow. The rest of mankind Ṣāʿid dismisses contemptuously as the northern and the southern barbarians. Of the former he remarks:

> The other peoples of this group who have not cultivated the sciences are more like beasts than like men. For those of them who live furthest to the north, between the last or the seven climates and the limits of the inhabited world, the excessive distance of the sun in relation to the zenith line makes the air cold and the sky cloudy. Their temperaments are therefore frigid, their humors raw, their bellies gross, their color pale, their hair long and lank. Thus they lack keenness of understanding and clarity of intelligence, and are overcome by ignorance and apathy, lack of discernment and stupidity. . . .[7]

In these remarks, Ṣāʿid was expressing the generally accepted view of Muslim scholars of his time. The center of the world was the lands of Islam, stretching from Spain across North Africa to the Middle East and containing within itself almost all the peoples and centers of ancient civilization. To the north the Christian empire of Byzantium represented an earlier, arrested stage of that civilization based on divine revelation which had reached its final and complete form in Islam. To the east, beyond Persia, there were countries which had achieved some form of civilized living, albeit of an inferior and idolatrous kind. Apart from that there were only the white and black barbarians of the outer world in the north and south. It is with the growth of Muslim knowledge about some of these northern barbarians that we are here concerned.

III

On Language
and Translation

In a fourteenth century Persian work on universal history the writer, discussing Europe, remarks that "the Franks speak twenty-five languages, and no people understands the language of any other. All they have in common," he adds, "is their calendar, script, and numbers."[1] It was a natural comment for a medieval Muslim, accustomed to the linguistic unity of the Muslim world in which two or sometimes three major languages served, not only the needs of a narrow clerical class (like Latin in western Europe), but as the effective means of universal communication, supplanting local languages and dialects at all but the lowest levels.

At first, only one language was in use among Muslims, and that was Arabic, the language of the Qur'ān and of the Arab conquerors. For a while, Arabic was virtually the sole language of government, commerce, and culture in the Muslim lands, replacing with astonishing speed such earlier cultural languages as Latin, Greek, Coptic, Syriac, and Persian, which had flourished in the territories now incorporated in the Islamic Empire.

Latin and Greek disappeared almost entirely; Coptic and Syriac survived as the liturgical but not the spoken languages of Christian minorities. Only Persian entered on a new phase in its development.

With the Islamization of Iran, a new form of Persian emerged, written in the Arabic script with an enormous loan vocabulary of Arabic words, differing from pre-Islamic Persian as English does from Anglo-Saxon. In time Persian became the second major cultural language of the Islamic world, widely used in Central Asia, India, and Turkey as well as in Iran proper.

The coming of the Turks from Central Asia to the Middle East and the establishment of a thousand-year-long Turkish ascendancy in the Muslim lands brought the third major Islamic language. Before their entry into the Islamic world, the Turks had included followers of a number of religions and had written their languages in several scripts. They became overwhelmingly Muslim, and various Turkic languages went through the same processes as Persian. A new Muslim Turkish emerged, written in the Arabic script, and with a vast loan vocabulary of Arabic and now also Persian words. Later other Muslim languages appeared in south and southeast Asia and in black Africa. But in the heartlands of Islam and the old centers of Muslim civilization in central and southwest Asia and in North Africa and Europe, only three languages, Arabic, Persian, and Turkish, were in common use.

In general, Arabs, even the most educated, knew only Arabic. Educated Persians knew Arabic and Persian. Educated Turks knew Arabic, Persian, and Turkish. Persian became a classical language; Arabic was both a classical and scriptural language, and an essential part of the formation of all educated Muslims of whatever ethnic and linguistic background. Both Persian and Turkish, as well as other languages used by Muslims, were written in the Arabic script and drew their intellectual and conceptual vocabulary almost entirely from Arabic sources.

The association between religious affiliation and writing was total. Jews used the Hebrew script, not only for Hebrew but for other languages they spoke. Christians used the Syriac script, not only for Syriac but for Arabic. And Muslims used the Arabic script to the exclusion of all others. For Muslims to learn an infidel script would involve an element of, so to speak, impiety, even of pollution, and few, indeed, were the Muslims who ever attempted to learn a foreign language. Non-Islamic languages were unknown except for previous knowledge brought into the fold by new converts to Islam.

This situation is in striking contrast with that prevailing in Europe, split into many countries and nations, each with its own language. Europeans found it necessary, at an early stage, to learn languages other than their own and to prepare tools for this purpose. In the Islamic world grammar and lexicography were for long limited to Arabic, for the religious task of enabling non-Arab converts to Islam to read and understand the sacred scriptures.

The general lack of interest in foreign languages was found even in border areas like Muslim Spain where, during the centuries of Muslim rule, the Romance vernacular which later developed into Spanish was in common use and was certainly known to Muslims and Jews as well as Christians. This is evidenced by the practice followed by both Muslim and Jewish poets of adding a refrain in Romance vernacular to their Arabic or Hebrew lyrics. This type of refrain, known as *kharja* and written in either Arabic or Hebrew script, constitutes an important source of information for the early history of Spanish language and literature. Even so, it does not seem to have fostered any deeper interest among Muslims in the society from which it emerged. The *kharja* is no more than a stylistic fashion—a refrain taken from the spoken language and probably used to indicate a popular tune. It was adopted in a certain type of poetic improvisation and nowhere beyond that. There is a class of literature in which Spanish Arab writers vaunt the glories of al-Andalus—the Arabic name for Muslim Spain—against the claims of the older Muslim East. They have much to say about the beauties of the Spanish landscape, the richness of its cities, and the achievements of its Muslim people. They do not think it worthwhile to mention its previous or other inhabitants. From the whole eight centuries of the Muslim presence in Spain only one document has survived that indicates any kind of interest in a European language. It is a very late fragment, no more than a sheet of paper, containing a few German words with their Arabic equivalents.[2] Of the countless scholars and philologists who flourished in Muslim Spain, only one, a certain Abū Ḥayyān of Granada who died in 1344, is reported to have interested himself in strange languages. He learned Turkish and Ethiopic.

This does not mean that the art of translation was unknown in medieval Islam. On the contrary, there was probably more translation activity into and out of Arabic than any other language in premodern times. Religious, legal and, later, some other texts were translated into Persian, Turkish, and other Muslim languages for the guidance of the believers; scientific and philosophical texts were translated into Hebrew and Latin for the instruction of Jews and Christians and through these, in due course, became available to the Western world.[3]

Of more immediate relevance are the translations made into Arabic from earlier literatures. According to the Arab tradition, the movement began at the turn of the seventh-eighth centuries when a prince of the reigning Umayyad family arranged for the translation of some Greek writings on alchemy. The translator was a certain Stephen, by his name clearly a Christian. The earliest translations appear to have been made for private use, and little if anything has survived. The choice was determined by practical considerations and concentrated on two fields, medicine and alchemy. Some religious material was also made available since knowledge of the Jewish and Christian religions could contribute to a better understanding of the Qur'ān.

The translation movement grew in scope under the Abbasid Caliphs who succeeded the Umayyads in the mid-eighth century. The transfer of the capital from Syria to Iraq led to a strengthening of Middle Eastern and a weakening of Mediterranean influences. Some works, dealing mainly with statecraft and court ceremonial, were translated from middle Persian into Arabic; others, on mathematics, from the languages of India. But the great bulk of the translations were of Greek origin, translated either directly from the Greek or indirectly via Syriac versions. The translators were without exception non-Muslims or new converts. Most were Christians, a few were Jews, and the remainder were members of the Sabian community.

The choice of works to be translated is instructive. The Arabic translations from the Greek consist in the main of books in two fields—philosophy and science. The one consists of the classical philosophical works of Plato and Aristotle, together with a number of other ancient philosophers, including hermetic, gnostic, and neo-Platonic writings. The other includes medicine, astrology and astronomy, alchemy and chemistry, physics and mathematics. Some attention was also given to technical literature, notably to works on agriculture. Two treatises on this topic were translated in the tenth century, one each from Aramaic and from Greek.

At the time when the Muslims came to the eastern Mediterranean lands, these were already overwhelmingly Christian, and to a large extent the Hellenistic heritage as it reached the Muslims had already passed through the filter of the eastern Christian churches. This is no doubt part of the explanation of the choices made by the Muslims, and by the translators working for them, concerning which Greek texts to translate. It is, however, only part and not the whole of the explanation. Some works cherished by the eastern Christians were tossed aside by the Muslims; others, neglected by the eastern churches, were recovered directly from ancient texts or through the classical scholars of Byzantium.

The basic criterion of choice was usefulness, though, as the progression from astrology to astronomy and from alchemy to chemistry shows, this could lead in time to a more detached scientific curiosity. The criterion of usefulness applied to philosophy no less than to science. Usefulness is not to be understood in a narrowly utilitarian sense. It includes works the purpose of which was to enable man to attain to what the Muslim philosophers called *sa'āda*, felicity, corresponding to the Greek concept of *eudaimonia*. Though expressed in abstract terms and concerned with abstract notions, this justification of philosphy is based on the pursuit of certain specific gains, spiritual as well as material. If science is concerned with the health and well-being of man in this world, philosophy helps to prepare him for the next. The translation and study of philosophic texts were essentially a religious activity and the influence of Greek thought on Muslim theology was very considerable.

There was no attempt to translate Greek poetry, drama, or history. Literature is both a personal and culture-bound experience. It is difficult to appreciate an alien aesthetic, and literary translation has, in the past, been extremely rare, occurring only where there is a close cultural symbiosis. There are translations from Greek into Latin, from Arabic into Persian, from Chinese into Japanese. Where there is no such link, science and even philosophy are sometimes translated, literature hardly ever. The transfer of poetry across the boundary from one civilization to another begins in early modern Europe. For medieval Muslims, the literature of an alien and heathen society could offer neither aesthetic appeal nor moral guidance. The history of these remote peoples, without prophets or scriptures, was a mere sequence of events, without aim or meaning. For the Muslim, literature meant the poetry and eloquence of his own rich cultural tradition. History was the working out of God's purpose for mankind as manifested in the life of His own Islamic community. The history of pre-Islam was of significance only insofar as it prefigured the Islamic revelation and helped to prepare for the advent of the Islamic community. It was not until Renaissance and post-Renaissance Europe that a human society for the first time developed the sophistication, the detachment and, above, all, the curiosity to study and appreciate the literary achievements of alien and even hostile societies.

Two other kinds of writing were of limited value and were translated in limited quantities—geography and politics. It was from translations of Greek works on geography that Muslims gleaned their first information on the geographical configuration of the world in which they lived; it was from Greek works on politics that they acquired certain basic notions on the nature of the state and the relationship between ruler and ruled. Greek political thought was, however, of restricted influence and Muslim writers on politics in Greek terms are marginal to mainstream Islam, where the dominant influences were the Qur'ān and the traditions of the early Muslims.

The translation movement from the Greek came to an end in the tenth century, by which time a considerable body of material had been translated. Thereafter, for a variety of reasons, this movement ceased. The reason was certainly not lack of material, since a good deal remained accessible and untranslated. The Byzantine Empire still offered great resources of Greek literature, the existence of which was known in Muslim lands. There are even cases on record of special emissaries being sent by Muslim rulers to Byzantium to find Greek texts required for translation. Nor can the cessation of the movement be attributed solely to the lack of translators. No doubt the progress of Arabization among the Christian minorities made it increasingly difficult to find scholars with the requisite knowledge of Greek. There were some, however, and translations continued to be made within the Christian communities for their own use. These, however, no longer passed into the common stock of Arabic culture which had, by this time, become resistant to such external influences.

The body of translated material from Greek is very extensive and was sufficient to give the Muslim reader a comprehensive view of ancient Greek philosophy, medicine, and science as well as of late Hellenistic accretions to them. In contrast to the large body of work translated from Greek, only a single book was translated from Latin in this period. This was the late chronicle of Orosius, exceptional not only in being Latin but also in dealing with history. This brief account of Roman history was translated in Spain and served as the basis of later treatments by Muslim writers on the history of Rome.[4]

If interest in ancient Rome was small, interest in medieval Europe and its languages was even less. When an ambassador from Italy arrived in Baghdad in 906, with a letter, presumably in Latin, there was some difficulty in getting it read. According to a contemporary Arab account:

> The letter was on white silk, in a writing resembling the Greek writing, but straighter . . . the authorities looked for someone to translate the letter, and there was in the clothing store, with Bishr the eunuch, a Frank who was able to read the writing of that people. The eunuch brought him into the Caliph's presence, and he read the letter and translated it into Greek writing. Then Isḥāq ibn Ḥunayn [one of the great scientific translators] was summoned, and he translated it from Greek into Arabic.[5]

The story illustrates graphically the remoteness and unfamiliarity of the Latin West among court circles in Baghdad. Later in the same century, when the great Arab scholar Ibn al-Nadīm compiled a comprehensive bibliographical survey of scholarly literature "both by

Arabs and non-Arabs" he listed sixteen languages, some of which are discussed at great length. Only three—apart from a passing mention of Russian—can be called European. The first is Greek, about which he has a great deal of information. The second is "the writing of the Lombards and Saxons, a people between Rome and Franja, near the ruler of Andalus. Their script is twenty-two letters. It is called "apostolic" [the word is transcribed in Arabic] and they start to write from left to right. . . ." The third is Frankish, and all that Ibn al-Nadim knows about it is the report of the embassy of 906, cited above. Latin is not mentioned by name; the "Lombard-Saxon" script is perhaps a distant echo of the Saxon Emperor Otto's campaigns in Italy.[6]

While the Muslim world rejected the study of non-Muslim languages and showed no interest in any works that might be written in them, Muslims were, nevertheless, obliged to communicate with Westerners for a variety of noncultural purposes. Even before the Crusades, trade between Islam and Western Christendom had resumed across the Mediterranean, and from Crusading times onwards it grew steadily in volume and scope. Some form of communication must obviously have existed between European merchants and the Middle Eastern buyers, sellers, or middlemen with whom they dealt. Diplomacy, too, gives rise to conversation and occasional exchanges of letters and documents. The Muslim world did not adopt the European practice of continuous diplomatic relations through resident embassies until the last years of the eighteenth century. Some form of diplomatic contact, however, existed from early times.

During the eighteenth century, a third important channel of communication was added to commerce and diplomacy—instruction, chiefly military and naval. The modernization of the Ottoman army and navy required the importation of European military and naval officers to teach in Turkish military academies and even, on occasion, to serve with the Turkish armed forces. Obviously some common language was required.

For all these activities translators and interpreters were employed as intermediaries between the two sides. Someone had to make an effort to learn someone else's language. Overwhelmingly, it was the Europeans and not the Muslims who made this effort. First in Spain, then in Italy, later in more northerly countries, there were Europeans who, through the circumstances of their lives or professions, had had the opportunity to live in an Arabic or Turkish-speaking environment and acquire at least a working knowledge of the spoken language. While increasing numbers of European merchants resided in Muslim cities, there were few voluntary Muslim residents in Europe, and Muslims, therefore, lacked the opportunity as well as the desire to learn any of the languages of Europe.

Along the European borders of the Ottoman Empire there was probably rather greater linguistic versatility, and the chronicles make occasional reference to the use of interpreters in interrogations, parleys, and even negotiations during the wars of the sixteenth and seventeenth centuries, presumably using local languages. These languages were no doubt also known by the innumerable Balkan Christians and Muslims who for one reason or another went to Istanbul, and the Ottoman-Turkish language, particularly in fiscal and bureaucratic usage, absorbed quite a number of words of Balkan and even Hungarian origin. All this, however, had little or no effect on Turkish perceptions of the West.

Such information as we have about interpreters in the Muslim service indicates that these were either renegades, that is to say Western Christians who had settled in a Muslim country and embraced Islam, or else *dhimmis,* that is to say non-Muslim subjects of the Muslim state. These included both Christians and Jews, the latter in Ottoman times often being recent immigrants from Europe and, therefore, possessors of useful knowledge of European languages and conditions.

Very occasionally we hear of a Muslim-born interpreter, whom chance—or more likely mischance—had provided with an opportunity to learn a foreign language. One such is Osman Aga, a Turkish cavalry officer from Temesvar, in Ottoman Hungary, who spent eleven years as a prisoner-of-war in Austrian hands and was thereby enabled to acquire an extensive knowledge of the German language. His memoirs indicate that he already knew Serbian and Hungarian, samples of which, transcribed into the Turko-Arabic script, he quotes in his memoirs. After his escape, he served as interpreter to the Pasha of Temesvar in his dealings with his opposite numbers along the central European frontier between the Hapsburg and the Ottoman Empires.[7]

Apart from border diplomacy, interpreters were also employed in commerce, and an Ottoman tax register from Tripoli even mentions an "interpreter's tax"—the *terjumāniyya.* [8] This is derived from the Arabic *tarjumān,* meaning a translator or interpreter. The Western term, dragoman, usually used to designate these interpreters, is derived from it.

The most important were, of course, those directly in the service of the Muslim sovereigns. Little is known about the dragomans employed by the Mamluk sultans of Egypt and other Muslim rulers of the Middle Ages, though what evidence exists indicates that these were, for the most part, renegades from Europe. An interesting case is the dragoman Taghri Berdi who served first as dragoman and later as ambassador of the Mamluk sultan to Venice, where he arrived in 1506. His name is Turkish and means "God gave." His patronymic is given as ibn 'Abdallah, a form commonly used by converts to Islam whose real fathers' names would have been too alien to fit into the Muslim pattern of nomenclature.

Taghri Berdi was clearly of European origin though there is some uncertainty as to his previous religion and nationality. Some contemporary authors describe him as a former Christian, others as a former Jew. A Christian traveler says that he was of Jewish birth and was subsequently converted, first to Christianity and then to Islam. An Italian Jewish visitor to Egypt, Meshullam da Volterra, says that Taghri Berdi was of Jewish descent but was "a Christian to Christians and a Jew to Jews." There is general agreement that he was born in Spain, though some sources say that he was born in Sicily.[9]

An early Ottoman interpreter about whom we have some information was a Hungarian, known after his conversion to Islam as Murad. Although he was only seventeen years old when he was captured by the Turks at the battle of Mohacs in 1526, he seems to have had a good Latin education, and thanks to this was able to make a career as interpreter in the Turkish service. On behalf of his new religion he composed a missionary treatise in Turkish and later in Latin, and in 1559–1560, at the request of the Venetian envoy to Istanbul, made a Turkish version of Cicero's *De Senectute,* for presentation to the Sultan Süleyman the Magnificent. The next time we hear of him is when he was dismissed from his post as interpreter to the Porte for persistent wine drinking. Very short of money, he accepted a commission, from a European employer, to make a Latin translation of selected Turkish works on Ottoman history.[10]

Under the Ottomans, the post of official interpreter or dragoman was an essential part of the governmental apparatus for the conduct of foreign affairs. The interpreter formed part of the staff of the chief secretary *(Reis ül-Küttab* or *Reis Efendi)* who, within the office of the grand vizier, was responsible for dealings with foreign governments. From the sixteenth century onwards we have a fairly full list of names of interpreters. The earliest named are all converts to Islam, mostly of European origin. They include Poles, Austrians, Hungarians, and Greeks. In the seventeenth century the office, under the name of grand dragoman *(Terjüman-başı),* became an institution, and was long the exclusive preserve of a group of Greek families living in the Phanar district in Istanbul. These were not converted to Islam but, through the holding of this office as well as some others under the authority of the sultans, acquired a position of great power and influence in the Ottoman system. The opening of the first resident Ottoman embassies in European capitals, in the last years of the eighteenth century, extended the scope of their activities. Virtually every one of these ambassadors was accompanied by an Ottoman Greek interpreter, who appears to have conducted a substantial part of the embassy business and no doubt reported to the grand dragoman in Istanbul.

Other Islamic states were somewhat haphazard, and seem to have relied largely on non-Muslims, sometimes not even their own subjects. Thus, a Moroccan ambassador to Spain at the end of the seventeenth century had to use an Arabic-speaking Syrian Christian, who was an interpreter in the Spanish service. As late as the early nineteenth century, a Persian envoy to Europe was accompanied by a Christian, probably an Armenian from Iran, who was his only link with the outside world.

European interest was not limited to the practical needs of commerce and diplomacy, nor could even these be adequately met by interpreters who had learned their trade in the field. The systematic study of Arabic and the preparation of scholarly tools for this purpose began very early. The first Latin-Arabic glossary was prepared in the twelfth century. By the thirteenth we find a number of European scholars engaged in the study of Arabic, and there were even attempts to translate parts of the Qur'ān into Latin. This was followed by the publication of further glossaries and dictionaries and, in 1538, by the first Latin treatise on Arabic grammar.

These formed the starting point of a much more extensive wave of Arabic studies in European universities during the great intellectual expansion of the sixteenth and seventeenth centuries. The same period also saw the publication of grammars and dictionaries for Persian and Turkish as well as critical editions, from manuscripts, of texts in these languages. The purpose of these activities was partly practical, related to the needs of commerce and diplomacy, and also partly scholarly, to gratify the boundless intellectual curiosity unleashed by the Renaissance. A characteristic figure is William Bedwell (1561–1632), the first major English Arabist. In an essay on the importance of Arabic and the need to learn it, he describes it as "the only language of religion and the chief language of diplomacy and business from the Fortunate Isles to the China Seas." He speaks at length of its value for letters and science.

Despite the establishment of a number of chairs of Arabic in European universities and the growth of a scholarly literature on the subject, the products of these schools were quite insufficient to meet the needs of Western diplomacy and commerce in the Middle East. For a long time the Western powers relied on local Christians recruited as dragomans and employed in the consulates and embassies. In the eighteenth century the French resorted to a new method, choosing young Frenchmen at an early age and instructing them in the relevant languages. For more than a century the French dragomans in the Levant were trained in this way, and French governments were thus able to draw on a reserve of officials who on the one hand were educated, metropolitan Frenchmen, and on the other possessed a knowledge of the Middle East and its languages that was both scholarly and practical. Their role, especially during the Revolutionary and Napoleonic Wars, was considerable.

There was no comparable interest on the Muslim side. While some Muslims, particularly in North Africa, appear to have acquired a working colloquial knowledge of French, Spanish, or Italian, this was purely for practical purposes and, in the main, at a low level of society with little or no cultural influence. Knowledge of foreign languages was not an esteemed qualification—if anything, the reverse—and it did not lead to high office. Rather was it a specialized craft belonging to the non-Muslim communities and, like some other such occupations, marked with a stigma of social inferiority. Merchants might have needed to talk to Europeans—but merchants could employ interpreters and often were themselves foreigners or non-Muslims. Sailors might need to talk to other sailors or to harbor officials, but for this the pan-Mediterranean jargon known as the *lingua franca* sufficed. In any case, the seamen of the Ottoman Empire and its neighbors did not serve as a conduit for cultural influences.

Of intellectual interest in Western languages and the literatures enshrined in them, there is not the slightest sign. We know of no Muslim scholar or man of letters before the eighteenth century who sought to learn a Western language, still less of any attempt to produce grammars, dictionaries, or other language tools. Translations are few and far between. Those that are known are works chosen for practical purposes and the translations are made by converts or non-Muslims.

Only one Ottoman Muslim writer, the great and ever-curious traveler Evliya Çelebi, shows some interest in European languages, and even offers his readers a few samples. In the course of a long account of his visit to Vienna, Evliya notes that the inhabitants of the Austrian empire speak two main languages, Hungarian and German, the latter, in Turkish called Nemçe, being the more important. Evliya notes the "Nemçe is a very difficult language, in which there are many Persian words." The reason for this curious fact, according to Evliya, is that "these people" came from Persia with the children of Manučihr. A likelier explanation is that Evliya had noticed certain lexical similarities, e.g., German *tochter,* Persian *dukhtar,* German *bruder,* Persian *birāder,* due to the common Indo-European origin of the two languages. Evliya then goes on to give some specimens of the German language—a few prayers transcribed in the Turco-Arabic script, together with a list of numbers, words, and simple expressions. Evliya notes that although the Nemçe are Catholics and follow the rule of the pope in Rome, their language is different from the speech of the Roman pope, which is Spanish.[11] The name Nemçe, commonly used by Ottoman writers for Austria and the Austrians, is derived from a Slavic word meaning dumb, and in most Slavic languages applied to the Germans. Evliya offers a different explanation: "The word *Nem* in the Hungarian language means 'I am not,' and Nemçe thus means 'I am not a Czech, I am a German.' "[12] Evliya's display of linguistic knowledge is not limited to his German verses and vocabulary. He also offers some samples of a language which he calls Jewish, and collected among Sephardic Jews in Ottoman Palestine. He seems quite unaware that this is in fact Spanish.[13]

In general, the Muslim world seems to have taken little trouble even to inform itself about the identity of the languages of Christendom, let alone learn them. The large number of languages spoken in Europe seems, not surprisingly, to have puzzled and confused Muslim observers. A few years before Evliya, Kâtib Çelebi, one of the greatest Muslim scholars of his time, offers his readers this account of the linguistic map of Europe. In former times, he says, "this accursed crew" used to speak Greek, which besides being the language of the scholars and the ancients was in actual use. But then the people who spoke it declined and after that the Latin language appeared. This, derived from Greek, became an esteemed language. But that people too declined. These two remained the languages of the scholars of Europe, and most learned books used to be written in these two languages. But afterwards the people of every region began to use their own language [a fate which the Islamic world had escaped] and a large number of different languages came into common use. Thus in England there are three languages, Hibernia, Anglia, and Scosia (sic). In Spain and Portugal, too, there are many languages, and also in France, where for example on the Mediterranean coast (sic) they speak Gascon and Provencal, on the Atlantic coast, Breton, and in the interior, French. Similarly, in Austria they speak Czech and Hungarian and Austrian (Nemçe). There are, says Kâtib Çelebi also other languages such as Muscovite and Dutch. In the middle of Italy they speak the Swiss language and the Italian language, which besides being spoken in Italy is also spoken by Jews in Turkey. It is also called the Frankish language. In eastern Europe they also speak such languages as Slav, Albanian, Bosnian, Greek (Rūmī), Bulgarian and Serb. All these languages are independent of one another and differ, not only from each other, but within themselves. Thus, the best and clearest Italian is called Tuscan and the language of Venice is condemned as bad. The purest form spoken in France is the language called French. Kâtib Çelebi notes that Latin is still the language of education and learning and has a place in Christendom like that of Arabic among Muslims. A similar observation was made by a seventeenth-century Moroccan ambassador who, noting the importance of Latin in Spanish education, describes it as "the equivalent of accidence and syntax [i.e. of classical Arabic] among us."[14] Kâtib Çelebi's account of the languages of Europe is surprising both in its detail and in its ignorance. He has heard of such local languages as Breton and Basque, and makes no distinction between them and such major languages as French and German. Better informed than Evliya, he knows that the language spoken by Jews in Turkey is not "the Jewish language" but European—and he identifies it with Italian instead of Spanish. His notions about the Romance languages are in any case somewhat confused. Kâtib Çelebi's information obviously came from some European traveler. His tone in discussing these barbarous and insignificant idioms is remarkably similar to that of later European explorers discussing the tribal dialects of the dark continent.[15]

A few Muslims did, however, take the trouble to learn an European language, and by late Ottoman times they began to increase in numbers. The introduction of printing in the early eighteenth century, and the employment of European instructors in Ottoman and, later, other Muslim military schools provided new opportunities and incentives.

Which languages, if any, did Muslims learn? Probably the earliest statement on this subject comes from a passage in the German chronicler of the Crusades, Arnold of Lübeck, quoting a German envoy who visited Syria and Palestine in 1175. Speaking of the mysterious Assassins, he explains that the Assassin chief had young men brought up from early childhood and specially trained for their dreadful task. Among other things, "he has them taught the various languages, such as Latin, Greek, Roman, Saracen, as well as many others."[16] Roman presumably refers to the Romance vernaculars spoken in the Crusader camp. While this account of the training of young Assassins is probably fantastic, it gives some indication of what languages might have been thought useful. In general, the only indications we have from the Middle Ages of the use of foreign languages by Muslims refer to the mother tongues of new converts.

It is not until Ottoman times that we have any more solid information. Mehmed II, the conqueror of Constantinople, is said by a contemporary Venetian visitor to have spoken Greek and Slavonic, as well as Turkish. He is also said to have entertained Italian humanists and shown interest in their work, and is accorded by his Greek biographer the title of philhellene. It is very unlikely that the sultan knew any non-Islamic language, but Greek was certainly in common use among the early Ottomans, and a knowledge of Slavonic languages was widespread among the new recruits and converts who formed so large a part of the Ottoman establishment. There are even fermans in Greek issued from the chancery of Mehmed the Conqueror in which the Sultan himself is called *O Megas Authentes,* the great lord.[17] The Italian title, *il Gran Signor* and the Turkish word *efendi* are probably both derived from this. Various forms of Italian, including the bastardized *lingua franca,* were in common use in the central and eastern Mediterranean and it seems likely that Turkish seamen, many of them of local or Christian origin, had at least a working knowledge.[18]

By the sixteenth century, Turkish maritime parlance had already borrowed a considerable number of Italian words, some directly and others via Greek. They include such words as *kapudan* for a sea captain and hence, in the form *Kapudan Pasha,* the Lord High Admiral of the Ottoman fleet; *lostromo* or *nostromo,* a common Mediterranean word for the boatswain of a ship, probably originating from the slang of Spanish or Portuguese galley slaves and meaning our boss; and *fortuna,* which in Turkish comes to a mean a storm; *mangia,* a Turkish sailor's term, of obvious Italian origin, used to designate food (rather like English "grub" or American "chow"). Most of these maritime loan words were of Italian, especially Venetian, origin but some came from Spanish, Catalan, or even Portuguese. The number of such loan words in colloquial Turkish and, particularly, in all that is connected with the sea— the language of shipbuilding, navigation, and fishing—testify to some Western influence. It is significant that there is no comparable borrowing of Western words in other areas of the Turkish language and virtually none at all in Arabic or Persian until comparatively modern times.

Italian seems to have remained the best-known European language among Turks for some time, and as late as the nineteenth century, European loan words in Turkish are almost invariably Italian in form. They included political, mechanical, and sartorial terms needed to designate the garments, gadgets, and institutions adapted from Europe.[19] Documents involving Turkish and European parties were drawn up in Latin as long as this was the formal, legal, diplomatic language of Europe. Thus, the Treaties of Carlowitz of 1699 and of

Passarowitz of 1718 are in Latin and, of course, in Turkish. Italian was, however, gaining ground and later treaties in the eighteenth century, such as the Treaty of Küçük Kaynarca of 1774, are in that language.

In the eighteenth century, we hear for the first time of a Turkish diplomat speaking French. The person in question, Said Efendi, had accompanied his father who went to Paris as ambassador in 1721, and later went on several diplomatic missions himself. An Ottoman chronicler of the time says that Said "studied and knows Latin." It is in the highest degree improbable that an eighteenth-century Ottoman official would spend his time acquiring an infidel dead language. A contemporary French observer notes that the diplomat in question spoke "excellent French, like a native," and it is probably to this that the chronicler was alluding.[20] Even by then, Ottoman ideas about the language map of Europe were still remarkably vague.

The rise of French seems to have begun with the employment of French-speaking officers in the military training schools in the eighteenth century; its position was confirmed by the increasing involvement of France in the internal affairs of the empire during the late eighteenth and early nineteenth centuries. The growth of Austrian and Russian influence worked in favor of the French language, as the diplomatic correspondence of the Russian and, in the nineteenth century, the Austrian Foreign Ministries with their embassies in Constantinople was largely written in that language. From the nineteenth century onwards, Turkish loan words of European origin begin to assume a French rather than an Italian form. Such words as *senato* and *parlamento* were clearly earlier borrowings and survive in modern Turkish in this Italianate form. The Turks heard of senates and parliaments in distant Europe at a relatively early stage. They did not meet senators until some time after and these are consequently known in Turkish as *senatör*. Sometimes an Italian form is replaced by a French equivalent. Thus, the heroine in Turkish romantic fiction at first wore a *roba di camera*; subsequently, she exchanged it for a *robe de chambre*. English came much later. In 1809, the British ambassador in Constantinople explained to Canning why he had to draw up a treaty with the Turks in French: "Even if the negotiations had been carried on at Constantinople, I should have found no dragoman employed by the Porte sufficiently master of the English language to render himself responsible for affixing the signature of the Turkish plenipotentiary to an instrument of so much importance."[21] It is not until the age of sport, technology, and air travel that English makes any impact.

A parallel process can be discerned in the countries of North Africa where Italian and, also, Spanish were at first the most widely known and used European languages and where both, in due course, gave way to French. In Iran and India, Italian had slight impact. The Portuguese seem to have left little impression, and for most Persian and Indian Muslims the West presented itself predominantly in an English or French form. The prevalence of French perceptions can be seen in the Persian name for the United States—Etāz Ūnī.

The Western-style military schools established by the reforming sultans and pashas, and the parallel training of young civilians for the modern diplomatic service created a new element in Muslim society —a class of young officers and officials acquainted with a Western language, usually French, professionally interested in the study of some aspects of Western civilization, and trained to look up to Western Christian experts as their teachers and guides to better ways. A text published in Üsküdar (Scutari) in 1803, probably the work of a Greek dragoman of the Porte, puts these words in the mouth of a young Ottoman engineer officer:

> Learning of the wonders of European science, I formed the idea of making an approach to them. Losing no time I applied myself to the study of the French language as being the most universal and capable of leading me to a knowledge of the authors on the sciences. . . . I was drunk with joy to see my native land in the condition that I so ardently desired, illuminated more brightly every day by the torch of the sciences and of the arts.[22]

The transition from the old attitude of contempt for the barbarous dialects of the infidels to a new one of respect for the means of access to superior skills and knowledge was by no means easy. In the early years of the nineteenth century, the Ottomans were still relying very heavily on Greek employees for their knowledge of Western languages and therefore also, to no small extent, for their information on current events and affairs in Europe. The dangers of this situation for the Porte were dramatically revealed in 1821 when the rising in Greece placed Greek and Turk in a state of war. Believing—probably wrongly—that he could not be trusted, the sultan's government decided to hang the last of the Greek grand dragomans, Stavraki Aristarchi, and to appoint a Muslim in his place.

This was easier said than done. The reforms at the end of the eighteenth and beginning of the nineteenth century had produced a very few Turks competent in Western languages, but by this time most of them were dead and the few survivors had either hidden or forgotten their skills. A contemporary Turkish historian tells us that for two or three weeks papers in Greek or "Frankish" accumulated at the chief dragoman's office at the Sublime Porte. To deal with this emergency the Sultan turned to the only other place where foreign languages were required and used—the military school. An order was issued transferring Yahya Efendi, at that time a teacher in the military school of engineering, to the office of dragoman. The contemporary historian Şanizade lays some stress on the importance of this transfer, which for the first time placed the business of translation and with it the conduct of foreign relations in Muslim hands, and thus made the knowledge and use of foreign languages a respectable Muslim profession.[23] Even Yahya was a convert to Islam and is variously described as of Bulgarian, Greek, or Jewish origin. Yahya Efendi, the founder of a dynasty of dragomans and ambassadors who played a great role in nineteenth century Turkey, was succeeded on his death in 1823 or 1824, by another teacher transferred from the School of Engineering, Hoja Ishak, a Jewish convert to Islam who held the office until 1830, when he returned to his teaching.[24]

The reliance on new Muslims shows that there were still many difficulties and considerable resistance. In 1838, the reforming Sultan Mahmud II, in a speech to the students at the opening of his new medical school, still had to apologize for the inclusion of French in the curriculum:

> You will study scientific medicine in French . . . my purpose in having you taught French is not to educate you in the French language; it is to teach you scientific medicine and little by little to take it into our language . . . therefore work hard to acquire a knowledge of medicine from your teachers and strive by degrees to adopt it into Turkish and give it currency in our language. . . .[25]

In these remarks, the sultan had raised one of the central problems of the whole process of Westernization. Even as late as 1838, the year in which the speech was delivered, the number of Turks with a serious knowledge of a Western language was still infinitesimally small. Much of the process of instruction in the schools, even of command by technical advisers in the armed forces, had to pass through the prism of translation. To a large extent the translators were still native Christians, and their presence served to strengthen rather than weaken the barrier. It was bad enough to be taught or commanded by a Frank. It was even worse when his instruction or command was mediated through a Greek or Armenian interpreter whose familiar appearance and accent would not, among Turkish listeners, command respect.

For many reasons, it was necessary for Muslim students to learn foreign languages. The purpose was for them to acquire useful knowledge—medical, technical, scientific, and military—and no more.

But it is difficult to draw such lines. The cadets and, later, students learned French and were taught to look up to Frenchmen and other Europeans as teachers. By the mid-nineteenth century, a knowledge of a European language had become an essential tool for ambitious young Muslims aspiring to a career in government service, and the Translation Office was joining the army and the palace as one of the avenues to preferment and power.

IV

Media
and Intermediaries

The Muslims were near neighbours of the Europeans, with whom they shared—or divided—the Mediterranean basin and much else besides. Most of the older Islamic lands had for long formed part of the Roman Empire, and like Europe had known the heritage of the Greco-Roman and Judaeo-Christian past, as well as of a remoter antiquity.[1] Culturally, racially, even religiously, they had far more in common with European Christendom than with the more distant civilizations of Asia and Africa, and might have been expected to know more about them. In fact, however, the medieval iron curtain between Islam and Christendom seems to have kept cultural exchanges to a minimum and to have greatly restricted even commercial and diplomatic intercourse. The Muslim world had its own internal lines of communication by land and sea, and was thus independent of Western routes and services. Muslim civilization, proud and confident of its superiority, could afford to despise the barbarous infidel in the cold and miserable lands of the north, and for the medieval Muslim in the Mediterranean lands, the European, at least to the north and west, was a remoter and more mysterious figure than the Indian, the Chinese, or even the inhabitant of tropical Africa.

In principle, Muslim travel to infidel lands was disapproved, but some exchanges could not be avoided. A tenth century Muslim geo-graphical writer describing Rome gives a number of reports from un-named travelers whom he cites simply as a Jew, a Christian monk, and a merchant—probably the three classes most likely to travel between the Christian and Muslim worlds.[2] There were Christian and Jewish pilgrims visiting Jerusalem, and Christian clergymen on their way from the east to Rome. These last became more numerous with the establishment of closer links between the Roman Curia and the vari-ous Uniate churches of the East. There were even some intrepid Mus-lims who dared to venture into darkest Europe. Sometimes the journey was involuntary. One of the most interesting early accounts comes from a ninth-century Arab prisoner of war called Hārūn ibn Yaḥyā, who was captured in the east, taken to Constantinople, kept there for a while, and then sent by land to Rome.[3]

Such Muslim prisoners in Christian hands became more numerous, or at least better documented, in Ottoman times. The centuries-long wars between the Ottomans and their rivals in southeastern and cen-tral Europe, as well as the constant naval warfare in the Mediterranean between the Barbary Corsairs and their Christian adversaries, left Muslim, as well as Christian, captives in enemy hands. From time to time, we hear of Muslim diplomatic missions to Spain and elsewhere to arrange for the release of these captives. However, while Christians returning from Turkey or North Africa produced an extensive litera-ture describing their experiences and the peoples among whom they had lived, Muslim ex-prisoners returning from Europe have left virtu-ally no record. Only two exceptions of any significance have so far come to light in the period to the end of the eighteenth century. One was a Turkish Kadi who was captured in April 1597 by the Knights of St. John while on his way to take up an appointment in Cyprus, and was kept prisoner in Malta for over two years. His brief account of his captivity was published from the unique manuscript.[4] The other was one Osman Aga, a Turkish prisoner of war who became an interpreter in the Ottoman service. Osman Aga is the author of two autobio-graphical works dealing with his captivity and his subsequent career, written in 1724 and 1725. Though interesting and informative, they seem to have aroused little interest among his compatriots, and are never cited by Ottoman authors nor even mentioned by Ottoman bibliographers. Both are preserved in unique autograph manuscripts, the one in London, the other in Vienna, and were virtually unknown until discovered by modern scholarship.[5] It seems unlikely, therefore, that the reports of returning captives were a significant source of new information.

Probably the two most important groups of travelers were merchants and diplomats. Both categories deserve more detailed treatment. During the early formative centuries, Muslims displayed an extraordinary reluctance, grounded in law as well as tradition, to travel in Christian Europe. This is in striking contrast with their attitude to the non-Muslim countries of Asia and Africa, also technically part of the House of War, and therefore subject to the same ban. Nevertheless Muslims traveled extensively in these countries, and sometimes even formed resident communities. The reasons are not difficult to find. One obvious difference is that western Europe, unlike Asia and Africa, had little to offer and few attractions. From India, southeast Asia, and China, the Muslim world imported a wide range of important commodities including silks and other textiles, spices and aromatics, timber, metals, and ceramics. From black Africa came two major commodities—gold and slaves—which between them gave rise to a far-flung commercial network. With the Byzantine Empire, based on a comparable economy, trade was limited, but from eastern and northern Europe there was, for a while, a significant importation of furs, amber, and fish products. Slaves, too, figure among importations from Europe, but these came mostly from central and eastern Europe, and on a far smaller scale than from Africa or Central Asia. All in all, western Europe did not have much to sell besides its own people. A few minor items receive occasional mention in medieval Muslim sources. The only west European commodity of importance, apart from weapons and slaves, was English wool. Otherwise, it is not until the end of the Middle Ages and the beginning of the modern period that the development of manufactures and the colonization of the New World gave Europe, for the first time, a range of goods for export to the lands of Islam.

Another factor which would certainly have discouraged the Muslims from traveling in western Europe was the ferocious intolerance of its rulers and peoples. In any regions conquered from heathendom or reconquered from Islam, Christianity was imposed by force and Muslims sooner or later forced to choose between conversion, exile, and death. The fate of the Jews in medieval Europe would not have encouraged followers of other non-Christian religions to settle or even travel in these lands. There were thus no resident Muslim communities in Christian Europe. This, in turn, made life very difficult for the Muslim visitor whose special needs, such as mosques, bathhouses, food slaughtered and prepared according to Muslim usage, and other essentials of the Muslim way of life, could not be met.

The Muslim horror of venturing among infidels is vividly expressed by Usāma ibn Munqidh, a twelfth-century Syrian Muslim who left a volume of memoirs. One of his neighbors in Syria was a Frankish knight with whom he established "bonds of amity and friendship." When the knight was about to leave Syria and return to Europe he suggested—apparently with the best of intentions—that Usāma's fourteen-year old son should accompany him to his own country "to live among the knights and learn wisdom and chivalry." To the Frank the suggestion must have seemed, at the very least, a gesture of friendship and goodwill. To Usāma, it was monstrously absurd: "Words struck my ears such as would never come out of the head of a man of wisdom. If my son were taken prisoner no greater misfortune could befall him from his imprisonment than being taken to the land of the Franks." Usāma found a courteous way to head off this suggestion: "I said to him: by your life this is just what I was thinking. But what prevents me from agreeing is that his grandmother loves him and would not let him come out with me until she made me promise that I would bring him back to her." He asked me: "Is your mother still living?" I answered: "Yes" and he said: "Then do not disobey her."[6]

In these circumstances it was not surprising that when a journey to Europe was necessary for either commercial or diplomatic purposes, Muslim rulers preferred to send one of their Christian or Jewish subjects, who was able to establish contacts with communities of his own coreligionists beyond the frontier and thus to ease his journey and the performance of his task. This same consideration made it relatively easier for Christians or Jews from Europe to travel in the Muslim lands.

The Frankish chronicles relate a famous story of an exchange of embassies by Charlemagne and Hārūn al-Rashīd between 797 and 807. According to these chronicles, two missions were sent by Charlemagne to Hārūn al-Rashīd in 797 and 802 and two from Hārūn al-Rashīd to Charlemagne in 801 and 807. In addition, the Frankish king is said to have sent one or possibly two missions to the Christian Patriarch of Jerusalem in 799 and perhaps also in 802, and to have received four in return from the Patriarch between 799 and 807.[7]

Considerable doubt has been expressed about whether these exchanges ever took place. If they did, they were of insufficient importance to attract the attention of the Arabic chroniclers, since these make no mention of them. They do, however, tell us something of a later embassy from the West, from a Frankish queen called Bertha to the Caliph al-Muktafī in Baghdad in the year 906. This is how the Arabic chronicler describes the arrival of the embassy:

> Bertha, daughter of Lothar, queen of Franja and its dependencies, sent
> a present to al-Muktafī Billah by ʿAli the Eunuch, one of the eunuchs

of Ziyādatallāh ibn Aghlab, in the year 293 [= 906], consisting of fifty swords and fifty shields and fifty Frankish spears; twenty garments woven with gold; twenty Slavonic eunuchs and twenty Slavonic slave-girls, beautiful and gracious; ten dogs so big that neither wild beasts nor any other could prevail against them; seven hawks and seven falcons; a silken tent with all its appurtenances; twenty garments made from a wool which comes from a shell which is brought up from the seabed in those parts and which changes to all colors like a rainbow, changing color every hour of the day; three birds that are found in the land of the Franks such that if they look at food that is poisoned they utter a strange screech and beat their wings until this becomes known; and beads that painlessly draw out arrowheads and lance points even after the flesh has grown together over them.

'Ali the Eunuch brought the present and letter of the Queen of Franja to al-Muktafi Billah, and also a further message not included in the letter lest anyone other than the Caliph become aware of it. . . . The message was a request to al-Muktafi for marriage and for his friendship. . . .[8]

Nothing very much seems to have come from this embassy, either by way of friendship or of marriage.

The earliest diplomatic report that we have from the Muslim side is of an embassy sent from Spain to the far north. This was at the beginning of the ninth century, when the Viking raids in Andalusia, as elsewhere in western Europe, had been causing havoc and devastation. Then, at one stage, a truce was patched up, Viking envoys were sent to the Muslim emir 'Abd al-Raḥmān II of Cordova, and a Muslim embassy sent in return. The ambassador was a certain Yaḥya ibn al-Ḥakam al-Bakrī of Jaen, known as al-Ghazāl, the gazelle, for his beauty. He told his story to a friend called Tammam ibn 'Alqama, from whose account it was cited by the early thirteenth-century chronicler, Ibn Dihya. The embassy could have taken place in about 845 to one of the Viking courts in Ireland or Denmark. Modern scholarship is divided on whether the report is authentic or a literary fabrication.

Al-Ghazāl's account of his embassy tells us very little about the people whom he visited. He does, however, tell us something about his arrival at the Viking court and is at pains to show how he preserved his honor and that of Islam despite the attempt by his hosts to humble him:

After two days the king summoned them to his presence, and al-Ghazāl stipulated that he would not be made to kneel to him and that he and his companions would not be required to do anything contrary to their customs. The king agreed to this. But when they went to the king, he sat before them in magnificent guise, and ordered an entrance, through which he must be approached, to be made so low that one could only enter kneeling. When al-Ghazāl came to this, he sat on the ground, stretched forth his two legs, and dragged himself through on his rear. And when he had passed through the doorway, he stood erect. The king had prepared himself for him, with many arms and great pomp. But al-Ghazāl was not overawed. . . . He stood erect before the king and said: "Peace be with you, O king, and with those whom your assembly hall contains. May you not cease to enjoy power, long life, and nobility which leads you to the greatness of this world and the next." The interpreter explained what al-Ghazal had said and the king admired his words, and said: "This is one of the wise and clever ones of his people." He was astonished at al-Ghazāl's sitting on the ground and entering feet foremost and he said: "We sought to humiliate him, and he greeted us with the soles of his shoes [to show these is insulting]. Had he not been an ambassador we would have taken this amiss."⁹

This passage is strikingly reminiscent of similar accounts by early European envoys to the barbarous lands of the East. The historian of al-Ghazāl's mission goes on to note that the ambassador "had noteworthy sessions and famous encounters with them when he debated with their scholars and silenced them, and contended against their champions and outmatched them."

After a somewhat perfunctory and rather improbable account of al-Ghazāl's activities among the Vikings, there comes what was obviously, either to al-Ghazāl or his narrator, the main theme of the embassy—a flirtation with the Viking queen.

Al-Ghazāl's mission, if it took place, was one of a number of diplomatic exchanges between Muslim and Christian states in Spain and the north, which have left no record beyond an occasional mention in chronicles. The only Muslim embassy of medieval times that has left any extensive documentation was one sent from the caliph of Cordova to the Holy Roman emperor in the middle of the tenth century. A party of Muslim freebooters had established themselves in the Alpine passes and had caused a great deal of trouble by raiding traffic passing to and from Italy. In 953, the Emperor Otto I sent an embassy to Cordova asking the caliph to call them off. Discussions of one sort or another seem to have gone on for several years and then, in circumstances which are not clear, the caliph sent a return embassy to Germany.

One member of this embassy was a certain Ibrāhīm ibn Yaʿqūb al-Isrāʾīlī al-Ṭurṭūshī—Abraham the son of Jacob, the Jew from Tortosa, a small town on the coast of Catalonia near Barcelona.¹⁰ Whether he was the ambassador or merely a member of the embassy is not known; nor is his profession, though on internal evidence it seems likely that he was a physician. He traveled through France, Holland,

and northern Germany, visited Bohemia and Poland, and probably returned via northern Italy. He seems to have written a narrative of his travels through Europe, which unfortunately is lost. However, lengthy excerpts from it were quoted by two eleventh-century Spanish Arab geographers, Bakrī and ʿUdhrī. Bakrī preserves the account of the Slav peoples in what is now Poland, Czechoslovakia, and eastern Germany; it is an important source for the early history of these countries. ʿUdhrī's work is lost but extracts from it, fragments of descriptions of Germany and western Europe, are cited by a yet later writer, the thirteenth-century Persian geographer Qazvīnī, who was chiefly interested in wonders and marvels. Bakrī cites his source as Ibrāhīm ibn Yaʿqūb al-Isrāʾīlī; Qazvīnī cites his simply as al-Ṭurṭūshī, and for a long time it was thought that these were two different authors, one a Jew, the other a Muslim. Georg Jacob, a German scholar who studied these texts, was even able to discern professional and ethnic differences between them. Since one account is longer than the other and names the emperor as source, this, he observed, illustrates a characteristic difference between the reticence of the Arab diplomat and the preening of the Jewish trader.[11] The late Tadeus Kowalski, however, established conclusively that the two are one and the same, and that the passages in Bakrī and Qazvīnī derive from the same source.

There is some uncertainty as to whether Ibrāhīm ibn Yaʿqūb was a professing Jew or a Muslim of Jewish origin. The form of his name would allow either possibility. There is also some uncertainty about the precise date and purpose of his visit to Otto. The most likely date is about 965 A.D., and it seems probable that he travelled as part of an embassy sent by the Caliph of Cordova to Otto I, perhaps in some way connected with the emperor's embassy to Spain in 953.[12]

Ibrāhīm's account of western Europe, whatever its limitations, is obviously far superior to those of his predecessors and would probably appear still better had it not survived only in the form of extracts assembled by a professional collector of tall stories.

But if the Muhammadans would not come to Europe, Europe was preparing to come to the Muhammadans. During the age of the Reconquista and the Crusades, Christian armies conquered and governed Muslim territories from Spain to Palestine, and Muslims had the opportunity to observe Frankish culture and Frankish ways without leaving their own homes. The results are astonishingly meager, though the Arab chronicles tell us of missions to Crusader kings and princes and even of embassies to Christian courts as far away as Sicily and southern Italy. One such was an embassy sent by the Egyptian Sultan Baybars to the Sicilian ruler Manfred in 1261, carried out by the well-known Syrian historian Jamāl al-Dīn ibn Wāṣil (1207–1298) and described by him in his chronicle.

Ibn Wāṣil visited Manfred in Barletta, a city on the Italian mainland in a region not long previously reconquered from Islam. He describes Manfred as "a man of distinction, a lover of the speculative sciences who knew by heart ten propositions from Euclid's book on geometry." He speaks approvingly of his friendly attitude towards the Muslims under his rule and notes that this had got him into trouble with the Pope.[13]

One reason why this brief account is preserved is no doubt that the ambassador himself was also an eminent historian, and therefore had a personal interest as well as firsthand information. But this reason in itself is not sufficient, since there were other historians who went on missions. No less a historian than the great Ibn Khaldūn went on an embassy to Pedro I of Castile in 1363–1364. In a memoir he gives this mission little more than a bare mention.[14] More probably the reason for Ibn Wāṣil's recording of his mission was the information which it produced on the survival and practice of the Islamic religion in the lost territories in Italy.

There are some other exceptions to the general lack of interest. One of the most remarkable is the memoirs of Usāma ibn Munqidh (1095–1188), cited above, one of the very few human documents illustrating the impact of the Crusaders on Middle Eastern Islam. Usāma, in describing a long and varied life, has much to say about his Frankish neighbors. While full of contempt for the barbarism of the Franks, he does not regard them as entirely beyond redemption and several times concedes that by long residence in the east and assimilation to Muslim ways they may acquire some tincture of civilization. The adventures of an agent of his whom he sent to the Christian-occupied city of Antioch on business illustrates this point:

> Among the Franks there are some who have settled down in this country and associated with Muslims. These are better than the new-comers, but they are exceptions to the rule, and no inference can be drawn from them.
> Here is an example. Once I sent a man to Antioch on business. At that time, Chief Theodore Sophianos [an eastern Christian] was there, and he and I were friends. He was then all-powerful in Antioch. One day he said to my man: "One of my Frankish friends has invited me. Come with me and see how they live." My man told me: "So I went with him, and we came to the house of one of the old knights, those who had come with the first Frankish expedition. He had already retired from state and military service, and had a property in Antioch from which he

lived. He produced a fine table, with food both tasty and cleanly served. He saw that I was reluctant to eat, and said: 'Eat to your heart's content, for I do not eat Frankish food. I have Egyptian women cooks, and eat nothing but what they prepare, nor does pig flesh ever enter my house.' So I ate, but with some caution, and we took our leave.

"Later I was walking through the market, when suddenly a Frankish woman caught hold of me, and began jabbering in their language, and I could not understand what she was saying. A crowd of Franks collected against me, and I was sure that my end had come. Then, suddenly, that same knight appeared and saw me, and came up to that woman, and asked her: 'What do you want of this Muslim?' She replied: 'He killed my brother Hurso.' This Hurso was a knight of Afamiya who had been killed by someone from the army of Hama. Then the knight shouted at her and said: 'This man is a *burjāsi* [bourgeois], that is, a merchant. He does not fight or go to war.' And he shouted at the crowd and they dispersed; then he took my hand and went away. So the effect of that meal that I had was to save me from death."[15]

Usāma's memoirs represent a form of literature that is, unfortunately, extremely rare in the world of Islam. There are, however, a few other writings recording some sort of personal impression of contact with European Christians. One of them comes from an almost exact contemporary of Usāma, but from the opposite end of the Islamic world. Abū Ḥāmid (1081–1170) was a scholar and geographer, a native of the Muslim city of Granada in Spain. He went on a long journey through North Africa to the Middle East, and from there northward into Russia. From Russia he penetrated westward into Europe as far as the country which is now called Hungary, and stayed there for three years.[16]

Most of what Abū Ḥāmid has to say concerns eastern Europe. His description of Rome, though lengthy, is of no great interest and seems to be based on earlier literary sources. Though by origin an Andalusian, he entered central Europe from the east and does not seem to have gone further west than the Hungarian plain. Yet with all his limitations he remains a landmark in the history of Muslim knowledge about Europe, for he is the only traveler from the lands of Islam to Europe whose name is known and whose writings have survived, between the tenth century diplomat Ibrāhīm ibn Yaʿqūb and the first Ottoman reports in the late fifteenth century.

An impression of the Crusaders comes from another traveler from the far west of the Muslim world. Ibn Jubayr, a native of Valencia in Spain, visited Syria in 1184 and traveled through the Frankish as well as the Muslim possessions. Among other places he passed through Acre, the chief port of the Crusaders:

> The city of Acre, may God destroy it and return it to Islam. This is the chief city of the Franks in Syria . . . the assembly point of ships and caravans, the meeting place of Muslim and Christian merchants from all parts. Its streets and roads are thronged with such crowds of people, that one can hardly walk. But it is a land of unbelief and impiety, swarming with pigs and crosses, full of filth and ordure, all of it filled with uncleanliness and excrement. . . . [17]

Ibn Jubayr is probably referring to the wine jars, pigs, musical instruments, churches, and other things offensive to Muslim eyes rather than to literal dirt, though it may be noted that Muslim standards at that time were very much higher than those of European Christians, and Muslim visitors to Europe into the early nineteenth century comment adversely on the European lack of personal hygiene.

Not everything he saw in the Frankish cities displeased him. He was delighted by the spectacle of a Christian wedding in Tyre, and particularly by the beauty of the bride:

> She walked with grace and dignity, swaying her jewels and adornments, stepping like a dove or a passing cloud—and may God save me from evil thoughts provoked by such sights.[18]

Ibn Jubayr found more serious things to trouble him than a beautiful Frankish bride. He notes with perturbation that the Franks treat their Muslim peasants humanely and justly and that these are better off than their neighbors still under Muslim rule:

> Seditious thoughts have caused the hearts of most of the Muslims to falter, when they see the state of their brothers in Muslim territory and under Muslim rule, and observe that the way they are treated is the reverse of the kindliness and forebearance of their Frankish masters. It is one of the misfortunes that befall the Muslims that the Islamic common people complain of the oppression of their own rulers, and praise the conduct of their opponents and enemies, the Franks, who have conquered them and who tamed them with their justice. It is to God that they should complain of these things. We may find sufficient consolation in the words of the Qur'ān: "This is only Thy trial; Thou wilt thereby lead into error whom Thou pleasest, and Thou wilt guide whom Thou pleasest into the right path."[19]

The observations of Ibn Jubayr, like those of Usāma and Abū Ḥāmid, are isolated phenomena and seemed to have had little effect on the development of Muslim knowledge concerning the West.

Of greater importance and impact was the growth of diplomatic relations between European, particularly west European, powers and the countries of the Middle East and North Africa. Two important factors contributed to the growth of these relations. One of these was the rise of European commerce. European merchants, at first mostly from the Italian states, later from Spain, France, the Netherlands and England, were becoming increasingly active in the Muslim ports and extending their range of activity even to some of the cities of the interior. The Frankish merchant, sometimes a long-term resident, became a familiar figure. The growth of European commercial activity also necessitated a stepping up of diplomatic relations. The merchant communities at an early date acquired the right to have consuls in Muslim cities. From the point of view of the Western states these discharged quasi-diplomatic functions and represented them in dealings with the host government and other authorities. On the Muslim side they were seen as heads of their respective communities and responsible for them to the Muslim authorities. A fifteenth-century Arabic writer makes the point clear. "The consuls are the chiefs of the Franks and are hostages for each community. If anything happens from any community dishonoring to Islam, the consul is answerable."[20]

The needs of commerce gave rise to frequent diplomatic discussions between European and Muslim states, to the granting of privileges of various kinds, and to the negotiation and signature of commercial treaties. These negotiations seem to have been carried out almost entirely by European consuls and envoys in Muslim lands. Visitors from Islam to Christendom remained extremely rare.

The other incentive to closer diplomatic relations came from quite a different source. Since the emergence of Egypt as an independent center of power within the Islamic world, there had been a recurring rivalry between the eastern and western halves of the Middle East—between the successive regimes ruling in the Nile Valley, which often dominated Syria and Palestine too, and those deriving their main support from Iraq and Iran. The coming of the Mongols in the thirteenth century gave a new acuteness to this rivalry. The establishment of a rival power to the east of the traditional Islamic adversary of Christendom raised hopes in Europe of an alliance and a second front, which were not immediately dispelled by the conversion of the Khans of Persia to Islam. A flurry of diplomatic activity resulted,[21] which produced a few passing references in Islamic literature.

The dealings between Europe and the Mongol rulers of Persia seem to have produced no great results. They may, however, have encouraged the Mamluk rulers of Egypt to pay rather more attention to Europe and to their diplomatic relations with the various rulers of Christendom. In about 1340, Shihāb al-Dīn al-ʿUmarī, an Egyptian

official, wrote a manual of diplomatic correspondence for the use of
scribes in the Egyptian chanceries.[22] It contains lists of the sovereigns
with whom the sultan of Egypt was in correspondence, with the approved titles and forms of address for each. Most of the sovereigns
named are Muslim but there is a section on "the kings of the infidels"
including such potentates as the Byzantine emperor, the kings of
Georgia and lesser Armenia, of Serbia, Sinope, and Rhodes. Of Western rulers only two are named: Alfons, King of Andalus and the Rid
Frans. The latter clearly represents the king of France in a Romance
vernacular, though there is no indication how the author of the manual
understood this term. A later, revised version of ʿUmarī's book, known
as the *Tathqīf,* adds a few more names; rather more than half a century
later, another chancery scribe, Qalqashandī, in a work of similar scope
but on a much greater scale, gives a somewhat longer list including the
pope, the rulers of Genoa, Venice and Naples, and some of the lesser
states of Christian Spain.

> Section II. On the forms of address to be used in correspondence
> from the kings of the Egyptian territories in accordance with established
> protocolar usage to the kings of the infidels.
> Know, that the infidel kings to whom letters are sent from this realm
> are all Christians, such as the Greeks, the Franks, the Georgians, the
> Ethiopians, and others . . . [23]

Qalqashandī then goes on to discuss the Christian kings of the East,
of the Balkans and of Spain, after which he comes to:

> Section IV. On correspondence to the kings of the infidels of the
> northern side of Rome and Franja, according to their various species. The
> religion of all of them is that of the Melkite Christians.
> 1. The form of address to the Pope.
> 2. The form of address to the king of the Romans, the ruler of Constan-
> tinople . . .
> 3. The form of address to the rulers of Genoa . . .
> 4. The form of address to the ruler of Venice . . .
> 11. The form of address of the woman ruler of Naples . . . [24]

From Qalqashandī's account, and a few references in the chronicles,
one may reasonably infer that correspondence with European monarchs was something of a rarity. As regards missions to Europe,
Muslims probably shared in some degree the views of the Mongols
who, we are told, used to punish criminals deemed worthy of death
by sending them as ambassadors to foreign parts where the climate
was unhealthy and their safe return problematic.[25]

The age of the Renaissance and of the great discoveries brought a rapid and extensive increase in European interest in the Islamic world. While Islam was no longer perceived as a serious rival to the Christian religion, the Ottoman Empire was still a redoubtable enemy, and its advance into the heart of Europe seemed at times to threaten the very survival of Christendom. The emergence at the beginning of the sixteenth century of a new and hostile Islamic power in Iran, under the Shiʿite Shahs of the Safavid dynasty, again seemed to offer the possibility of creating a second front or, at least, a diversion on the far side of the Ottoman Empire. For these reasons, reliable and accurate information concerning both the Ottoman and Persian states was of great importance to the powers of Europe, and a number of visitors traveled in various capacities to the east to find it.

But that was not all. There were other motives which impelled Europeans in ever greater numbers to journey to the east and even to reside there for extended periods. The age of the great discoveries which brought European exploration to the remotest parts of Asia, Africa, and the Americas, brought them also to the Asian and African, as well as the European, approaches to the world of Islam, and gave them new opportunities as well as new incentives to explore it. The intellectual curiosity of the Renaissance was soon extended to the great neighbor of European Christendom. The expansion of European manufactures and the growing supply of commodities available for export from the European colonies in the new world encouraged European traders to look to the Islamic East as a market for their wares. The resulting commercial and political rivalries between the various European powers led to a more direct and more intensive European involvement in Middle Eastern countries.

Not the least important development was the extension to Istanbul, the Ottoman capital, of the practice which had in the meantime been developing in Europe of continuous diplomacy through resident embassies. By the end of the sixteenth century, most of the states of both eastern and western Europe were sending frequent and regular envoys to Istanbul; several of them, including Venice, France, England, and the Empire, had already established permanent resident missions. During the course of the seventeenth and eighteenth centuries, most of the remaining European states followed suit. The result was to create a sizable resident community of middle- and upper-class Europeans in the Ottoman capital with a somewhat larger number of local aides and dependents, recruited mainly from among the non-Muslim residents of the city. In addition to the three local communities of Greeks, Armenians and Jews, a new community came into being. It was mostly Catholic by religion, drawn from various nationalities and

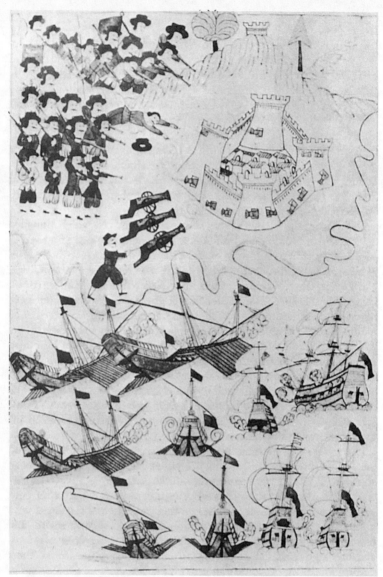

4. *Venetians bombard Tenedos*

5. *Procession of the Venetian Bailo in Istanbul to his audience*

6. *The Bailo is perfumed during his audience with the grand vizier*

7. *Audience of the Bailo with the grand vizier*

communities, speaking many languages but most commonly Italian and Greek and enjoying, or claiming, the citizenship of one or other European states, with which its connections were often somewhat tenuous. The members of this community came to be known in Europe as Levantines, in Turkey as *tatlı su Frengi,* sweetwater Franks, to distinguish them from the saltwater Franks who had actually come from Europe.

The development of diplomatic relations with Iran and Morocco proved somewhat more difficult. Visiting envoys to those countries were not infrequent but the establishment of resident missions was delayed until a very late date.

The growth of European interest and activity in the Islamic lands can hardly have passed unnoticed. European commerce and diplomacy brought a steady increase in the number of European residents in Islamic cities and in the number of local residents who, in one way or another, came in contact with them. While these, for the most part, were non-Muslims, they, in turn, remained in some measure connected with the larger Middle Eastern societies of which, however segregated and isolated, they were still a part. Even the growth of Orientalist scholarship in Europe must have had some effect. From the sixteenth century onwards, European presses were producing editions of Arabic books which in cost and convenience of handling compared favorably with the manuscripts on which readers in the Muslim lands were still compelled to rely. We do indeed find occasional complaints in the Muslim sources about the importation of these European editions of Arabic texts.

But, on the whole, the response to all these activities remains small. The communities of European residents, traders, diplomats and others, remained isolated. Their local circle of native associates served to insulate them from rather than to connect them with the Muslim population, which indeed seems to have regarded their position in this light. Dealing with infidel foreigners was a dirty and dangerous business and best left to other infidels.

Given these attitudes, it is not surprising that the old reluctance to visit the House of War persisted. For such dealings as were felt to be necessary with the infidel world, most Muslim rulers were content to rely on infidels calling on them—a natural tribute from the lower to the higher order—and to make use, even at home, of intermediaries to shield them from too close contact.

For a long time, Ottoman relations with Europe were conducted almost entirely through such intermediaries. For one thing, the task required skills which Muslims either did not possess or did not care to acquire. It also involved duties which Muslims found unattractive. As is usual in most human societies, distasteful tasks were left by the dominant group to others. Thus we find non-Muslims well represented, particularly in the later centuries, in what one might call the "dirty trades." These included what was, for a strict Muslim, the dirtiest trade of all, namely dealing with unbelievers. This led, at times, to fairly large numbers of Jews and Christians in such occupations as diplomacy, banking, and espionage. In general, negotiations with foreign representatives in Istanbul were carried on by non-Muslim employees of the Sublime Porte; travel abroad, whether for diplomacy or for trade, was also normally left to non-Muslims. Only occasionally did an Ottoman dignitary go on a mission and he was usually accompanied by a non-Muslim interpreter.

The sixteenth century brought a significant change in Turkish attitudes. Under the early sultans southeast Europeans—Greeks, Slavs and Albanians—figured prominently in the Ottoman ruling establishment, not only as converts to Islam but even as professing Christians. Ottoman princes contracted dynastic marriages with Christian princesses, and several of the most ancient and distinguished Ottoman aristocratic families were of Byzantine descent. Lists of fiefholders preserved in the Ottoman archives include many Christian names, and show that the Christian gentry was accommodated in the Ottoman military ruling class. The evolution of the Ottoman state from a border principality to an Islamic empire inevitably transformed both government and society. The process was accelerated by the acquisition of the Arab heartlands, especially the Muslim holy places in Arabia, with a resulting shift eastward of the weight of territory, population and tradition. Converts of Balkan and other origins continued for another century or so to play a major part, but they were increasingly overshadowed by men of the old Muslim families, while unconverted Christians were gradually extruded from the apparatus of power and restricted to their legally correct position as *dhimmis*.

Dealings with the unconquered Christian world continued, however, and in these the Turks were in the forefront. From the sixteenth until the early nineteenth century, the eastern Arabs depended almost entirely on the Ottomans for their political contacts with Europe, and in Iran, further away to the east, such information as reached them was often filtered through Ottoman channels.

In the development of Ottoman relations with Europe and the role of the intermediaries who, in effect, conducted them, two stages can be discerned. In the first, the intermediaries were, for the most part, people who had come from Europe; in the second, they were people native to the region who were moving towards Europe. In the first phase, these intermediaries consist largely of renegades and refugees, most of them of European origin. Apart from the Spanish Moriscos who were quickly absorbed into the Muslim community, the refugees were mainly, though not exclusively, Jewish. The persecution of Jews in Spain and Portugal and in the territories under Spanish influence provided the Ottomans with a windfall. From the late fifteenth and during the sixteenth centuries, large numbers of European Jews flooded into the Ottoman dominions. They brought with them useful skills, a knowledge of European languages and conditions and, in addition, some arts and crafts. The Western traveler Nicholas de Nicolay, who visited Turkey in 1551, has some interesting observations on the role of the Spanish and Portuguese Marranos, forced converts to Christianity who fled to Turkey in order to revert to Judaism:

> "They [the Turks] also have among them very excellent practitioners of all the arts and manufacturers, especially the Marranos not long since banished and expelled from Spain and Portugal, who to the great detriment and injury of Christianity have taught the Turks several inventions, artifices and machines of war such as how to make artillery, arquebuses, gunpowder, balls, and other arms. Similarly, they have set up a printing press never before seen in these regions, but it is not permitted to them to print in Turkish or in Arabic."[26]

Jews had an important advantage over Christians from the Muslim point of view. They were not suspected of complicity with the major European adversaries of Islam. That meant that the Turks often preferred them to Christians for politically or economically sensitive tasks. Immediately after the Turkish conquest of Cyprus, which was mainly inhabited by orthodox Greek Christians with a small minority of Italian Catholics, we find orders in the Ottoman archives to send Jewish families to the island. One order speaks of five hundred, another of a thousand "prosperous Jewish families" to be sent to Cyprus "in the interests of the said island."[27] What this meant was that the Ottomans wanted to have a productive industrial and commercial element in the island which was not Greek or Italian or Christian and which was not likely to be sympathetic to Christian Europe. They could rely on the Jews in their dealings with the West. They could not then rely on Greeks or Armenians. Similar consideration led to the beginnings of what eventually developed into the massive Jewish settlement in Salonika, after its conquest by the Ottomans. This settlement was in part due to deliberate Ottoman policy aimed at creating an economically useful and politically reliable population in this strategic seaport.

During the sixteenth century, European Jews appear in the Ottoman service in a number of capacities. We find them in the customs service—in which Jews were already numerous in Mamluk Egypt and in which their knowledge of European languages and conditions served their masters in good stead. We find them engaged in diplomatic activities of various kinds, sometimes at a high level. We find them as traders, traveling and working under Ottoman protection. Finally, there is evidence from the Spanish archives that Ottoman espionage in Christian Europe relied in some measure on Jewish agents.[28]

The Greeks, though not over-friendly to the West, might still cherish hopes of a restored Byzantine Empire. The Armenians, still mostly in southern and eastern Asia Minor, were almost as isolated from the West as the Turks themselves. The Jews were better placed to render these services and the Turks preferred them.

In addition to Jews, there were other refugees, from persecuted Christian groups, such as Unitarians, and a significant number of renegades or, as they are called in Muslim history, *muhtadī*, those who have found the right path.

By the seventeenth century, the supply of both renegades and refugees had seriously diminished. For one thing, conditions in Europe were improving. After the wars of religion, Europe had at last learned some tolerance in religious matters, and heretical Christians and even Jews had less reason to flee their homes and move to remote countries. For those adventurous spirits who had previously sought fame and fortune in the Ottoman Empire, the great European discoveries and the colonisation of the New World offered better opportunities, and many who might previously have made a career in the Ottoman or other Muslim service now found their way to the Americas and to the newly acquired colonial territories.

While Europe and its overseas possessions were becoming more interesting, the Middle East and the Islamic world, in general, were becoming less attractive and, entering on a period of economic and political decline, offered fewer and fewer temptations. The movement of renegades, however, still continued. The last important group was the pirates who, in the early seventeenth century, moved from western Europe to North Africa and placed their navigational and predatory skills at the disposal of the Barbary Corsairs.

Jews, once so important, ceased to come from Europe. Those who were already in Turkey gradually lost their skills and their contacts. A trickle of refugees and adventurers continued to seek safety or fortune in Turkey, but of these only one group made a contribution of any significance. These were the Hungarians, including some Poles, who fled from Hungary after the unsuccessful rising of 1848 and found a home and a career in the Ottoman Empire. The refugees of 1848, some of whom were converted to Islam and rose high in the Ottoman service, played a not unimportant role in the modernization of the Turkish administrative and military apparatus in the mid-nineteenth century.

As the renegades and the refugees ceased to come, and those who were already in the empire lost the qualities which had made them useful, they were replaced by others. Though few were now coming from Europe, there were others who were going to Europe, notably the Greeks. By the mid-seventeenth century, these had lost their hopes of restoring the Byzantine Empire and had overcome their previous hostility to Western Christendom. Greek Christians from the Ottoman territories began to send their sons to Europe, usually to Italy, to study, and Greek graduates of Italian universities, in particular of medical schools, were playing a role of growing importance. The Greeks were followed by other Ottoman Christians, especially from the Eastern churches in communion with Rome. From the late sixteenth century the Vatican was increasingly active among the Christians of the Middle East. The monastic orders sent missions to Lebanon and elsewhere, and colleges for the Eastern communities were established in Rome. Catholic and Uniate Christians of the Greek, Armenian, Coptic, Maronite, Chaldean and Syrian rites were influenced in growing numbers by these European connections, which sometimes also touched their orthodox and even their Muslim neighbours. The School and order founded in Venice by the Catholic Armenian Mekhitar became for a while the center of Armenian intellectual life throughout the East; the Westernization of the Arabic-speaking Maronites of Mount Lebanon in time affected, to a greater or less degree, all Syria and beyond. Unlike the Jews, the Greeks were able to maintain and extend their contacts with Europe and to institutionalize and give a permanent form to the positions of power and influence which this new knowledge enabled them to acquire in the Ottoman state. The Jewish physicians from the West who had once served the sultans and the grand viziers were replaced by Ottoman Greeks with Italian diplomas. They were in every way better placed than the Jews. Being native to the area, they had a better understanding of the Turks and their language. Being Christians they had better contacts with Europe, and enjoyed the protection of Christian governments and trading companies in Europe, which naturally tended to favor local Christians at the expense of Jews. This became the more important in a period when it was the preferences of Christian Europeans rather than those of Muslim Turks which mattered.

While diplomatic relations between Christian and Muslim states were conducted almost entirely through Christian envoys to Muslim courts, occasional ventures into infidel territory could not be entirely avoided, and from the sixteenth century onwards the three Muslim countries with most dealings with Europe—Turkey, Iran, and Morocco—began with increasing frequency to send envoys or merchants to various European countries.

At first, these too were largely drawn from the local non-Muslim communities or even from renegades and adventurers coming from Europe. When Muslims were sent, they were more often than not newly converted to Islam and, thus, still in possession of useful knowledge concerning Europe, its peoples, it governments, and its languages. So new were the ways of European diplomacy to the Muslim world that sometimes Muslim sovereigns even sent foreigners who had come to them back to their own countries as envoys bearing messages. Such, for example, was the case of the brothers Antony and Robert Sherley, who traveled from England to Iran in 1598. Antony Sherley had been sent by the Earl of Essex to win Persian support for an alliance against the Ottomans, and stayed to instruct Persian troops in the European art of war. In 1599, the shah sent Antony Sherley as his own envoy to Europe on a mission which, however, produced no results. His brother, Robert Sherley, remained in Iran where, in 1607, the shah gave him the daughter of a Circassian chief as wife and, in 1608, sent him on another diplomatic mission to Europe which led to the establishment of diplomatic and commercial relations between England and Iran. That such missions were entrusted to foreigners and infidels shows how little importance was attached to them.

Occasionally, Muslim officials were sent on missions to Europe. The Turkish Sultan Bayezid II sent an envoy called Ismail with letters and gifts to various European courts, including Florence, Milan, and Savoy. We hear of a Moroccan ambassador to London in Shakespeare's day who may perhaps have inspired the figure of Othello, and of Turkish missions to Vienna, Paris, and other capitals in the late sixteenth and early seventeenth centuries. In 1581, no less than two Turkish envoys reached Paris. The first was instructed to bring the French King Henry III an invitation from the Turkish Sultan Murad III to the circumcision of his young son Mehmed. The mission consisted of four çaşnigirs— literally, tasters, the title of a high official at Muslim courts. The second mission was carried out by a certain Ali Çelebi, who brought a copy of the capitulations, just renewed, with a letter to Henry III. The episode indicates a certain reluctance on the French side to receive this mission. The Turkish emissaries were kept waiting for three months at Venice before being allowed to proceed to France. Even the French ambassador in Venice, so he wrote to the king, was unwilling to receive the Turks, "given that the purpose of this embassy is quite contrary to the Christian religion." To send Christian embassies to the sovereigns of Islam was acceptable; to receive Muslim envoys in the capitals of Christendom was not. Later, however, the French ambassador changed his mind and the king was persuaded to allow the Turks to proceed to Paris, where they seem to have been given a warm welcome. Another Turkish mission to France is recorded in 1607 when a *çauş*—an Ottoman pursuivant—brought a letter from the sultan to King Henry IV, apparently with a purely ceremonial mission.[29]

A *çauş* was little more than a messenger—*çauşes* were routinely sent with orders to provincial governors—and the choice indicates the low esteem accorded by the Ottomans to these "diplomatic" exchanges. It was not until some time later that the sultans began to send emissaries with the title of ambassador—*elçi*—first to Vienna and then to other European capitals.

In general, Europeans as well as Turks seem to have preferred to conduct their business in Istanbul rather than in European capitals. Discussions in Istanbul could be held in secrecy and the presence of European envoys could be passed off as concerned with trade. The visit of Turkish envoys to Europe raised a suspicion of attempts by one Christian power to make an alliance with the Turks against its Christian rivals, and while most were willing to try this, few were willing to be seen trying. As a result of this reluctance on both sides, missions to Europe remained few. A Turkish envoy is reported in Paris in 1640, and another in 1669; his appearance is said to have inspired the Turkish ceremony scene in Molière's play, *Le Bourgeois Gentilhomme.*

Missions from other Muslim countries were even fewer. A Persian envoy in Paris in the time of Louis XIV attracted considerable attention.[30] Moroccan embassies also appear on various occasions. Some missions appear to have been concerned with negotiating the ransoming of captives taken at sea in the Mediterranean. One such was the first Ottoman mission to The Hague in 1614. The emissary was a certain Ömer Aga who held the ranks both of Çauş and Müteferrika; he was accompanied by two dragomans, one a Roman Catholic from Naxos whose name is given as Gian Giacomo Belegro, the other presumably a Spanish Jew, whose name, Abraham Abensanchio, reflects the mixed culture of the Iberian peninsula. No doubt the two dragomans, the one a Christian and the other a Jew, served as a check on one another.[31]

It is noteworthy that all these early missions from Islamic lands to Europe are known to us only from Western sources. The dispatch and business of such missions did not reach the level of events calling for the attention of Muslim chroniclers. The first embassy of which Muslim accounts have survived is that of the Turkish ambassador Kara

Mehmed Pasha, who went to Vienna in 1665.[32] The occasion was the signature of the treaty (or truce) of Vasvar between the Ottoman and Austrian sovereigns; the purpose allegedly to establish friendly relations between the two. This appears to have been the first such Ottoman embassy on a grand scale. The ambassador was accompanied by a suite of 150 persons of whom no less than one-third are named as holding specific offices. The interpreter was a well-known European scholar, François de Mesgnien Meninski, at that time chief interpreter to the Austrian emperor. A lengthy report by Meninski in Italian, entitled *Relazione di Cio, che e passato circa l'ambasciata solenne Turchesca nell-'anno 1665 e 1666,* is preserved in the archives in Vienna and seems to have served as guide for the ceremonies and procedures followed in the welcoming of subsequent Ottoman embassies in that city. Two Turkish accounts of the embassy survive, one of them being the official report of the ambassador himself.[33]

Although the embassy stayed in Vienna for nine months, Kara Mehmed Pasha's report is brief and dry, restricted to an account of his own official actions and telling little or nothing of the country he visited. His visit did, however, provide the occasion for another, and far more famous, Turkish traveler and writer to describe the Austrian capital. Evliya Çelebi was indeed a great traveler but unfortunately also a great romancer. He does not hide from his readers that his purpose was to entertain rather than to instruct, and if a story was amusing it did not greatly matter whether it was true. In the ten volumes of his *Seyahatname*—book of travels—he describes the many countries he visited and many more in which he never set foot. Besides what he saw himself he tells of things that he had heard from authorities both sound and unsound, and makes no attempt to distinguish between them. In the sixth volume of his travels, he describes an obviously mythical expedition in which he took part, riding with 40,000 Tatar horsemen through Austria, Germany, and Holland to the North Sea. In the seventh volume he describes Vienna and Austria to which he traveled, so he tells us, as a member of Kara Mehmed Pasha's embassy. Evliya Çelebi's somewhat sophisticated attitude to the truth makes it difficult to evaluate the veracity of his statements. It was at one time suggested that he never even went to Vienna, but put together his narrative from information gleaned from members of the returning embassy, rearranged and amplified to serve his own purpose. This accusation has been proved false by a contemporary document attesting Evliya's presence in Vienna.[34] Most of what he says indicates firsthand observation, though his style and presentation are not always unduly serious.

His description of the Austrian emperor may serve as an example of his literary manner:

> One may almost doubt whether the Almighty really intended, in him, to create a man. . . . He is young, of medium height, beardless, narrow-hipped, not really fat and corpulent, but not exactly haggard.
>
> By God's decision he has a bottle-shaped head, pointed at the top like the cap of a dancing dervish or like a gourd pear. His brows are flat as a board, and he has thick, black eyebrows, set far apart, under which his light brown eyes, round as circles and rimmed with black lashes, gleam like the orbs of a horned owl. His face is long and sharp like a fox, with ears as big as children's slippers, and a red nose that shines like an unripe grape and is as big as an eggplant from the Morea. From his broad nostrils, into each of which he could stick three fingers at a time, droop hairs, as long as the moustachios of a thirty-year old swashbuckler, growing in confused tangles with the hair on his upper lip and with his black whiskers, which reach as far as his ears. His lips are as swollen as a camel's, and his mouth could hold a whole loaf of bread at a time. His ears too are as big and as wide as a camel's. Whenever he speaks, the spittle spurts and splashes over him from his mouth and camel lips, as if he had vomited. Then the dazzlingly beautiful page boys who stand by him wipe away the spittle with huge, red handkerchiefs. He himself constantly combs his locks and curls with a comb. His fingers look like cucumbers from Langa.
>
> By the will of Almighty God, all the emperors of this house are equally repulsive in appearance. And in all their churches and houses, as well as on their coins, the emperor is depicted with this ugly face; indeed, if any artist depicts him with a handsome face, he has that man executed, for he considers that he has disfigured him. For these emperors are proud and boastful of their ugliness.[35]

Despite such obvious caricatures, Evliya Çelebi was the first to break away from the traditional pattern of uninformed contempt. His description of Austria shows glimpses of a society not only different from that of the Ottomans, but in several respects rather better. With one or two exceptions, such as when he contrasts European timepieces with those in use among the Ottomans, or when he speaks of the large and well-kept library of the St. Stephen's cathedral in Vienna, Evliya is careful to avoid any explicit comparison between what he saw in Austria and what he and his readers knew at home. But in the tall stories with which he regaled his audience, important features can be seen—a well-disciplined army, a well organized system of judicature, a flourishing agriculture, a prosperous population, and a well-designed, well-ordered, and thriving capital city.

A similar concern to imply rather than state the points of difference, especially those in which infidel practices might appear superior, inspires some later visitors. From this time onwards it became a custom for Turkish ambassadors to Europe to write reports on their return, describing what they had seen and, more particularly, what they had done. A number of these reports, known in Turkish as *sefaretname,* embassy-book or embassy-letter, survive from the late seventeenth and eighteenth centuries. By far the most interesting is the report of Mehmed Efendi, known as Yirmisekiz Çelebi, Mister Twenty-Eight (he had served as an officer on the twenty-eighth company of the corps of Janissaries) who went to Paris in 1720–1721 as Ottoman Ambassador to the Court of the child king Louis XV. Mehmed Efendi was a person of some consequence, having been plenipotentiary in the negotiations that led to the signing of the Treaty of Passarowitz in 1718. He had then served as ambassador to Vienna and as chief treasurer of the empire. His mission, according to French sources, was to inform the Regent that the sultan would agree to permit necessary repairs to the Church of the Holy Sepulchre. He also discussed the depredations of the knights of Malta, the ransoming of their captives, and some other diplomatic and political matters. In addition to his more immediate mission, he was instructed "to make a thorough study of the means of civilization and education, and report on those capable of application" in Turkey. This additional task is reflected in his embassy-letter, which is of unusual length and interest.[36]

Mehmed Efendi was the first Ottoman envoy in Paris for a long time and was an object of great interest and curiosity whenever he went. While he was traveling to Paris along the canals, crowds gathered on the banks to look at him. Some of the curious fell into the water, some were even shot by the guards. In Bordeaux he saw a truly remarkable sight, the like of which he had never seen before:

> In this place we were able to see the ebb and flow of the tide, of which we had heard. It rises and falls twice in the ocean in twenty-four hours . . . I personally, with my own eyes, witnessed the waters of the river rise and fall by more than a cubit . . . no one who has not seen this with his own eyes could believe it.[37]

In Paris he was appropriately received by the king and the court, and was again troubled by the curiosity of both the vulgar and the noble:

> They stood shivering in the cold and rain until three or four in the night and would not go away. We were astonished at their curiosity.[38]

In due course the ambassador presented his credentials to the French Regent:

I told him that in the joy of meeting so distinguished a personage as himself we forgot all the trouble of our journey, but I said this out of politeness. In fact, if I had to relate all the discomforts we suffered between Toulon and Paris, the heavens could not contain it. . . .[39]

Throughout his long and interesting description of what he saw in France, Mehmed Efendi at no point attempts any direct comparison with Ottoman society. But he was not an unobservant man and comparisons are frequently implicit. His descriptions of the observatory with its scientific instruments, of the hospital and its dissecting room, of such cultural activities as the theatre and the opera, of French industry and manufactures, of the architecture and design of palaces and gardens; the roads and canals, the bridges and locks through which he passed, together amounted to a picture of a whole, perhaps a brave, new world. As a modern Turkish historian has said, when Mehmed Efendi went on his mission in 1720 he could no longer see Paris as Evliya Çelebi had seen Vienna, "with the proud eye of a frontier warrior." Evliya's view was still dominated by the glorious and recent memories of the time of Süleyman the Magnificent. Mehmed Efendi's experience was one of defeat and humiliation—the second failure at Vienna, the withdrawal from Hungary, the peace treaties of Carlowitz and Passarowitz. Not only were the Ottomans in retreat from central Europe; they now confronted a new and terrible danger, barely perceived in the previous century—that posed by the advance of Russia.

The Duke de St. Simon, who seems to have met the Turkish ambassador during his stay in Paris, notes that "he observed with taste and discernment all that Paris could offer him . . . he seemed to understand machines and manufacturing, especially coins and the press. He seemed to know a great deal and have a great knowledge of history and good books."[40] St. Simon also notes that the Turkish ambassador intended on his return to Istanbul to establish a printing press and a library, and that he succeeded in this aim. In fact, this last task seems to have been accomplished by his son, Mehmed Efendi, who accompanied him to Paris and later had a distinguished career of his own as diplomat and briefly even as grand vizier.

Other Ottoman ambassadors visited London, Paris, Berlin, Vienna, Madrid, and St. Petersburg, and duly reported on their activities. These embassy-letters tend to be rather stylized, and indeed the writing of such reports became a kind of minor literary genre. Their political content is disappointing. They tell us very little about the dealings in which the ambassadors were involved and not a great deal about general political conditions in Europe; instead they become stereotyped compositions, with an almost standard sequence of activities and topics. One reason for this lack of political comment may be that these reports were by no means confidential documents. When Mehmed Efendi returned to Istanbul from Paris in 1721, as a matter of courtesy he sent a copy of his report to the French ambassador in Istanbul, who had it translated into French by his dragoman and later published in both capitals. The Ottoman ambassador was obviously unlikely to say anything of political significance in a report receiving such a distribution. One may reasonably assume that the Ottoman ambassadors, in addition to their embassy-letters, presented some further reports to their masters on what they had accomplished. To judge, however, by the level of information available to the Ottoman chancery, even in the late eighteenth and early nineteenth century, such additional reports cannot have amounted to very much.

There was, however, some change, and from about the middle of the eighteenth century, we see a notable improvement in the quality of the reports written by Turkish ambassadors, who become more observant and are better informed. They show a keener awareness of the politics of Europe and sometimes attempt an analysis of diplomatic moves and even, occasionally, of long-term historical trends. At least two Turkish envoys find an analytical tool in the Prolegomena of the great Arab historian Ibn Khaldūn, a work that had for some time been well known in Turkey and much of which had not long previously been translated into Turkish. Interestingly, they offer explanations in Khaldunian terms of events in Europe. Resmi Efendi, who went as ambassador to Vienna in 1757 and to Berlin in 1763, discusses the changes in the situation in Europe following the Diplomatic Revolution and notes the rise of Prussian power and the victories of Prussia over her enemies. "In the words of Ibn Khaldūn, the complete victory of a newly created state over an old established state depends on the length of time and the recurring sequence of events."[41] Some decades later, in 1790, another Ottoman ambassador to Berlin, Azmi Efendi, attributes the European love of comfort and tranquility to the loss of virility characteristic of what Ibn Khaldūn calls the period of decline. Both their notes on German politics and conditions show knowledge and perspicacity, though Resmi was probably mistaken in thinking that the Berliners were on the point of embracing Islam.[42]

One of the best known of these late-eighteenth-century Ottoman diplomats was Vasif Efendi, who was in Madrid from 1787 to 1789.[43] He was a leading man of letters of his time and for some years held the post of imperial historiographer. Later he became chief secretary (*Reis Efendi*) to the grand vizier, a post which involved some attention to foreign affairs. During his stay in Spain, he made the acquaintance of the English writer William Beckford, who speaks of him in his diary. His own account of his adventures indicates some disillusionment with the Spaniards. He begins with the usual difficulties encountered by Ottoman visitors to Europe in passing through quarantine—the barrier which most European governments had erected to protect themselves against infections brought by visitors from the East. He landed at Barcelona, and from there went on to Valencia, where an exchange of gifts with the Spanish commandant caused him great annoyance. He had given "the general" in Barcelona "a richly furnished purse," and therefore felt obliged to offer the same present to the commandant of Valencia, whom he describes as "the second man to the prime minister." Vasif was not happy with the result: "In return he sent me two bottles of olive oil. From this alone one may judge the mean and base character of the people of Spain."[44]

Another key figure was Ebu Bekir Ratib Efendi, who was sent to Vienna as ambassador in 1791–1792. His embassy reports have not been published but are frequently quoted or alluded to by later writers. He wrote at some length on both political and military affairs, describing in detail the structure of the Austrian government, the organization of the Austrian armed forces, and even adding some comments on Austrian society. Among many Ottoman writers of the late eighteenth century who addressed the problem of Ottoman backwardness and weakness, he is one of the first to suggest that the problem may not be so much that the Ottomans have fallen back as that the Christians have pressed ahead, with the implication that the practices of Christian Europe may deserve closer study and possible imitation.[45]

The Ottoman sultan was not the only Muslim sovereign who felt the need to send emissaries to Europe. The sultans of Morocco sent occasional envoys to Europe, some of whom wrote accounts of their travels and activities. Their purpose was usually to ransom Muslim captives held in Christian lands, though it is possible that this was a legal device to justify their missions in terms of Mālikī law.[46] One of the earliest to leave an extended record was the Wazir al-Ghassānī, Moroccan ambassador to King Charles II of Spain, who visited Madrid in 1690–1691. The Moorish sultan had just captured the Spanish North African possession of Larache and now proposed to release the garrison in exchange for 500 Muslim prisoners held in Spain and 5,000 Arabic manuscripts from the Escurial library. Eventually the ambassador, with the consent of the sultan, agreed to forego the manuscripts and take another 500 prisoners instead. One prisoner would thus seem to be worth ten manuscripts.

Ghassānī was a man of intelligence and discernment, and his description of Spain, the first extant written by a Moorish visitor since the completion of the Reconquest, is of quite extraordinary interest. He has something but not a great deal to say concerning the lost glories of Moorish Spain and the tragic fall of Granada, and keeps mainly to recent and contemporary conditions and affairs, not only in Spain but in Europe generally.[47]

Ghassāni was followed by other Moroccan ambassadors to Europe, especially to Spain, the country with which they were most concerned. Their reports are often interesting, though in Morocco as in Turkey the writing of such embassy letters seems to have become a literary genre, with an accepted sequence of themes, places, and events. Nevertheless, the reader of the Moroccan and Ottoman Embassy reports of the seventeenth and eighteenth centuries cannot but be struck by the superior quality of Moroccan reporting on Europe. The Moroccan envoys show an interest in European affairs extending beyond the surface movements of personalities and events. They seek and obtain often good information about political and religious as well as commercial and military affairs, not only in the countries to which they are sent but in other European countries too; not only of immediate and current events, but sometimes extending back into the history of the previous century. Ottoman visitors in contrast seem basically uninterested. Their observations in European politics are few and those that they make are usually superficial and often inaccurate. Their reports are mostly limited to the places and persons that they encountered and they rarely, if ever, make any attempt to see these in a larger perspective, whether of time or of place. Only towards the end of the eighteenth century do Ottoman envoys to Europe begin to offer serious discussions of European affairs.

The difference is not difficult to explain. In the world of Islam, Morocco, in Arabic called al-Maghrib al-Aqṣā, the Far West, was a remote and isolated outpost and a comparatively small and weak country at that. Moreover, the Moroccans could not but be keenly aware of the threat of Europe. They had seen the loss of Spain and Portugal, for centuries part of the world of Islam, to the Christian reconquest, and had received many of its victims. What was still more alarming, they were witnessing the continuation of that process of reconquest by the Spaniards and the Portuguese carrying the banners of Christendom across the straits onto the North African mainland. In a sense, they encountered in the sixteenth century some of the problems which the Turks and Egyptians confronted in the nineteenth. They were aware of European expansion and of the military and economic power that made it possible. It was, therefore, natural that the Moroccans should seek and obtain good intelligence about the countries from which this perceived threat was coming.

The Ottoman situation was quite different. Unlike Morocco, the Ottoman Empire was not a single country but a whole world. Moreover, it was not a remote periphery but embraced the very heartlands of Islam. The only Europeans the Ottoman knew well were those he had conquered and subjugated. More recently, they had been supplemented by other Europeans who came to his court as suppliants and petitioners for the advancement of their commercial and diplomatic interests. The Ottoman world was vast, varied, and in most respects self-sufficient. The remoter lands of Europe and, in particular, those of western Europe were seen as offering neither gain nor risk and therefore unworthy of closer attention. Only towards the latter part of the eighteenth century, when a series of military defeats finally impressed on the Ottoman governing elite the changes which had taken place in the relationships of power, did they begin to seek out information about this outer world, still mysterious, still contemptible, but now also dangerous.

The shahs of Iran were much less interested than their colleagues in either Turkey or Morocco in sending embassies to Europe. The first Persian diplomatic agent to visit England was Naqd ʿAlī Beg, who appears to have accompanied Sir Robert Sherley in 1626.[48] The only one to attract any attention was Muḥammad Riżā Beg, sent by the shah to Paris in 1714. His activities led to the signature of a Franco-Persian treaty the following year. The personality and activities of the ambassador caused a furor in France, where they produced a considerable iconography and literature, and helped to inspire the *Lettres Persanes* of Montesquieu.[49] There is no evidence that the embassy evoked even a ripple of attention in Iran.

Persian diplomatic activity in Europe did not really begin until the nineteenth century, when the extension of the Napoleonic Wars on the one hand and the advance of Russia on the other forced even the inward-looking rulers of Iran to look outwards towards the West. The first notable figure among these Iranian visitors to the West was Ḥajjī Mīrzā Abu'l-Ḥasan Khān ibn Mīrzā Muḥammad ʿAlī Shīrāzī, usually known as Abu'l-Ḥasan Shīrāzī. The nephew and son-in-law of the late chief minister, he left Tehran for London on 7th May 1809, accompanied by the famous James Morier, author of the immortal *Hajji Baba of Isfahan*. The main purpose of his mission was to make sure about the payment of the subsidy promised by Britain to Persia under the preliminary treaty of March 1809, and the manner of its payment. He left London on his return journey on the 18th July, 1810, in the company of James Morier and Sir Gore Ouseley, an orientalist. In 1815, he went as special envoy to St. Petersburg and in 1818 returned on a special mission to England. Later he was placed in charge of relations with foreign powers and held this office until 1834, the year in which Fath ʿAlī Shah died. In addition to a number of English accounts, there is an unfinished and unpublished diary written by Shīrāzī himself of his mission to England in 1809–1810.[50]

A second Persian envoy to the West was Ḥusayn Khān Muqaddam Ājūdān-Bāshī, a military officer who rose to the rank of Adjutant General, whence his title. In 1838, he was sent by Muḥammad Shah on a mission to Europe, apparently for the purpose of securing the recall of the British Minister in Tehran, Sir John McNeill. He traveled via Istanbul and Vienna to Paris and then London, which he reached in April 1839. Ḥusayn Khān himself seems to have left no record of his adventures, but an account of his mission was written by a member of his staff.[51]

This shows some awareness of the need for some better preparation for relations with the Western world:

> While we were in Paris, I tried to get a book which would contain a description of the countries of the inhabited world, and their true condition, so as to quote extracts from it on each country in these pages. When we were leaving Paris for Iran, M. Jouannin, interpreter to the French government, brought in, as a present, a geography book which described the whole world. . . . I had a provisional translation made by Mr. Jabrā'īl, a Christian who was the first interpreter to our mission. . . .
>
> In fact, since the Europeans always want to inform themselves about the true situation of all the countries in the world, they have for a long time been sending expert persons to all parts to note and record the situation and have assembled this information in this geography book. . . . If His Majesty the Shahinshah . . . would order the translation of this book into the Persian language, it would be of lasting value for the realm of Iran and for all the peoples of Islam.[52]

These Muslim diplomats were not, of course, the only visitors from the Islamic lands to the West. As in medieval times, members of the Christian and Jewish minorities continued to travel to Europe either for religious or commercial purposes. One of them, the Chaldean priest Ilyās ibn Ḥannā of Mosul, traveled in 1668 to Italy, France, and Spain and from there took ship to the American colonies. He was almost certainly the first Middle Easterner to visit and describe the New World, where he traveled extensively in Peru, Panama, and Mexico.[53]

The Jews, as one might expect, adopted the general attitudes of the societies of which they were part. Throughout the Middle Ages and into early modern times, the Jews of Christendom were fewer in numbers, lower in culture, and less in importance than their coreligionists in the lands of Islam. Nevertheless, though we have a number of accounts by Jewish travelers from Europe to the Middle East, we have hardly any by Jewish travellers from the Middle East to Europe. There was, of course, the attraction of the Holy Land, which drew learned and pious Jews eastward on pilgrimage. These were more likely to leave written accounts of their travels than were diplomats and merchants. Even so, the lack of travel books by westbound Levantine Jews is remarkable. Apart from the surviving extracts of the travels of Ibrāhīm ibn Yaʿqūb—who may possibly have been a convert to Islam—the only work of any significance is by a Jerusalem rabbi called Haim David Azulay, who traveled extensively in western Europe to collect funds for the rabbinical seminary in Hebron. He made three journeys in all, the first, between 1753 and 1758, to Italy, Germany, Holland, England, and France; the second in 1764 to the same countries; the third, in 1781, to Italy only, where he remained until his death at Livorno in 1806. He wrote a book about his first journey, which was published some years ago from the autograph manuscript now at the Jewish Theological Seminary in New York.[54]

There were also merchants, even Muslim merchants, who traveled to Europe, though their numbers—for good reason—were very small compared with the European presence in the lands of Islam. In Venice, at least, they were of some importance and even achieved something which, though normal for Christian visitors to Muslim lands, was virtually unique for Muslims in Europe, namely a permanent resident establishment. An Arabicized word of Greek origin, *funduq,* is used to describe the hostelries with accommodation for humans and animals and storage space for merchandise which were common in the Muslim world. In the later Middle Ages, the various groups of European traders in Muslim countries were allowed to maintain their own *funduqs,* which came to be known by their various national or regional names. There were, thus, Venetian, Genoese, French, and other *funduqs* in Muslim cities.

The only parallel in Europe is the Fondaco dei Turchi in Venice. There is evidence from Venetian sources of the existence of a small colony of Ottoman merchants in Venice in the late sixteenth century. On the outbreak of war between Venice and Turkey in 1570, the Venetian Senate, receiving a report that the Venetian Bailo, or envoy, Marcantonio Barbaro, along with some Venetian merchants, had been arrested in Istanbul, decided "to do the same in Venice to Turkish subjects and their wares which were in that city so that in any case their persons and property could make easier the recovery of our own men and their possessions."[55] There is no indication of the number of merchants or the value and quantity of their goods. They would appear to have been substantial, however, since in the spring of 1571 Mehmed Pasha sent a message to Venice proposing that they be exchanged against the Venetians and their goods detained in Istanbul. Some of these "Turkish merchants" detained in Venice may have been Jews. In May 1571, according to the Venetian report, the detainees were released and allowed to resume business activities on the Rialto. This was probably part of a deal allowing the Venetians to go back to work in Istanbul.

Another report on the Turkish presence in Venice comes at the time of the Western naval victory over the Turks at Lepanto, when, according to an Italian historian, the Turkish community indulged in "noisy scenes of despair, typically Oriental in their theatricality." The "Turkish merchants" fled from the Rialto and closed themselves in their houses for four days in fear of being stoned by the children.[56]

With the conclusion of peace between Venice and Turkey in March 1573, business was resumed as usual. The number of Ottoman businessmen in Venice increased and now certainly included at least a proportion of Muslims. In 1587 the Venetian Senate decided to increase the number of Turkish dragomans in its service from one to two. The practical needs of a resident colony of Muslims finally induced the Venetian authorities to grant the Turks a *funduq,* similar to those enjoyed by the Christian merchants in Muslim countries. A precedent already existed for this in the famous *funduq* granted to Germans in Venice, the Fondaco dei Tedeschi. According to one Italian source, as early as August 1573, that is to say shortly after the signing of the peace, the Turks requested "for the convenience of trade a place of their own like that which the Jews have in their ghetto." The parallel is one more likely to have occurred to a Venetian than to a Turk. In the following year a Greek resident in Venice, claiming knowledge of Turkish manners and customs, sent a letter to the Doge in which he pointed to the disadvantages of having the Turks scattered through the city. The Turkish merchants, he said, do not fail to "rob, seduce boys, misuse Christian ladies." At the same time, they themselves are frequently robbed and murdered. Therefore, with the example of the facilities provided for Christian merchants in the East, he proposes to provide for "the Turkish nation a resort and hostelry for themselves."

The proposal was accepted by the Venetian Senate on the 16th August 1575. On the 4th August 1579, the Hostelry of the Angel,

Osteria del Angelo, was selected and for some years served as the Fondaco dei Turchi. Before long it was found too small to accommodate numerous merchants with large numbers of attendants and great quantities of goods. The sources note that these quarters were sufficient to accommodate only "Bosnian and Albanian" Turks while "Asiatic" Turks, then rather few in number, still had to seek accommodation elsewhere in hostelries or private houses. The Turks apparently still suffered some inconvenience at the hands of the mob, to such a degree that the legal authorities, the Avogadori di Comun, published a proclamation in August 1594, threatening any who offended against them, by word or deed, with exile, imprisonment, or the galleys. It was, they said, the wish of the republic that they "be able to live and do business quietly and satisfactorily as they have done hitherto."[57]

The establishment of the Fondaco dei Turchi was not unopposed. An anonymous petition, presented to the government of Venice in April 1602, states the case against it with some vigor, using religious as well as political and economic arguments. The presence of a large number of Turks, together in one place, would be dangerous. It could lead to the construction of a mosque and the worship of Muḥammad, an even greater scandal than that already offered by the presence of Jews and of Protestant Germans. The lascivious behavior of the Turks would turn the Fondaco into "a den of vice and a sink of iniquity." Their presence would also serve the political ambitions of the Turks who, possessing great naval power and headed by a mighty sultan, could inflict far greater danger on Venice than the despised and leaderless Jews. There could be no commercial advantage from such an institution since the goods sent from Istanbul by the Turks were of scant value. Despite these and other objections, the project continued and the Fondaco dei Turchi was given a new and larger seat to which it transferred in March 1621. The more extensive accommodation made it possible to transfer the "Asiatics" from their lodgings in the city to this new center. There was apparently some resistance among the Asiatics to this transfer, and a division seems to have been maintained in the Fondaco dei Turchi between the two communities of "Asiatic and Constantinopolitan Turks" and "Bosnian and Albanian Turks."

During the seventeenth and eighteenth centuries, there was some decline in the activities of the Fondaco. From time to time it was closed because of the outbreak of hostilities between the Venetian Republic and the Ottoman Empire. The reopening was often long delayed and the return of Ottoman merchants slow and limited. There are reports of complaints to the proprietors of the building that it was falling into disrepair. They refused repeated requests for repairs and improvements on the grounds that the limited number of visitors made the operation unprofitable. It was not until 1740 that some repairs were carried out. A petition signed by fifty guests complained of excessive rents and declining amenities and, after much argument and a public inspection, the proprietors of the establishment finally agreed to effect some minimal repairs.

The evidence is that, from the end of the seventeenth century, the Ottoman merchant community in Venice decreased steadily in numbers, no doubt as a consequence of the economic decline which in the course of the seventeenth and eighteenth centuries struck both the Venetian and Ottoman economies. Ottoman export trade, now limited almost entirely to raw materials, was particularly affected. After the signature of the Treaty of Carlowitz in 1699, the Turkish merchants were slow to return to Venice and most of them preferred to send their goods through correspondents or agents, thus avoiding the need to stay abroad in the lands of the infidels. When, later in the eighteenth century, the Ottoman merchants reappear in Venice, their composition is changed. The so-called "Asiatics," always a minority, virtually disappear. Most of the visitors mentioned in the mid- and late eighteenth century are from the Balkans. There is also a change in the quality of the visitors. In 1750 the custodian of the Fondaco notes that among the Turkish newcomers there are more servants than merchants.[58]

The safety of these visitors from the fanaticism or hostility of the Venetians was a continuing concern. A law of 1612 imposed severe penalties on anyone who offended, by word or deed, against foreign merchants working in the city. Repeated references to this matter indicate that the protection of Muslim travelers or residents from insult or injury was no easy matter. If Venice, which lived by the Levant trade, had difficulty in tolerating a Muslim presence in its midst, it is hardly surprising that others found it impossible. From Spain to Sweden, royal and local edicts prohibit the entry of Jews and Muslims, the latter usually designated as Moors or Turks, and their settlement. In the Treaty of Utrecht of 1713, by which the government of Spain relinquished its claims on Gibraltar in favor of England, Spanish recognition of British sovereignty was on condition that "Her Britannic Majesty, at the request of the Catholic king, does consent and agree, that no leave shall be given under any pretence whatsoever, either to Jews or Moors, to reside or have their dwellings in the said town of Gibraltar." Her Britannic Majesty's governors, it may be noted, disregarded this pledge almost from the beginning.[59]

Elsewhere, the unwillingness of Europeans to receive Muslim visitors was paralleled by the unwillingness of Muslims and even other Middle Easterners to go to Europe. A trickle of Levantine Jews settled, for business reasons, in Italy or Vienna, maintaining their contacts with their Ottoman homeland. Apart from the occupants of the Fondaco dei Turchi in Venice and small group of Turks later reported in Marseilles and Vienna, few Muslims stayed for very long in Christian lands, for commerce or any other reason. A good indication of the relative situations of the two worlds is the movement of refugees. While great numbers of Jews and dissenting Christians of various kinds fled from Christendom to the lands of Islam, there were very few who cared to move in the opposite direction. A limited number of Greek Christians migrated from Greece to Italy during the decline and fall of the Byzantine Empire; later, small groups of Maronite Christians from Lebanon and some Armenians and Greeks, mostly Uniates, settled in Rome, Venice, and other European cities. In general, Eastern Christians found it more comfortable to be unbelievers in Muslim Turkey than schismatics in Christian Europe.

Only one group of refugees from east to west was of any significance. These were a few Ottoman princes who, unsuccessful in dynastic disputes at home, sought refuge and sometimes support in Europe, always without effect.[60] The most famous among them was Prince Jem, son of Mehmed the Conqueror, and brother of Bayezid II.[61] After a unsuccessful bid for the succession, Jem took refuge on the Island of Rhodes, then governed by the Knights of St. John, and in 1482 sailed from there to France. He tried, without success, to win support among the European rulers, who seem to have regarded him rather as a hostage or as a pawn to be used against the Turkish sultan. For a while he was virtually interned in France in the care of the Knights of St. John. He was accompanied by a small group of Turkish companions, one of whom, probably a certain Haydar, left a memoir which may well be the earliest surviving narrative by a Turkish visitor to Christian Europe. His brief notes on places and people in France and Italy show a characteristic mixture of surprise, distaste, and indifference.

The prince stayed in Nice for four months, and seems to have amused himself quite well. Part of his entertainment consisted of going to balls where the author of the memoir, like many later Muslim travelers, was deeply shocked by this strange European custom:

> They brought the beautiful maidens of the city, and they cavorted around like cocks. In their customs, the women do not cover themselves decently, but on the contrary are proud to kiss and embrace. If they grow tired of their games and need to rest, they sit on the knees of strange men. Their necks and ears are uncovered. Among them, the prince had

relations with many beautiful girls. While he was in Nice the prince composed the following couplet:

> What a wonderful place is this city of Nice
> A man who stays there can do as he please.[62]

Later the Knights and Pope Innocent VIII deemed it advisable "for the general good of Christendom" to transfer Prince Jem to Rome, which he reached on 4th March 1489. He was received with due ceremony by the Pope ten days later, but then became the object rather than the subject of a great deal of jockeying and bargaining among his Christian custodians. In 1494, the French King Charles VIII went to Rome and took possession of Jem from the Pope. He accompanied the king on his expedition against Naples, but was taken ill on the way and died in Naples on 25th February 1495. Rumor had it that he had been poisoned at the orders of the Pope or, according to some later versions, of the sultan. The exiled Ottoman prince left a will in which he asked that his death be made public so that the unbelievers could not use his name in their plans to attack Islam. He also requested that his brother take his body back to the Ottoman lands, pay his debts and take care of his mother, his daughter, and the other members of his household. This was done.

Jem's adventures among the Franks left some record among the Turks. He was, after all, an Ottoman prince. He was also a poet of some distinction whose poems were collected in two divans, one in Persian and the other in Turkish. In addition to the memoirs cited above, a number of documents including some of Jem's own letters are preserved in the Turkish archives, and there is even a short account of the debriefing of an Ottoman spy who was sent from Istanbul to keep an eye on Jem's activities.

Another, less famous, exile was the Lebanese prince Fakhr al-Dīn Maʿn. An adaptable man, he has been variously described as a Muslim, a Druze, and a Christian. Forced out of Lebanon after an unsuccessful attempt to defy the Ottomans, he spent the years 1613 to 1618 in Italy. Arriving in Livorno, he lived much of the time in Florence, moving to Sicily and finally Naples before his return home. An account of his travels and impressions, probably edited from his own verbal statements, was preserved by his biographer. The impact of his stay in Europe revealed itself in several ways. He built an Italian style palace in Beirut, brought Tuscan experts in different fields to work in Lebanon, and—an interesting innovation—deposited money in a Florentine bank for his children.[63]

But apart from ambassadors these are about the only records of any substance that remain of Ottoman travelers in Europe. The Turkish community in Venice can be traced through Venetian documents and chronicles; it is virtually unmentioned in the Turkish sources that have so far come to light. Certainly, in the circles from which the authors of the Turkish chronicles were drawn, the movements and activities of small groups of Balkan merchants would have offered no interest. Only the occasional intervention of Ottoman power to protect Ottoman subjects abroad receives a passing mention.

In addition to diplomats, merchants, and pilgrims, there must have been another category of informants concerning the West—spies. In the nature of things, little information is available about their activities. A secret service which is not secret does not serve, and the activities of espionage organizations are not normally publicly documented. There are, however, some indications in the sources which indicate first that the Muslim states did engage in some espionage activities in Christendom, and second, that these were on a small and ineffectual scale as contrasted with Christian activities in Islam.

Occasionally, a fortunate chance gives us some insight into the spies who were sent and the work that they did. One example has already been mentioned—the report of an Ottoman secret agent sent to France in 1486, to observe the exiled Prince Jem. The arrival of an Ottoman prince—the brother of the reigning sultan and a defeated candidate for the sultanate—presented an obvious temptation and opportunity to the rulers of Christendom. During his twelve-year stay in Europe, Prince Jem was the focus of a whole series of plots and intrigues, the purpose of which was to use him in some way against the Ottoman state. The sultan, naturally, was anxious to keep a watch on his rival, and there are many indications of Ottoman efforts, by both diplomacy and espionage, first to find the exiled Prince and then either to recapture or remove him. Among the numerous documents in the Topkapi Palace archives dealing with Jem, there is the report of a certain Barak, a Turkish sea captain who was sent to Italy and then to France, where he found the missing Prince. Of all the different branches of the Turkish service, a seaman was the most likely to have some smattering of a European language and some knowledge of European conditions. He might also find it easier to travel in Europe without attracting undue attention. The document reads like a deposition and is concerned mainly with Barak's journey to his destination. Presumably, he made a fuller verbal report on the purpose of his mission.[64]

Another interesting figure is that of the first Ottoman emissary known to have visited England. His name is given in various forms, the commonest being Gabriel de Frens. Though a native of France, Gabriel had a Middle Eastern connection in that his father had been French consul in Alexandria. While still a young man, he was captured by Dalmatian brigands and sold as a slave to the Turks. Adopting Islam, he took the name Mahmud Abdullah and entered the service of the sultan, where he was particularly useful in conducting and organizing espionage in the Ottoman interest.[65]

The states of Christendom were in every way better situated for this purpose. They had at their disposal persons with a knowledge of Middle Eastern languages. From an early date, they had resident communities in Middle Eastern countries and, perhaps most important of all, there were large communities of potential sympathizers and employees in the native Christian communities of the Islamic lands. From occasional scraps of information in the sources, it is clear that, from the Byzantine emperors to the states of modern Christendom, the European adversaries of the empires of Islam were engaged in extensive espionage.

The Muslims, though no doubt with equal need, did not have equal opportunity. There were no Muslim communities in Christian Europe. Those who remained in reconquered territories, as in Spain, Portugal, and southern Italy, were soon extirpated. There is some evidence that during the sixteenth century the Ottomans were able to draw on Jewish sympathizers in the Spanish realm—to what extent is not known. They had no residents and few visitors in Europe and were virtually bereft of any firsthand knowledge of European languages and conditions. Such information as they possessed seems to have come in the main from two sources: from Jews, particularly Jews newly arrived from Europe, and from Christian renegades or adventurers who entered the service of one or another Muslim state.

A few surviving texts give some kind of indication of the kind of person involved and the kind of knowledge which they could offer. The fourteenth-century Egyptian author ʿUmarī, in his work already cited above, includes a description of the Christian states of Europe, derived, he says, from a Genoese whom he names as Balban and describes as a liberated slave. Balban identifies himself as Domenichino, son of Taddeo (the reading is uncertain) of the great Genoese family of Doria. ʿUmarī's description begins with the emperor and the king of France, reviews Provence and the states of Italy in some detail, notes the arrival and departure of the Franks in Syria, and ends with an apology for including such matters.

We have given this brief account of the conditions of the Franks only because it comes within the scope of what we have already indicated concerning the division of climates as to the lands of the Franks. Otherwise, it would have fallen outside the scope of this book, though it is not entirely lacking in usefulness. . . . [66]

There were practical as well as ideological barriers to Muslim travel to Europe. As early as the fourteenth century, first Venice and Ragusa, and later Marseilles and other Christian seaports began to take measures to protect themselves against the plague. This developed into a system which came to be known as quarantine from the waiting period of forty days imposed by the Venetian authorities in the fifteenth century on all visitors from the Ottoman lands. With the growing disparity in standards of public health and hygiene between West and East, quarantine became a permanent institution, seen as necessary to protect Europe from contamination. It was applied with the utmost rigor, without reference to religion or nationality, status or position. Ambassadors and great merchants were subject to it no less than humble pilgrims, returning dignitaries no less than visiting Muslims. Most of the Muslim ambassadors have something to say about the quarantine stations, which not unnaturally they found to be both insulting and irritating. Part of the problem was that their incarceration in quarantine provided an opportunity for the local population to come and stare at them. Mehmed Efendi was detained for some time at Cette, a quarantine station in the south of France, where, he tells us, "when I took my walk great multitudes of men and especially women came to watch me . . . the women began in groups of ten and did not desist until five hours after sunset, for all the ladies of quality of the neighborhood . . . had assembled at Cette to have a look at me."[67] Vasif Efendi describes how "The lazaretto being surrounded by a stockade, spectators who came from round about greeted us from afar. Since they had never in their lives seen the men or attire of our realm, they were greatly astonished."[68] Sometimes these ambassadors were offered specious excuses for this indignity. Thus in 1790 Azmi reported from Berlin: "The general himself came to our house and said: 'For you it would not have been necessary to wait in quarantine, but if we had not submitted you to quarantine, this would have aroused much talk among the population.' With these words he tried to excuse himself."[69] In time the quarantine came to be a major barrier to closer intercourse and communication between the two worlds of Christendom and Islam. The material and psychological impact of this barrier are well described by an early-nineteenth-century English traveler to the East:

> The two frontier towns are less than a gunshot apart, yet their people hold no communion. The Hungarian on the North, and the Turk and the

Servian on the Southern side of the Save, are as much asunder as though there were fifty broad provinces that lay in the path between them. Of the men that bustled around me in the streets of Semlin, there was not, perhaps, one who had ever gone down to look upon the stranger race dwelling under the walls of that opposite castle. It is the Plague, and the dread of the Plague, that divide the one people from the other. All coming and going stands forbidden by the terrors of the yellow flag. If you dare to break the laws of the quarantine, you will be tried with military haste; the court will scream out your sentence to you from a tribunal some fifty yards off; the priest, instead of gently whispering to you the sweet hopes of religion, will console you at duelling distance, and after that you will find yourself carefully shot, and carelessly buried in the ground of the Lazaretto.

When all was in order for our departure, we walked down to the precincts of the Quarantine Establishment, and here awaited as the "compromised"* officer of the Austrian Government, whose duty it is to superintend the passage of the frontier, and who for that purpose lives in a state of perpetual excommunication. The boats with their "compromised" rowers are also in readiness.

After coming in contact with any creature or thing belonging to the Ottoman Empire, it would be impossible for us to return to the Austrian territory without undergoing an imprisonment of fourteen days in the Lazaretto. We felt therefore that before we committed outselves, it was important to take care that none of the arrangements necessary for the journey had been forgotten; and in our anxiety to avoid such a misfortune we managed the work of departure from Semlin with nearly as much solemnity as if we had been departing this life. Some obliging persons from whom we had received civilities during our short stay in the place came down to say their farewell at the river's side; and now, as we stood with them at the distance of three or four yards from the "compromised" officer, they asked if we were perfectly certain that we had wound up all our affairs in Christendom, and whether we had no parting requests to make. We repeated the caution to our servants, and took anxious thought lest by any possibility we might be cut off from some cherished object of affection: were they quite sure that nothing had been forgotten—that there was no fragrant dressingcase with its gold compelling letters of credit from which we might be parting for ever? No, every one of our treasures lay safely stowed in the boat, and we—we were ready to follow. Now therefore we shook hands with our Semlin friends, and they immediately retreated for three or four paces, so as to leave us in the center of a space between them and the "compromised" officer. The latter then advanced, and asking once more if we had

---

*A "compromised" person is one who has been in contact with people or things supposed to be capable of conveying infection. As a general rule the whole Ottoman Empire lies constantly under this terrible ban. The "yellow flag" is the ensign of the Quarantine Establishment. [A.W.K.]

done with the civilized world, held forth his hand. I met it with mine, and there was an end to Christendom for many a day to come.[70]

The first really detailed descriptions of western Europe by Muslim travelers did not come from any of the countries of the Middle East or North Africa but from further afield—from India. While the rulers of Turkey and Iran were fighting a desperate but on the whole successful rear guard action to preserve the Muslim heartlands of the Middle East from the advance of Europe—Russia from the north, the maritime powers from the south—the remoter lands of Islam had lost the struggle and fallen under foreign rule. The advance of the Russian and British empires in northern and southern Asia brought millions of Muslims under their control. For the first time, Muslims now met Europeans not just as neighbors or visitors but as masters. It was a chastening experience, but some of them set out to discover the homelands of these new and strange beings who had come to them out of the West.

Two Muslim visitors from India to Britain are particularly interesting. The first was Sheikh I'tisām al-Dīn, a Bengali Muslim who traveled to England in 1765 and is said to have been the first Indian ever to visit London. He left an account of his travels in Persian. It includes a description of places he saw in England and Scotland, and some observations on religious and social institutions and customs, on education, law, on military matters, and on places of entertainment. It also includes an account of St. James's Palace and the Houses of Parliament. Sheikh I'tisām al-Dīn traveled via France and also has some comments on the manners and customs of the French people.[71]

The second, and more interesting, visitor was Mīrzā Abū Ṭālib Khān, who was born in Lucknow in 1752 to a family of Perso-Turkish origin, and was employed as a revenue officer by the British. Between 1799 and 1803 he traveled extensively in Europe and on his return to India wrote a book describing his adventures. Though he wrote in Persian he seems to have had an eye on possible English readers and, as a subject of a European government and an official in European service, took a somewhat different view from that of other Muslim writers. Abū Ṭālib Khān began his European travels in Ireland and spent most of his time in London. He returned via France, Italy, and the Middle East. Unlike most other travelers from the lands of Islam, he attempted a detailed description of the nations and countries he visited.[72]

An entirely new phase in Muslim travel began in the late eighteenth century with the program of reforms initiated by Sultan Selim III. In 1792, as part of a general program of change designed to bring Turkey into line with common European practice, the sultan decided to establish resident Ottoman embassies in the major European capitals. The first Ottoman embassy was established in London in 1793. This was followed by Vienna, Berlin, and Paris where, in 1796, Seyyid Ali Efendi arrived as the first ambassador of the Ottoman sultan to the French Republic. In addition to normal diplomatic duties, these ambassadors were instructed to study the institutions of the countries to which they were posted and to acquire "languages, knowledge and sciences useful to servants of the Empire."[73]

Most of these first Ottoman resident diplomats in Europe were officials from the palace or the chancery brought up and educated in the old way, ignorant of Western languages or conditions and mostly conservative in outlook. To judge by their despatches, they learned little of the countries to which they were sent and were not favorably impressed by what they did learn.

But there were exceptions. One of the most interesting of these Ottoman diplomats was Ali Aziz Efendi, a native of Crete and the son of a high Ottoman official. He, himself, held various appointments in the Ottoman administration and was in due course appointed ambassador to Prussia. He arrived in Berlin in June, 1797, and died there in October the following year. Ali Aziz Efendi knew French and even some German, and had some acquaintance with Western literature. During his stay in Berlin he met the German orientalist Friedrich von Diez, with whom he corresponded on various scientific and philosophic subjects. Though only part of the correspondence has survived, it is sufficient to show that the Ottoman ambassador knew virtually nothing of the experimental sciences or of the rational philosophy of the Enlightenment. He was, however, acquainted with another form of Western literature. Apart from some mystical writings, his most famous book is a collection of fairy tales written in the last year of his life. This is in part translated, in part freely adapted from a work entitled *Les Mille et un jours* by the French orientalist Pétis de la Croix, first printed between 1710 and 1712. Pétis de la Croix's book is a kind of imitation of *A Thousand and One Nights* (not long previously translated into French), based at least in part on Persian or other Islamic original sources; it was therefore more accessible to a Middle Eastern reader than any other Western book.[74]

These ambassadors did not travel alone. Besides the Greek dragomans who served as their main channels of communications, they also took with them young Turkish secretaries whose principal task was to learn languages, mainly French, and to discover something about Western society. These missions thus provided, for the first time, an opportunity for a number of young Turks of the educated elite to spend some time in a European capital, master a Western language and acquire some first inklings of European civilization. On their return to Turkey, most of them became government officials, and together they constituted a new and significantly different group within the Ottoman bureaucratic hierarchy, having both some Western training and some Western interest. They were thus in many ways a civilian parallel to the new Westernized officers graduating from the reformed military and naval academies.[75]

One such was Mahmud Raif, who went to London as chief secretary to the first resident Ottoman ambassador, Yusuf Agah Efendi, and served as chief secretary (Reis ül-küttab) to the grand vizier from 1800 to 1805. Mahmud Raif became enough of an expert on England to be known after his return to Turkey as Ingiliz Mahmud. He wrote a description of England and her institutions which is preserved in manuscript in the Saray Library in Istanbul. Curiously enough, it was in French. So, too, was another book which he wrote on the proposed Ottoman reforms and which was printed in Üsküdar (Scutari) in 1797. His very modest Westernizing did him no good, and in 1808 he was killed by mutinous Janissaries.[76]

Officer cadets and apprentice diplomats were both students sitting at the feet of European teachers. Before long, Muslim rulers were ready to go one step further and send students to Europe to take advantage of the formal educational facilities offered there. The first to take this vital step was Muḥammad ʿAlī Pasha, the governor of Egypt, who sent his first Egyptian student to Italy in 1809. By 1818, some twenty-eight students had gone, and in 1826 he sent the first large Egyptian student mission to France. Forty-four in number, they were escorted by a sheikh from the great mosque university of al-Azhar whose task was to act as their religious preceptor. Many of the students sent from Egypt were Turks and other Ottoman subjects. But some were native Arabic-speaking Muslims, as was their preceptor, Sheikh Rifāʿa Rāfiʿ al-Ṭahṭāwī (1801–1873), who stayed in Paris for about five years, mastered French, and seems to have accomplished far more than any of his wards. Through his books and teachings, he became a key figure in the new intellectual opening to the West that began in the nineteenth century.[77] The Ottoman Sultan Mahmud II, in this as in many other respects, followed the lead of his Egyptian vassal, and in 1827 sent the first Turkish student missions of 150 students to various European countries. His purpose was to train them to serve as teachers in the new schools which he proposed to establish in Turkey. Small groups of students were also sent from Iran to Europe in 1811 and 1815. One of them, Mīrzā Muḥammad Ṣāliḥ Shīrāzī, left an account of his travels which is of considerable interest.[78]

Needless to say, these moves encountered very strong opposition from conservative religious circles. Nevertheless, the movement gained force, and in the early decades of the nineteenth century increasing numbers of students from the Muslim lands of the Middle East began to appear in European staff colleges and even universities. For many of them, these were years of exile and isolation from which they returned happily to reimmerse themselves in their traditional ways. But not for all. As is often the way of students, they learned more from their fellow students than from their teachers. Some of the lessons which they learned were to transform the history of the Middle East.

V

Muslim Scholarship
about the West

In 1655, the Ottoman geographer and polymath Kâtib Çelebi was moved to write a little book entitled *Guide for the Perplexed on the History of the Greeks and the Romans and the Christians.* [1] He explains his reasons for writing this booklet in his preface. The Christians had become very numerous and were no longer confined to that part of the inhabited world in which they had previously lived. Though the sects of Christians were one *Millet,* they had spread out and become so numerous that they had gone to many parts of the world. Sailing with their ships across the eastern and western seas, they had become masters of a number of countries. They had not been able to encroach on the Ottoman Empire, but they had won victories in the New World and had prevailed in the ports of India of which they had taken control. They were thus approaching nearer to the Ottoman realms. In the face of this growing threat, all that the Islamic histories offered about these people was manifest lies and grotesque fables. This being so, it was necessary to provide better information so that the people of Islam should no longer be totally ignorant concerning the affairs of those hellbound people, nor unaware and uninformed concerning these hostile neighbors, but should, on the contrary, awaken from their sleep of neglect, which had already allowed these accursed people to take certain countries from the hands of the Muslims, and thus turn Muslim lands into the House of Unbelief.

To provide this information, Kâtib Çelebi says, he relied on the Frankish *Atlas Minor* and other works which he had had translated.

The first part of the book is introductory and consists of two sections. One is an outline of the Christian religion based on works written in Arabic by medieval converts from Christianity to Islam, frankly hostile in tone and polemical in purpose. The second part of the introduction gives the reader an outline of European systems of government. This is presented in the form of a series of definitions with explanations of a number of European political terms, such as emperor *(imperator)*, king *(kıral)*, etc., followed by a variety of ranks in the church and state, among which he is careful to distinguish. They include pope, cardinal, and patriarch as well as count and other secular titles. The introductory section concludes with a brief statement on the languages used by "this reprobate crew." Kâtib Çelebi comments on the large number of languages spoken in Europe and their mutual unintelligibility.

The remainder of the book consists of nine chapters, dealing with the Papacy, the Empire, France, Spain, Denmark, Transylvania, Hungary, Venice, and Moldavia, these apparently being the countries of Europe to which Kâtib Çelebi thought it necessary to draw attention. The information given consists of a little more than numbered lists of popes or rulers interspersed with odd scraps of information of varying provenance. The only system of government discussed in any detail is that of Venice. For two countries, France and Spain, he was also able to provide some limited amount of historical and geographical information.

Kâtib Çelebi was well-intentioned. His writings on geography and cartography attest to this and indicate the efforts which he made to obtain information from such informants as were available to him. He is no doubt right in his description of the earlier literature, on which his own accounts of Europe do represent a substantial advance. Certainly nothing comparable is available in Arabic or Persian until the nineteenth century. Even so, his presentation of European history and current affairs, written in 1655, seems naive and trivial when compared with the European picture of the Ottomans. More than a century before Kâtib Çelebi wrote his treatise, the European reader had at his disposal a wide range of detailed and well-informed accounts of Ottoman history and institutions, including translations made from manuscripts of some of the major early Ottoman chronicles. Nor was European interest limited to the Ottoman Turks, who presented them with current problems of some urgency. They had also for some time been interested in the earlier history and culture of Islam and had already produced an extensive literature that included editions and translations of Arabic texts as well as studies of Muslim history, thought, and letters. By Kâtib Çelebi's day, chairs of Arabic already existed in a number of west European universities, and such scholars as Jacob Golius in Holland and Edward Pococke in England were laying the foundations of classical orientalism. When, towards the end of the seventeenth century the Frenchman Barthélemi d'Herbelot prepared his *Bibliothèque orientale,* an alphabetical dictionary of oriental civilization, he was able to make use of a substantial body of published scholarly literature in Latin as well as in several European vernaculars. Some of the information came from escaped or redeemed captives, some from diplomatic and commercial travelers. But more and more it was drawn from a new breed of scholars who were applying to the languages and literatures of Islam the methods which Europe had perfected for the recovery and study of classical and scriptural texts. To all this there was nothing remotely comparable among the Muslims where scholarship, whether philological or other, was confined to the monuments of their own faith, law, and literature.

Something, however, was known about the West, and it may be useful to look at the sources and content of the "lies and fables" which Kâtib Çelebi so cavalierly and so justly condemns.

The first serious reports in Arabic about western Europe that have survived appeared during the ninth century. They derive largely from Greek sources, and especially from the geography of Ptolemy. This seems to have been translated several times into Arabic. The extant text is an adaptation made at the beginning of the ninth century by the famous central Asian mathematician and philosopher, Muḥammad ibn Mūsā al-Khwarezmī.[2] It was he who gave his name to the algorism, a medieval European term for decimal numeration. Al-Khwarezmī was not content with merely translating Ptolemy, but incorporated in his version a number of corrections and additions deriving from the geographical information available to the Persians and Arabs. This is true even for the brief account of western Europe, though far less than for those of other parts of the world. Unfortunately, European place names are badly distorted in the one surviving manuscript, to the point that some of them are unrecognizable.

From this and, perhaps, from some other translated works, including Syriac as well as Greek writings, Muslim scholars were able to get some idea of the geographical configuration of western Europe and even of a few place names. Soon they began to produce geographical works of their own which, though generally they devote little space to so remote and unimportant a region as western Europe, do nevertheless illustrate the gradual extension of knowledge.[3]

The first Muslim geographer whose work has come down to us was a certain Ibn Khurradādhbeh, a Persian who wrote in Arabic towards the middle of the ninth century. He was a senior official in the state postal service, responsible for couriers, relay services, and intelligence, and his book, like much of the geographical literature of medieval Islam, was at least in part inspired by the needs and informed by the files of that service. It is naturally concerned in the main with the territories under Islamic rule. It does, however, also devote some attention to the Byzantine Empire, which had a postal service linked with that of the Caliphate, and even provides a brief account of the remoter parts of Europe.

"The inhabited world," says Ibn Khurradādhbeh, "is divided into four parts, Europe, Libya, Ethiopia, and Scythia." This classification occurs in a very few other early Arabic texts, citing Greek sources, and soon disappears entirely from Islamic geographical literature. Ibn Khurradādhbeh's Europe, spelled "Urūfa", consists, somewhat surprisingly, of "Andalus [i.e., Muslim Spain], the lands of the Slavs, Romans, and Franks, and the country from Tangier to the border of Egypt."[4]

On Muslim Spain, part of the House of Islam, Ibn Khurradādhbeh is fairly well informed. Of the countries beyond the Muslim frontier, he has this to say:

> To the north of Andalus lie Rome, Burjān [Burgundy], and the lands of the Slavs and Avars.
> The things that come from the western Sea are Slavonic, Greek, Frankish, and Lombard slaves, Greek and Andalusian slave girls, beaver skins and other furs, of perfumes, styrax, and of drugs, mastic. From the bottom of that sea, near the shores of the land of the Franks, they bring up *bussadh,* which the common people call coral [*marjān*]. On the sea which is beyond the land of the Slavs lies the city of Tūliya [Thule]. No ship or boat goes there and nothing comes from there.[5]
> There are Jewish merchants . . . who speak Arabic, Persian, Greek, Frankish, Andalusian, and Slavonic. They travel from West to East and from East to West, by land and by sea. From the West they bring eunuchs, slave girls and boys, brocade, beaver skins, glue, sables, and swords.[6]

Ibn Khurradādhbeh's Jewish merchants have given rise to a considerable scholarly literature and many attempts have been made to identify and locate them and assess their importance. It seems likely that they were of Middle Eastern and not Western origin.

Parallel passages may be found in the writings of two other Muslim geographers of the time. One of them, Ibn al-Faqīh (d. 903) follows his predecessor but has this to add:

> In the sixth climate are Frankland and other peoples. There are women there whose custom it is to cut off their breasts and cauterize them while they are small to prevent them from growing big.[7]

The other, Ibn Rusteh (d. 910) also tells much the same story but adds a new and intriguing detail:

> In the northern part of the ocean are twelve islands called the Islands of Baraṭiniya. After that one goes away from inhabited land, and no one knows how it is.[8]

All three of them mention the name of Rome, of which they have some rather strange stories to tell.

By the tenth century, rather fuller information was available to Muslim readers. By far the greatest geographical writer of his time was Masʿūdī (d. 956). His remarks about the peoples of Europe contain some echoes of Greek geographical notions, but with interesting additions:

> As regards the people of the northern quadrant, they are the ones for whom the sun is distant from the zenith, as they penetrate to the north, such as the Slavs, the Franks, and those nations that are their neighbors. The power of the sun is weakened among them, because of its distance from them; cold and damp prevail in their regions, and snow and ice follow one another in endless succession. The warm humor is lacking among them; their bodies are large, their natures gross, their manners harsh, their understanding dull, and their tongues heavy. Their color is so excessively white that they look blue; their skin is fine and their flesh coarse. Their eyes, too, are blue, matching their coloring; their hair is lank and reddish because of the damp mists. Their religious beliefs lack solidity, and this is because of the nature of cold and the lack of warmth. The farther they are to the north the more stupid, gross, and brutish they are. These qualities increase in them as they go further northward. . . . Those who dwell sixty odd miles beyond this latitude are Gog and Magog. They are in the sixth climate and are reckoned among the beasts.[9]

The same author in another work remarks:

> Franks, Slavs, Lombards, Spaniards, Gog, Magog, Turks, Khazars, Bulgars, Alans, Galicians, and other peoples whom we have mentioned as occupying the area of Capricorn, that is, the north, are, according to the unanimous opinion of men of authority and understanding among the doctors of the divine law, all descended from Japhet, the son of Noah. . . . The Franks are the most courageous of these peoples, the best

defended, the most plentifully equipped, with the widest lands and the most numerous cities, the best organized and the most submissive and obedient to their kings—except that the Galicians are even bolder and more vicious than the Franks, for one man of the Galicians can withstand a number of Franks.

The Franks are all subject to one king, and there is no dispute or faction among them in this matter. The name of their capital at the present time is Bāriza, which is a great city. They have some 150 cities, apart from country towns and villages.[10]

From these and other Arabic and Persian geographical writings of the time it is possible to reconstruct some sort of picture of the European scene as it appeared to Muslim eyes. To the north of the civilized lands of Muslim Andalusia, in the mountains of northern Spain and the foothills of the Pyrenees, were wild and primitive Christian peoples called Galicians and Basques. In Italy, north of the areas under Muslim control was the territory of Rome, ruled by a priest-king called the pope. In the country beyond that was the realm of a savage people called the Lombards. At the eastern end of the Mediterranean, north of the Muslim frontiers, was the kingdom of Rūm, the Greek Christian Empire, and beyond that the broad lands of the Slavs, a great race subdivided into many peoples, some of whom were fairly well known to Muslim merchants and travelers. West of the Slavs, reaching all the way to the northern approaches of the Alps and the Pyrenees, was the vast Kingdom of Franja, the land of the Franks. Among these some authorities, though not all, distinguish another people called the Burjān or Burgundians. Yet further to the north, beyond the Franks, were the fireworshiping Majūs or Magians, a name and description which the Arabs had quite arbitrarily transferred from the ancient Persians to the Norsemen.[11] A few names of these remoter northern lands appear in Islamic writings—Britain, sometimes Ireland, and even Scandinavia.

Occasionally, Muslim authors used the term Rūm even for central and western Europe, making it roughly the equivalent of Christendom. More commonly, however, western Europeans are known by a different set of terms. The commonest of these is *Ifranj* or *Firanj,* the Arabic form of the name Franks. This name probably reached the Muslims via Byzantium and was originally applied by them to the inhabitants of the Western empire of Charlemagne. Later it was extended to Europeans in general. In medieval usage, it was not normally applied to Spanish Christians, to Slavs, or to the Norse peoples but was otherwise used in a loose and general sense of continental Europe and the British Isles. The land of the Franks was known in Arabic as Franja or Ifranja, in Persian and later in Turkish as Frangistan.

A term sometimes used in medieval texts to designate the peoples of Europe is Banu'l-Aṣfar, which could mean "sons of the yellow [one]." At first applied by the ancient Arabs to the Greeks and Romans, it was later extended to the natives of Spain and then to Europeans in general. Muslim genealogists usually derive this term from a personal name—Aṣfar, the grandson of Esau and the father of Rūmīl, the ancestor of the Greeks and Romans (Rūm). Some scholars have explained the terms as referring to the lighter skin color of Europeans, seen as yellow, i.e., blonde, in contrast to the brown and black of Asia and Africa. This seems unlikely. Arab and Persian authors usually call whites, white, not yellow. Moreover, they rarely speak of Europeans in terms of race or color. While aware, sometimes sharply, of the contrast between themselves and their darker-skinned neighbors to the south and east, they attach much less importance to the somewhat lighter complexions of their neighbors to the north. Occasional references, usually derogatory, to the blanched or leprous coloring of the northern races included Slavs, Turks, and other steppe peoples, as well as—indeed, more often than—Franks. In Ottoman times the term Banu'l-Aṣfar is sometimes used for the Slavic peoples of central and eastern Europe, but more especially for the Russians, whose czar is sometimes called al-Malik al-Aṣfar, the yellow king.[12]

What were the sources of Muslim information about Europe? The literary sources which they used were chiefly Greek, with some meager additions from Syriac and Persian. Certainly they did not learn much from Western books. As far as we know only one Western book was actually translated into Arabic in medieval times.

One or two other books may have become known by indirect means. Thus, Masʿūdī, giving a brief account of the kings of the Franks from Clovis to Louis IV, draws, he says, on a book written by a Frankish Bishop in 939 for the information of al-Ḥakam, the amir of Cordova:

> In Fusṭāṭ in Egypt in the year 336 [947], I came across a book composed by Godmar, Bishop in the city of Gerona, one of the cities of the Franks, in the year 328, for al-Ḥakam ibn ʿAbd al-Raḥmān ibn Muḥammad, heir apparent of his father, ʿAbd al-Raḥmān, sovereign of Andalus at this time. . . . According to this book, the first of the kings of the Franks was Kludieh. He was a heathen and his wife, whose name was Ghartala, converted him to Christianity. After him came his son Ludric, then his son Dakoshirt, then his son Ludric, then his brother Kartan, then his son Karla, then his son Tebin, and his son Karla. He ruled for twenty-six years and he was in the time of al-Ḥakam, the sovereign of Andalus. His sons fought after him, and dissension arose among them to such a point that the Franks were destroying themselves

because of them. Then Ludrik, the son of Karla, became their sovereign and ruled for twenty-eight years and six months. It was he who advanced on Tortosa and laid seige to it. After him came Karla and then the son of Ludric and it is he who sent gifts to Muḥammad ibn ʿAbd al-Raḥmān ibn al-Ḥakam, who was addressed as al-Imām. He ruled for thirtynine years and six months and after him his son Ludric ruled for six years. Then the Frankish Count Nusa rose up against him and seized the kingdom of the Franks and ruled there for eight years. It was he who bought off the Normans from his country for seven years at a cost of 700 ratls of gold and 600 ratls of silver, to be paid to them by the King of the Franks. After him, Karla, the son of Takwira, ruled for four years; then another Karla who stayed for thirty-one years and three months; then Ludric, the son of Karla, and he is the king of the Franks at this time, that is, in the year 336. He has ruled over them now for ten years, according to the information that has reached us.[13]

Of the sixteen names in Masʿūdī's list, the last ten, from Charles Martel to Louis IV, can be identified with fair certainty. Of the first six names, Clovis, his wife Clotilde, and his great-great-grandson Dagobert, present no difficulty; the remainder are impossible to identify among the mass of Merovingian and Carolingian monarchs.

The interest of the passage, however, does not lie in the actual list of names, teeming as it does with corruptions, errors, and omissions. Its importance lies in its mere existence. The classical historiography of the Islamic world is of enormous bulk, probably greater than that of all the states of medieval Europe put together and on a far higher level of sophistication. It is all the more remarkable that, despite the long confrontation of Islam and Christendom across the Mediterranean from Spain through Sicily to the Levant, there should have been such a complete lack of interest and curiosity among Muslim scholars about what went on beyond the Muslim frontiers in Europe. From the first millennium of Islam, only three writings have survived that offer the Muslim reader any information about the history of western Europe. Masʿūdī's list is the first of them.

If the history of western Europe was almost completely neglected, its geography continued to receive some attention. Muslim scholarship devoted great attention to geography and produced a vast and ramified literature on the subject. Starting with adaptations and amplifications of Greek works, it was enriched by a number of travel books, and eventually Muslim scholars produced more systematic statements, some in the form of treatises on geography, others of alphabetical geographical dictionaries. These often include some European names.

The mighty name of Rome was, of course, known to the Islamic world where it was, however, usually confused with Byzantium, to which the term Rūm was more commonly applied. Some scholars were, however, aware of a Rome in Italy, too. An early Arabic author gives a lengthy quotation from Hārūn ibn Yahyā, an Arab prisoner of war who seems to have spent a little while in Rome in about 886. Hārūn describes the city and the churches in somewhat fanciful terms and then continues:

> From this city you take ship and sail for three months until you reach the land of the King of the Burjān [? Burgundians]. From there you travel through mountains and valleys for one month until you reach the land of Franja, and from there you go forth and travel another four months until you reach the city of Baratīnīya [Britain]. This is a great city on the shore of the Western Sea and it is ruled over by seven kings. At the gate of the city there is an idol, and when a stranger tries to enter, he falls asleep and is unable to enter until the people of the city seize him and ascertain his purpose and his aim in entering the city. They are Christian people, and theirs is the last of the lands of Rūm. Beyond them there is no inhabited place.[14]

It is clear that Hārūn did not venture far beyond Rome. It is interesting that he had heard of Britain and of the Anglo-Saxon heptarchy and was even able to give what is probably the first account of Anglo-Saxon immigration procedures. His information was, however, somewhat out of date since the heptarchy had ceased to rule some thirty years previously.

Much of Hārūn's information about Rome obviously came from collections of wonderful stories of Rome, examples of which are current in medieval literature. Some of these were assembled by Ibn al-Faqīh and cited by Yāqūt, one of the greatest of Muslim geographers, who died in 1229. Yāqūt has grave doubts about some of the stories he repeats. In his geographical dictionary, the entry on Rome begins as follows:

> Rūmiya. This is the pronunciation established by trustworthy authorities. Al-Asmaʿi [a famous philologist] says: "The name is of the same pattern as Antākiya [Antioch] and Afāmiya and Niqiya [Nicaea] and Salūqiya [Seleucia] and Malatiya. Such names are numerous in the language and country of the Rūm.'
>
> There are two Romes, one of them in Rūm and the other in Madāʾin, built and named after a king. As for the one which is in the land of Rūm, it is the center of their sovereignty and their learning. . . . The name in the Rūmi language is Romanus. This name was then put into an Arabic form, and those who lived there were called Rūmi.
>
> The city lies northwest of Constantinople, at a distance of fifty days or more. At the present day it is in the hands of the Franks, and its king is called the king of Almān. In it lives the Pope. . . .
>
> Rome is one of the wonders of the world, in its buildings, its size,

and the number of its inhabitants. For my part, before I begin to speak of it, I disclaim responsibility to whoever may look into my book for what I am going to relate about this city, for it is indeed a very great city, beyond the ordinary, and it can have no equal. But I have seen a number of those who have won fame by transmitting learning and they have related what I shall tell. I follow them in what they say, and God knows best what is the truth.[15]

After this careful and, one may say, scholarly disclaimer, Yāqūt goes on to quote extensively from medieval narratives—most of them probably of European origin—about the wonders and marvels of Rome, and then concludes:

All that I have said here describing this city is taken from the book of Aḥmad ibn Muḥammad al-Hamadānī, known as Ibn al-Faqīh. The most difficult part of the story is that the city should be of such enormous size that its countryside for the distance of several months journey does not produce sufficient food to feed its population. Many, however, relate of Baghdad that in size and extent and populousness and the number of baths it used to be the same as this, but such things are difficult to accept for one who only reads about them but has never seen their like, and God knows best what is true. As for me, this is my excuse for that I did not copy all that was said but shortened some of it.[16]

It is easy to sympathize with Yāqūt's point of view.

Most medieval Islamic descriptions of western Europe derive directly or indirectly from the account given by the ambassador Ibrāhīm ibn Yaʿqūb in the mid-tenth century. Two samples must suffice of Ibn Yaʿqūb's descriptions:

Ireland: an island in the northwest of the sixth climate . . . the Vikings have no firmer base than this island in the whole world. Its circumference is 1,000 miles, and its people are Viking in customs and dress. They wear burnooses, the price of each of which is 100 dinars, and their nobles wear burnooses encrusted with pearls. It is said that on their shores they hunt the young of the whale [bālina], which is a very large fish of which they hunt the young and eat it as a delicacy. It is said that these young ones are born in the month of September and they are caught in October, November, December, and January. After that their flesh grows tough and is unfit to eat. As regards the manner of hunting them . . . the hunters assemble on ships, taking with them a large, iron hook with sharp teeth. On the hook there is a large, strong ring and in the ring a stout cord. If they come across a young whale they clap their hands and shout. The young whale is diverted by the clapping, and approaches the ships in a sociable and friendly manner. One of the sailors then leaps onto it and scratches its brow vigorously. This gives pleasure to the young whale. Then the sailor places the hook in the center of the whale's head, takes a strong, iron hammer and with it strikes the hook three times with the utmost vigor. The whale does not feel the first blow, but with the second and third it becomes greatly agitated, and sometimes it hits some of the ships with its tail and shatters them. It goes on struggling until it is overcome by exhaustion. Then the men in the ships help one another drag it along until they reach the shore. Sometimes the mother of the young whale perceives his struggles and follows him. For this case they prepare a great quantity of ground garlic, which they mix into the water. When she smells the odor of the garlic she finds it revolting, turns around, and goes away. Then they cut up the flesh of the young whale and salt it. Its flesh is as white as snow, and its skin is as black as ink.[17]

Ibn Ya'qūb's account of whaling in the Irish Sea obviously has some factual base, and reveals knowledge that whales have mothers and are caught with harpoons. It is doubtful, however, whether he set foot in Ireland, and his account is probably secondhand. His description of Bohemia, on the other hand, is obviously based on direct experience:

> Bohemia: This is the land of King Boyslav. Its length from the city of Prague to the city of Cracow is a three-week journey, and its march is lengthwise with the land of the Turks. The city of Prague is built of stone and chalk and is the richest in trade of all these lands. The Russians and the Slavs bring goods there from Cracow; Muslims, Jews, and Turks from the land of the Turks also bring goods and market weights; and they carry away slaves, tin, and various kinds of fur. Their country is the best of all those of the Northern peoples, and the richest in provender. For one penny, enough flour is sold there to suffice a man for a month, and for the same sum enough barley to fodder a riding animal for forty nights; ten hens are sold there for one penny.
>
> In the city of Prague they make saddles, bridles, and the flimsy leather bucklers that are used in those parts. And in the land of Bohemia they make light, fine kerchiefs like nets, embroidered with crescents which are of no use for anything. Their price there at all times is ten kerchiefs for a penny. With these they trade and deal with one another and they possess vases of them. They regard them as money, and the most costly things are bought with them, wheat, slaves, horses, gold, silver, and all things. It is remarkable that the people of Bohemia are dark and black-haired; blonds are rare among them. . . . [18]

The Reconquest and the Crusades brought Muslims and Westerners into closer contact, in peace as well as in war. In this period one would expect the Muslims to have more detailed and more accurate knowledge of their European Christian neighbors—more substantial

information than the vague reports, rumors, and imaginings of an
earlier time. Certainly the Muslims of the twelfth, thirteenth, and
fourteenth centuries knew more about the West than did their predecessors in the period before the Crusades, but we still cannot be but
astonished at how little in fact they did know, even more at how little
they cared.

One of the greatest of the geographers of the time, the Persian
Zakariyā ibn Muḥammad al-Qazvīnī (d. 1283), relies in the main on
Ibn Yaʿqūb for his account of Europe and, indeed, it is in part thanks
to him that Ibn Yaʿqūb's narrative has survived. Of the Franks, he has
only this to say:

> Frankland: A mighty land and a broad kingdom in the realms of the
> Christians. Its cold is very great and its air is thick on account of the
> excess of cold. It is full of good things, of fruits and harvests, rich in
> rivers, plentiful of produce, possessing tillage and cattle, trees and
> honey. There is a wide variety of game there and the swords of Frank-
> land are keener than the swords of India.
>
> Its people are Christians and they have a king possessing courage,
> great numbers, and power to rule. He has two or three cities on our shore
> of the sea in the midst of the lands of Islam and he protects them from
> his side. Whenever the Muslims send forces to them, he sends forces
> from his side to defend them, and his soldiers are of mighty courage and
> in the hour of combat do not even think of flight, rather preferring
> death.[19]

Part of this no doubt comes from an earlier writer, possibly even
Ibn Yaʿqūb, but the latter part, with its reference to Frankish possessions "in the midst of the lands of Islam" and its involuntary testimony to the power of Frankish arms, would seem to date from the time
of the Crusades. Qazvīnī's observations have the merit of reflecting the
impressions received from direct contact—something very different
from the travelers' tales, old legends, and refurbished fragments of
Greek learning that make up the bulk of the earlier accounts of the
West.

Somewhat better information was available in the Islamic West, in
North Africa, and Spain, where the advance of the Christian reconquest had brought the Muslims into closer if unwelcome contact with
Europe. A twelfth-century geographer called Zuhrī, probably writing
in Spain, speaks of Venice, Amalfi, Pisa, and Genoa, with some notes
on their merchants and their products. Of Genoa he remarks that it is
"one of the greatest of the cities of the Romans and Franks, and its
people are the Quraysh of the Romans." Since Quraysh, the Meccan
tribe to which the Prophet belonged, are the noblest of the Arabs, this
is an extravagant compliment. And that is not all. It is said, Zuhrī

continues, that the Genoese are descended from the Christianized Arab tribe of Ghassān, who lived in the Syrian-Arabian borderlands before the advent of Islam. "These people do not resemble the Romans in their appearance. Most of the Romans are fair, while these people are dark, curly-haired and proud-nosed. That is why it is said that they are descended from Arabs."[20]

Meanwhile, another Muslim Westerner, living under Christian rule in Norman Sicily, had written a work which represents the high water-mark of medieval Muslim geographical knowledge of Europe as well as of the rest of the world. Abū 'Abdallah Muhammad al-Sharif al-Idrīsī, a scion of a former Moroccan ruling house, was born in Ceuta in Morocco in 1099. After studying in Cordova and traveling extensively in Africa and the Middle East, he accepted an invitation from the Norman King of Sicily, Roger II, and settled in Palermo. There, on the basis of his own travels and of information collected from other unknown informants, he compiled his great geographical masterpiece known as the *Book of Roger*. It was completed in 1154. This work, as one might expect, contains much information on Italy and also includes detailed descriptions of most of western Europe. In these chapters, Idrīsī pays only limited attention to earlier Muslim geographical writings and seems to rely directly on western Christian informants and perhaps also on western maps. These would have been readily accessible to him in Norman Sicily. This is how Idrīsī begins his description of the British Isles:

> The first part of the seventh climate consists entirely of the ocean and its islands are deserted and uninhabited. . . .
> The second section of the seventh climate contains a part of the ocean in which is the island of l'Angleterre [England]. This is a great island, shaped like the head of an ostrich; in it are populous cities, high mountains, flowing streams, and level ground. It has great fertility and its people are hardy, resolute, and vigorous. The winter there is permanent. The nearest land to it is Wissant in the land of France, and between this island and the continent there is a strait twelve miles wide. . . . [21]

Idrīsī then goes on to describe, briefly, Dorchester, Wareham, Dartmouth, and "the narrow part of the island called Cornwall which is like a bird's beak," Salisbury, Southampton, Winchester, Shoreham, Hastings "a city of considerable size and numerous inhabitants, flourishing and splendid, with markets, artisans and prosperous merchants," Dover, London, Lincoln, and Durham. Beyond these lies Scotland, of which Idrīsī remarks that:

> It adjoins the island of England and is a long peninsula to the north of the larger island. It is uninhabited and has neither town nor village. Its length is 150 miles. . . . [22]

Idrīsī has heard of an even remoter place:

> From the extremity of the empty peninsula of Scotland to the extremity of the island of Ireland there is a distance of two days sailing towards the west . . . the author of the *Book of Wonders* [an earlier, Eastern work] says that there are three cities there, and that they used to be inhabited, and that ships used to call and put in there and buy amber and colored stones from the natives. Then one of them tried to make himself ruler over them, and he made war against them with his people, and they fought back against him. Then an enemy arose among them, they exterminated one another, and some of them migrated to the mainland. Thus their cities were ruined, and no inhabitants remain in them.[23]

Idrīsī's information about the British Isles is meager; by comparison, he is far better informed about the European continent, even its northern and eastern extremities. His description of the islands— shaped like the head of an ostrich, like a bird's beak—clearly indicates that he had looked at maps. It was probably from these also that he gleaned the numerous place names which he mentions.

Idrīsī's example was followed—and his material used—by later Arab geographers. Ibn 'Abd al-Mun'im, an author of uncertain date from somewhere in the Islamic west, compiled a geographical dictionary, including parts of Europe; Ibn Sa'īd (1214–1274), a native of Alcala la Real near Granada wrote a *World Geography* which was extensively quoted by later Muslim writers in both West and East.

Ibn Sa'īd's account of the West contains a number of interesting novelties. Speaking of England, he remarks that "the ruler of this island is called al-Inkitār in the history of Saladin and the wars of Acre."[24] The ruler who is mentioned in the history of Saladin is, of course, Richard Coeur de Lion who, under the curious name of al-Inkitār, obviously from l'Angleterre, appears in all the Muslim accounts of the Third Crusade. The Muslim chroniclers have a good deal to say about the military and political activities of the Crusaders in the East; they show, however, remarkably little interest in the internal affairs of the Crusading states, still less in the differences between the various national contingents, and none at all in their countries of origin. Ibn Sa'īd's identification of these remote and mysterious islanders with a figure in Syro-Palestinian history is, therefore, unusual. For most Muslim chroniclers they were all Frankish infidels who came from the northern lands of barbarism, and the sooner they went back there the better. Frankish rulers and leaders are rarely mentioned by name, but are designated by some loose and vague title or description, usually followed by the formula "God speed his soul to Hell" or some equivalent.

The historians hardly ever troubled to correlate their knowledge of the Franks in Syria with the scanty information about Europe available in the writings of the cosmographers, geographers, and travelers. The idea that Frankish religion, philosophy, science, or literature might be of any interest does not seem to have occurred to anyone at all. It is not until the late fourteenth century, after several centuries of commercial and diplomatic relations, that we first encounter in an Arabic writer the merest hint of the possibility that such things might even exist in Europe. It comes, as one might expect, from one of the greatest and most original minds that Islamic civilization has ever produced, and even then it is expressed in terms of scholarly reserve. In the geographical section of his famous *Muqaddima,* or prolegomena to history, the great Tunisian historian and sociologist Ibn Khaldūn (1332–1406) includes a description of western Europe which says no more than can be found in the writings of Idrīsī and other Muslim geographers. Towards the end of the *Muqaddima,* however, there is an account of the origin and growth of the rational sciences which contains a revolutionary admission. After describing the genesis of science among the Greeks and Persians and other peoples of antiquity, Ibn Khaldūn goes on to discuss its development under Islam and its spread westward across North Africa into Spain and then concludes:

> We have heard of late that in the lands of the Franks, that is, in the country of Rome and its dependencies on the northern shore of the Mediterranean Sea, the philosophic sciences are thriving, their works reviving, their sessions of study increasing, their assemblies comprehensive, their exponents numerous, and their students abundant. But God knows best what goes on in those parts. "God creates what He wishes and chooses."[25]

The point of the concluding quotation from the Qur'ān seems to be that even something as extraordinary as the birth of learning among the Franks is not beyond the scope of God's omnipotence.

Ibn Khaldūn was also the author of a universal history to which his better known *Muqaddima* was an introduction. It is, as one would expect, fullest on North Africa, and includes an account of the ill-fated Crusade led by the sainted King Louis IX of France against Tunis. This account is remarkable in a number of ways. Ibn Khaldūn gives the name of the French monarch as "Sanluwīs ibn Luwīs," and his title as Rīdā Frans "which in the Frankish language means king of France."[26] He was thus aware that the king was known as Saint Louis—though one may wonder how much this meant to him—and that his father was also called Louis. More significantly, though like other Muslim historians Ibn Khaldūn does not use the word "Crusade," he nevertheless presents the expedition to Tunis as part of a historic struggle between Christendom and Islam, extending over centuries and including such remote but related events as the earlier Arab-Byzantine wars and the more recent clashes in Palestine and Spain. Perhaps most remarkably, he begins his account with a brief discussion of the invaders' country of origin, which, however, does not go beyond the limited stock of available geographical information.

He has little else to say about Europe. The second volume deals mainly with the pre-Islamic and non-Islamic peoples, including ancient Arabia, Babylon, Egypt, Israel, Persia, Greece, Rome, and Byzantium. In Europe only the Visigoths are mentioned—a brief account of them is necessary as an introduction to the Muslim conquest of Spain and is part of the tradition of Spanish-Arab historiography. Ibn Khaldūn's universal history did not extend north of Spain nor east of Persia; that is to say it was limited to his own civilization and its direct predecessors and thus resembled most of the so-called universal histories written in the Western world until very recently.

But nearly a century earlier, far away to the east in Persia, an attempt had been made to produce a truly universal history covering the whole of the inhabited world as it was known at that time—an attempt that was without precedent and for long without parallel. The opportunity and the occasion were provided by the great Mongol conquests which, for the first time in history, had united both eastern and western Asia in a single imperial system and brought the ancient civilizations of China and Persia into close and fruitful contact.

In the opening years of the fourteenth century, Ghāzān Khan, the Mongol ruler of Persia, invited his physician and adviser Rashīd al-Dīn, a Jewish convert to Islam, to prepare a universal history of mankind, embracing all the peoples and kingdoms that were known. The resulting work places Rashīd al-Dīn among the very greatest historians of Islam and, indeed, of mankind. He seems to have set about his work in a remarkably conscientious and efficient way. For Chinese history, he consulted two Chinese scholars brought to Persia for the purpose, for Indian history a Buddhist hermit summoned from Kashmir. In an historical work on so vast a scale, even the remote barbarians of western Europe were found worthy of a brief description, the more so since several of them were in diplomatic negotiations with Rashīd al-Dīn's master. His informant on European matters would appear to have been an Italian, probably one of the emissaries of the Papal Curia then frequenting the Mongol courts. Through him, Rashīd al-Dīn made the acquaintance of a European chronicle which has recently been identified as that of the thirteenth-century chronicler Martin of

Troppau, also known, despite his Czech origin, as Martinus Polonus.[27]

Rashīd al-Dīn's section on the Franks is divided into two parts. The first consists of a geographical and political survey of the countries and states of Europe, the second of a brief chronicle of the emperors and the popes. Rashīd al-Dīn obviously made use of earlier Arabic and Persian writings on Europe, but much of his information is new and firsthand. His account of the relations of pope and emperor is detailed and clearly comes from a papal envoy; he has fairly good information on imperial coronations; he has heard of the wool and scarlet cloth of England; the universities of Paris and Bologna; the lagoons of Venice; the Republics of Italy, and the absence of snakes from Ireland. All this represents a considerable advance in knowledge. Even his curious statement that the ruler of the two islands [Ireland and England] is called Scotland and that they are tributary to the King of England may have a grain of truth.[28]

His chronicle of the emperors and popes ends with the Emperor Albert I and Pope Benedict XI, both of whom are correctly described as living at that time. This contains no more than an abridgement of Martin of Troppau brought up-to-date. His account of Europe is flimsy, superficial and sometimes inaccurate, and in comparison with his long and exhaustive treatment of other civilizations—for example, those of India and China—it seems a poor thing. But after the brief list of Frankish kings given by Masʿūdī, it appears to be the only attempt made by a medieval Islamic author to outline the history of Christian Europe. The third was not made until Ottoman times, in the sixteenth century. Right through the medieval period Islam remained indifferent, uninterested in the backward and infidel peoples who lived in the lands to the north of the Mediterranean. It is remarkable that even so great and original a thinker as Ibn Khaldūn himself—a native of Tunisia, one of the Muslim lands with most direct experience of the West —shared the general indifference. The great debate of the Crusades, so significant in Western history, stirred hardly a ripple of curiosity in the lands of Islam. Even the rapid growth of commercial and diplomatic relations with Europe after the Crusades seems to have evoked no desire to penetrate the secrets of the other side.

While the old Muslim states of Spain and the East were declining and falling under foreign rule, in Anatolia a new and vigorous principality was arising which was soon to grow into the last and greatest of the universal Muslim empires. The Ottoman state was born on the frontier between Islam and Christendom, and from the first the Ottomans, though perhaps more wholeheartedly devoted to Islam than any of their predecessors, had a closer and more intimate acquaintance with at least some parts of Christian Europe. For the advancing Otto-mans, Frankish Europe was no longer the remote and mysterious wil-derness that it had been for the Arabs and Persians of medieval times. It was their immediate neighbor and rival, replacing the defunct Byz-antine Empire as the emblem of Christendom, the millennial and ar-chetypal adversary of the House of Islam.

It was mainly in the arts of war that the Turks were ready to turn to Europe for information and even instruction. In naval construction in particular they followed closely on Western models and made not a few improvements of their own. With European naval techniques, however, they also acquired a working knowledge of European maps and navigation, and were soon able to copy, translate, and use Euro-pean sailing charts and to make coastal charts of their own. Piri Reis (d.c. 1550), the first noteworthy Ottoman cartographer, seems to have known some Western languages and to have made use of Western sources. As early as 1517, he presented a world map to Sultan Selim I which included a copy of Columbus' map of America made in 1498. Since Columbus' original is lost, this map—probably captured in one of the numerous naval encounters with the Spaniards and the Por-tuguese—survives only in the Turkish version, which is still to be found in the Topkapı Palace Library in Istanbul.[29] It was followed in 1580 by an account of the discovery of the New World apparently compiled from European sources by the Ottoman geographer Muham-mad ibn Hasan Su'udi and presented to Sultan Murad III.[30]

A Turkish sailing book for the Mediterranean, compiled in the year 1521, and revised in 1525, contains detailed sailing instructions for the Mediterranean coasts. The version of 1525 includes a preface and an appendix, both in verse, which give some idea of the geographical knowledge and concepts then in use among the Turks. A later *map-pemonde* of 1559 appears to have been drawn by a certain Ḥājji Aḥmad of Tunis, who studied at the mosque university of Fez in Morocco and was later a prisoner in Europe, probably in Venice. It was there, in any case, that he prepared his Turkish planisphere covering Europe, Asia, Africa, and the known parts of America. He also gives a few details about himself, from which it would appear that he prepared his map while the captive of a "virtuous and learned gentleman." Describing his book, he says, "I have made a reproduction in Muslim script by translating the Frankish languages and writings. They promised to free me in exchange for my toils and labors, which are such that words fail me to describe them . . . I have written it [or perhaps dictated it] in Turkish according to my means and at the orders of my master, for this language has great authority in the world."[31]

The first major Ottoman work on general geography was the *Jihan-nüma* (World Mirror) of Kâtib Çelebi, who tells us in his preface that he almost gave up hope of being able to compile a universal geography when he realized that the British Isles and Iceland could not be described without having recourse to European works since all those available to him in Arabic, Persian, and Turkish were incomplete and inaccurate. He had, he said, consulted, through intermediaries, the geography of Ortelius and the *Atlas* (Major or Minor) of Mercator. Just at the moment when he hoped to find a copy of Ortelius "he had the good fortune to find the *Atlas Minor,* an abridgement of the *Atlas Major*" and at the same time to make the acquaintance of a certain Sheikh Muhammad Ihlasi, "a former French monk who had come over to Islam". With the help of the Frenchman, he began to translate the *Atlas Minor,* which he completed in 1655.[32]

Towards the end of the century another writer on geography, Abū Bakr ibn Bahrām al-Dimashqī (d. 1691), a protégé of the grand vizier Fazil Ahmed Pasha, worked on the various drafts of Kâtib Çelebi's *Jihannüma* and himself added some material to it. His major work is a translation of the *Atlas Major* of Joan Blaeu.[33] Dimashqī seems to have been interested mainly in Blaeu's geography, to a lesser extent in his geometry. Significantly, his account of the cosmic theories of Tycho Brahe and of Copernicus is reduced to a brief statement that "there is another doctrine according to which the sun is the center of the universe and the earth turns around it."[34]

The trend initiated by the work of Kâtib Çelebi and Dimashqī continued into the eighteenth century. Several other geographical works appear mostly in the form of appendices or addenda to the *Jihannüma.* Of some interest is the work of an Armenian, Bedros Baronian, who served as dragoman to the Netherlands legation and later to that of the kingdom of the Two Sicilies. He is said to have prepared a Turkish translation of a French manual by Jacques Robbs entitled *La Méthode pour apprendre facilement la géographie.*[35]

This literature, although of interest, seems to have had only a limited impact, and it is doubtful whether Turkish mariners or geographers knew much beyond the Mediterranean. In 1770, when a Russian fleet sailed round western Europe and suddenly confronted the Ottomans in the Aegean, the Ottoman government made a formal protest to the Venetian representative, complaining that his government had allowed the Russian fleet to sail from the Baltic into the Adriatic. This refers to a feature of some medieval maps which shows a channel between these two seas with its southern terminal at Venice. Though Kâtib Celebi and his disciples certainly knew better, and the *Jihannüma* was already in print, the officials at the Porte were still apparently guided by medieval geographical notions.

The eighteenth-century Ottoman chronicler Vasif remarks that the Ottoman ministers could not conceive that there was any way for the Muscovite fleet to go from St. Petersburg to the Mediterranean Sea.[36] The Austrian interpreter and historian Joseph Hammer tells of a similar expression of incredulity "under my own eyes" in the year 1800, when the grand vizier, Yusuf Ziya, refused to believe that British reinforcements could be brought from India by the Red Sea. Hammer remarks: "Sir Sidney Smith, to whom I served as interpreter during this meeting, had all the trouble in the world to demonstrate to him by the inspection of maps that there existed a junction between the Indian Ocean and the Red Sea."[37] The modern history of Europe and North America offers equally dramatic examples of geographical ignorance on the part of politicians and even statesmen. Such ignorance, however, though sometimes found among rulers, was not characteristic of the political elite and was usually corrected by a well-trained and well-informed civil service.

Of the human geography of Europe—the different peoples who inhabited the countries that loomed vaguely on the Ottoman horizon, there is little information in Ottoman literature. An interesting exception is a certain Mustafa Âli of Gallipoli (1541–1600), a well-known historian, poet, and polymath of his time. In at least two places, Âli attempts a kind of ethnology of Europe. In the fifth volume of a work on universal history which does not include Europe, he offers a longish digression on the various races encountered by the Ottomans inside and outside their borders. A parallel passage occurs in another work by Âli, in which he discusses the different types of slaves and servants, and the racial qualities and aptitudes of the peoples from whom they are drawn. Âli is naturally best informed about the races within the empire, and richly reflects the normal prejudices of the slaveowner. To expect good manners and dignity from Albanians or loyalty from Kurds is like asking a broody hen to stop cackling. It is equally impossible for a Russian slave-girl not to be a whore, or a Cossack man not to be a drunkard. Âli thinks rather better of the Balkan Slavs. The Bosniaks, and more especially the Croats, are decent people. Of other Europeans he mentions only the Hungarians, the Franks, and the Germans (Alman). The Franks and the Hungarians somewhat resemble one another. They are clean in their habits regarding eating, drinking, clothing, and household appurtenances. They are also ready of understanding, quickwitted and agile. They are, however, inclined to be devious and cunning and are very crafty in acquiring money. As regards good breeding and dignity—qualities to which

Âli attaches importance—they are middling. They are, however, capable of connected and intelligible conversation. While often marked by beauty and elegance of appearance, few of them enjoy good health and many are subject to various diseases. Their physiognomies are open and easy to interpret. They are extremely capable in commerce and, when gathered together for drinking and jollity, take their pleasures judiciously. All in all, says Âli, they are smart people. The Germans, on the other hand are stubborn and ill-disposed, skilled in handicrafts and the like, but otherwise rather backward. They are heavy of tongue and slow of movement. Few of them come over to Islam, and they prefer to persist in their error and unbelief. They are, however, excellent fighters, both as cavalry and as infantry.[38]

Âli was, of course, writing from hearsay. Half a century later, Evliya Çelebi attempted a comparison between the Hungarians and the Austrians, based on direct observation. Evliya notes that the Hungarians had been weakened by the Ottoman conquests of the previous century, and those not conquered by the Turks had fallen under Austrian domination. Despite this, he regarded them as far superior to the Austrians, who in his view were very unwarlike. "They are just like Jews. They have no stomach for a fight." The Hungarians are finer people.

> Though they have lost their power, they still have fine tables, are hospitable to guests, and are capable cultivators of their fertile land. Like the Tatars, they ride wherever they go with a span of horses, with from five to ten pistols, and with swords at their waists. Indeed, they look just like our frontier soldiers, wearing the same dress as they, and riding the same thoroughbred horses. They are clean in their ways and in their eating, and honor their guests. They do not torture their prisoners as the Austrians do. They practice sword play like the Ottomans. In short, though both of them are unbelievers without faith, the Hungarians are more honorable and cleaner infidels. They do not wash their faces every morning with their urine as the Austrians do, but wash their faces every morning with water as the Ottomans do.[39]

If the infidel present offered little of value, the infidel past offered even less, and Ottoman historians did not normally concern themselves with the history of Europe.

There is, however, an occasional glimmer of interest. If we may believe an early Ottoman chronicle, the capture of the great, historic city of Constantinople in 1453 aroused some slight curiosity about the city's past. It was quickly satisfied.

> After Sultan Mehmed had conquered Constantinople, he saw Aya Sofya and was amazed. He questioned the people of Rūm and of Frangistan and the monks and the patriarchs and those of the Romans and the

Franks who knew their histories and he wanted to know who had built Constantinople and who had ruled there and who had been kings *(padişah)*. . . . He gathered the monks and other people of Rūm and the Franks who knew history and questioned them: 'Who built this city of Constantinople, who ruled it?' They on their part informed Sultan Mehmed to the extent of their knowledge from their books and chronicles and from the information handed down.[40]

It is not clear who these monks and chroniclers, these Franks and Greeks whom the Sultan consulted might have been. The pre-Ottoman history of the city, with which the Ottoman chronicler follows this passage, is entirely fantastic, and bears no relation to the Greek, Roman, or Byzantine history of the city. Sultan Mehmed's interest in earlier history is independently attested by both Greek and Italian writers, some of whom were at one time or another in his service. His interest, however, such as it was, seems to have been unique, and in any case left no trace in Ottoman historiography.

The first Turkish historical work about western Europe was written in the late sixteenth century. It consists of a history of France from the legendary founder King Faramund to the year 1560. According to the colophon it was translated into Turkish by order of Feridun Bey, who held the office of chief secretary to the grand vizier from 1570 to 1573, and was carried out by two men, the translator Hasan ibn Hamza and the scribe, Ali ibn Sinan. The translation was completed in 1572. Since it survives in a single manuscript and that in Germany, it is clear that the work did not arouse much interest among Turkish readers.

During the seventeenth century, there are signs of a change, and a few Turkish historians and other scholars show interest in Europe and even some acquaintance with European sources. A certain Ibrahim Mülhemi (d. 1650) is reported to have written a history of the kings of the Romans and the Franks, of which no copy appears to have survived. His better known contemporary, Kâtib Çelebi, who devoted some attention to Europe in his geographical works, also wrote on history, and mentions in one of his works a translation of "a Frankish history of the infidel kings." At least one copy of this translation has survived in private possession in Turkey, and parts of it were published in serial form in a Turkish newspaper in 1862–1863. In his introduction Kâtib Çelebi names his source—the Latin chronicle of Johann Carion (1499–1537), which he used in the Paris edition of 1548. The choice of a Lutheran work, much used in Protestant propaganda, might possibly indicate that Kâtib Çelebi's French collaborator, though described by him as a former monk, had a Protestant and not a Catholic background.[47]

In addition to this translation, Kâtib Çelebi wrote an "original" work on Europe which survives only in manuscript and is cited at the beginning of this chapter. His purpose, he explains, was to give the Muslims much-needed accurate information about the peoples of Europe. Despite this aim, his treatise serves, in the words of Professor Victor Ménage, "by its very triviality, as an index of the ignorance of Europe which prevailed in his day among Ottoman men of learning."[42]

Meanwhile, there was some little interest in Western history, although in a low key. It seems to have increased somewhat in the second half of the seventeenth century, when a new kind of society emerged in the villas around Istanbul. Turkish scholars could now meet with westernized but Turkish-speaking Ottoman Christians, and even an occasional European, and had the opportunity to learn something of Western scholarship and science. A key figure was the Roumanian prince Demetrius Cantemir, at home in both Ottoman and European society, and himself the author of a history of the Ottoman Empire. These encounters were, however, of limited scope, and seem to have had little effect on the general Ottoman perception of the outside world. One of the exceptions was a little-known historian of the late seventeenth century called Hüseyn Hezarfen (d. 1691), most of whose works are still unpublished. Like Kâtib Çelebi, whom he cites with admiration, he was a man of wide-ranging curiosity, interested in the geography and history of distant lands as well as the earlier history of his own. He is known to have been acquainted with such figures as Count Ferdinand Marsigli and Antoine Galland and probably knew Cantemir and the great French orientalist, Pétis de la Croix. It was perhaps in part through the good offices of these and other European acquaintances that Hüseyn Hezarfen was able to gain access to the contents of European books and to incorporate some of them in his own works.

One of these is the *Tenkih al-Tevarih,* completed in 1673. It is a historical work divided into nine parts, of which the sixth, seventh, eighth, and ninth deal with history outside the Islamic oecumene and its accepted predecessors. This is a remarkably high proportion. Part six deals with Greek and Roman history, part seven with the history of Constantinople since its foundation, part eight with Asia, China, the Philippines, the East Indies, India, and Ceylon, part nine with the discovery of America. Oddly enough, Hüseyn Hezarfen does not seem to have included Europe in his survey but his descriptions of both Asia and America are based almost entirely on European sources, most of them via the *Jihannüma* of Kâtib Çelebi. His accounts of Greek, Roman,

and Byzantine history are also drawn from European sources, which
served to augment the slender stock of Islamic knowledge of classical
antiquity.[43]

With the work of Ahmed ibn Lutfullah, known as Münejjimbaşi,
the Chief Astrologer (d. 1702), we return to universal history in the
grand style. His major work is a universal history of mankind from
Adam to the year 1672, based, so he tells us, on some seventy sources.
Münejjimbaşi elected to write his work in Arabic, and, apart from a
few excerpts, the original text is still unpublished. A Turkish translation, however, prepared under the direction of the great early eighteenth-century Turkish poet Nedim, was printed in Istanbul in three
volumes in 1868. The greater part of the book, as one would expect,
is devoted to Islamic history. A substantial part of the first volume,
however, deals with the history of pre-Islamic and non-Islamic states.
The former, as usual, included the Persians and ancient Arabians on
the one hand and the Israelites and ancient Egyptians on the other,
discussing them on more or less traditional lines.

Münejjimbaşi's ancient history goes beyond the common Islamic
stock. His accounts of the Romans and of the Jews clearly derive from
Roman and Jewish sources. These were, in part, already available in
the Arabic adaptation of Ibn Khaldūn. His information, however, is
much fuller than that of the great North African historian and includes
such entities as the Assyrians and Babylonians, the Seleucids and the
Ptolemies, previously barely known to Islamic historiography.

Clearly, he must have used a European source for these. This
becomes certain in Münejjimbaşi's chapter on Europe, which includes
sections on the divisions of the "Frankish" peoples and on the kings
of France, Germany, Spain, and England. His source would appear to
be the Turkish translation of the chronicles of Johann Carion, though
since Munejjimbaşi continues his narrative down to the reigns of Louis
XIII of France, the Emperor Leopold in Germany, and Charles I of
England, he must have had later supplementary material at his disposal. He reports on the English Civil War and the execution of King
Charles and ends:

> "After him the people of England did not appoint another king over
> them; we have no further information about their affairs."[44]

Kâtib Çelebi, Hüseyn Hezarfen, and Münejjimbaşi provide virtually the whole of Ottoman historiography on western Europe in the
sixteenth and seventeenth centuries. Their information is scanty and
derives mainly from the same group of sources of information. And
even that limited degree of interest is lacking in other Ottoman writ-

ers. For most Ottoman Muslims, the only achievements of Europe worthy of attention were in the arts of war, and these could be studied in captured guns and ships with the aid of prisoners and renegades. That the languages, literatures, arts, and philosophies of Europe could be of any interest or relevance to them did not enter their minds, and such European movements of ideas as the Renaissance and the Reformation awoke no echo and found no response among the Muslim peoples—no more than did Muslim movements of ideas in the Europe of that time.

These writings, devoted specifically to Europe, its people, and its affairs, are of minor importance. They survive in few copies, sometimes only in a single copy, and were for the most part never printed. Their impact on Ottoman opinion must have been very slight. A much better idea of the Ottoman perception of Europe can be gathered from the series of major Ottoman historians, some of them holding the rank of *Vakanüvis* or Imperial Historiographer, others without official status. Together, these historians produced a series of chronicles covering the history of the empire from its origins to its end. Most of them were printed at a fairly early date, and in sum they constitute the most important formative influence on the Ottomans' perception of themselves, their place in the world, and their dealings with others.

While the Ottoman chroniclers, like those of virtually every other society known to history, were concerned mainly with their own affairs, even these involved some dealings with Europe in war, trade, diplomacy, and otherwise. Such contacts find occasional expression in Ottoman historical literature, the character of which reflects the changes of successive centuries.

During the period of the great Ottoman advances into Europe in the fifteenth century, Ottoman historiography was still somewhat meager, consisting in the main of simple narratives in simple Turkish, reflecting the outlook and aspirations of the gazis, the frontier fighters of Islam. They see the Europeans first as enemies and then as tribute-paying subjects, and show little knowledge or concern about what happens on the other side of the battlelines. They were, however, aware that they were confronting others beside their local Christian adversaries, and the word "Frank" occurs not infrequently in the lists of enemies who have been met and vanquished. In early Ottoman writings, it normally appears to mean the Italians and, more especially, the Venetians, whom the Turks encountered in their expansion into Greece and the eastern Mediterranean islands. The Franks were, of course, always duly defeated, and provided the victors with impressive booty. Describing a victory won in the year 903/1497, the early Ottoman historian Oruç lists the enormous amounts taken from the defeated Franks in gold and silver coin, ermine and other furs, silks and satins and gold and silver brocades—"these they found and plundered in such unlimited quantities that no one cared to bother with carts, horses, mules, camels, or prisoners. So many prisoners were taken that no one could count them." The only times, says Oruç, that such splendid booty was found were in the jihāds at Varna [1444] and at Kosova [1389] and at the conquest of Constantinople [1453]—"or so it was said." The two richest people in the world, he goes on to observe, are the Poles and the Franks, "richer than any others in worldly goods and therefore yielding immense and unequalled booty to the warriors of the faith."[45]

A more sophisticated view of Europe occurs, somewhat surprisingly, not in a chronicle or document, but in an epic poem written at the beginning of the sixteenth century and celebrating the defeat of a European naval expedition against the Turks. The episode in itself was a minor one. Turkish forces had captured Modon and other Venetian outposts on the Greek coast. The Venetians succeeded in rallying support from many parts of Europe, and in the course of the war a naval expedition, mainly French but with some allies and auxiliaries, launched an attack on the Turkish-held island of Lesbos, at the end of October 1501. The expedition was repelled, and the occasion gave rise to a lengthy narrative poem celebrating the Turkish victory. The poet, who modestly adopted the soubriquet of Firdevsi of Turkey (after the great Persian epic poet Firdawsi), explains that the Turkish conquest of Modon had caused great distress among the Franks and especially to their leader, Rin-Pap, barely recognizable as the pope in Rome. When Sultan Bayezid conquered Modon, says the poet, the Franks were so terrified of his sword that the Nine [Ionian] islands sank in the sea like a crocodile. When "the great chief of irreligion, Rin-Pap," heard about this he set to work to form an alliance for the recovery of Modon, and sent messages to all the rulers of the Frankish infidels. He then introduces a curious cast of Frankish leaders, who from time to time reappear in the ensuing narrative. They include the kings of France and Hungary, of Bohemia and of Poland, the latter two named, echoing the slavic myth, as Czech and Lech. Other European figures are Kız-khan, the Girl khan—that is, Isabel of Castile—who sends her "ban" (a Hungarian term for chief, often used by Ottoman writers), the officer commanding the Spanish contingent in the fleet; Doza, the Doge of Venice; the rulers of Andalusia and Catalonia, the Knights of Rhodes, and even the Prince of Muscovy, Ivan III.[46] In true epic style, the leaders of the enemy are also allowed to make speeches and write letters, and these present in a somewhat startling light what the poet conceived to be the beliefs and attitudes of the Franks. These naturally see and speak of themselves as infidels. A particularly remarkable statement is attributed to a slavic prince:

> I am a servant of Christ, I am a slave of the idol of Mark [St. Mark of Venice], I am a greater idolater and infidel than the king of Hungary.[47]

During the sixteenth century the Ottoman Empire was at the height of its power, and its historians reflect the confidence of Muslims in their unchallenged superiority and unbroken success. Only the rusticated Grand Vizier Lûtfi Pasha, pondering the woes of the empire after his dismissal, warned his ungrateful sovereign of the twin dangers of corruption at home and the rise of Frankish naval power. Most other historians were untroubled by such concerns. If the Franks are mentioned at all, it is with contempt, as barbarian enemies, or with condescension, as tributaries. In the late sixteenth and seventeenth centuries, there are references to the appearance of Frankish merchants and shipping, and sometimes to the arrival of Frankish diplomats in Istanbul. The Ottoman historian Selaniki Mustafa Efendi records the arrival in 1593 of the second English ambassador to Istanbul, Edward Barton, in these terms:

> "The ruler of the country of the island of England, which is 3700 miles by sea from the Golden Horn of Istanbul, is a woman who governs her inherited realm and maintains her state and sovereignty with complete power. She is of the Lutheran religion. She sends her letters of homage, her envoy, her gifts, and her presents. That day there was a meeting of the Council and the ambassador was entertained and honored according to law. A ship as strange as this has never entered the port of Istanbul. It crossed 3700 miles of sea and carried 83 guns, besides other weapons. The outward form of the firearms was in the shape of a swine. It was a wonder of the age worthy to be recorded."[48]

Selaniki's English ship with its eighty-three pig-shaped guns seems a little fanciful. But at least, he knew that there was a Protestant queen in England and either he or his informant had observed the heavier armament carried by ships built to sail the Atlantic.

During the seventeenth and eighteenth centuries, Ottoman chroniclers devote some though not a great deal of attention to relations with Europe. The various European nations are still referred to invariably as "the English infidels," "the French infidels," etc., though the curses and insults customary in earlier historiography become less frequent and less vehement.

In general, however, the Ottoman historians, while beginning to devote rather more attention to affairs on their European borders, have little to say about what goes on inside Europe. There is a remarkable consistency in this, partly due to the fact that the Ottoman chroniclers regarded the narrative of past events as a kind of immutable documentary record rather than an individual statement, and therefore felt free to copy each other at length. Even the seventeenth-century scholar Kâtib Çelebi, who in other historical and geographical writings shows some interest in Europe, departs very little from the norm in his general Ottoman chronicle. His account, for example, of the arrival in Turkey of news of the Thirty Years War is brief and characteristic, and appears almost verbatim in several other authors. It is inserted in the chronicle of events for the Muslim year 1054. In the month of Shawwal of that year, corresponding to December 1644, he tells us, reports were received in Istanbul "from the notables of the border fortress of Buda" with the following story. The Roman Emperor Ferdinand had wished to induce the seven electors, known in Turkey as the seven kings, to agree to the nomination of his son as successor to the imperial title during his life time. One of these electors being a partisan of the French, the emperor, in agreement with the king of Spain, seized and killed him. The French king, greatly angered, made an agreement with the Swede, who invaded the German lands and seized the old city of Prague. The war continued until the year 1057 [1647], when peace was made. By its terms the Austrian, greatly weakened, was obliged to cede Alsace to France and Pomerania to Sweden.[49]

This account misdates both the Swedish entry into Prague (when, incidentally, they failed to take the old city) and the Treaty of Westphalia, and shows a remarkable unawareness of the earlier phases of the war, not to speak of its religious and political complexities. In another passage, under the heading the "war of the French and the Swedes against the Austrian infidels" Kâtib Çelebi gives a slightly more detailed account. It is placed among the events of the year 1040 (1630–31). The French King Louis (Ludoricus) XIII, he says, had wanted to become emperor. The emperor was appointed by seven kings called electors, each of whom has his own land. The said King Louis succeeded in winning over two of them. The emperor at that time was the father of the present Emperor Ferdinand [Ferdinand III died in 1657]. He arranged to have his son nominated as successor during his own lifetime. Some of the electors disapproved of this nomination, saying it would do them no good and was contrary to law. The French king made war in protest and allied himself with the Swedish king, saying that such a nomination during the lifetime of the emperor was contrary to the laws of the infidels. Philip IV [d. 1665], "who is still king of Spain . . . was the maternal uncle of the king of France and there was peace between them. But the kings of Spain, like the Nemçe, are of the house of Dostoria [presumably from the Italian d'Austria], and he therefore took the side of the emperor." A brief account of the Thirty Years War follows up to final peace of Westphalia.[50]

Kâtib Çelebi offers several other reports on French affairs. Under the year 1018 he notes that an envoy came from the French King Henry to request the renewal of the capitulation.[51] The French ambassador, whose name is given as Franciscus Savary, refers to the friendship which had existed between earlier French and Ottoman monarchs and to the capitulations given in the time of Sultan Mehmed the Conqueror [they were in fact somewhat later]. François Savary, count de Brèves (1560–1628), left Istanbul in 1605. The capitulations were renewed 20 May 1604. Kâtib Çelebi notes that others besides the French had received such capitulations and he lists the Venetians, the English, the Genoese, the Portuguese and the Catalan merchants, Sicily, Ancona, Spain, and Florence. Many of these had come under the French flag and in the name of the French king. Other questions discussed by the ambassador, he says, included a possible pilgrimage to Jerusalem, the activities of the Barbary Corsairs, and earlier military cooperation.

The arrival of a Venetian envoy in January 1653 to sue for peace, with the help of the English ambassador, prompts the Ottoman chronicler to a rare personal comment. The Venetian, he says, was "a ninety-year-old infidel with trembling head and hands, but a cunning ambassador."[52] The ambassador was Giovanni Cappello (1584–1662), who was in fact 69 years old at the time.

An exceptional figure among the Ottoman historians of the seventeenth century is Ibrahim-i Peçuy, commonly known as Peçevi, whose history covers the years 1520–1639. He was born in 1574 in the Hungarian city of Pecs, whence his name. On his father's side he came from a Turkish family which had been in the service of the sultans for generations. His mother belonged to the Sokollu, i.e., Sokolovič family and was thus of Islamized Serbian origin. Apart from some service in Anatolia, he seems to have spent the greater part of his life in the Hungarian and adjoining Sanjaks of the empire. His birth and upbringing in the European border provinces gave him a degree of knowledge and also of interest that is rare among Ottoman historians. Peçevi was not concerned with universal history or geography, still less with writing or translating the histories of the kings of the infidels. His prime concern, like that of most Ottoman and, for that matter, most Western historians, was with the history of the empire of which he was a subject, and, more particularly, with its wars against its adversaries in Europe.

For the earlier period he seems to have followed the common practice of using his predecessors; for the later period he relied mainly on firsthand evidence—his own experiences and the reports of old soldiers. But in addition to these more normal sources of information, Peçevi had the revolutionary idea of consulting the historians of the enemy. He was interested above all in military history and dwells lovingly on the details of the great battles fought in the plains of Hungary. But sometimes the Ottoman chronicles are lacking in detail, and so Peçevi had a recourse to the other side: "In our country" he says, "there are Hungarians without number able to read and write [he uses the Hungarian word *deak*, one able to read Latin]."[53] There were, no doubt, numerous Hungarians in the empire, either as captives or as converts to Islam, sufficiently literate for Peçevi's purpose. His procedure, it would seem, was to have Hungarian chronicles, presumably written in Latin, read to him and rendered into Turkish. He incorporated a number of passages in his own chronicle, among them accounts of the great battle of Mohacs and some other events in the Hungarian wars. Though he does not name his sources, two of them have been identified by modern scholars.[54] Peçevi seems to have been the first Ottoman historian to compare enemy accounts of battle with those of his own side and to weave them into a single narrative. In this he can have had few predecessors anywhere; he certainly had few successors for a long time.

Peçevi's chronicle includes several other references to events in Europe, mostly to those which have some Ottoman or Islamic concern. He speaks briefly of the joint French and Turkish naval operations against Spain in 1552 and has an account of the Morisco rising in Spain in 1568–1570. He has, of course, much to say about the wars on the frontier and also about the naval war in the Mediterranean against Venice and her allies. Occasionally, he even ventures away from the political and military matters which were the chief concern of most of the chroniclers. Thus he describes the introduction of tobacco to Turkey by English merchants and its consequences, and even gives brief accounts of the invention both of printing and of gunpowder in Europe.[55]

Probably the most distinguished of the great series of Ottoman imperial histories is the *Tarih-i Naima,* covering the period from the year 1000 to the year 1070 of the Islamic era, corresponding to the years 1590 to 1660. Naima, who edited this history as well as writing a good deal of it, was one of the greatest of Ottoman historians. Unlike so many of his colleagues, who were mere chroniclers of events, Naima had a philosophical conception of the nature of history, and had thought very deeply about it. One of the major themes of his history was the war in Europe, both in the Balkan peninsula and the Black Sea area. His account of these struggles is very detailed, and local European leaders in Hungary and Transylvania who were involved in these wars figure prominently. The Hapsburg emperor for the most part remains a vague, shadowy, and usually nameless figure, while the kings and kingdoms of the West hardly appear at all. Of the Thirty Years War in Germany, a central event in the period he covers and a major convulsion which should have been of direct concern to the Ottomans, Naima offers no more than a transcript of the earlier chronicles, copied so negligently that he refers to the Spanish King Philip IV as "still King of Spain at this time," a hundred years later. It is hardly surprising that he is even less interested in more remote events, such as the activities of Louis XIV and Richelieu in France or the civil war and common-wealth in England.

In one respect, however, Naima marks an interesting departure from the norms of Ottoman historiography—in his interest in the history of a more distant past and in his desire to draw parallels between past and current events. This is not entirely without prece-dent in Ottoman historiography. The sixteenth-century historian Kemalpaşazade, describing how Sultan Süleyman the Magnificent set forth in 1521 to do battle against the emperor, presented this as a kind of reprisal for the invasion of Asia Minor by medieval German Cru-saders. Naima, writing in the early eighteenth century, when the Otto-man Empire was badly shaken by its defeats at the hands of Austria and Russia, tried to find comfort in the story of the early successes and final defeat of the Crusaders, centuries earlier.

> "After six centuries of the Islamic era [Naima's chronology is slightly wrong], because there was no accord or agreement among the kings of Islam, strife and discord appeared, and while they were busy fighting each other, the French infidels and other kings of the infidels, and especially numberless soldiers sent from Austria [a curiously clumsy attempt to link the Crusades with the current Austrian wars] came with a great fleet to the shores of the Mediterranean and occupied them."

Naima goes on to describe how the victorious Franks were at first able to establish themselves along the Syrian and Palestinian coasts and even to threaten Damascus and Egypt. This danger was averted by Saladin, who held and confined them until they were eventually driven out by his successors, and "the pure lands which they had occupied were cleansed of their pollution." Naima seems to find guid-ance in this for the Ottomans in his own time. The medieval sultans of Egypt had found it necessary to make accommodations, and one of them was even willing to sign a treaty ceding Jerusalem to the Franks. The implication seems to be that the Ottomans too, having suffered a series of shattering defeats, must be prepared to make peace even on disadvantageous terms in order to save what they could from the ruin and prepare themselves for an ultimate recovery.[56]

In another place Naima is more explicit: "This has been written . . . for the purpose of showing how important it is to make armistices with infidel kings and, indeed, to make peace with the Christians of the whole earth, so that the [Ottoman] lands may be put in order and the inhabitants may have respite."[57]

Naima's successor as imperial historiographer, Raşid Efendi, begins where Naima leaves off, in the year 1070, corresponding to 1660, and continues to 1720. His chronicle thus covers a series of major events in Ottoman relations with Europe: the second unsuccessful siege of Vienna and the retreat which followed it, the Treaty of Carlowitz of 1699, the war with Peter the Great of Russia in 1710–1711, and with Venice and Austria in 1714–1718, and the curious and complicated dealings with King Charles XII of Sweden, including his stay in Turkey as a somewhat unwelcome guest of the Sultan. Not surprisingly, Raşid Efendi devotes rather more attention than his predecessors to diplomatic relations, including peace negotiations with the immediate adversaries of the Ottomans, Russia, Austria, and Venice, and even has a little to say about some of the more distant states of Europe. Raşid is also the first to report in any detail on Ottoman emissaries to European states. His predecessors, at most, reported their departures and returns. Raşid introduced a new practice by incorporating in his chronicle lengthy excerpts from the reports which these envoys, now ranking as ambassadors, presented after their return to Istanbul. Despite, however, this increase of interest in diplomatic relations with Europe, he remains almost totally unconcerned with the internal affairs of the European states and, like his predecessors, passes over in silence the major events of European history in that period.

Much the same may be said of most of his contemporaries and of his successors who covered the middle decades of the eighteenth century, though one notes a slight increase in the space allotted to diplomatic relations with Europe and the degree of detail provided about European rulers. There is even a beginning of interest in European affairs. The Ottoman historian Sılıhdar gives an extensive Turkish version of the recently concluded Treaty of Ryswick of 1697.[58] Several Ottoman historians are willing to devote a page or two to the war of the Austrian succession and the enumeration of the parties involved and their interests. Apart from the very brief accounts of the Thirty Years War, this is the first European struggle to receive such attention from Ottoman historiography. Another historian of the time, Şem' danizade Süleyman Efendi, explains the electoral system of the Holy Roman Empire in Ottoman terms: "The realm of the Nemçe consists of nine kingdoms, three of which are the Sanjaks of Mainz, Cologne and Trier in the Eyalet of the Rhine. These are the first three electors and bear the stamp of priesthood." The fourth and subsequent are the Eyalets of Czech, Bavaria, Saxony, and Prussia, the Sanjak of the Palatinate, and the Eyalet of Hanover. In addition to these nine provinces, there is the Sanjak of Savoy, now under the rule of the King of Sardinia, the Sanjak of Hesse which is an independent duchy and the Eyalet of Swabia, which is an independent republic. Şem'danizade has a few notes on each of these provinces. The ruler of the Eyalet of Prussia, he notes, is a certain Grandebur. This name, he explains, is a corruption of Brandenburg, which is the name of a castle in this province; his proper name is Fredoricus. Of the ninth Eyalet, that of Hanover, Şem'danizade notes that it is "the inherited property of the present king of England, Jojo."[59] This last, obviously a corruption of Giorgio, suggests an Italian informant. The account of Austria and of the circumstances leading to the war of the Austrian succession occupies two whole pages of the printed edition of Şem'danizade and is by far the most detailed that has so far come to light in Ottoman historiography. Şem'danizade also gives brief notices on other events in Europe, and, while mainly concerned with Austria and Russia, makes occasional allusion to remoter and more mysterious countries such as France, England, Holland, and Sweden. Though aware of differences and even of rivalries between them, he tends to assume a common hostility to the Muslim state. Thus, in the crisis with Russia in 1736, when the English and Dutch ambassadors, fearing an Ottoman debacle, advised caution, they were seen as deviously abetting Russian plots and plans.[60]

Further change can be seen in the chronicle of Vasif, which covers the years 1166/1752 to 1188/1774 and thus deals with a period of strain and danger to the Ottoman Empire, culminating in the disastrous Treaty of Küçük Kaynarja imposed on the Turks by a victorious Russia. Vasif himself lived during the period of the Revolutionary and Napoleonic Wars and was the witness of such major events as the French invasion and occupation of Egypt, about which he wrote a separate book. In his chronicle, Vasif reports on the Ottoman missions to Vienna and Berlin and quotes at some length from their accounts of middle European politics.

In the early eighteenth century, when the Ottoman Empire was much more involved in the affairs of Europe, the attention given to them by the chroniclers is still remarkably small. Apart from actual wars, which are described at some length, the chroniclers devote less attention to Ottoman dealings with Russia, Austria, and the West than to relations with Persia, and far less than to provincial news concerning the various actions and quarrels of the pashas and notables of the empire. The interest in foreign affairs is slightly greater than before, but is still very limited, and the information used by the different Ottoman chroniclers seems to come from the same small pool of informants, foreigners, renegades, and local non-Muslims. An eighteenth-century Ottoman knew as much of the states and nations of Europe as a nineteenth-century European about the tribes and peoples of Africa—and regarded them with the same slightly amused disdain. Only the growing sense of threat begins to bring a change in this attitude, and even then it is slow and gradual.

By the end of the eighteenth century, Ottoman accounts of Europe had not yet amounted to anything very substantial. They represent, however, a considerable advance from what had gone before, and are still in marked contrast with the total lack of any such literature in Persian or—with the exception of a few Moroccan embassy reports—in Arabic.

The new situation in the eighteenth century—the knowledge of defeat and awareness of danger—brought a change in the nature of Ottoman interest in Europe. It was now primarily concerned with defense. But once the barriers separating the two civilizations had been breached, it was no longer possible to keep a strict control over the traffic passing through. An interest in military science on the one hand and a need for political and military intelligence on the other led to an interest in recent European history which, though at first desultory and sporadic, became more urgent as Turks gradually came to realize that the very survival of their empire might depend on an accurate understanding of what was happening in Europe.

The books printed at the first Turkish printing press established in 1729 and closed in 1742 include a number dealing with history and geography. Among them are the account of the Ambassador Mehmed Efendi of his embassy to France, a treatise on the science of tactics as applied in European armies written by the founder of the press, Ibrahim Müteferrika, and a translation of a European narrative of the wars in Persia. Ibrahim also printed some earlier works, including the sixteenth-century history of the discovery of the New World and part of the geographical writings of Kâtib Çelebi.

In addition to these books printed at the Ibrahim Müteferrika press, a few manuscripts, preserved in Istanbul collections, attest the emergence of a new interest in European history. A manuscript dated 1722 gives an outline history of Austria from 800 to 1662 and was translated from the German by the interpreter Osman Aga of Temesvar. More directly concerned with current affairs are two anonymous manuscripts written in about 1725 giving firsthand and almost up-to-date information about contemporary Europe.

One of them, a short, anonymous survey of affairs in Europe, survives in Turkey in at least four manuscripts, indicating some degree of interest. It begins with definitions of both secular and clerical ranks and consists, in the main, of a kind of statistical survey of the states of Europe. The exposition starts with an enumeration and classification of the territories of the Holy Roman Empire, followed by the states of Italy (Venice, Genoa, etc.) and then Switzerland, France, Spain, Portugal, Malta, "the realms of the English," Holland, Denmark, Sweden, Poland, and Russia. The author is ill informed about England—he names the reigning monarch as William II (William III died in 1702, certainly before this text was written) and despite a carefully written and vocalized text of foreign place names, distorts most of those in Britain. He is better informed about continental affairs noting, for example, that the Archbishop of Cologne was the son of the Duke of Bavaria, that Mecklenburg had "recently" undergone a Russian occupation (in fact in 1716), that the "late czar" (Peter the Great died in 1725) had taken most of the Baltic lands from Sweden (by the treaty of 1721) and other similar changes.

A parallel text, also surviving in several manuscripts, deals with the navies of the world. According to a note on the manuscripts, "a learned monk recently came from Toulouse in France and embraced Islam in the presence of the grand vizier. Since he had made numerous voyages and was fully acquainted with world affairs, this treatise has been drawn up from his deposition."[61]

The two treatises are obviously written by the same author, presumably the editor who prepared the information on naval matters obtained from the French renegade. The form in which Western names are spelled and transcribed suggests that the redactor in question might have been of Hungarian origin—perhaps none other than Ibrahim Müteferrika.[62]

Another report, dated 1733–1734, deals with "some historical circumstances of the states of Europe" and was made by Claude-Alexandre de Bonneval, later Ahmed Pasha, a French nobleman who joined the Ottoman service and was converted to Islam. Dealing with events in Austria, Hungary, Spain, and France, it was translated into Turkish, presumably from the author's French original. A historian, Abd al-Rahman Münif Efendi (d. 1742), included in an outline survey of major dynasties not only the monarchs of Islam but also pagan and Christian Roman emperors, Byzantine emperors, the kings of France, and the kings of Austria. A manuscript of the late eighteenth century, entitled "A Survey of European Affairs," discusses Prussia under Frederick William II and France under the Revolutionary governments, and in 1799 an Istanbul Christian called Cosmo Comidas prepared a Turkish handlist of reigning European sovereigns with their dates of birth and accession, their capitals, titles, heirs, and other useful information.[63]

In the Arab countries, almost all of which were under Ottoman domination or suzerainty, interest in the West, except to a limited extent among the Christian minorities, was even less. In Morocco, a few reports from ambassadors sent to various European capitals provided some basic information for the inner political circle, but of historical interest there was none until the nineteenth century. In the Ottoman-dominated Arab east, only the irruption of the French and the English at the turn of the eighteenth and nineteenth centuries briefly awakened some interest in these peoples. But accounts written at the time are few in number and are almost exclusively concerned with the activities of the Franks in the East and not with the events at home which had impelled them to go there. It is not until the 1820s that for the first time we find in Egypt translations of Western books issuing from the printing press established in Cairo by the modernizing ruler Muḥammad ʿAlī Pasha. In other Arab countries, and in Iran, the awakening of Muslim interest in the West came much later, and was the result of an overwhelming Western presence.

VI

Religion

For the Muslim, religion was the core of identity, of his own and therefore of other men's. The civilized world consisted of the House of Islam, in which a Muslim government ruled, Mulim law prevailed, and non-Muslim communities might enjoy the tolerance of the Muslim state and community provided they accepted the conditions. The basic distinction between themselves and the outside world was the acceptance or rejection of the message of Islam. The conventional nomenclature of physical and even human geography was at best of secondary significance. Muslim writers, as we have seen, were aware of the fact that there were peoples beyond the northern border called Romans, Franks, Slavs, and other names, speaking a bewildering variety of languages. But this in itself was unremarkable. There were many races and nations within the Islamic oecumene and, although the Muslims had preferred to establish a very limited number of languages as the media of government, culture, and commerce, they too could parallel the profusion of local dialects and idioms characteristic of the European continent.

The real difference was religion. Those who professed Islam were called Muslims and were part of God's community, no matter in which country or under what sovereign they lived. Those who rejected Islam

were infidels. The Arabic word is *kāfir,* from a root meaning to disbelieve or deny, normally used only of those who disbelieve in the
Islamic message and deny its truth.

Strictly speaking, the term *kāfir* applies to all non-Muslims. In Arabic, Persian, and Turkish usage, however, it came to be virtually synonymous with Christian. In the same way the House of War was seen
more and more as consisting principally of the rival faith and polity
which thought of itself first as Christendom and later as Europe. Muslims were of course aware of other infidels besides the Christians.
Some, like the Hindus and Buddhists of Asia, were too remote to have
much impact on the perceptions and usage of Middle Eastern and
Mediterranean Islamic communities. Others, like the non-Muslim inhabitants of black Africa, had much closer relations with them but
were seen primarily as polytheists and idolaters, and are commonly so
designated. Only two other religions were known in the Middle East,
Zoroastrianism and Judaism, and both were too small to be of much
significance. Both had lost their political power and were no longer
considered to be in a state of war with Islam. Jews were seen only as
dhimmīs, and the dwindling remnant of the Zoroastrians were more or
less admitted to the same status. By Ottoman times the term *kāfir,* even
in official usage, does not include Jews. In innumerable fiscal and other
documents dealing with the affairs of the non-Muslim communities,
the customary Ottoman formula is "*kāfirs* and Jews", with the obvious
implication that the first term does not include the second. This is in
part a testimony to the preeminence of the Christians, in part a recognition of the unflawed monotheism of the Jews. In Ottoman (and
modern) Turkish usage the term *kāfir* is often replaced by *gavur,* applied
to infidels in general and Christians in particular. The word is no doubt
a popular mispronunciation of *kāfir,* perhaps affected by the older
Persian word *gabr,* which originally meant Zoroastrians but was sometimes transferred to Christians.

The same basic religious classification can be seen even in Ottoman
customs regulations, which usually laid down three rates of customs
duty, determined not by the merchandise but by the merchant, and
more specifically by his religion. Of the three rates, the lowest is for
Muslims, Ottoman or other, the intermediate rate is for *dhimmīs,* and
the highest rate is for *harbīs,* those coming from the House of War.
Curiously, Jews of whatever nationality or political allegiance paid the
dhimmī rate even if they come from Europe. The same principle, applied
in the opposite direction, may be seen in the interpretation given by
the Persians to the extraterritorial privileges exacted from them by the
Russians in the early nineteenth century. These were accorded to

Russian Christians, but refused to Sunni Muslims from the Russian empire.

The *kāfir* par excellence was thus the Christian, and the countries which in their own self-image constituted Europe were perceived by Muslims as "the lands of the infidels", meaning Christendom. The religious definition of identity and difference is almost universal. While visitors from Europe to the Muslim world saw themselves as Englishmen, Frenchmen, Italians, Germans, etc., among the Moors or Turks or Persians, Muslim visitors to Europe in contrast, whether coming from Morocco or Turkey or Iran, see themselves rather as Muslims in Christendom and do not normally refer either to themselves or to their hosts by national, territorial, or ethnic titles. Almost invariably they speak of their own country as "the lands of Islam," and of their own ruler as "the sovereign of Islam" or synonymous expressions.

Only towards the end of the eighteenth century do Ottoman envoys to Europe begin to speak of themselves and their country more specifically as Ottoman, as distinct from the common Islamic identity. And just as the travelers refer to themselves as Muslims and to their community as Islam, so do they almost invariably speak of their European hosts and interlocutors simply as infidels. "The Austrian ambassador" says an eighteenth-century Turkish visitor to Austria "sent three infidels to meet us. . . ."[1] This means that the ambassador (labelled as Austrian, since only governments can appoint ambassadors) had sent three men to meet them. The term infidel not only occurs where a European would use some national or political designation; it also occurs with great frequency to replace more basic words like person, man, or human being.

The European is different, but not because he belongs to another nation, is subject to another ruler, lives in another place, or speaks another language. He is different because he follows another religion. As a result of this difference he is presumed to be hostile and known to be inferior. No doubt resorting to a well-known device of modern propaganda and advertising, writers on Christendom use infinite repetition to emphasize and drive home these points. With rare exceptions no European nation, group, or even individual is mentioned without the term infidel, either as substantive or adjective. Sometimes in both official dealings and historical writings it becomes necessary to distinguish between the different states or nations of Christendom. In such case, they are referred to as the English infidels, the French infidels, the Russian infidels, and the rest. Often the point is further emphasized by some insulting epithet or imprecation, usually in the form of a

rhyme or jingle. In Ottoman usage, each nation has its own little jingle
—Ingiliz dinsiz (Englishman without religion), Fransız jansız (soulless
French), Engurus menhus (inauspicious Hungarian), Rus ma'kus (per-
verse Russian), Alman biaman (merciless German), etc. For Muslim
nations, both positive and negative jingles are available, for use according to circumstances. For the *gavur,* all are negative, and good will
is expressed by omitting them.[2] In medieval writings the names of
European individuals are invariably accompanied by curses. These are
by no means perfunctory but are obviously deeply meant and often
reasserted with considerable emphasis.

   This practice of referring to Europeans as infidels was remarkably
persistent and pervasive. It occurs, for example, even in letters intended to be friendly and courteous, addressed by Muslim sovereigns
to Christian European monarchs. Thus Sultan Murad III, writing to
Queen Elizabeth of England, informs her of his victories against "the
Austrian and Hungarian infidels" and the advance of his army into
"the land of the base infidels," urges the queen to "turn and proceed
against the Spanish infidels, over whom with the help of God you will
be victorious," and expresses qualified goodwill towards the Polish
and Portuguese infidels "who are your friends." Even Kâtib Çelebi,
writing in the mid-seventeenth century, still finds it necessary to accompany almost every reference to the Franks by some such formula
as accursed, doomed to destruction, foreordained to hellfire, and the
like. As late as the mid-eighteenth century, an Ottoman official reporting on his work on a frontier demarcation commission with the Austrians, begins his report by referring to the liberation (i.e., recovery) of
Belgrade, "the house of jihād" from "the thievish hands of the Austrian infidels."[3] In general, the policies and actions of European governments and individuals are characterized by such words as evildoing,
mischief, intrigue, plots, wiles, and other expressions indicating vil-
lainy. While this evaluation might often have been well-founded, in
the texts it is usually taken as axiomatic. These verbal habits continue
well into the period when the Ottoman Empire was directly involved
in the affairs of Europe, with allies as well as adversaries, and when
Ottoman officials and even historians begin to pay some attention to
the finer points of European international relations. It is not until the
late eighteenth century that these expletives are finally deleted, and
even then Muslim diplomats in their reports continue to apply the
derogatory term infidel to every person, group, or institution that they
encounter. In the course of the nineteenth century, this language began
to die out of documentary and historiographic usage though remaining
in popular and colloquial use until much later.

Given the primacy of religion in Muslim considerations, even of state, we might expect to find some attention given to religion in the Western world. Muslim envoys and historians do, for the most part, make reference to religious matters but show no great interest in European Christianity and offer very little information. They knew that the Europeans were Christians and for most of them that was enough. Christianity was after all not new to them—it was the immediate predecessor of Islam and was still represented by sizable minorities in the Muslim lands. The Christian religion was, so to speak, from a Muslim point of view, known, accounted for, and disposed of.

In medieval times the Muslim scholar had at his disposal, in Arabic, a sizable body of literature on Christian beliefs and practices, from which it was possible to gather a fairly detailed knowledge of the early history of Christianity and of the different schools and sects within the Christian church. This early interest was not, however, sustained, and discussions of Christianity by Ottoman authors seemed to depend on earlier Arabic Muslim texts rather than on new observations or information. Thus Kâtib Çelebi in his treatise on Europe, written in 1655, begins with an account of the Christian religion, which is almost purely medieval. This religion, he tells his readers, is based on four gospels, which he correctly enumerates, and, by a tacit analogy with Islam, rests on five basic principles, namely baptism, trinity, incarnation, eucharist, and confession. He devotes a brief section to each of these and under the heading "trinity" discusses the Christological controversies of the early churches, about which fairly extensive information was available in classical Arabic writings of Christian provenance. He gives a text of the Nicene Creed in an Arabic version (omitting the *filioque* clause) and explains that the Christians were divided into three main schools or sects—the word he uses is the Islamic term *madhhab* (Turkish *mezheb*), normally applied to the four schools of Sunni jurisprudence. The three Christian schools are the Jacobites, the Melkites, and the Nestorians, and Kâtib Çelebi offers an explanation of their differing doctrines on the human and divine natures of Christ. By the Jacobites—strictly speaking the followers of the Syrian church of Jacob Baradeus—he appears to mean the Monophysites in general, as is shown by his remark that "most of the Jacobites are Armenians." The Melkites are the followers of the school which is approved as orthodox by the state and the hierarchy and is thus the school of the Rūm—the Greeks and Romans. The Nestorians, he explains, were a later group who broke away from the commonly accepted creed and formed a separate sect. By Kâtib Çelebi's own day, the churches of Jacob Baradeus and of Nestorius had dwindled into insignificance and even the Armenian and Coptic monophysite churches were safely subject to Islamic rule. Of such later differences as the schism which split the Melkite church into the Greek orthodox east and the Roman Catholic west, or the new division in the Roman Catholic west caused by the Protestant reformation—matters which one would have thought more important to an Ottoman observer than the long forgotten polemics of the Jacobites and the Nestorians—Kâtib Çelebi has nothing to say.[4]

The differences between Catholics and Protestants did not, however, entirely escape attention, and one Ottoman historian even has an explanation of the wars of religion in central Europe. One day, he tells us, the Austrian emperor was profoundly melancholy and his eyes were full of tears, so that his wife, who was the daughter of the king of Spain, asked him what ailed him. The trouble, he said, was the difference between himself and the sultan of the Ottomans. Whenever the sultan sent orders summoning the princes under his suzerainty to come with their forces and serve in his armies, they came at once and placed themselves without reserve at his disposal. The Austrian emperor, in contrast, might send such messages to the princes of Hungary, but it would not occur to them that they owed him any service or obedience. To this complaint the empress replied: "The warriors of the Padishah of the Ottomans belong to his own faith and rite, and that is why they obey him. Your Hungarian princes refuse you obedience because they have another faith than yours." The emperor, impressed by this argument, at once sent envoys and priests to the Hungarian princes, and commanded them "to go over to his own deluded faith." Some did, but many refused, and this gave rise to much tyranny and oppression. "And that is why Almighty God, who overlooks no mortal even if he is a *gavur,* sent the armies of Islam against him."[5] Evliya Çelebi, who had traveled through Hungary and Austria a little earlier, also noted that the two belonged to different churches, the Hungarians following the Lutheran rite, while the Austrians "obeyed the pope." For this reason, he notes, they were bitterly opposed to one another. However, both being Christians, they held together against the Muslims, since, in the words of a Muslim tradition which Evliya quotes: "All unbelievers are one religion."[6]

Ottoman officialdom seems to have been rather more alert than Ottoman scholarship to the significance of the clash between Protestants and Catholics and its possible value to the Islamic cause. In part this may have been due to information brought by Muslim refugees from Spain; in part also to the effort made by some emissaries of the Protestant powers to present themselves as austere monotheists, closer to Islam than to the image-worshipping and polytheistic Catholics, and therefore worthy of favorable consideration in trade and perhaps in other respects. The Ottomans do not appear to have been greatly impressed by such arguments, but occasionally they put them to the test. When the Moriscos rose in revolt in Spain in 1568–1570, the sultan sent them a special envoy to draw their attention to the continued struggle of the Lutherans against "those who are subject to the pope and his school." The rebels were advised to establish secret contacts with these Lutherans and, when the latter made war against the pope, to inflict losses on the Catholic provinces and soldiery in their own area.[7] Selim II went so far as to send a secret agent to meet the Protestant leaders in the Spanish Netherlands. An Ottoman royal letter noted a common interest between Muslims and Lutherans, who also make war against the Catholics and reject their idolatry: "Since you have raised your swords against the papists and since you have regularly killed them, our imperial compassion and royal attention have been devoted in every way to your region. As you, for your part, do not worship idols, you have banished the idols and portraits and "bells" from churches, and declared your faith by stating that God Almighty is One and Holy Jesus is His Prophet and Servant, and now, with heart and soul, are seeking and desirous of the true faith; but the faithless one they call Papa does not recognize his Creator as One, ascribing divinity to Holy Jesus (upon him be peace!), and worshipping idols and pictures which he has made with his own hands, thus casting doubt upon the Oneness of God and instigating how many servants of God to that path of error."[8] Later, Ottoman correspondence with Queen Elizabeth of England shows a similar interest in the Protestants, not—God forbid—as allies, but as a useful distraction of the Catholic powers.

The institution of the papacy could hardly escape Muslim attention, and many Muslim writers comment on the strange phenomenon of the ruler of Rome, a kind of priest-king whom they call al-Bāb, the pope. Islam has neither priesthood nor ecclesiastical hierarchy, and the phenomenon of the elaborately organized Christian church was difficult for Muslims to apprehend. Only by Ottoman times did closer acquaintance with the hierarchy of the eastern church make such institutions intelligible. The first to mention the pope is the Arab prisoner of war, Hārūn ibn Yaḥyā, who visited Rome in about 886. He notes simply that: "Rome is a city governed by a king who is called al-Bāb, the pope." He offers no explanation of this title and seems to have assumed that this was the personal name of the monarch. The account of Rome contained in the geographical dictionary of Yāqūt is somewhat fuller. "At the present day Rome is in the hands of the Franks, and its king is called the king of Almān. In it lives the pope, whom the Franks obey and who is to them in the position of an Imam. If anyone of them disobeys him, they consider him a rebel and an evildoer, deserving of exile, banishment, and death. He imposes prohibitions on them in what concerns their women, their ablutions, their food, and their drink, and none of them can gainsay him."[9]

Some word of this remarkable institution seems to have traveled even to the eastern parts of the Islamic world. A thirteenth-century Persian poet, Khāqānī, in a satirical ode, speaks of Batrīq-i Zamāne Bāb-i Buṭrus, the patriarch of the time, the gate (or pope) of Peter.[10] He appears to confuse the institution with the patriarchate of the eastern churches, a common error in later Muslim authors.

One of the first accounts of papal authority comes from the Syrian historian Ibn Wāṣil, who visited the southern Italian mainland as a diplomatic envoy in 1261, and has this to say of the pope: "He is for them the Vicar *(khalīfa)* of Christ and his lieutenant, with powers to forbid and to permit, to decide and to annul." Similar comments are made by several later writers; one of them, the Turkish author of the adventures of Jem, noted something even more extraordinary—the Christian belief that the pope could remit sins. The possession of such powers by the pope is something which never fails to astonish visitors from the lands of Islam. Muslims are familiar with religious authority—indeed, in a sense, they recognize no other. Islam has, however, never recognized spiritual as distinct from religious authority among mankind, and for them the powers attributed to the pope properly belong to God alone. Ibn Wāṣil continues: "It is he (the pope) who crowns and enthrones kings, and nothing in their religious law *(sharīʿa)* can be carried out except through him. He is a monk, and when he dies, another with the same monkly character succeeds him.[11]

Qalqashandī (d. 1418) includes a brief note on the pope in his manual of chancery usage:

> The form of address to the pope: he is the patriarch of the Melkites who occupies among them the position of a caliph. It is remarkable that the author of the *Tathqīf* [an earlier work on chancery usage] puts him in the position of the great khan among the Tatars, whereas in fact the khan occupies the position of great king among the Tatars, while the pope is nothing of the kind but has authority in religious matters, including even the power to declare what is permitted and what is forbidden. . . .
>
> The form of address to him . . . is as follows: "May Almighty God redouble the felicity of his high presence, the exalted, holy, spiritual, humble, active pope of Rome, mighty one of the Christian nation, exem-

plar of the community of Jesus, enthroner of the kings of Christendom
. . . protector of bridges and canals . . . refuge of patriarchs, bishops,
priests, and monks, follower of the gospel, who declares to his community what is permitted and what is forbidden, friend of kings and sultans
. . .

The author of the *Tathqīf* as quoted by Qalqashandī remarks:

This is what I found in the records, but nothing was written to him
during my period of service, and I do not know on what subjects he was
written to previously . . .[12]

An account of the papacy which is both historical and contemporary occurs in the *Universal History* of Rashīd al-Dīn, written in Iran in
the early years of the fourteenth century and derived, as has already
been noted, from a papal envoy and a propapal chronicle. Prince Jem
had personal contact with the papacy, and the author of the memoir
offers a somewhat lurid account of the procedures followed when a
new pope was installed, and the outbreaks of popular violence that
accompanied this event. Kâtib Çelebi, in his short treatise on Europe,
includes a chapter on the papacy consisting in the main of a numbered
list of popes with the dates of their election and the length of their
tenure, beginning with Peter and ending with Paul III, of whom it is
noted that he became pope in 1535.[13] Since Kâtib Çelebi's account of
the popes makes no mention of Paul III's death, which occurred in
1549, or of any of his successors, one may assume that whatever source
of information he used was rather more than a hundred years old. In
this as in many other matters, the Muslim author felt no need—or
perhaps found no opportunity—to obtain more up-to-date information. Since Kâtib Çelebi's account of Christian theology is a millennium old, it is hardly surprising if his list of popes is obsolete by little
more than a century.

A very much better account of the papacy and, indeed, of European
Christianity in general is given by the Moroccan ambassador, al-Wazīr
al-Ghassānī, who visited Spain at the end of the seventeenth century.
He has a great deal to say, not only about the pope but the organization
of the papacy, the role of the cardinals, and even the manner in which
a new pope is elected. The whole institution seems to arouse his special
ire, and every mention of the pope is followed by insults and curses.
Ghassānī goes on to discuss such matters as the Inquisition, the persecution of Jews, the history of the Reformation, and the subsequent
religious conflicts in Christendom. He even has something to say about
the Reformation in England, which he attributes to the marital problems of King Henry VIII, a point of view no doubt gathered from his
Spanish hosts. He discourses at some length on Catholicism as prac-

ticed in Spain, speaking of nuns and monks and of the Catholic practice of confession and the evils to which it can give rise.[14] Subsequent Moroccan envoys to Spain follow his example in discussing the church and its institutions and several of them dwell at length on the topic of the Inquisition.

One of the few subjects that seems to arouse any real interest among these Muslim visitors to Europe is anything connected with Islam itself. In a few places Muslim populations had managed to hold out in countries restored to Christian rule, and these naturally receive some attention. Ibn Wāṣil was interested to find a Muslim population still living on the southern Italian mainland under Norman rule:

> Near the place where I lived there was a city called Lucera, the inhabitants of which are all Muslims of Sicilian origin. The Friday prayer is observed there and the Muslim religion openly professed. This has been so since the time of Manfred's father, the Emperor [Frederick II]. Manfred began to build a house of science there, for the cultivation of all branches of the speculative sciences. I found that most of his intimates, who attend to his personal affairs, are Muslims, and in his camp the call to prayer and the prayer itself are open and public.

Ibn Wāṣil notes that the pope "had excommunicated Manfred because of his sympathy for the Muslims."[15]

The Muslims were in due course evicted from Sicily and mainland Italy. A decree of 11 February 1502 gave all Muslims in the Kingdom of Castile the choice of conversion, exile or death. Similar decrees followed in all the other territories under the Spanish crown. But even after these expulsions, a kind of crypto-Muslim community known as the Moriscos managed to survive for some time and to mount several rebellions, at one time even briefly seizing the city of Granada. The Spanish Muslims, both before and after their final defeat, turned for help to the Ottomans, the greatest Muslim power of the time, but without much effect. The Ottomans did indeed enter into negotiations with the Moriscos and attempted in various ways to provide them with advice and even occasional help. An Ottoman secret envoy was sent to coordinate communications, information and action between Spain, North Africa, and Istanbul. But it was a lost cause, and in due course the Moriscos followed their predecessors into exile.

A similar situation began to arise with the Ottoman retreat from central Europe. In most places Christian reconquest was followed by a Muslim exodus, and, except in the Russian-conquered Tatar lands, it was not until the nineteenth century that substantial Muslim populations were left under Christian rule. Elsewhere, all that remained to arouse the nostalgic interest of Muslim visitors were the monuments and memories of the Islamic past. Moroccan envoys to Spain and Ottoman envoys to central and southeastern Europe often had to pass through former Muslim territories that had been lost to Christian reconquest. The two groups show remarkable similarities. Just as European visitors to the East look for traces of the classical and Christian past, so Muslim visitors to Europe are interested in Muslim remains, are moved by Muslim inscriptions, offer reminiscences about the Muslim past, and even try to find some relics, or better survivals, of the Muslim presence. Thus the Moroccan ambassador al-Ghazzāl notes that the inhabitants of a place in Spain called Villafranca-Palacios are survivors of "the Andalusians," a term by which he means the former Muslim inhabitants of Spain: "Their blood is the blood of the Arabs, their ways are different from those of the foreigners (ʿAjam). Their inclining towards the Muslims, their desire to be with us, their sadness at parting, show conclusively that they are remnants of the Andalusians. But a long time has passed during which they have dwelt amid unbelief, may God preserve us." Al-Ghazzāl even claims to have found a crypto-Muslim, a certain Belasco, who came with his daughter, "a girl of very Arab appearance," and who made "mysterious signs" which the ambassador believed, though without confirmation, to indicate that he was really a secret Muslim.[16] The Ottoman ambassadors also found expressions of sympathy among their former subjects in Hungary and even in southern Poland. Thus, Azmi Efendi, passing through Hungary in 1790, notes the extreme friendship and goodwill shown by the Hungarians towards him and his mission and more generally towards the Ottoman Empire.[17] Other Ottoman envoys passing through the lost provinces in central and southeastern Europe claim to have discerned warm feelings among these peoples for their former masters. More surprisingly, similar sentiments were discovered by Moroccan ambassadors to Spain as late as the eighteenth century. Keenly aware of the many Islamic remains in that country, now desecrated for secular, or worse, for Christian use, some of the envoys from Morocco believed that the Christianization of Spain was but skin deep, and that old Muslim loyalties were waiting to reappear.

Muslim visitors are often troubled by the defacement or profanation of Muslim remains. The Moroccan al-Ghazzāl, visiting Granada, demanded that a stone with an Arabic inscription be put the right way up, so that it could be more easily read and presented a better appearance. He even claims to have insisted, while visiting the mosque in Cordova, on the removal of a stone with Arabic pious inscriptions which was used as a paving block. Minarets were a particular concern; one in Spain used as a lighthouse, one in Serbia used as a clocktower, distressed visiting Muslims. Even bathhouses were not safe from profanation, and a Turkish visitor to Belgrade, shortly after its occupation by the Austrians, noted with distaste that some of them were being used as dwellings.[18] This was another indication of the dirty habits of the unbelievers.

One feeling which appears very strongly in the writings of Muslim visitors to the lost provinces in both eastern and western Europe is that these are Islamic lands, wrongfully taken from Islam and destined ultimately to be restored. Even a brief occupation is sufficient to establish this right. Thus in 1763 Resmi Efendi, visiting the Polish fortress of Kameniets, which was held by the Ottomans from 1672 to 1699, was moved by the sight of a minaret with an Islamic date of construction and a Koranic quotation: "When I read this inscription, I uttered a prayer from my heart that it might please the Creator soon to return these places to Islam, so that the word of truth may resound from this minaret."[19] As late as 1779 a Moroccan ambassador to Spain, Muḥammad ibn ʿUthmān al-Miknāsī, still follows the first mention of every place-name with the formula "may God restore it to Islam."[20]

In general, the Muslims did not see Christianity as a religious threat to Islam, and even when Christian armies were reconquering province after province in Spain and, later, in southeastern Europe, the danger was seen in political and military rather than in religious terms. The idea that Muslims, even in defeat, should choose to adopt an earlier and incomplete form of God's revelation was too absurd to contemplate. And, indeed, voluntary conversions from Islam to Christianity are exceedingly rare. In Muslim lands apostasy—as such conversion would be in Muslim eyes—is a capital offence. But even in Christian lands Muslims were encouraged by their own laws to emigrate rather than submit to Christian rule, and where forced conversions occurred they were of doubtful sincerity.

The first perceived threat from the West to Muslim beliefs came with the French Revolution when for the first time propaganda was addressed to Muslims in the name not of an old religion but of a new and seductive ideology. Signs of Ottoman awareness of such a danger already appear in a memorandum drafted by the Ottoman chief secretary in the spring of 1798 for the guidance of the High Council of State. Explaining the origins of the recent events in France, the chief secretary explains: "The known and famous atheists, Voltaire and Rousseau, and other materialists like them, had printed and published various works consisting, God preserve us, of insults and vilification against the pure prophets and great kings, of the removal and abolition of all religion, and of allusions to the sweetness of equality and republicanism, all expressed in easily intelligible words and phrases, in the form of mockery, in the language of the common people . . ."[21]

The French invasion of Egypt brought the new menace closer to home, and induced the Ottoman Empire to venture on what would nowadays be called psychological warfare. In proclamations addressed to the Sultan's Muslim subjects in both Arabic and Turkish, the wickedness of the Revolutionaries is described at length:

> The French nation (may God devastate their dwellings and abase their banners, for they are tyrannical infidels and dissident evildoers) do not believe in the oneness of the Lord of the Heaven and Earth nor in the mission of the intercessor on the Day of Judgment but have abandoned all religion and deny the afterworld and its penalties. They do not believe in the day of resurrection and pretend that only the passage of time destroys us and that there is nothing but the womb that emits us and the earth that swallows us and that beyond this there is no resurrection and no reckoning, no examination and no retribution, no question and no answer. . . . They assert that the books which the Prophets brought are manifest error and that the Qur'ān, the Torah, and the Gospels are nothing but lies and idle talk and that those who claim to be Prophets . . . lied to ignorant people . . . that all men are equal in humanity and alike in being men, none has any superiority of merit over any other and everyone himself disposes of his soul and arranges his own livelihood in this life. And in this vain belief and preposterous opinion they have erected new principles and set laws and established what Satan whispered to them and destroyed the basis of religions and made lawful to themselves forbidden things and permitted to themselves whatever their passions desire and have enticed into their iniquity the common people who have become as raving madmen and have sown sedition among religions and thrown mischief between kings and states.

The author of the proclamation warns his readers against French blandishments:

> With lying books and meretricious falsehoods they address themselves to every party and say: "We belong to you, to your religion and to your community," and they make them vain promises and also utter fearful warnings.

Having wrought havoc in Europe, the French turned their attention eastward. "Then their wickedness and evil plots were turned against the community of Muḥammad . . ."[22]

They were indeed. For the first time since its beginnings, Islam faced an ideological and philosophical challenge that threatened the very foundations of Muslim doctrine and society. There had been nothing like it before in Muslim experience. After conquering and absorbing the ancient societies of the Middle East, Islam had confronted three major civilizations, in India, China, and Europe. Only one of these, the third, was seen as possessing a religion worthy of the name and as constituting a serious political and military alternative to Islamic power. But the Christian religion had always retreated before Islam, and Christian power was at best able to hold its own against the advance of Muslim arms. True, in the high Middle Ages Islamic theology had faced the challenge of Hellenistic philosophy and science, but this challenge, limited in scope and coming from a conquered culture, had been held and contained. Part of the Hellenistic heritage was incorporated in Islam, the rest discarded.

The new challenge presented to Islam by European secularism was a very different matter—far greater in scope, power, and extent, and, moreover, coming not from a conquered but a conquering world. A philosophy free from visible Christian connotations and expressed in a society that was rich, strong, and rapidly expanding, it seemed to some Muslims to embody the secret of European success and to offer a remedy for the weakness, poverty, and retreat of which they were becoming increasingly aware. In the course of the nineteenth and twentieth centuries, European secularism, and a series of political, social, and economic doctrines inspired by it, exercised a continuing fascination on successive generations of Muslims.

VII

The Economy: Perceptions and Contacts

In the ninth century, an author in Baghdad wrote a short treatise entitled "A Clear Look at Trade" in which he discusses the different commodities that form the basis of trade, their types and qualities and their places of origin. One section is devoted to a list of commodities and merchandise imported from "other countries" into Iraq. The "other countries" consist almost entirely of the various provinces of the far-flung Muslim Empire in Asia and Africa. Only four of the territories mentioned are outside the Muslim realms: the lands of the Khazars, a Turkic kingdom in the Eurasian steppe; India; China; and Byzantium. From the Khazars came "slaves, slave women, armor, helmets, and hoods of mail"; from India "tigers, leopards, elephants, leopard skins, red rubies, white sandalwood, ebony, and coconuts"; from China "aromatics, silk, porcelain, paper, ink, peacocks, fiery horses, saddles, felts, cinnamon, and unmixed rhubarb" and from Byzantium "silver and gold vessels, pure imperial dinars, simples, embroidered cloths, brocades, fiery horses, slave girls, rare articles in red copper, strong locks, lyres, water engineers, specialists in plowing and cultivation, marble workers, and eunuchs." There is no reference to Europe, the exports of which were too few and too insignificant to deserve mention, though possibly some of them may have been included in the list for Byzantium.[1]

185

The accounts given by medieval Muslim geographers of the commodities coming from western Europe are unimpressive. Imports from Scandinavia via Russia appear to have had rather greater importance. In addition to literary mentions, this trade has left behind it a substantial record in the form of large finds of Muslim coins, most of them from central Asian mints, in Scandinavian, especially Swedish, hoards.

Medieval authors do give a few scraps of information about economic conditions in the West.

Ibn Ya'qūb, speaking of Utrecht, notes that:

> It is a great city in the land of the Franks with extensive lands. Its soil is saline, and no seeds or plants can grow there. The people obtain their livelihood from cattle, their milk and their wool. There is no firewood in their country to burn for their needs, but they have a kind of mud which they use as fuel. What happens is this; in the summer when the water is dry, they go to their fields and cut out the mud with axes, in the shape of bricks. Each man cuts as much as he needs and spreads it in the sun to dry. It becomes very light, and if it is brought near a flame it catches fire. The fire seizes it as it seizes wood, and it gives out a great flame with a great heat, like the flame of the glassblowers' bellows. When a piece of it is burned up, it leaves ashes but no carbon.

Ibn Ya'qūb has similar observations on other cities which he visited or of which he heard. Bordeaux, he says, is "rich in water, trees, fruit and grain. By the shores of this city excellent amber is found." Rouen is a city . . .

> built of symmetrically arranged stones by the River Seine. Vines and trees do not grow there at all, but there is plenty of wheat and spelt. In the river they catch a fish which they call "salmon" and another small fish that tastes and smells like a cucumber. . . . In the winter in Rouen when the cold is extreme, a kind of white goose with red feet and beak comes out . . . this species only hatches on an uninhabited island. Sometimes, when ships are wrecked at sea, those who reach this island can subsist on the eggs and chicks of this bird for a month or two.

Of Schleswig he remarks:

> The town has few good things or blessings. Their food consists chiefly of fish, which is plentiful. When children are born to any of them, he throws them into the sea to save the expense.

He was more impressed by Mainz:

> A very great city, some of it inhabited and the rest sown. It is in the land of the Franks, by a river called the Rhine. It is rich in wheat, barley, spelt, limes, and fruit. There are dirhams there, struck in Samarkand in

the years 301–302 [934 and 935], with the name of the ruler and the date of issue. . . . An extraordinary thing is that, though this city is in the farthest West, they have spices there which are only to be obtained in the farthest East; such as pepper, ginger, cloves, spikenard, costmary, and galingale; these are brought from India where they are to be found in plenty.[2]

In the later Middle Ages, Muslim authors are somewhat better informed, and Idrīsī, for example, offers quite detailed information. Even a place as remote as England begins to appear. Thus Ibn Saʿīd notes, as a peculiarity of England, that:

> There is only rainwater in this island, and it is by rainwater that they grow their crops. . . . In this island there are mines of gold and silver and copper and tin. They have no vineyards because of the great cold. The people transport the produce of these mines to the land of France and exchange them for wine. That is why the ruler of France has so much gold and silver. . . .[3]

The Persian historian, Rashīd al-Dīn, was also impressed by the wealth of England, which "contains numberless mines of gold, silver, copper, tin, and iron as well as a great variety of fruits. . . ." Rashīd al-Dīn also notes that there were Frankish merchants who traveled to Egypt, Syria, North Africa, Anatolia, and Tabriz and who embarked from Genoa.[4]

Of the commodities produced in central and western Europe, only three attracted the attention of Muslim writers. They are Slavonic slaves, Frankish weapons, and English wool. Since Islamic law prohibits the enslavement of any free Muslim or of any free non-Muslim who is a lawful, tax-paying subject of the Islamic empire, the slave population of the Islamic lands could be recruited only in two ways; by birth (children of a slave parent irrespective of religion were slaves) or from outside. Natural increase soon proved to be a wholly inadequate source of additional slave labor. The Muslim empire, unlike the Roman and other ancient empires, could not add to its slave population by enslaving criminals and debtors or by the sale into bondage of free but impoverished persons. New slaves, therefore, had to come from beyond the Islamic frontiers and could be acquired as tribute, by capture, or simply by purchase.

This gave rise to a significant difference between the Islamic and earlier empires. In antiquity, except after a successful campaign or repression, the majority of the slave population was of local origin. In the Islamic empire, in contrast, the majority of the slave population came from outside the lands of Islam and, in due course, this gave rise to a massive development of the slave trade in all the countries adjoining the Islamic world, in order to provide for its steadily growing needs.

The two major sources of the slave population of Islam were the Eurasian steppes to the north, from which white slaves, mostly Turkish, were imported and used principally for military purposes, and tropical Africa to the south, from which black slaves were captured or bought for domestic and other labor. There were, however, some secondary areas of recruitment and Europe was one of these. Naturally enough, slaves of European origin were more prominent in the western lands of Islam and especially in Muslim Spain. As on the other frontiers they were at first recruited mainly by warfare. The infidel enemy captured on the battlefield is lawfully enslaved and, for a while, this sufficed to maintain the supply.

With the halting of the Islamic advance, followed by a period of stalemate and then by a gradual Islamic retreat, supplies of prisoners of war were no longer adequate, and those who were captured could be turned to better advantage by ransom or exchange. Slaves were then acquired by purchase, and a flourishing trade developed for the supply of European slaves, both male and female, to meet the domestic and other needs of Muslim Spain and North Africa. These white slaves in the Muslim west are collectively known as Saqāliba, the Arabic plural of Saqlabī or Slav; as in the languages of Europe, the term Slav, slave, seems to have combined an ethnic with a social content. In the writings of the geographers, the term Saqāliba refers to the various Slavonic peoples of central and eastern Europe. In the chronicles of Muslim Spain, it becomes a technical term for the slave praetorians of the Umayyad caliphs of Cordoba, thus corresponding to the Turkish Mamlūks in the eastern caliphate. The first Saqāliba in Spain appear to have been prisoners captured by the Germans in their raids into eastern Europe and sold by them to the Muslims of Spain. In time, the range of meaning of the term was extended to include virtually all foreign white slaves serving in the army or in the households. The tenth-century Arabic author, Ibn Ḥawqal, a traveler from the east who visited Muslim Spain, remarks that the European slaves whom he encountered there came not only from eastern Europe but also included natives of France, Italy, and northern Spain. Some were still supplied by capture—no longer by military expeditions beyond the frontier but, now, mainly by the raids from the sea. A commercial importation of slaves continued overland from France where, to borrow an expression from the Dutch historian Reinhart Dozy, there was an important "manufactory of eunuchs" at Verdun.[5]

The peculiar structure of Muslim society, which allowed slaves to occupy positions of great influence and power, enabled the Saqāliba in Muslim Spain to become a very important element in Spanish-Arab society. We find them serving as generals and as ministers, possessing great wealth, and sometimes owning estates and slaves of their own. Adopting the Arabic language, they even produced scholars, poets, and scientists in such numbers, and of such significance, that one of them during the reign of Hishām II (976–1013) composed a whole book on the merits and achievements of the Slavs of Andalusia. No copy appears to have survived.

When the Fatimids established their caliphate in Tunisia, in the early tenth century and advanced eastward to the conquest of Egypt some fifty years later, Slavonic slaves played a role of some importance in their successes. Jawhar, who commanded the armies which conquered Egypt and ranks as one of the founders of Cairo, may have been a Slav.[6]

Many Europeans were engaged in the export of slaves to the Muslim world. They included Christians and Jews, and citizens of the great merchant cities of Italy and France as well as Greek slavers operating in the eastern Mediterranean. An important part was played by the Venetians, who as early as the eighth century began to compete with the Greeks in this trade.

The Europeans seem to have had no compunction in selling Christian slaves to the Muslims in Spain, North Africa, and as far east as Egypt, although this traffic had already been banned by Charlemagne and, after him, by Popes Zachary and Hadrian I, who tried to end it. The Venetians were undaunted and even went so far as to buy slaves of both sexes in the city of Rome.[7] Venice was also the main supplier, to both the Islamic and Byzantine courts, of eunuchs. The trade reached such dimensions as to become a public scandal and was at times forbidden, apparently not very effectively, by the doges of Venice themselves.

All these bans and condemnations were ineffective in stopping so lucrative a business. The geographical situation of Venice, on the edge of the Slavonic lands and in easy maritime communication with the Muslim states, gave Venetian merchants a competitive edge, and the Adriatic island of Pola, then a Venetian possession, became a major slave market.

There were other sources of supply. Muslim corsairs from Spain, Sicily, and North Africa raided the Christian coasts of the Mediterranean, especially during the tenth, eleventh and twelfth centuries, and carried off great numbers of captives. In the year 928, a single expedition to the Adriatic is said to have returned to the port of al-Mahdiyya in Tunisia with 12,000 captives. It was commanded by one Sabir, a manumitted Slavonic slave of the governor of Sicily and a frequent raider on the Italian and Dalmatian coasts.

This traffic continued right through the Middle Ages, and did not begin to die out until the fifteenth century. One reason for this change was that Muslim merchants in search of Slavonic slaves, like Westerners in search of spices, were now gaining direct access to the sources of supply. The Mediterranean middleman was circumvented on both sides. While the Portuguese, sailing round Africa, went and bought their spices from the source in India and the East Indies, the Turks, advancing in the Balkans and the Black Sea area, were able to levy their supplies of slaves directly from the central and east European populations, and thus dispense with the services of the mostly European middlemen who had previously conveyed Slavonic slaves from Europe to the Middle East and North Africa. During the fifteenth and sixteenth centuries, the main source of supply was in southeastern Europe, where the advance of the Ottoman jihād brought a steady and ample supply of Albanian, Slavonic, Wallachian, Hungarian, and other Christian slaves. Some were recruited by the famous devshirme, the levy of Christian boys from the subject populations of the empire; others were captured in battle. In the seventeenth century, the devshirme were gradually abandoned. At the same time, the stalemate in the wars between the Ottomans and the Hapsburgs meant that conquest no longer provided an adequate flow of slaves to meet the needs of Ottoman society.

A substitute was found. The Tatar khans of the Crimea, an autonomous Muslim dynasty recognizing a loose Ottoman suzerainty, developed a vast apparatus of slave raiding and slave trading. Tatar raiders captured slaves from the Russian, Polish, and Ukrainian populations of eastern Europe and brought them to the Crimea, where they were sold and shipped to Istanbul for further distribution through the slave markets of the Ottoman Empire. "The harvesting of the steppes" as the Tatars called their activities, provided a regular and extensive supply of male and female slaves that continued into the latter part of the eighteenth century, when Tatar depredations were finally ended with the Russian annexation of the Crimea.[8]

The role played by the Balkan Christian boys recruited into the Ottoman service through the devshirme is well known. Great numbers of them entered the Ottoman military and bureaucratic apparatus, which for a while came to be dominated by these new recruits to the Ottoman state and the Muslim faith. This ascendancy of Balkan Europeans into the Ottoman power structure did not pass unnoticed, and there are many complaints from other elements, sometimes from the Caucasian slaves who were their main competitors, and more vocally from the old and free Muslims, who felt slighted by the preference given to newly converted slaves. The poet Veysi, writing in the early seventeenth century on the troubles that had befallen the empire and their causes, notes among other grievances: "How strange it is that those who enjoy rank and power are all Albanians and Bosnians, while the people of the Prophet of God [i.e., the old Muslims, or perhaps the Arabs] suffer abasement."[9]

The influence of the devshirme recruits was indeed enormous. Many of them rose to the highest offices in the Ottoman State; others achieved eminence as scholars, poets, and even as Muslim jurists and theologians. The role of the east European peasants taken by Tatar raiders and dispatched across the Black Sea is less well known and appears to have been less happy. Unlike the recruits of the devshirme, they rarely penetrated the Ottoman ruling elite, but served instead in humbler and often menial capacities. These were not limited to the familiar forms of service in the household and the harem. Contrary to a widely accepted assumption, slaves were often used also for economic purposes. The employment of slaves in plantations and in mines is already attested in the Middle Ages, though this does not appear to have been the most common form of production in either. By Ottoman times, however, there is extensive information about the use of slave labor in large plantations, mostly though not exclusively owned and operated under government auspices.

Some idea of the relative importance of the different ethnic groups of slaves may be gathered from Muslim literature on the subject. We possess a number of texts written in Arabic, Persian, and Turkish, extending from the early Middle Ages to the eighteenth century and describing the attributes of different races of slaves and the purposes for which they could most appropriately be used. The earlier works speak almost exclusively of slaves of Asian and, more especially, African origin. Ottoman writings on this topic give some attention to Slavonic and other east European slaves, but with few exceptions do not discuss west Europeans.[10]

In later times, virtually the sole source of west European slaves in the Islamic world was the Barbary Corsairs, who continued to capture ships at sea and occasionally raided the coasts of Christendom. These entered a new period of intensive activity in the early seventeenth century, when they sailed as far as the British Isles and Iceland. Their captives, however, were taken mainly for ransom rather than for use and no longer constituted a commercial commodity of any significance.

Some of them, however, voluntarily or involuntarily, stayed among their Muslim captors. The first group, predominantly male, consisted of Europeans who adopted Islam and made a career in the service of the Corsairs. These, like the former European pirates who, in the early seventeenth century, continued their careers as privateers under the Crescent, certainly brought useful skills to their new masters, in shipbuilding, gunnery, and navigation. They also served in a number of instances to lead them to some of the remoter and less defended coasts of western Europe where they found rich booty. There is no evidence that such adventurers had any beyond the most limited impact on their host countries.

There was another group of captives taken by Muslim Corsairs whose stay in Muslim lands was involuntary but permanent. These were women who, because of their beauty, were retained as concubines or sent—by sale or as gifts—to the harems of the Middle East. The choicest often found their final destinations in the Imperial Seraglio in Istanbul as concubines of the sultans or other dignitaries. The fathers of the Ottoman sultans are famous and amply documented, but little is known about their mothers. Most of them were slaves of the harem whose identities, origins, and even names are hidden from history by the discreet reticence of the Muslim household. This has given rise to some speculation about the origins of some of these ladies, who arrived in the palace as insignificant slave girls and rose to positions of great power and dignity as mothers of a reigning sultan. There are many stories concerning the sultans' mothers, some of whom are said to have been of European origin. The most famous is Nakşidil, the name given in the harem to the mother of the great reforming Sultan Mahmud II. According to a widespread legend, she was Aimée du Buc de Rivery, a French lady from Martinique and a cousin of Josephine de Beauharnais, but there is no reliable evidence to support this story. There is better evidence in the case of Nur Banu, a concubine of Selim II and the mother of his successor Murad III. A Venetian lady of patrician birth, she was, according to some accounts, Cecilia Venier-Baffo, the daughter of the Venetian governor of Corfu. Captured at the age of twelve by a Turkish raider, she was sent as a gift to Sultan Süleyman the Magnificent, who passed her on to his son Selim. Later, she and her successor Safiye, the mother of Mehmed III, entered into correspondence with Venice and even England.[11]

It is unlikely that these ladies can have contributed very much to Muslim knowledge of Europe, or even to that of their sons, royal or otherwise. In the nature of things they entered the harem at a very early age; in the nature of Muslim society, their impact and influence, outside the harem, were minimal.

The trade in weapons, unlike that in slaves, exhibits uninterrupted growth. Even before the Crusades, passages occur in Arabic texts praising the high quality of Frankish and other European swords. By the time of the Crusades, this had become an important export commodity that helped to redress the otherwise unfavorable balance of trade between Europe and the lands of Islam. The export of arms to the Muslims, even more than the export of Christian slaves, aroused the ire of the ecclesiastical and, sometimes, even of the royal authorities, but to little effect.

It was not only Frankish weapons that were found useful by the Muslims, but also the men who made and used them. An Egyptian chronicler speaks of Franks employed as craftsmen making weapons for the navy and other services in Cairo under the Fatimids.[12] Frankish soldiers of fortune turn up in the armies of Muslim rulers from Spain to the Levant and Asia Minor. Some of the early Turkish rulers of Anatolia are said to have employed thousands of Christian mercenaries, including Westerners. We also hear of Genoese and other European sailors in the service of Middle Eastern rulers and, in particular, of the Mongols.[13]

By Ottoman times, the trade in weapons was very extensive and included vital raw materials. A papal bull issued by Clement VII in 1527 pronounced excommunication and anathema on "all those who take to the Saracens, Turks, and other enemies of the Christian name, horses, weapons, iron, iron wire, tin, copper, bandaraspata, brass, sulphur, saltpeter, and all else suitable for the making of artillery, and instruments, arms, and machines for offense, with which they fight against the Christians, as also ropes and timber and other nautical supplies and other prohibited wares. . . ." A hundred years later a similar bull of Pope Urban VIII includes a slightly longer list of prohibited war materials; it further excommunicates and anathematizes those who directly or indirectly give aid, comfort, or information to the Turks and other enemies of the Christian religion.[14]

It was not only the Vatican that was concerned about this traffic. There are frequent complaints by European governments of the supply of war materials and military skills to the Turks by rival European powers. In the late sixteenth and early seventeenth centuries, the Catholic powers frequently accuse the Protestants, and especially the English, of supplying a wide range of war materials, and especially tin. "The Turks are also desirous of friendship with the English on account of the tin which has been sent thither for the last few years, and which is of the greatest value to them, as they cannot cast their guns without it, whilst the English make a tremendous profit on the article, by means of which alone they maintain the trade with the Levant." An English ship seized at Melos with a cargo of merchandise bound for Turkey was found to contain "200 bales of kerseys, English woolens, 700 barrels of gunpowder, 1000 harquebuss barrels, 500 mounted harquebusses, 2000 sword blades, a barrel full of ingots of fine gold, 20,000 sequins, many great dollars, and other things of value. Further there was found a note written in Turkish character on parchment, issued by the sultan's orders."[15]

Decrees of excommunication and threats of worldly punishment failed, however, to deter those engaged in these highly profitable trades. The supply of weapons and war materials by the Christian powers to the Ottomans and other Muslim states grew steadily, and in time reached enormous proportions.

Apart from slaves and war materials, Europe seems to have had little to offer that would interest the Muslim purchaser. There was, however, one other commodity which is mentioned several times by Muslim writers; that is English cloth, already famous in the Western world in the High Middle Ages. Ibn Yaʿqūb, the tenth-century traveler to the West, remarks, in speaking of the Island of Shāshīn, presumably Anglo-Saxon England:

> There is a kind of wool there of exceeding beauty, the like of which is to be found in no other land. They say that the cause of this is that their women grease the wool with pig fat, which improves its quality. Its colour is white or turquoise, and it is of exceeding beauty.[16]

A later writer, the geographer Ibn Saʿid, has a little more information:

> Fine scarlet (ishkarlaṭ) is made there [in England]. In this island they have sheep with wool as soft as silk. They cover their sheep with cloths to protect them from the rain, the sun, and the dust.[17]

This passage is also quoted from Ibn Saʿid by later geographical writers.

An independent reference occurs in the description of Frankish Europe by Rashīd al-Dīn, who remarks:

> In both islands [Ireland and England] they have ewes from whose fleece woollen cloth and fine scarlet are made.[18]

The word scarlet is of disputed origin, though it seems probable that the Arabic and Persian forms derive from the West rather than the reverse. There has been much discussion as to whether in the thirteenth century this word denoted a color or a particular quality of cloth. The latter seems more probable. Scarlet, whatever it was, was one of England's major products in the thirteenth century, and these remote eastern echoes of this English trade are of some interest. The three sources quoted above indicate that this scarlet was something known by hearsay and found only in distant Europe. By the fifteenth century, however, Ottoman documents contain explicit references to English cloth as a commodity imported into the Ottoman dominions.[19]

By the later eighteenth century, the balance of trade had changed decisively in favor of Europe and against the Islamic lands of the Middle East and North Africa. This process was initiated by the great efflorescence of European industry and trade in the late Middle Ages and early modern centuries. The opening and development of the oceanic routes bypassed the Middle East, and even the Persian silk trade, which had once been important as a source of raw materials and also of tax revenue to Turkey, was now diverted and to a large extent controlled by west European merchants. The establishment of European colonies in the New World and commercial outposts in the East, added to the new industrial capacity in Europe itself, at last gave European merchants something substantial to offer to Middle Eastern customers.

In a real sense, the composition of trade between Islam and Christendom was being reversed. Where once Europe had imported cloth from the Middle East it now sold cloth and imported raw materials. The changing commercial relationship is graphically illustrated in that familiar Middle Eastern indulgence, a cup of coffee. Both coffee and the sugar used to sweeten it were first introduced to Europe from the Middle East. Coffee, which originally came from the southern end of the Red Sea, probably from Ethiopia, was brought to the eastern Mediterranean lands during the sixteenth century and spread from there to Europe. Until the last quarter of the seventeenth century, coffee was an important item among exports to Europe from the Middle East. By the second decade of the eighteenth century, the Dutch were growing coffee in Java for the European market and the French were even exporting coffee, grown in their West Indian colonies, to Turkey. By 1739, West Indian coffee is mentioned as far east as Erzurum in eastern Turkey. Colonial coffee brought by Western merchants was cheaper than that coming from the Red Sea area and greatly reduced its share of the market.

Sugar, too, was originally an eastern innovation. First refined in

India and Iran, it was imported by Europe from Egypt, Syria, and North Africa, and transplanted by the Arabs to Sicily and Spain. From there it was taken to the mid-Atlantic islands and thence to the New World. Here again the West Indian colonies provided an opportunity which was not missed. In 1671, the French built a refinery in Marseilles from which they exported colonial sugar to Turkey. Consumption there increased enormously when the Turks took to sweetening their coffee, perhaps as a consequence of the bitterer flavor of the West Indian bean. Hitherto they had relied largely on Egyptian sugar. West Indian sugar was cheaper and soon dominated the Middle Eastern market. By the end of the eighteenth century, when a Turk or an Arab drank a cup of coffee both the coffee and the sugar had been grown in Central America and imported by French or English merchants. Only the hot water was of local provenance.

Another important commodity in this new trade was tobacco. This was entirely new to the Islamic world, and was brought by English merchants from the American colonies. The historian Peçevi, writing in about 1635, has this to say on what he calls "the coming of the fetid and nauseating smoke of tobacco": "The English infidels," he says, "brought it in the year 1009 [A.D. 1601], and sold it as a remedy for certain diseases of humidity." Its use, however, rapidly extended beyond its allegedly medicinal purposes. It was seized upon by "pleasure seekers and sensualists" and even by "many of the great ulema and the mighty." In a vivid passage, Peçevi describes the immediate popularity of this new vice and its effects. "From the ceaseless smoking of the coffeehouse riffraff, the coffeehouses were filled with blue smoke, to such a point that those who were in them could not see one another." Even in public places, the addicts poisoned the air. "Their pipes never left their hands. Puffing in each other's faces and eyes, they made the streets and markets stink." Despite these and many other ill effects "by the beginning of the year 1045 [A.D. 1635–36], its spread and fame were such as cannot be written or expressed."[20]

By the end of the eighteenth century, the economic weakness of the Middle East as contrasted with Europe was overwhelming and helped to prepare the way for political and military domination in the following century. But Muslim writers show little awareness of this. The economic literature of the West remained totally unknown to Muslim readers. Not a single work of economic content was translated into Arabic, Persian, or Turkish until well into the nineteenth century. Even the limited accounts of Europe that are available are concerned mostly with political and military matters, and have little to say about the economies of European nations. Perhaps the one exception is the

Moroccan ambassador Ghassānī, who visited Madrid in 1690–1691. His comments on the effects of Spanish expansion in America show some perspicacity, and an echo of Ibn Khaldūn's social philosophy:

> The Spaniards still own many provinces and vast territories in the Indies, and what they bring from them every year makes them rich. By the conquest and exploitation of the Indian lands and the great riches they draw from them, the Spanish nation today possesses the greatest wealth and the largest income of all the Christians. But the love of luxury and of the comforts of civilization have overcome them, and you will rarely find one of this nation who engages in trade or travels abroad for commerce as do the other Christian nations such as the Dutch, the English, the French, the Genoese and their like. Similarly, the handicrafts practiced by the lower classes and common people are despised by this nation, which regards itself as superior to the other Christian nations. Most of those who practise these crafts in Spain are Frenchmen, and this is because their own country offers them only a poor livelihood; they flock to Spain to look for work and make money. In a short time they make great fortunes. . . .[21]

The Ottoman ambassador Vasif, who was in Spain in 1787–1788, also notes some economic effects of American bullion: "every three years," he observes, "the Spaniards send some five or six thousand workers to the mines of the New World. This has become a necessity of state, since most of the miners cannot adapt to the climate and die. The gold and silver come to the mints of Madrid, but the population is thin and agriculture languishes, forcing the Spaniards to import foodstuffs from Morocco. That is why they seek the good will of the Moroccan ruler. He sells them supplies at a high price in unminted gold and silver, which he then has minted for him in Madrid from matrices supplied by him, with his own inscriptions."[22]

The Wazīr al-Ghassānī has much else to say on economic matters. Mehmed Efendi also discusses, and was particularly impressed by, the factories which he visited for the manufacture of tapestries and of glassware.[23]

By the latter part of the eighteenth century, such envoys as Resmi and Azmi make frequent reference to trade and manufactures in the countries which they visited. Resmi, who went to Berlin in 1777, traveling through Rumania and Poland, has a number of comments. "In the Polish kingdom," he notes, "besides the Poles, there are two other nationalities, the Russians and the Jews. The former take care of agriculture and other hard work, while the Jews in the towns carry on all the trade in wheat and other commodities, as well as profitable enterprises in buying and selling; but the greatest profit is in the hands of the already very wealthy Pole, who dresses in a gold-braided, broad-sleeved coat and a light lamb cap." In Prussia he saw sugar and cloth factories and noted that the machines used in these factories were also made in the city of Berlin. Resmi remarks on the Prussian liking for porcelain, which was previously imported from China and India until they learned to make it themselves, first in Saxony and more recently in Berlin.[24] His successor Azmi, who went to Berlin in 1790, was more concerned with military and political matters but also has something to say about the successful Prussian effort to establish industries and about the strength which this confers on the country.[25]

References to Europe in Ottoman belles-lettres before the nineteenth century are exceedingly rare. One example occurs in a literary work written by the poet Hashmet on the occasion of the accession of Sultan Mustafa III in 1757. In this work, the poet, to honor the new sultan and glorify his accession, uses the common literary device of a dream and the well-known Muslim theme of the kings of the earth who come to pay homage to the lord of Islam. In his vision the poet sees the kings arrive in state to offer obeisance to the new sultan and to request the privilege of serving at his court. The kings come one by one to the poet, explain their purposes, and solicit his good offices in obtaining the appointments which they seek. Each monarch describes the speciality of his own country and asks for a corresponding appointment at the court of the new sultan. The emperor of China asks for custody of the palace porcelain, the imam of the Yemen wants to be chief coffee maker. Then come six European rulers numbered in the following order—the Russian czar, who asks to be chief furrier; the Austrian emperor, who boasts of his country's skill in glassware, crystalware, and mirrors and asks to be made chief glazier; the "chief of the Republic of Venice," who speaks of the long-standing skill of his people in precious metals, and seeks appointment as chief assayer; the king of England, who speaks of his country's production of powder and weapons of war, and asks to be put in charge of the powder magazine; the "king" of Holland, who speaks with pride of tulips and other flowers, and seeks appointment as a gardener; and finally, the king of France, who describes his country's production of broadcloth and satin and other cloths, and asks for appointment as master of the wardrobe. No other European ruler is listed.[26]

Hashmet's vision may have little value as economic history, but it provides interesting evidence of a mid–eighteenth-century Ottoman's perception of the states of Europe and their products.

Abū Ṭālib Khan, who visited England at the end of the eighteenth century, devotes a whole chapter in his book to the beginnings of industry which he was able to see at that time. In the number and perfection of machines he saw the prime cause of English wealth and greatness. It was this that had enabled the English to extend their power to so many distant places; this too that made it impossible for their neighbors, the French, despite their great strength and courage, to accomplish anything against them. Abū Ṭālib describes several types of machinery, beginning with the simplest, the mills for grinding corn, and continuing with the great iron-foundries, "driven by steam." He comments on the manufacture of cannon, flat metal sheets, and needles, and admires the speed and efficiency of the spinning jenny. He describes its action, and notes that by means of this device it is possible to produce cloth far more quickly and with far fewer hands. He was, however, less impressed by the quality, which he found to be inferior to that of the handmade cloths of India. Abū Ṭālib also visited a brewery, a paper factory, and other establishments, and has much to say about the hydraulic pump used to supply London with water. He had even heard of machines invented for use in the kitchen. "The men of this kingdom," he remarks, "are extremely impatient and averse to trivial and time-consuming work," and have therefore invented machines for use in the kitchen, to perform such tasks as roasting chickens, mincing meat, and chopping onions.[27]

Abū Ṭālib seems to have visited a number of factories in different parts of the country. He was duly impressed by what he saw, and even comments in his opening remarks on the economic foundations of military and political power. The connection was seen more clearly and discussed more explicitly by a slightly later visitor, Halet Efendi, Ottoman Ambassador in Paris from 1803 to 1806. Halet Efendi was a resolute reactionary, contemptuous of the French and other Europeans and opposed to the idea of imitating them in any significant way. For him the remedy is clear and simple:

> God knows, I am of the opinion that if, as an emergency measure once every three or four years, 25,000 purses of aspers were to be set aside, and five factories for snuff, paper, crystal, cloth, and porcelain as well as a school for languages and geography set up, then in the course of five years there will be as good as nothing left for them to hold on to, since the basis of all their current trade is in these five commodities. May God bestow some zeal on our masters, amen.[28]

Halet's stress on the need for improved education was anticipated by the eighteenth-century reformers. His pointing to manufactures as one of the sources of European power, however simplistically expressed, raised a new and important issue for Middle Easterners. In the course of the nineteenth century, this became part of the accepted wisdom, and reforming rulers in Turkey, Egypt, Iran, and elsewhere saw science and industry as magic talismans with which to conjure up the gorgeous treasures of the mysterious Occident.

VIII

Government and Justice

For the Muslim, the community to which he belonged was the center of the world, defined by the possession of God's truth and the acceptance of God's law. In this Muslim world, there was in principle only one state, the caliphate, and only one sovereign, the caliph, the legitimate head of the House of Islam and the supreme sovereign of the Muslim polity.

For the first century or so of Islamic history, this perception corresponded to reality. Islam was indeed one community and one polity; its advance was rapid and unimpeded, and it must have seemed clear and certain to contemporaries that the swift progress and imminent completion of the parallel processes of conquest and conversion would before long bring all mankind into the Islamic fold.

In the course of the eighth century, Arab Islam reached its limits, and gradually the idea was admitted that there was a pause in the inevitable expansion of the Muslim state and faith. The grand design of capturing Constantinople was postponed; it was resumed only many centuries later, by the Ottoman Turks, in a new wave of Islamic conquest which in turn came to a halt in central Europe. Gradually, Muslims came to accept the notion that Islam had a frontier, and that there were other societies and other polities beyond it. The concept of the single universal Islamic community to embrace all mankind was preserved, but its accomplishment was left to a messianic future.

In the harsh world of reality, the unity as well as the universality of the Islamic polity was tacitly abandoned. Sometimes conflicting sovereignties arose within the Islamic Empire, giving, at best, token recognition to the suzerainty of the caliph. In time, even rival caliphates emerged, and after the destruction of the Baghdad caliphate by the Mongol invaders in 1258, the theoretical political unity of Islam was at an end. Even so, the ideal of a single Islamic sovereignty still dominated the minds of the Muslims and is expressed in the titulature of the Muslim monarchs who arose in the post-caliphal age. One of the most striking features of the Islamic lands from medieval times right through to the nineteenth century is the absence of established and continuing territorial or ethnic entities or even of ethnic and territorial regnal titles such as are found in Europe where, from an early time, we find a king of France, a king of England, a king of Denmark, and many others.

In the Islamic Middle East, there is no such thing. In part, this reflects the great variation and instability of realms in the medieval period, when it was quite uncommon for two successive rulers to rule over precisely the same territory. But it remained a feature of Islamic royal titulature even in the post-Mongol period, when states were on the whole relatively stable and enduring. By 1500, there were only three states of any importance in the Middle East, Turkey, Iran, and Egypt, and with the Ottoman conquest of Egypt and its dependencies this was reduced to two. But the terms we use—the sultan of Turkey, the shah of Persia, the sultan of Egypt—were applied to these rulers by outsiders or by rivals, never by themselves. In European practice, the use of such titles was merely descriptive. Applied by these rulers to one another, a territorial title was a term of abuse, intended to show that their sovereignty was local and limited. When the rulers of Egypt, Turkey, and Persia alike spoke of themselves, they called themselves sovereign of Islam or of the people of Islam or of the lands of Islam but never of Turkey, Persia, or Egypt.

In this as in other respects, among Muslims as among other peoples, there was a tendency to see others as a reflection of themselves. While Islam was conceived as a single entity, it was natural to think of the House of War in the same terms. The subdivisions among the infidels, particularly those of them who lived beyond the Islamic frontier, were of no interest or significance.

But while historians could concentrate on the truly significant parts of history, that is to say the affairs of God's own community and the rulers appointed by Him, and disregard the meaningless gyrations of the infidel barbarians beyond the frontier, the rulers of Islamic states were increasingly compelled to enter into dealings of one sort or another with these barbarians and were therefore obliged to collect some minimal information about them.

The first point of concern in dealing with infidel polities was to name and identify the various rulers. This, in itself, raised some interesting problems. The earliest Muslim traditions, referring to a time when Islam was still confined to parts of the Arabian Peninsula, name three sovereigns as dominating the surrounding areas—Kisrā, Qayṣar, and Najāshī. None of these appears by name in the Qur'ān but the occasional Qur'anic allusions to the surrounding states are explained and elaborated in commentary and tradition. All three are loan words filtered into Arabic, probably through Aramaic. Kisrā derives from Chosroes or Khusraw, one of the last and greatest of the Sasanid rulers of Iran; Qayṣar is of course Caesar and Najāshī is the Negus of Ethiopia. All three seem to have been regarded by the early Muslims as personal names rather than titles—the designations of the sovereigns ruling at that time in the three important countries known to them. According to a prophetic utterance attributed to Muḥammad: "If Kisrā perishes, there will be no Kisrā after him. And if Qayṣar perishes, there will be no Qayṣar after him. By Him in whose hand my soul lies, you will spend their treasures in the way of God."[1]

Kisrā perished and, indeed, there was none after him. The Sasanian realm was overwhelmed and incorporated in the House of Islam, and the line of Zoroastrian emperors came to an end. The Ethiopian Christian monarchy survived but was surrounded and reduced to relative insignificance. Only the east Roman Empire remained as a neighbor and adversary of Islam. The title Qayṣar, however, was rarely used to designate the Byzantine emperors. Sometimes they were known by frankly insulting titles. A common one is *ṭāghiya,* tyrant, later also used of European monarchs, especially by North African writers. Another form of address is typified in a famous letter sent by the Caliph Hārūn al-Rashīd to the Byzantine emperor Nikephoras, which begins "From Hārūn, Commander of the Faithful, to Nikephoras, dog of the Romans, greeting."[2]

The most common term used, however, to designate the Byzantine emperor along with all the other rulers of Christendom is *malik,* king. The Arabic word *malik* in Qur'ān and tradition, like its Hebrew equivalent *melekh* in the earlier books of the Old Testament, has a very negative connotation when applied to human rulers, conveying a suggestion of worldly and irreligious authority. In the early Muslim centuries, within the Muslim lands, it was used as a term of condemnation to distinguish between the impious and arbitrary rule of worldly sovereigns and the divinely authorized and divinely regulated rule of the caliphs. It was not until the reemergence of the distinctively Persian political tradition within Islam that the notion and terminology of monarchy began to recover some respectability among Muslims. Even then it still retained something of a negative connotation. This is clear from the contemptuous lumping together of the monarchs of Christendom in the expression *mulūk al-kuffār,* the kings of the unbelievers, or *mulūk al-kufr,* the kings of unbelief.

For one class of rulers even the term king is too much. The Christian principalities established by the Crusaders in territories taken from the Muslims are seen as lacking even the minimal legitimacy of the rulers of Europe. In the models of usage listed in the Egyptian chancery manuals for addressing the kings of Cyprus and of Lesser Armenia, the word *malik* is replaced by *mutamallik,* an Arabic form meaning one who pretends to be a king without actually being one. The same word *malik* is used indiscriminately of Frankish princes, African tribal chiefs, Byzantine, Indian, and Chinese emperors and the monarchs of Europe.

For correspondence with these monarchs, some greater precision was necessary. The earliest Islamic examples of such correspondence are letters alleged to have been exchanged between the Prophet Muḥammad and the rulers of the three surrounding countries. Though the authenticity of these documents has been challenged, they are certainly of very early origin and served as proof texts for dealings with a non-Muslim ruler. The three monarchs are addressed by name, followed by a title, usually king, sometimes an early equivalent such as lord *(ṣāḥib)* or mighty one *('aẓim),* and by the name of the domain or people ruled. Thus the Byzantine emperor is addressed as *malik* or *ṣāḥib* or *'aẓim* of the Romans, the *Negus* as *najāshī* or king of Ethiopia, etc. The form of greeting is different from that used for Muslim sovereigns. When one Muslim sovereign writes to another, he uses the classical Islamic salutation, "Peace be with you"; when addressing a non-Muslim monarch, this is replaced by "Peace with those who follow the right path." This somewhat ambiguous greeting came to be standard in correspondence with non-Muslim rulers. The Moroccan ambassador Ghassānī makes a point of his insistence on greeting the king of Spain with these words when he was received in audience. The Spanish *ṭāghiya,* he notes, was surprised at this unprecedented form of address, but perforce accepted it, since he knew that the ambassador was firmly resolved to give him no other.[3] Centuries earlier, the author of the memoir on Jem emphasized that the captive Prince refused to kiss the Pope's hand, foot or even knee, consenting finally only to kiss his shoulder, in accordance with eastern courtesy.

Information about diplomatic correspondence with non-Muslim powers in the early centuries is lacking, though it seems likely that Hārūn al-Rashīd's discourteous "Dog of the Romans," written on the eve of an outbreak of war, is the exception rather than the rule. Our best information on such matters in medieval Islam comes from Egypt, where the earliest report of an exchange of letters with a non-Muslim sovereign, the Byzantine coemperor, dates from the tenth century.[4] Thereafter we have fairly good accounts in Egyptian bureaucratic literature as well as a number of documents, preserved mostly in European archives.

Really full information is not available until the Ottoman period when, for the first time, we have not only chronicles but also numerous documents. From the chronicles, one would gather that the Ottomans were little concerned with correct European titles. Thus, even Kemalpaşazade, the historian of Süleyman the Magnificent, refers to the major European monarchs as the bey of France, the bey of Spain, the bey of Alaman, using the title given in the Ottoman Empire to a mere provincial governor. In the same spirit, the realms over which these European monarchs ruled are usually designated—even in royal letters addressed to them—by the term vilayet, normally applied to the subdivisions of the Ottoman Empire.

More commonly, however, Ottoman texts use the term *kiral* of European monarchs and show some concern to address European sovereigns by their correct titles as defined by themselves, without, however, compromising basic Muslim positions. Letters to Queen Elizabeth I of England begin "Glory of the virtuous followers of Jesus, elder of the revered ladies of the Christian community, moderator of the affairs of the Nazarene sect, who draws the trains of majesty and reverence, Queen of the land of England, may her end be blissful."[5] This *intitulatio,* common to virtually all letters addressed to Christian, European monarchs, indicates the basic religious classification assumed in the Ottoman chancery. Queen Elizabeth's Christian identity is asserted no less than three times before the writer of the document gets down to speaking of England. The queen is one of the rulers of Christendom. Within that larger entity, she governs the land (vilayet) of England. The invocation, like the prophetic formula cited above, expresses the hope that she will become a Muslim before her death and thus earn eternal bliss.

In Elizabeth's day, little was known in Turkey about the land of England and the claims of its ruler. Not surprisingly, they knew more about central Europe, where such dignitaries as the emperor in Vienna and, later, the king of Prussia are addressed with the same formula, but followed by an approximation to their correct titles.

For a long time, Ottoman chancery practice refused to accord any title greater than king to Christian rulers. While the sultans of Morocco were content to use the term sultan rather loosely for other Muslim and even for Christian European rulers, the Ottomans jealously guarded that title exclusively for themselves, calling other Muslim sovereigns, not to speak of European sovereigns, by lesser designations. Even the Holy Roman emperor was normally addressed as the king of Vienna, a protocolar device for cutting him down to size. The first European monarch to be accorded a somewhat more dignified title was Francis I of France who, in a Franco-Ottoman treaty, is designated as padishah, a term of Persian origin indicating supreme sovereignty and sometimes used by the Ottoman sultans themselves. Its application to the French king was thus a considerable concession. It was not until the following century that more exalted titles were allowed to the Austrian, Russian, and other European monarchs. The normal practice was to accord them their own titles. The Austrian emperor is usually addressed çasar, from kaiser, the Russian as czar.

The Russians thought the matter important enough to incorporate it in the Treaty of Küçük Kaynarja of 1774, in which they imposed their will on a defeated Ottoman Empire. Article 13 of the Treaty provides that henceforth "the Sublime Porte promises to employ the sacred title of The Empress of all the Russias in all public acts and letters, as well as in other cases, in the Turkish language, that is to say, 'Temamen Roussielerin Padischag.' " The inclusion of the transcribed Turkish phrase in the text of the article is noteworthy. A contemporary Russian memorandum on the treaty notes this point, along with the more obvious economic, strategic, and political gains, as one of the achievements of the treaty. The Ottoman reluctance to accord this title to foreign rulers was more than merely a matter of official protocol. It had deep roots in the Ottoman Muslim sense of propriety. This can be seen in a report written by a Turkish officer who accompanied the Ambassador Ibrahim Pasha to Vienna in 1719. The writer—no diplomat or bureaucrat but a soldier writing in simple, straightforward Turkish—refers to the Austrian emperor with the word "kaiser," written in the Turkish script. To explain this unfamiliar word to his readers, he notes that "in the German language this means padişah." To avoid even the appearance of an unseemly comparison, he adds the phrase la-teşbih, the purport of which is something like the English expression "God save the mark."[6]

The Ottoman concern to differentiate between their own Islamic sovereignty and that of the lesser potentates of Europe is clear in the style as well as the headings of their letters. "Our Sublime Porte" writes Sultan Murad III to Queen Elizabeth in 1583, "is open in grace and benevolence to those who offer loyalty. Our hearts, enkindled with felicity, are always ready and prepared for those who make submission . . . your envoy . . . like the envoys of the other kings who . . . offer devotion and fidelity to our Lofty Lintel and Illustrious Threshold, will be cared for and protected . . . therefore you on your part always remain in loyalty and friendship with our Court . . . firm-footed on the path of devotion and fidelity, constant on the highway of friendship and loyalty. . . ."[7] These formulas, together with other even stronger terms common in Ottoman correspondence with European monarchs, reflect a perhaps premature expectation of European acquiescence in such a relationship.

The Muslim ambassadors, not surprisingly, devote their attention mainly to the sovereigns to whom they were accredited and say little about lesser personages. These are normally mentioned chiefly in the context of their own meetings and exchanges with them. Ghassānī discusses the remarkable phenomenon of the inheritance of titles, even in the female line, and the great eagerness of the Spaniards to acquire them, whether by merit or by matrimony.[8] Mehmed Efendi offers a brief explanation of the French system of government for the use of his readers:

> They have several viziers who are called "ministres," and who rank below marshals and dukes. Each of them is entrusted with a specific matter. No one of them interferes with any other, and each is independent in the service which is entrusted to him. The above-mentioned [the archbishop of Cambrai] was in charge of foreign affairs and had the power to deal with such matters as arranging war and peace, looking after all commercial affairs, dealing with the ambassadors who came from other parts, and appointing and dismissing the French ambassadors to the Threshold of Felicity [Istanbul].[9]

It is not until the latter part of the eighteenth century that Muslim envoys and other visitors to Europe begin to pay any attention to the actual structure of government, and to functionaries below the top level. Certainly the most interesting of these is Azmi Efendi, the Ottoman ambassador in Berlin from 1790 to 1792. Like other Turkish visitors and writers of this period, he reflects a perceptible change in attitude towards Europeans, who are no longer seen as benighted infidels only worth mentioning, if at all, for their amusing oddities. On the contrary, they are seen as powerful and advancing rivals whose ways must be studied in order to guard against them and perhaps even, for this purpose, to imitate them. Azmi's report begins with a fairly standard form of description of his travels and activities. Of much greater interest is the second part of his report, in which he offers an account of the kingdom of Prussia under various headings: the administration of the country, its inhabitants, the high government offices, the state of treasury, the population, the governmental food depots, the military, the munitions arsenal, and artillery magazines. Azmi Efendi was clearly greatly impressed by the organization of the Prussian government and in particular by the efficiency of the state apparatus, the competence of its officials, the absence of unqualified and unnecessary officials, and the system of salaries and promotions. He speaks of the Prussian effort to establish industries and expatiates on the internal calm and security of the Prussian kingdom. He bestows particular praise on the financial order and on the treasury. His description of the Prussian army and of its system of training came to be an important source for Ottoman officials pressing for a better military organization. Azmi Efendi is not content to make his suggestions by implication but ends his report with a series of recommendations for the improvement of the Ottoman state, suggested to him by his Prussian experiences. They are as follows:

1) Corruption, a cause of tyranny and ruination in the Ottoman realm, is to be entirely eliminated.

2) The state apparatus is to be pruned and only competent persons employed in it.

3) Every official is to be assured a regular salary in accordance with his work.

4) As long as officials commit no offense damaging to the order and principles of the realm, they are not to be dismissed from their posts.

5) Unqualified persons should not be allowed to occupy posts for which they are unsuited.

6) The lower classes, who now strive in vain to imitate the great, must be educated.

7) The armed forces, and in particular the artillery and the navy, should be properly trained and ready for all emergencies in summer and winter alike. If this is ensured, the allies of the Ottoman state will grow in strength and zeal, and its opponents will be defeated. In this way, it would be possible to overcome the enemies of the Ottoman state.[10]

From time to time Muslim writers on western Europe observe deviations from the normal human pattern of kingship. One of these is the rule of a queen. In a society in which polygamy and concubinage were normal and were, in particular, extensively practiced by monarchs, the institution of female sovereignty was unlikely to emerge. There were, indeed, a very few remarkable women who managed to achieve supreme power even in this inauspicious context, but their reigns were of brief duration. Queens were not, however, entirely unknown to the Muslim world. They had seen queens in neighboring Byzantium and seem to have understood the principle of succession. A near-contemporary Muslim historian, speaking of the Byzantine empress Irene, who reigned from 797 to 822, remarks: "A woman came to rule over the Romans because at the time she was the only one of their royal house who remained."[11]

A Muslim historian records the arrival in Baghdad in the year 906 of an embassy from a Lombard monarch in Italy called Bertha, daughter of Lothar, but offers no information about her or her country. Qalqashandī, in his chancery manual, includes among the monarchs he discusses the "woman ruler of Naples." Quoting an earlier source, he says that her name was Joanna and that a letter was sent to her towards the end of the year 773 [1371] with the following titles: "To the exalted, honored, revered, venerated, magnificent, glorious Queen, learned in her religion, just in her kingdom, great one of the Nazarene religion, helper of the Christian community, protectress of the frontier, friend of kings and sultans." Qalqashandī goes on to remark that "if she be succeeded in her kingdom by a man, then it will be proper for him to be addressed with the same titles in the masculine form, or with higher titles, in view of the superiority of men over women."[12]

The Ottomans were well acquainted with European queens regnant from Elizabeth of England to Maria Theresa of Austria. It is curious that while Muslim visitors comment frequently and unfavorably on the high place accorded to women in Christian society, they appear to be untroubled by female sovereigns.

Several Muslim authors discuss the temporal power of the popes, and one of them, the Persian historian Rashīd al-Dīn, even attempts, in his universal history written in the early years of the fourteenth century, a definition of the relations between the pope, the emperor, and the other kings of Christendom:

> The order of the sovereigns of the Franks is as follows: The first in line is the *Pāp,* which means father of fathers and they regard him as the caliph of Christ. After him comes the emperor *(Chasar],* which in the language of the Franks they call *Āmperūr,* meaning sultan of sultans. After him comes the Rēdā Frans, which means king of kings. The emperor retains his sovereignty from the day he becomes emperor until his death. They choose him for his piety and worthiness from among a number of worthy men, and they enthrone him. The Rēdā Frans reigns by inheritance from father to son and at the present time he is very powerful and respected. Under his command there are twelve sove-

reigns, and to each of these sovereigns three kings submit. Then comes the Rē, which means king or lord.

The rank of the pope is very high and great. Whenever they wish to appoint a new emperor, seven of their great men whose task it is meet and take counsel—three marquises, three great princes, and one sovereign. They consider all the notables of the Franks, and choose ten persons from among them, and then among the ten, after careful examination, they choose one possessed of piety, authority, competence, and chastity, and distinguished by faith, piety, constancy, dignity, good character, nobility, and perfection of soul. They put a silver crown on his head in Allemania, which the Franks believe to be one-third of the world. From there they go to the land of Lombardia and put a crown of steel on his head, then from there they go to great Rome, the city of the pope, and the pope, standing on his feet, lifts up a golden crown and puts it on his head. Then he throws himself down and grasps the stirrup, so that the pope puts his foot on his head and neck and steps over him and sits on his horse. Thereupon he is given the title of Emperor, and the sovereigns of the Franks become submissive and obedient to him, and his sway extends over the lands and seas of the realms of the Franks."[13]

Rashīd al-Dīn's information is fairly good and obviously comes from a papal source. He follows it with a brief account of the history of the popes until his own time.

Even stranger than the rule of a woman or a priest was a third type of sovereignty which the Muslims encountered in Europe and to which they occasionally refer in their books. The notion of a republic was by no means unfamiliar to medieval Muslims. It appears in Arabic versions and discussions of Greek political writings where the Greek term *politeia* (cf. the Latin *res publica*), i.e., polity or commonweal, was rendered by the Arabic term *madīna*. The "democratic polity" of Plato's classification appears in classical Arabic texts as *madīna jamā'iyya*. Even in the Islamic community itself, according to the law as formulated by the Sunni jurists, the caliphate was to be a nonhereditary, elective office, subject to and not above the law.

In fact, however, after the first forty years and the first four caliphs, sovereignty in Islam as in most other places in the world at that time was almost invariably monarchical. Nor did the republican concepts carried over from Greek philosophical writings have much influence outside a narrow circle of writers and readers of philosophy. Their lack of impact is clear from the fact that when, at a later stage, a new terminology was needed to designate republican forms of government in Europe, it was devised without knowledge of or reference to the philosophic literature.

The republican form of government obviously offered some problems of comprehension. An early account comes in the report of ʿUmarī, drafted in about 1340.

> The Venetians have no king, but their form of rule is a commune. This means that they agree on a man whom they appoint to rule over them by their unanimous consent. The Venetians *(Banādiqa)* are called Finisin. Their emblem is a human figure with a face which they believed to be that of Mark, one of the Apostles. The man who rules over them comes from one of the noted families among them. . . .

After noting that the Pisans, Tuscans, Anconitans, and Florentines have the same system of government by commune, ʿUmarī gives rather more detail about Genoa, the country of origin of his renegade informant:

> The form of government of the people of Genoa is a commune. They never have had or will have a king. Rule over them at the present time is held by two families, one is the House of Doria from which my informant Balban comes and the other is the House of Spinola. Balban also said that after these two families in Genoa, there are the Houses of Grimaldi, Mallono, de Mari, San Tortore (?), and Fieschi. The members of these families are the counsellors of whoever rules over them. . . .[14]

Qalqashandī, following the *Tathqīf,* gives instructions for correspondence with two Italian republics, those of Genoa and Venice. On the first he says:

> The form of address to the rulers of Genoa: They are a group of people of various positions namely the podestà, the captain, and the elders. According to the *Tathqīf,* letters to them should be written on quarto and using the following style: "This correspondence is addressed to their excellencies, the exalted, respected, honored, venerated, and esteemed podestà and captain, so-and-so and so-and-so, and to the great and honored elders (sheikhs), the wielders of judgment and counsel, of the Commune of Genoa, the glorious ones of the Christian community, the great ones of the Nazarene religion, the friends of kings and sultans, may Almighty God inspire them to follow the right path, make their endeavours auspicious and lead them to good counsel. . . .

The *Tathqīf* adds:

> At the beginning of the year 767 [1365–1366], they discontinued the form of address to the podestà and captain, who had themselves been discontinued, and correspondence was addressed to the doge, who replaced them.

On Venice, Qalqashandī remarks:

The form of address to the ruler of Venice; the author of the *Tath-qif* says: The established formula was adopted when a reply was sent to him in the year 767. His name at that time was Marco Cornaro. . . . We have received the letter of his Excellency the exalted, respected, esteemed, brave, venerated, magnificent doge, Marco Cornaro, Pride of the Christian Community, Splendor of the sect of the cross, doge of Venice and Dalmatia. . . . Upholder of the religion of the sons of baptism, friend of kings and sultans. . . .

After quoting further examples, Qalqashandī adds his own comment:

From all this it follows that the doge is different from a king. In the first and second examples, the form of address is much the same, but in the third it is lower than in the first two. . . .

If the doge is indeed the king, then the difference in form of address is due to some circumstances, or some difference in the purpose of the scribes, or their lack of information concerning the rank of the addresses, such as could occur from the rush of business at any time, as is obvious.[15]

Further east, Rashīd al-Dīn also appears to have heard about the Republics of Italy. "In these cities" he says, "there is no hereditary king. The notables and great ones appoint a pious man of good life and by agreement make him sovereign for a year, and at the end of the year a crier cries out 'whoever has suffered an injustice during this year, let him make his complaint'. All those who have suffered injustice present themselves and absolve him. Then they call in another and make him their ruler. . . . Beyond this country [the neighborhood of Genoa], there is another, called Bologna, and its capital is a great city . . . and beyond that on the seashore is a city called Venice and they have built most of their buildings rising out of the sea. Their ruler also has three hundred galleys. There, too, there is no sovereign established by force or by descent. The merchants of the city appoint by agreement a good and pious man, and set him up as their ruler, and when he dies they choose and set up another."[16]

By Ottoman times, republican institutions were more familiar and perhaps better understood. The Ottoman Empire maintained extensive relations with the Republics of Ragusa on the Dalmatian coast, Venice, Genoa, and other Italian states and later, also, with the United States of the Netherlands. The form of address, however, is still normally personal. The head of the Republic of Ragusa, who used the title "rector," is addressed in Ottoman documents with the Slavic word *knez,* sometimes in the form "to the knez and knights of Ragusa" or "to the knez and merchants of Ragusa." Similarly, in letters to Venice or discussions of Venetian affairs, Ottoman writers normally speak of the doge or the signoria, (Venedik Beyleri), rather than of the republic.

Kâtib Çelebi, writing, in 1655 was even able to distinguish between the oligarchic republic of Venice and the democratic republics of the Netherlands and of Cromwell's England, as well as to give a brief account of electoral procedures.

In matters of the organization of government, he says, the states of Europe are divided into three schools, or *madhhab,* each founded by a highly regarded sage; they are called *monarchia,* founded by Plato, *aristocratia,* founded by Aristotle, and *democratia,* founded by Democritus. Monarchy means that all the people obey a single wise and just ruler. This system is followed by most of the rulers of Europe. In *aristocratia* the conduct of government is in the hands of the notables who are independent in most matters but choose one of their number as chief. The state of Venice is organized on this principle. In the third, *democratia,* the conduct of government is in the hands of the subjects *(reaya),* who in this way are able to protect themselves from tyranny. They proceed by election so that the people of every village choose one or two men whom they judge to be wise and competent and send them to the place of government where they form a council and choose leaders among themselves. This is the system followed by the Dutch and the English.

Kâtib Çelebi gives a brief description of the various councils *(Divan)* in Venice and even of voting procedures. Each council member has in his hand two balls like buttons, one white and one black. They are called *ballotta.* After discussion in the Divan, those who sit there indicate their wishes by dropping these black or white balls.[17]

An early eighteenth-century writer on the affairs of Europe even attempts an explanation of the term republic *(jumhūr),* which is used of Venice, Holland, and other republics. "In such a state" he says "there is no single ruler, but all affairs are dealt with by the agreement of its leading men; and these leading men are elected by the choice of the populace." The same author defines Switzerland as "associated republics", each canton being a separate republic. This term, he says, is also used of Holland, but with a slightly different system, being rather a *stadt,* in which the leading men indeed make the decisions but one man is entrusted with the task of applying them. Poland, he notes with some justification, is at the same time both a kingdom and a republic.[18]

By the eighteenth century, even such curiously European institutions as free cities are noted by Ottoman visitors. Mehmed Efendi, visiting Toulouse and Bordeaux on his way to Paris, describes them as free *(serbest)* cities, in that the city was garrisoned by its own locally raised troops and administered by a *parlement* headed by a *president*. Both words are given in French, in Turco-Arabic transcription.[19] The author of the early eighteenth-century survey of the conditions of Europe uses the same term, "free," to describe the port of Danzig, which enjoyed exemption from both imperial authority and taxation. Another eighteenth-century author, describing the structure of the holy Roman empire, uses the terms "free" and even "republic" to describe such privileged entities within the empire as Swabia.[20] Some Ottoman visitors to Hungary even talk of how the Hungarians lament the loss of their former liberties.

The perception of republican institutions entered a new phase after the French Revolution, when the Ottoman Empire had to deal not only with the new republic in France but also with other republics, some of them on the borders of Turkey, that were formed on the French model. While France and Turkey were at war, the communication of French ideas to the Turks was somewhat impeded. Nevertheless, the speed and ease with which an army of fewer than 30,000 Frenchmen was able to conquer and hold Egypt for over three years made a deep impression. So, too, did the tolerance and justice of French rule. These are noted among other things by an Egyptian historian, Jabartī, who in several historical works preserves a contemporary record of the impressions made on a member of the Egyptian ulema class by the French occupiers of Egypt.

By the peace of 1802, France withdrew from both Egypt and the Ionian islands, and a new Ottoman ambassador Halet Efendi was sent to Paris, where he stayed until 1806. His comments are instructive:

> Since the French had no king, they could have no government. Furthermore, as a result of the interregnum which had occurred, most of the high positions are held by the scum of the people and although a few nobles remain, effective power is still in the hands of the vile rabble. They were, thus, unable to organize even a republic. Since they are no more than an association of revolutionaries or, in plain Turkish, a pack of dogs, it is in no way possible for any nation to expect loyalty or friendship from these people. Napoleon is a mad dog, striving to reduce all states to the same disorder as his own accursed nation . . . Talleyrand is a spoilt priest . . . and the rest are mere brigands. . . .[21]

On 29th May, 1807, the first great reforming sultan, Selim III, was deposed and the triumph of the reactionary forces was celebrated with a massacre of the partisans of reform. A year or two after these events, Ahmed Asim Efendi, the imperial historiographer, wrote a chronicle of the years 1791–1808 which conveys some impression of the reform movement in general and of the effect of French influence in particular. Asim was, on the whole, in favor of the reforms, which he hoped would restore the failing military strength of the empire and enable it to confront its enemies. In an interesting passage, he cites the example of Russia which, he says, emerged from weakness and barbarism and became a great power by adopting Western sciences and techniques. But his readiness to accept Western methods does not prevent him from being anti-Christian and from considering all the Christian powers as enemies of Islam. In his view; nothing but evil could arise from agreements with these powers. He is particularly hostile to the French and derides the pro-French element in Turkey as deluded fools. He has little to say about the internal affairs of France, and that is negative. The French Republic, he says, was "like the rumblings and crepitations of a queasy stomach." Its principles consisted of "the abandonment of religion and the equality of rich and poor."[22]

One of the most incomprehensible of Western institutions for the Muslim observer was the elected representative assembly. Kâtib Çelebi, as we have seen, offers a few notes on republican and democratic institutions, but his information is scanty, and his treatise on Europe was in any case little known. Other Ottoman writers have virtually nothing to say on the subject, and occasional brief references to elected bodies in Italy, France, the Netherlands, or elsewhere show little interest or understanding.

The first attempt at a description is that of Abū Ṭālib Khān who visited England at the end of the eighteenth century. Even he, in the course of a long and, in general, factual and friendly account of the British political system discusses the officers of state and their functions at some length, but makes only two brief references to the House of Commons, which he visited in the company of English friends.

In the first, after remarking somewhat unkindly that the orating members reminded him of a flock of parrots in India, he observes that the Commons serve a threefold purpose—to facilitate the collection of taxes for the State, to preserve contractors from error, and in the third place to exercise supervision of the affairs of the sovereign and the ministers and matters in general.[23] In a second passage Abū Ṭālib comments briefly on the members of the House of Commons, their manner of election, and the range of duties and functions assigned to them. Among these, he notes with some astonishment, are the fixing of penalties for wrongdoers and the establishment of laws, this being necessary since, unlike the Muslims, they possess no divine law revealed from heaven and are therefore obliged to make their own laws in accordance with the necessities of time and circumstance, the state of affairs, and the experience of judges.[24]

In this reference to the legislative function of Parliament, Abū Ṭālib touches on one of the profounder differences between Islam and Christendom. For the believing Muslim, there is no human legislative power. God is the sole source of law which He promulgates through revelation. The divine law—in Arabic *sharīʿa*—regulates all aspects of human life. Earthly powers have no right to abrogate or even to modify the law. Their duty is to maintain and enforce it, no more. The only latitude left, in principle, is that of interpretation, and this is the task of the qualified interpreters, the doctors of the holy law. In practice, the situation was somewhat different from the theory. In a wide range of matters, the prescriptions of the holy law were disregarded, either tacitly or through ingenious reinterpretation. And as changing circumstances made the holy law either inappropriate or inadequate, it was in fact supplemented or modified by customary law or simply by the will of the ruler. But all this was practice, not theory. In principle, God was the sole legislator. Human authorities could do no more than interpret, regulate, and enforce.

Some early Muslim references to Christian practice assume a similar view on the Christian side and even go so far as to speak of "the *sharīʿa* of the Christians," which is seen as analogous to that of the Muslims. But in time it came to be understood that the Christian world had a different concept of the nature of law and a different way of perceiving and applying justice.

Not surprisingly, early Muslim references to European judicial procedures are hostile or, rather, contemptuous. For example, a medieval visitor to central Europe has a description of trial by ordeal in its various forms:

> They have strange customs. For example, if one of them accuses another of falsehood, they are both tested by the sword. This happens as follows: the two men, the accuser and the accused, go forth with their brothers and their clients, and each of them is given two swords, one of which he girds about his waist and the other he holds in his hands. Then he that is accused of falsehood swears by such oaths as are esteemed among them that he is guiltless of the charge brought against him; the other swears that what he said was true. Then they both kneel, a short distance apart, facing towards the east. Then each goes up against his adversary, and they fight until one of them is killed or disabled.
>
> Another of their strange customs is the ordeal by fire. If a man is accused in matters of property or of blood, they take a piece of iron, heat it in the fire, and recite something from the Torah and something from

the Gospels over it. Then they fix two upright sticks in the ground, take the iron out of the fire with tongs, and place it on the ends of the two sticks. Then the accused comes, washes his hands, picks up the piece of iron, and walks with it three paces. Then he drops it, and his hand is bound with a bandage and marked with a seal, and he is kept under surveillance for a night and a day. If on the third day they find a blister from which liquid comes forth, then he is guilty, and if not, then he is innocent.

Another of their customs is the ordeal by water. This means that the accused is bound hand and foot, and he is secured with a rope. If he floats, he is guilty, if he sinks, he is innocent, for they consider that the water has accepted him.

Only slaves are tested by water and fire. As regards free men, if they are accused in matters of property worth less than 5 dinars, the two parties go forth with sticks and shields and fight until one of them is disabled. If one of the parties is a woman or a cripple or a Jew, he appoints a deputy for 5 dinars. If the accused falls, he must inevitably be crucified, and all his possessions taken. His opponent receives 10 dinars from his property.[25]

This passage is quoted by Qazvīnī from ʿUdhrī and, therefore, probably forms part of the report of Ibrāhīm ibn Yaʿqūb.

Usāma ibn Munqidh, a Syrian contemporary of the Crusaders, gives an eyewitness description of an encounter in the Crusader-occupied town of Nabulus in Palestine:

One day in Nabulus I saw one of their ordeals by battle. The cause of this was that some Muslim bandits had raided one of the villages of Nabulus, and they had accused one of the peasants of having guided the bandits to this village. He fled, but the king had the man's children arrested, so he came back and said: "Give me justice, I challenge the man who said that I guided the bandits to the village." Then the king said to the lord who held that village in fief: "Bring someone to fight him." So he went to the village and there he found a blacksmith, and ordered him to fight; for the fiefholder wished to safeguard his peasants lest any of them be killed and his husbandry suffer.

I saw this blacksmith. He was a powerful young man, but without stomach for the fight. He would walk a little, then sit down and ask for something to drink. The challenger was an old man, but he was stout of heart, defiant and unconcerned. The viscount, who was the provost of the place, came and gave each one of them a cudgel and a shield, and placed the people round them in a ring. Then they met, and the old man pressed the blacksmith, and forced him back to the ring of spectators, and then he returned to the center. They went on striking one another until they looked like pillars of blood. This went on for some time, and the viscount hurried them on with cries of "make haste." The blacksmith profited from his experience in wielding the hammer, and the old man was weakening. Then the smith struck him a blow that felled him, and his cudgel fell under his back. Then the smith knelt on him and tried to put his fingers in his eyes, but he could not do so because of the great flow of blood from his eyes. So he stood up and beat his head with his cudgel until he killed him. Then he tied a rope round the dead man's neck and dragged him away and hanged him. The lord of the blacksmith came and gave him his own cloak, mounted him on the crupper of his horse, and rode away.

This is an example of their jurisprudence and legal procedure, may God curse them."[26]

It is easy to understand the contempt of a civilized Muslim, accustomed to the orderly procedure of a Qadi's court, for this kind of law and justice. But European legal procedures did not remain at the level of ordeal by battle, and later Muslim observers, who had the opportunity to observe them more closely, are somewhat more positive in their comments. As early as the twelfth century, Ibn Jubayr, a Spanish Muslim visitor to Syria, noted that the Franks treated their conquered Muslim subjects with justice, and he found this a cause of disquiet. Similar feelings are expressed at the end of the eighteenth century by the Egyptian historian Jabartī who, describing the French forces occupying his country, admires their disciplined restraint in dealing with the civil population and their submission of their own authority to judicial rules and procedures in contrast to the arbitrary and capricious despotisms to which he was accustomed. He was particularly struck by the way the French military authorities tried the Muslim assassin of General Kléber, Bonaparte's successor as commander in chief of the French forces in Egypt.

The French, he says, printed a full report of the trial in three languages, French and Turkish as well as Arabic. He would have preferred to omit it since it was very long and written in bad Arabic but decided that many of his readers would wish to know about it, not only for the information it provided about the actual event but also for the light that it would throw on the way the French administered justice and the way "the rules are enforced by this people, which follows no religion but which rules and judges by reason." The case, he remarks, is instructive: "A harebrained stranger from a far place treacherously attacked and killed their chief and they caught him red-handed. Yet they did not hasten to kill him or kill those whom he named, even though they caught him with the murder weapon in his hand, still dripping with the blood of their commander in chief. Instead, they set up a tribunal and conducted a trial to which they brought the killer and interrogated him both verbally and by torture. Then they brought those whom he had denounced and questioned them separately and together. Then they gave judgment upon them in accordance with their legal procedure and they released Muṣṭafā Efendi al-Bursali, the calligrapher, since there was no case against him." Jabartī is clearly deeply impressed by the insistence of the French on due process of law and by their readiness to acquit and release one of the accused against whom there was insufficient evidence. With obvious bitterness, he contrasts this with "the misdeeds which we later saw committed by ruffianly soldiers who claimed to be Muslims and pretended to be warriors in a holy war but killed people and destroyed human beings for no other reason than to gratify their animal passions."[27]

Not all Muslim observers were as admiring of Western judicial procedures. Abū Ṭālib Khan, who had the misfortune to be prosecuted by a tailor in London for ten shillings and ordered by a judge to pay this sum with a further fine of six shillings for not having obeyed the summons, had a somewhat less favorable view. He was not impressed by the jury system since jurors could easily be browbeaten by the judge, forced to adopt his opinion, or sent back to reconsider their verdict. Nor was that all. If these measures failed, the judges had the power to lock up the jury, without food, while they and the lawyers retired to another part of the courthouse to dine and wine lavishly at government expense. Even more disturbing than the jurors for Abū Ṭālib were the advocates, engaged in a profession alien to Islamic judicial procedures. Abū Ṭālib concedes that the English judges are "honorable and God-fearing, and protected against the cunning of the lawyers," but notes that nevertheless the long duration and high cost of English law suits often results in a denial of justice to a plaintiff. Even well intentioned judges may allow lawyers to confuse the issue and intimidate witnesses. He observes that often the rule of law transgresses against the dictates of natural justice, and even a God-fearing judge cannot give an equitable decision without himself violating this man-made law.[28]

In general, however, those Muslims who took the trouble to observe European judicial and legislative procedures were favorably impressed by them. The Egyptian Sheikh Rifā'a, who was in Paris from 1826 to 1831, even took the trouble to translate the full text of the French constitution.

Sheikh Rifā'a was not entirely taken in by the French doctrine of equality which, he noted, did not extend to economic matters: "Equality exists among them only in their words and their actions but not in their possessions. True, they do not refuse their friends, provided that they ask them for a loan and not a gift, and even then only if they are sure of being repaid." Sheikh Rifāʿa notes in passing that the French "are nearer to avarice than to generosity . . . in fact generosity belongs to the Arabs." He was, however, impressed by the French principle of equality before the law, and quotes this as "one of the clearest proofs of the attainment of a high degree of justice among them and of their advancement in the civilized arts. That which they call freedom and strive to attain is the same as that which we call justice and equity, and this is because the meaning of the rule of freedom is the establishment of equality before the law. . . ." Sheikh Rifāʿa was particularly struck by the existence of fixed laws, and draws attention to the significance of the constitutional guarantees of liberty and equality before the law, and the provision for an elected legislative chamber to make the laws.[29]

It was this last aspect—constitutional and parliamentary government—that came more and more to obsess the minds of visitors to Europe from the Muslim east, to a greater extent, in the beginning, than even economic development. It was here that many of them hoped to find the key with which to unlock the secrets of Western progress and share the benefits of Western wealth and power.

I X
Science and Technology

The great age of classical Muslim science was initiated by translations and adaptations of Persian, Indian and, above all, Greek scientific works. Though the translation movement came to an end in the eleventh century, the development of Islamic science continued for some time beyond that. Muslim scientists added greatly to the material transmitted to them, through their own researches and through practical experiments and observations in fields as diverse as medicine, agriculture, geography, and warfare. Of the external influences which, through translation or otherwise, contributed to the development of Islamic science, that of the Greeks is overwhelmingly the most important. There were, however, others, some of them substantial. Indian mathematics and astronomy, and especially positional notation—the so-called Arabic numerals which were, in fact, Indian—are of crucial significance. In addition, the Mongol invasions brought the Islamic world for the first time into direct relationship with China, and some elements of Far Eastern culture and science also began to affect Muslim practice and, to a lesser extent, Muslim thought.

The influence of the West in this period was virtually nil—perhaps for the very good reason that the West had so little to offer. So far only one Arabic text of scientific content based on a west European original has come to light. It is a Judeo-Arabic version—that is to say in the Arabic language but in the Hebrew script—of a set of astronomic tables showing the movement of the planets, apparently based on a book of tables from Novara, Italy, completed in 1327 A.D.[1] Though written in Arabic, it would have been inaccessible to Muslim Arabs who did not know the Hebrew script, and was clearly intended for the use of Jewish scientists. This prefigures a fairly common phenomenon in the late medieval and early modern centuries when Jewish scientists, and in particular Jewish physicians, formed virtually the only channel through which Western scientific knowledge penetrated to the Islamic world.

The twelfth-century Syrian writer, Usāma ibn Munqidh, gives us a vivid account of the impression made on the Muslim world by the medieval European practice of medicine:

> The Lord of Munaytira [a neighboring Crusader Baron] wrote to my uncle asking him to send a physician to treat one of his companions who was sick. He sent him a [Syrian] Christian physician called Thābit. He had hardly been away for ten days, when he returned, and we said to him: "How quickly you have healed the sick!" and he replied: "They brought me two patients, a knight with an abscess on his leg, and a woman afflicted with a mental disorder. I made the knight a poultice, and the abscess burst and he felt better. I put the woman on a diet and kept her humour moist. Then a Frankish physician came to them and said to them: "This man knows nothing about how to treat them!" Then he said to the knight: "Which do you prefer, to live with one leg or to die with two?' and the knight said: "To live with one." Then the physician said: "Bring me a strong knight and a sharp ax," and they brought them. Meanwhile I stood by. Then he put the sick man's leg on a wooden block and said to the knight: "Strike his leg with the ax and cut it off with one blow!" Then, while I watched, he struck one blow, but the leg was not severed; then he struck a second blow, and the marrow of the leg spurted out, and the man died at once.
>
> The physician then turned to the woman, and said: "This woman has a devil in her head who has fallen in love with her. Shave her hair off." So they shaved her head, and she began once again to eat their usual diet, with garlic and mustard and such like. Her disorder got worse, and he said: "The devil has entered her head." Then he took a razor, incised a cross on her head and pulled off the skin in the middle until the bone of the skull appeared; this he rubbed with salt, and the woman died forthwith.
>
> Then I said to them: "Have you any further need of me?" and they said no and so I came home, having learned things about their medical practice which I did not know before."[2]

Usāma's uncle would naturally have sent a local Christian physician rather than ask a Muslim to venture himself into Frankish hands. The Syrian Christian shared the disdain which the Muslim disciples of Galen and Hippocrates must have felt for the backward and barbarous practices of the Frankish doctors. Usāma also noted a couple of cases in which Frankish medical treatments worked. Of one of them, a prescription for scrofula, Usāma observes that the Frankish physician first required his patient to swear a Christian oath that he would not himself prescribe this medicine to others, for money. In general, his view of the Franks is remarkably negative.

Only in one area did the medieval Muslims show any respect for the achievements of the Crusaders, and that is in the arts of war. Muslim practice in weaponry and, still more, in fortification shows signs of Frankish influence both through the adaptation of Frankish models and the employment of Frankish prisoners of war.

By Ottoman times, the importance of mastering the Frankish art of war was becoming painfully obvious. This was particularly so in the artillery and in the navy. Though gunpowder had been invented centuries earlier in China, the dubious credit for recognizing and realizing its military potential belongs to Christian Europe. The Muslim lands were at first reluctant to accept this new device. It would appear that guns were used in the defense of Aleppo when it was besieged by Tamerlane, but in general the Mamluks of Egypt and Syria rejected a weapon which they found unchivalrous and which they realized to be destructive of their social order. The Ottomans were much quicker to appreciate the value of firearms, and it was largely thanks to their use of musketry and cannon that they were able to defeat their two major Muslim rivals, the sultan of Egypt and the shah of Persia. The effective use of cannon played an important part in the conquest of Constantinople in 1453 and in other victories won by the Ottomans over both their European and their Muslim adversaries. Significantly, the majority of their gun-founders and gunners were European renegades or adventurers. While the Ottomans were well able to deploy this new weapon, they continued to rely on outsiders for the science and even the technology needed to produce it. Much the same is true of the related corps of bombardiers and sappers. The inevitable result was that, with the passage of time, the Ottoman artillery fell steadily behind that of their European rivals.

The Ottoman interest in guns and mines was paralleled by their concern to keep up with European shipbuilding and navigation. When a Venetian war galley ran aground in Turkish waters, Ottoman naval engineers examined it with great interest and wished to incorporate several features of its construction and armament in their own ships. The question was put to the chief Mufti of the capital—is it licit to copy the devices of the infidels in such matters? The reply came that in order to defeat the infidel it is permissible to imitate the weapons of the infidel.

The question raised is an important one. In the Muslim tradition, innovation is generally assumed to be bad unless it can be shown to be good. The word *bidʿa,* innovation or novelty, denotes a departure from the sacred precept and practice communicated to mankind by the Prophet, his disciples, and the early Muslims. Tradition is good and enshrines God's message to mankind. Departure from tradition is therefore bad, and in time the word *bidʿa,* among Muslims, came to have approximately the same connotation as heresy in Christendom.

A particularly objectionable kind of *bidʿa* is that which takes the form of imitating the infidel. According to a saying ascribed to the Prophet, "whoever imitates a people becomes one of them." This has been taken to mean that adopting or imitating practices characteristic of the infidel amounts in itself to an act of infidelity and consequently a betrayal of Islam. This dictum and the doctrine which it expresses were frequently invoked by Muslim religious authorities to oppose and denounce anything which they saw as an imitation of Europe and, therefore, as a compromise with unbelief. It was a powerful argument in the hands of the religious conservatives, and was frequently used by them to block such westernizing innovations as technology, printing, and even European style medicine.

There was, however, one important exception to this doctrine— warfare. The jihād, the holy war against the unbelievers, was one of the basic collective obligations of the Muslim state and community. When the war is defensive, it becomes an individual obligation of every Muslim. To strengthen the arms of the Muslims and make them more effective in waging jihād against the unbelievers is, therefore, in itself of religious merit and is, indeed, an obligation. To fight against the unbeliever, it may be necessary to learn from the unbeliever, and Ottoman jurists and other writers on the subject occasionally adduce a principle which they call *al-muqābala biʾl-mithl,* opposing like with like, that is to say fighting the infidel with his own weapons and devices.[3] Proponents of the modernization of warfare were able to find precedents in the sacred past and even in scripture. The Prophet himself, they argued, and the early Muslim warriors were willing to adopt the advanced military techniques of the time, from the Zoroastrian Persians and the Christian Byzantines, in order to fight against them more effectively. Later the armies of the caliphate had adopted Greek fire from the Byzantines, thus anticipating and justifying the subsequent adoption of gunpowder and firearms, also from Christendom. Authority was found even in a verse in the Qur'ān in which the believers are enjoined to "fight the polytheists completely, as they fight you completely."[4] This was reinterpreted to mean that the Muslims should use all weapons, including the weapons of the infidels, in order to defeat them.

On the whole, the Ottomans were willing to follow or adapt European practice in warfare and, more particularly, in artillery and in naval matters, where religious opposition was muted. They also made use of Western technology in mining. The Ottoman territories in southeastern Europe contained important mines for iron and, more especially, silver. The exploitation of these mines was largely in the hands of German experts, employed by the Ottoman state on a profit-sharing basis. They used the mining techniques familiar to them in Germany, and even the laws regulating these Ottoman mines were the Saxon mining laws. These are extant in a Turkish version known as the *Kanun-i Sas*—the Saxon law.[5]

For these and other purposes, the Ottomans were willing to employ European experts in sufficient numbers to form a recognized group in the palace establishment, known as the *Taife-i Efrenjiyan,* the Corps of Franks. The Ottoman sultans and their ministers were well able to see the importance of European technology and to seek out and employ Europeans to serve their needs. But there was always opposition from religious conservatives, and while this was not strong enough to prevent borrowing and some imitation, it was strong enough to prevent the emergence of a vigorous indigenous technology. The sultans had the power and the means to hire technologists from abroad; they did not have the power to produce their own technologists from the ulema-dominated educational system.

Despite their difficulties, the Ottomans were far better placed than other Islamic states. The Ottoman sultans and ministers could at least see the importance of Western technology, and for a while were even able to foster some limited measure of technological innovation. In the great centuries, the Ottomans were not only able to keep up with the most advanced European weapons, but at times even to improve on them through inventions and innovations of their own. Some European observers of the sixteenth and seventeenth centuries comment on the speed with which the Ottomans adapted, and sometimes modified, European weapons and munitions. As late as the second Turkish siege of Vienna in 1683, some contemporary Austrian observers noted that the Turkish muskets were as good as those of the Austrians and, in some respects, in range for example, even better. But the continued dependence on external skills and experts took its toll. The Ottomans found it more and more difficult to keep up with the rapidly advancing Western technological innovations, and in the course of the eighteenth century the Ottoman Empire, itself far ahead of the rest of the Islamic world, fell decisively behind Europe in virtually all the arts of war.[6]

The stages of change can be seen most clearly in the contrast between the Muslim and European fleets. As long as Ottoman naval operations were confined to the Mediterranean they managed to keep pace fairly well with European shipbuilding and navigation. In the early seventeenth century, with the extension of Ottoman power and influence into the western Mediterranean, they came into more direct contact with the Atlantic maritime powers. They were greatly helped in this by an important change in western Europe. After the death of Queen Elizabeth of England in 1603, the new King James I made peace with Spain, and by the treaty of 1604 the long maritime war between the two countries came to an end. About the same time, the Spanish struggle with the Netherlands ended, and in 1609 Spain recognized the independence of the Dutch. The many English and Dutch sea rovers, who had been so important in the struggle of both peoples against Spain, now became not only redundant but dangerous, and the English, Dutch, and other Western governments abandoned their previous tolerance and began to act with increasing severity against their own pirates. Many of these, finding conditions at home less favorable to the exercise of their profession, sacrificed their faith to their trade and fled to the Barbary Coast, where they received a ready welcome. West European pirates, accustomed to navigating the oceans on square-rigged sailing ships with their armaments disposed along their sides, introduced these vessels to their hosts and instructed them in their construction and use. The corsairs, quick to realize the advantage of the broadside over the meager armament of the galley, soon mastered the arts of navigation and warfare with these new vessels, and before long fleets from North Africa were sailing past the Straits of Gibraltar and ravaging as far away as Madeira, the British Isles, and beyond.

For a while the Muslim fleets were as good as, or better than, the Christian. But the advantage was gradually lost, and without the steady flow of refugees and of renegades to restore and maintain their standards, they began to fall behind. Ottoman and North African naval construction failed to keep pace with the major developments that took place in Europe in the seventeenth and eighteenth centuries, and by the late eighteenth century the Ottomans, for so long self-sufficient in armaments, found themselves obliged to place orders for ships in foreign shipyards. It was a portentous change.

Apart from weaponry and seafaring, there was one other useful art in which Europe was seen as able to make some contribution. This was in the science of medicine. By the fifteenth and sixteenth centuries, things had changed very radically since the days when Crusaders sought the help of Muslim or eastern Christian and Jewish physicians. By now it was Europe that was advancing, Islam that was falling back. The intimate and personal character of the services rendered by physicians gave to medical innovation an attraction lacking in the more public and impersonal branches of European science and technology. In medicine it was the individual welfare, and perhaps even the survival, of the patient that was at stake. As in other times and places, in seeking out the best doctors available self-interest was able to triumph over even the most extreme bigotry. All the same, however, it was not unresisted and the more conservative practitioners of traditional medicine fought back.

At first the penetration of European medicine into the Ottoman realms was due largely, if not entirely, to non-Muslims—mainly to Jews and occasionally to Christians. In the fifteenth century, Mehmed the Conqueror drew on the services of a Jewish physician from Italy, Giacomo di Gaeta, who later, as a convert to Islam, became Yaqub Pasha. By the sixteenth century, Jewish physicians, most of them of Spanish, Portuguese and Italian origin, were common in the Ottoman empire. Not only the sultans, but also many of their subjects had recourse to these physicians, whom they recognized as representing a higher level of medical knowledge. Temporary visitors from the Christian West remark, usually with disapproval, on the role played by these Jewish physicians, and especially on their influence at the Ottoman court. Some of these visitors deride the Jewish doctors for their poor knowledge of Latin and Greek, and their failure to keep up with Western medical science, then advancing rapidly.[7] Others note that they include some who are "well learned in theory and experienced in practice"[8] and familiar with standard medical and related literature in Greek as well as in Arabic and Hebrew.

Some of these Jewish doctors even went so far as to prepare treatises which they either wrote or had translated into Turkish for the use of their royal and other patients. One such little book, entitled *Asa-i Piran,* The Staff of the Old, discusses the illnesses to which old men are subject and offers advice for their prevention and cure. The author seems to have been a certain Manuel Brudo, sometimes called Brudus Lusitanus, i.e., Brudo the Portuguese, a crypto-Jew who left Portugal in the 1530s. He first went to London, then moved to Antwerp and then to Italy and finally settled in Turkey where he openly reverted to Judaism. Apart from medical advice, the book includes a number of observations drawn from the author's experience in various European countries. He notes, for example, how the English cook eggs and fish, and what firewood Londoners use in winter to get rid of dampness. He discusses the English and German habits of eating fresh butter and eggs for breakfast and the custom of serving cooked prunes before meals as a laxative. He disapproves the Christian practice of lunching at noon and commends Muslim wisdom in eating early in the morning. His book appears to have been written for Süleyman the Magnificent.[9]

Manuel Brudo was one of a number of Jewish doctors of European origin who entered the sultan's service. These became so important that the Ottoman palace archives indicate the existence of two separate corps of court physicians, one Muslim and the other Jewish. It may be assumed that the Muslims continued to practice according to the medical traditions of medieval Islam while the Jews, to a greater or lesser extent, followed the practice of Europe, probably with a steadily increasing time lag as contact was lost with their countries of origin and with European science. Other works of Jewish authorship of this time include a short Turkish treatise on dentistry written by Moses Hamon, a Jew of Andalusian origin who was appointed chief Jewish physician to Sultan Süleyman the Magnificent.[10] This would appear to be the first Turkish work on dentistry and probably one of the first published anywhere. Another book of the period is a brief treatise on pharmaceutical compounds written by a physician who modestly calls himself Musa Jalinus al-Isra'ili, i.e., Moses the Jewish Galen. The author indicates that his treatise is based on Muslim, Frankish, Greek, and Jewish writings.

Several of these Jewish doctors played a political role of some importance. Their access to the persons of sultans and viziers on the one hand, and their knowledge of European languages and conditions on the other, made them useful to both Turkish rulers and foreign envoys, and enabled some of them to achieve positions of power and influence. Some were even sent on diplomatic missions abroad.

By the following century, Ottoman doctors had a new and painful reason for paying attention to European medical skills. This was a previously unknown ailment which came to them from the West, and to which therefore they gave the name which it still retains in most Muslim countries—Firengi, the Frankish disease. The first Turkish treatise on syphilis, part of a collection of medical writings presented to Sultan Mehmed IV in 1655, is based largely on the famous work of

Girolamo Fracastro of Verona (1483–1553), and also includes some borrowings from Jean Fernel (d. 1558) on the treatment of this disease. Other parts of this work dealing with other diseases quote the names of several well-known European physicians of the sixteenth century. The book indicates some acquaintance with European medicine, and it is even possible that the author was able to read Latin or at least had someone at his disposal to render him this service. But the difference in approach is already noticeable. Though the collection was presented to the sultan in 1655, the European works cited in it all belong to the sixteenth century.[11] The Jewish doctors who came from Europe in the sixteenth century represented the highest level of sixteenth-century European medicine. The Ottoman Jewish doctors of the seventeenth century still represented the highest level of European medicine—of the sixteenth century. The renewal of contact through the training of Ottoman Greek physicians in Italian schools from the mid-seventeenth century onwards does not seem to have brought any fundamental change in this relationship. The leisurely pace and timeless framework of Ottoman scientific writing had already given rise to a serious time lag between Western and Ottoman science. It was to become much wider.

From these occasional Ottoman references to Western science, it is clear that they did not think in terms of the progress of research, the transformation of ideas, the gradual growth of knowledge. The basic ideas of forming, testing and, if necessary, abandoning hypotheses remained alien to a society in which knowledge was conceived as a corpus of eternal verities which could be acquired, accumulated, transmitted, interpreted, and applied but not modified or transformed. Their works on medical and other sciences consist mostly of compilations, adaptations, and interpretations of the corpus of classical Islamic learning preserved in Persian and, more especially, Arabic, sometimes supplemented by material derived from Western scientific writings but similarly treated. There is no attempt to follow new discoveries and little awareness even of the existence of such a process. The great changes in anatomy and physiology occurring at that time pass unnoticed and unknown.

According to Muslim belief there was, in the early days of Islam, a rule called *ijtihād,* the exercise of independent judgment, whereby Muslim scholars, theologians, and jurists were able to resolve problems of theology and law for which scripture and tradition provided no explicit answer. A large part of the corpus of Muslim theology and jurisprudence came into being in this way. In due course the process came to an end when all the questions had been answered; in the traditional formulation, "the gate of *ijtihād* was closed" and henceforth no further exercise of independent judgment was required or permitted. All the answers were already there, and all that was needed was to follow and obey. One is tempted to seek a parallel in the development of Muslim science, where the exercise of independent judgment in early days produced a rich flowering of scientific activity and discovery but where, too, the gate of *ijtihād* was subsequently closed and a long period followed during which Muslim science consisted almost entirely of compilation and repetition.

For a while Jewish refugees from Europe seemed about to initiate a new phase in Ottoman medicine. But in fact all they brought were some new details, new information to be added to the corpus and, in time, as they lost their contacts with Europe and became part of Middle Eastern society, the Ottoman Jews ceased to differ in any significant way from their Muslim neighbors.

To some extent, they were replaced by Ottoman Greeks now entering on a period of growth and development. Panagiotis Nicoussias was one of the first Ottoman Greeks to study medicine at the University of Padua, where he qualified in about 1650. After his return to Istanbul, he was so successful as a medical practitioner that he was appointed by the grand vizier Mehmed Köprülü as his personal physician. As had happened with the Jewish physicians in the previous century, the grand vizier came to rely on his Western-educated Greek physician for his knowledge of European conditions. Nicoussias became grand dragoman of the Sublime Porte, possibly the first holder of that important office. He was succeeded after his death in 1673 by another Greek doctor from Padua, the Chiote Alexander Mavrocordato, who had published a dissertation on the function of the lungs in the circulation of the blood. He published it, however, in Latin and his work belongs to the history of European not Ottoman medicine. It was as grand dragoman of the Porte that he earned his place in Ottoman history.

The early eighteenth century brought some changes. In 1704, a physician called Ömer Şifai wrote a little book on the use of chemistry in medical treatment, which he presents as a translation from Paracelsus. At about the same time, another Ottoman physician, a Cretan Greek convert to Islam called Nuh ibn Abdulmennan, translated another book on medical treatment. A third doctor of the time, Şaban Şifai, a teacher at the medical school attached to the Süleymaniye Mosque, wrote a treatise dealing with conception and birth and with antenatal and postnatal care. All these works reflect a new type of medical science and also a new approach to medical practice.

Inevitably, such innovations aroused strong resistance and, in 1704 a new decree prohibited the practice of "the new medicine *(Tibb-i Jedid)* by certain ignorant physicians." The decree speaks of "certain pseudo-physicians of the Frankish community who abandoned the way of the old physicians and used certain medicaments known by the name of the new medicine. . . ." The decree required Turkish physicians to submit to an examination and prohibited foreign physicians from practicing. This did not stop Ömer Şifai from continuing his work and writing a treatise in eight volumes on the so-called new medicine. Though the official Ottoman establishment still gave its support to the medicine of Galen and Avicenna, the disciples of Paracelsus were beginning to gather force.[12]

Several of the ambassadors who visited European countries show some interest in science and a little more in technology. Mehmed Efendi commented repeatedly and favorably on the French communications system, on the locks, canals, roads, bridges, and tunnels by which he passed on his way from the south coast to Paris. He was taken to the Observatory where he was much impressed by the wide range of astronomical and other instruments which he saw and the purpose of which he seems to have well understood. He speaks of "numberless machines" for the observation of the stars, "for raising large burdens with ease, for knowing when the moon is new, for raising waters from below above, and other admirable and marvellous things." He also saw concave burning mirrors "as big as one of our large dining trays of Damascus metalwork" where sufficient heat was generated to burn pieces of wood and to melt lead. He goes into some detail on astronomical instruments and, in particular, on a telescope which he greatly admired.[13]

Others were less interested. An example of a different attitude to science and to the gadgets which it produced may be found in the embassy report of Mustafa Hatti Efendi, who went on a mission to Vienna in 1748. While he was there, he and his party were invited to the Observatory to be shown the wonders of science of the day. He was not impressed:

> At the emperor's command we were invited to the Observatory, to see some of the strange devices and wonderful objects kept there. We accepted the invitation a few days later, and went to a seven- or eight-storey building. On the top floor, with a pierced ceiling, we saw the astronomical instruments and the large and small telescopes for the sun, moon, and stars.
>
> One of the contrivances shown to us was as follows. There were two adjoining rooms. In one there was a wheel, and on that wheel were two

large, spherical, crystal balls. To these were attached a hollow cylinder, narrower than a reed, from which a long chain ran into the other room. When the wheel was turned, a fiery wind ran along the chain into the other room, where it surged up from the ground and, if any man touched it, that wind struck his finger and jarred his whole body. What is still more wonderful, is that if the man who touched it held another by the hand, and he another, and so formed a ring of twenty or thirty persons, each of them would feel the same shock in finger and body as the first one. We tried this ourselves. Since they did not give any intelligible reply to our questions, and since the whole thing is merely a plaything, we did not think it worthwhile to seek further information about it.

Another contrivance which they showed us consisted of two copper cups, each placed on a chair, about three ells apart. When a fire was lit in one of them, it produced such an effect on the other, despite the distance, that it exploded as if seven or eight muskets had been discharged.

The third contrivance consisted of small glass bottles which we saw them strike against stone and wood without breaking them. Then they put fragments of flint in the bottles, whereupon these finger-thick bottles, which had withstood the impact of stone, dissolved like flour. When we asked the meaning of this, they said that when glass was cooled in cold water straight from the fire, it became like this. We ascribe this preposterous answer to their Frankish trickery.

Another contrivance consisted of a box, with a mirror inside and two wooden handles outside. When the handles were turned, rolls of paper in the box were revealed in stages, each depicting various kinds of gardens, palaces, and other fantasies painted on them.

After the display of these toys, a robe of honor was presented to the astronomer and money given to the servants of the Observatory.[14]

One may wonder whether European gentlemen and diplomats of the eighteenth century would have been any more responsive to the wonders of science than their Turkish colleague. The significant difference is that the latter expressed the attitude of his society, while they did not.

The Ottomans, no less than other Muslim peoples, despised the barbarous unbelievers to the west of them, but they were prepared to study and borrow some inventions of the ingenious barbarians which might serve their purposes without endangering their way of life. The point was well made by Ghiselin de Busbecq, ambassador of the Holy Roman Empire in Istanbul, in a letter dated 1560:

. . . No nation has shown less reluctance to adopt the useful inventions of others; for example, they have appropriated to their own use large and small cannons and many other of our discoveries. They have, however, never been able to bring themselves to print books and set up public clocks. They hold that their scriptures, that is, their sacred books, would no longer be scriptures if they were printed; and if they established public clocks, they think that the authority of their muezzins and their ancient rites would suffer diminution.[15]

In time the Ottomans gave way on these two points. Printing, as has been seen, was introduced for Turkish and Arabic in the eighteenth century and clocks were imported much earlier and eventually installed even in the Great Imperial Mosques.

The use of devices for measuring the passage of time was by no means new in Islam. On the contrary, starting with the two methods inherited from antiquity, the sundial and the water clock, the Muslims were able to develop an elaborate set of devices of their own. Ottoman interest in European mechanical clocks, production of which in the West began in the fourteenth century, dates from a fairly early period. By the sixteenth century, European clocks and watches were widely used in the Ottoman Empire and even found local imitators. One of the most notable was a Syrian called Taqī al-Dīn (1525–1585), whose treatise on clocks operated by weights and by springs, written in mid-century, is of major importance in the history of this science.

Not all the clocks and watches used in the Ottoman Empire were imports from Europe. From about 1630 to about 1700 there was a guild of watchmakers and clockmakers in the Galata district of Istanbul, whose products were up to the standards of the Swiss and English masters of the craft. These were, however, European emigrés, not local Muslims, and by the end of the seventeenth century, even they were no longer able to maintain themselves. Several factors contributed to their downfall. One was the growing difficulty of obtaining the necessary materials, aggravated by the mercantilist policies of the Western governments and producers, now manufacturing clocks and watches designed for Turkish taste and the Turkish market. Their practice was to export complete clocks and watches; they were no longer willing to provide movements or replacement parts for local watchmakers as they had done previously. Another reason, no doubt, was the steady improvement in pendulum-clocks and spring-driven watches in Europe, with which the Istanbul-based clockmakers were not able to keep pace. By the early years of the eighteenth century, watchmaking in Turkey virtually came to an end. One of the last Western watchmakers to go to Turkey was Isaac Rousseau, the father of the philosopher Jean-Jacques Rousseau, who remarks in his confessions that "my father, after the birth of my only brother, set off for Constantinople where he had received the appointment of watchmaker to the Seraglio."

By an odd coincidence, Voltaire too had a connection with the

Turkish market for watches. As squire of Ferney he made some effort to help the people of his estate, including a group of some fifty religious refugees from Geneva. These happened to be watchmakers, and Voltaire set to work to find new markets for them. In a letter written to Frederick the Great in 1771, Voltaire notes that Turkey was the perfect market: "It is now sixty years since they have been importing watches from Geneva, and they are still not able to make one, or even to regulate it."[16]

Besides clocks and watches, there was another European device which some Middle Easterners found useful. As far east as Iran, and as early as 1480, a poet, lamenting the onset of old age, notes among other infirmities that

> My two eyes now serve no purpose at all
> unless with the aid of Frankish glasses (Firangī shīsha) they become four.

The importation of glasses made in Europe seems to have continued on a small scale, and there are occasional references to their purchase and use.[17]

The system of filtration, designed to exclude those imports which might have threatened the traditional way of life, remained effective against the more dangerous penetration of ideas—of the Western conceptions of inquiry and discovery, experimentation and change which underlay both the science of the West and the technology to which it gave rise. The products of Western technology might, after due consideration, be admitted; the knowledge achieved by Western science might in certain cases be applied; but that was the limit of their acceptance.

The question arose again in an acute form in the eighteenth century, when a series of defeats in the battlefield convinced the Ottoman governing elite that the Christian enemies of the empire had somehow managed to achieve superiority in the arts of war and that changes were necessary to restore Ottoman power. Their feelings are well expressed in a memorandum written by one Janikli Ali Pasha after the crushing Ottoman defeat by the Russians in 1774. Ali Pasha addresses himself to two questions which he tells us had profoundly occupied his thoughts. Why had the empire, which was once so strong, become so weak, and what should be done to restore her former strength? The Turkish soldier, he said, was no less brave than before, the people no fewer, the territories no smaller, and the resources of the empire were still as great. Yet, where once the armies of Islam had invariably put the infidel to flight, it was now the Muslims themselves who were put to flight by the infidel.[18]

Janikli Ali Pasha's remedy was strictly conservative—a return to the good old ways. There were others, however, who saw the problem in the military superiority of the West and the answer in military reform. An important aspect of this was the establishment of training centers in modern warfare.

The new schools of military and naval engineering established in the eighteenth century gave a fresh stimulus to the acceptance and assimilation of at least some aspects of Western science. One of the teachers of the Üsküdar school of engineering established in 1734 was a certain Mehmed Said, the son of an Anatolian Mufti, who is said to have invented a two-part quadrant for the use of gunners and to have written a treatise illustrated with geographical drawings. There are other writings of the period, including a Turkish treatise on trigonometry, apparently based on Western sources, a translation of a well-known treatise on military science by the great Italian soldier Count Montecuccoli, and some medical works.[19]

This first school, and the corps of military engineers established at the same time, were bitterly opposed by the Janissaries, who in due course forced their abandonment. The objective of modernizing the armed forces was not, however, given up, and in 1773 a new start was made with the opening of a naval school of engineering. The teachers of this new school included a number of Europeans. The student body seems to have consisted in the first instance of surviving pupils of the earlier schools, together with some serving officers. A Western artillery officer who helped start the school speaks of his "white bearded captains" and "sixty-year-old pupils."[20]

This time the reactionary forces were not able to procure the closing of the school, which on the contrary grew and served as a model for other schools of military engineering, medicine, and similar matters established by Sultan Selim III and his successors. The Venetian priest, Gianbatista Toderini, who visited Istanbul between 1781 and 1786, described this school in some detail. He found a good number of nautical instruments as well as atlases and European naval charts, a Turkish version of the *Atlas Minor,* a celestial globe showing the constellations with signs and characters in Turkish (the work of a professor of the school), "a metal armillary sphere made in Paris, some Arab astrolabes, some Turkish and Frankish sundials, a very fine English octant made by John Hadley, various Turkish compasses with correction" and other navigational devices.

In a second room, Toderini was shown a "geographical map of Asia", printed on silk, with "a long Turkish legend" saying that it had been translated by Ibrahim Müteferrika in the year 1141 of the *hijra,* i.e. 1728–29, three terrestrial globes of various sizes, a rather fine theodolite from Paris, ancient and modern instruments for measuring distances, a telescopic quadrant, and various trigonometrical tables. Toderini notes that he did not see the model of the machine for installing and removing masts on ships, introduced by Tott. Among many European books, he found the astronomical tables of Monsieur de la Lande, with a Turkish translation. He pointed out to his guide that these were not recent and advised him to procure the latest edition. His guide also showed him Turkish tables on ballistics translated from European books, and codices on the astrolabe, on sundials, on the compass, and on geometry that he used in teaching his pupils.

Toderini's guide was the chief instructor of the school, an Algerian of mature years—"un Algerino uomo maturo"—who spoke Italian, French, and Spanish, and who told him that he had come to Istanbul after having sailed the Mediterranean, the Atlantic, the coasts of the Indies, and even as far as America. He was a skilled helmsman and pilot and expressed a preference for English instruments and French maps.

The pupils of the school, according to what the Algerian professor told the Venetian priest, were more than fifty in number, "sons of sea captains and of Turkish gentlemen" but only a few were assiduous and attentive in their studies.[21]

They became more attentive after the Russian annexation of the Crimea in 1783, which brought home to the Ottomans with a new urgency the nature of the menace that confronted them. In 1784, at the initiative of the grand vizier Halil Hamid Pasha, and with the assistance of the French Embassy, a new training program was initiated with two French engineer officers as instructors working through Armenian interpreters. But this initiative also came to an end when war broke out between the Ottoman Empire and Austria and Russia in 1787. The presence of French instructors being regarded as a breach of neutrality, they were withdrawn. The departure of the instructors and the strains of the war itself hampered progress, until the signing of peace with the empire's northern neighbors in 1792 enabled the new Sultan Selim III to make a fresh start. Again the sultan turned to France and, in the autumn of 1793, he sent to Paris a list of requirements, of officers and technicians whom he wished to employ. In 1795, the Reis Efendi Ratib sent a similar, but longer list, to the Committee of Public Safety in Paris. That it was no longer the king of France but the republic to which these requests were sent and by whom these officers were appointed, did not seem to trouble the sultan at all. In 1796, the new French ambassador, General Aubert du Bayet, a veteran of the American and French revolutions, arrived in Istanbul with a whole group of French military experts.[22] This time several schools were started, for both army and naval officers, offering instruction in gunnery, fortification, navigation, and the ancillary sciences. French officers were requested to serve as instructors and a knowledge of French was made compulsory for students. A library for the use of the trainees contained some 400 European books, most of them French. They included a set of the *Grande Encyclopédie.*

Once again, during the upheavals of the Revolutionary and Napoleonic Wars, these schools ran into difficulties and some were closed down under the pressure of the reactionary forces. When Mahmud II began his reforms in 1826 only two of them were left, the military and naval engineering schools. These were reactivated and others added, notably a Medical School in 1827 and a School of Military Sciences in 1834, intended to serve as the Sandhurst or Saint Cyr of the Ottoman armies. In all these schools, foreigners figured prominently among the teachers and knowledge of a foreign language, normally French, was a requirement for the students.

There was indeed an urgent task for Muslims with a knowledge of Western languages—to study the sciences of the West, to translate or write textbooks in Turkish and, as a prerequisite, to endow the Turkish language with the modern technical and scientific vocabulary which it lacked, and which it needed for this purpose.

Two men played a role of outstanding importance in this work. One was Ataullah Mehmed, known as Şanizade (1769–1826), imperial historiographer from 1819 until his death. By origin and education a member of the Ulema class, he nevertheless seems to have learned at least one Western language and to have made a study of European medicine and other sciences. His most important writing, apart from his history of the empire during the years of his office, is a Turkish translation of an Austrian medical textbook, probably made from an Italian version. Şanizade added an explanatory treatise of his own on physiology and anatomy and, later, another translation of an Austrian work, this time on vaccination. The appearance of this textbook in Turkish marks the end of one era and the beginning of another in Turkish medicine. Hitherto, despite some occasional additions of knowledge or methods from the West, Ottoman medical practice had basically remained faithful to the Hellenistic and classical Islamic tradition, to the medicine of Galen and Avicenna, as Ottoman philosophy and science had to Aristotle and Ptolemy and their commentators, and Ottoman religion had to the Prophet, the Qur'ān, and tradition. The discoveries of Paracelsus and Copernicus, of Kepler and of Galileo, were as alien and as irrelevant to the Ottomans as were the arguments of Luther and Calvin.

Now for the first time, Şanizade had created a modern medical vocabulary in the Turkish language (which was to remain in use until the recent linguistic reforms), and had provided Turkish medical students with a comprehensive textbook of modern medicine which served as the starting point of an entirely new medical literature and practice.

What Şanizade did for medicine, Hoja Ishak Efendi (d. 1834) did for mathematics and physics. A Jew by birth and a native of Greece, Ishak Efendi was at some stage converted to Islam and appointed a teacher at the School of Engineering where, in due course, he became the chief instructor. He is said to have known French, Latin, Greek, and Hebrew as well as Turkish and the two classical Islamic languages, Persian and Arabic. Hoja Ishak Efendi produced a number of works, mostly translations, the most important being a four-volume compendium of the mathematical and physical sciences which for the first time gave the Turkish student an outline of these sciences as practised and understood in the West. Like Şanizade, Hoja Ishak Efendi had to create his own vocabulary, and with him he was the creator of most of the scientific vocabulary used in Turkey in the nineteenth century, and, indeed, until the linguistic reforms undertaken under the Republic. Since the practise of Ottoman scholars of the time was to draw on Arabic, and to a lesser extent Persian, to create new terms, in the same way that European writers drew on Latin and Greek, some of this new vocabulary is still in use in Arab countries. Hoja Ishak Efendi's other writings deal chiefly with the military sciences and engineering.[23]

With the publication of the writings of these two men, the creation of new schools in which their works were used as textbooks, and ultimately, most important of all, the increasing number of students sent to study science in Europe, the old sciences—medicine, mathematics, physics, and chemistry—came to an end. The older sciences lingered on for a while in the remoter lands of Islam, but from this time onwards science means modern Western science. There is no other.

X

Cultural Life

The Nuruosmaniye Mosque stands at the entrance to the great bazaar in Istanbul. Completed in 1755 under the direction of the architect Çelebi Mustafa with a Christian master mason called Simon, it marks a turning point in Islamic cultural evolution. In its general plan, the Nuruosmaniye Mosque, with its single, central dome over a lateral space, remains in the tradition of the great imperial mosques with which the Ottoman Sultans from Mehmed the Conqueror onwards adorned the city of Istanbul. But in the minor architectural features and details there is significant change, clearly reflecting the influence of Italian baroque ornamentation.[1]

Such influences can already be discerned at an earlier date in some of the decoration at the Imperial Palace. The appearance of European influence in something as central to Ottoman Islam as the architecture of an imperial mosque reveals something new in Islam—a faltering of the self-confidence which had hitherto survived all the defeats and retreats which the Christian enemy had inflicted on the Ottoman state. The same feeling of self-doubt is expressed in a saying quoted by the Ottoman ambassador in Paris, Mehmed Efendi, on seeing the beautiful gardens of Trianon, "This world is the prison of the believers and the paradise of the unbelievers."[2]

The first sign of the wave of cultural influence which can be seen in the baroque decoration of the Nuruosmaniye Mosque dates from the early years of the eighteenth century, from the period known in Ottoman annals as *Lale Devri,* the Age of Tulips. This period, beginning with the signature of the Treaty of Passarowitz with Austria in 1718, derives its name from the universal passion for tulips which absorbed Ottoman society at the time. It was an era of peace. The sultan, Ahmed III, and his grand vizier, Damad Ibrahim Pasha, were keenly aware of the new danger that threatened the empire from the north and which had for a time been averted by the signing of the peace. In this situation, they pursued two objectives—to avoid war and to find new friends. The negotiation of the Peace of Carlowitz in 1699 had shown them the way. Threatened by their neighbors in central and eastern Europe, they looked towards western Europe for support and for the first time began to enter into closer relations.

In Ottoman history, the tulip era is seen as an age of peaceful and cultural development and of the opening of new ways. As one might expect, the Ottomans looked in the first instance to the sources of their own civilization and a program was undertaken to produce Turkish translations of some of the major Arabic and Persian classics, not previously available in Turkish.

The extension of this interest to Western writings was more remarkable. Only a few years earlier, in 1716, the grand vizier, Damad Ali Pasha, had died at the battle of Peterwardein, leaving a magnificent library. The chief mufti of the empire, Abu Ishak Ismail Efendi, issued a fetwa prohibiting the consecration of this library as a pious endowment (*waqf*) because it contained books (some of them perhaps in European languages) on philosophy, history, astronomy, and poetry. The books were therefore sent to the Imperial Palace.[3]

Such interest in the West as arose was still limited and practical. Its purpose was to strengthen the empire, the better to resist its enemies. The guidance, or rather information sought from the West was first and foremost military, to be supplemented by such political matters as might be necessary. By this time, however, there was a dawning awareness that some other elements beyond the military and political might be involved. Significantly, in the instructions given to Mehmed Efendi when he left for France in 1721, he was told to "visit fortresses and factories and make a thorough study of the means of civilization and education and report on those capable of application"[4] in Turkey.

Mehmed Efendi's embassy produced some ripples in social and cultural life on both sides. In Paris, the appearance of the Turkish ambassador and his suite started a fashion of *turquerie,* ranging from ladies' fashions to architecture and music, with parallels in other European capitals similarly visited. Less well known is the somewhat smaller wave of French fashions in Istanbul. The effects of this can be seen chiefly in the palaces built by the sultan and his ministers in the tulip era, and, more particularly, in their gardens. Mehmed Efendi expatiates at some length in his embassy report on the gardens of Versailles and elsewhere, which he enormously admired.[5] The influence of the formal French garden with marble fountains surrounded by symmetrically arranged walks and flower beds is clear. Some Western-style furniture, hitherto unknown, was introduced to the palace, mainly, it would seem, for the use of Western guests.

Mehmed Efendi is instructive on the response to the arts:

> The custom among these people is that the king gives ambassadors his own portrait adorned with diamonds, but since pictures are not permitted among Muslims, I was given instead a diamond-studded belt, two rugs made in Paris, a large mirror, a gun and pistols, a casket bound in gilded brass, a gilded brass table-clock, two thick porcelain vases with gilded brass handles for ice, and a sugar bowl.[6]

Mehmed Efendi clearly disapproved—or at least wished to be understood as disapproving—of portraits. His lack of interest in painting is confirmed by his very brief account of the pictures which he was shown in the palace:

> We then began to look at the wonderful pictures which were hanging in the council chamber. We went round with the King, who himself explained who they were.[7]

In contrast, he waxes truly eloquent on the subject of tapestry:

> There is a special factory for making tapestries which belongs to the King. . . . Knowing that an ambassador was coming, they had hung all the tapestries which were ready on the walls. Since the factory is very vast, there must have been more than a hundred pieces hung on the walls. When we saw them, we put the finger of admiration in the mouth. For example, the flowers are worked in such a way that they look like a vase of real flowers. The appearance of the persons depicted, their eyelids, their eyebrows and especially the hair and the beards on their heads are so well portrayed that neither Mani nor Behzad working on the finest Chinese paper could achieve such art. One appears laughing, to show his joy; another sad, to show his sadness. One is shown trembling with fear, another weeping, another stricken by some disease. Thus, at first glance the condition of each person is known. The beauty of these works is beyond description and beyond imagination.[8]

Mehmed Efendi's reactions to realistic art, even that of eighteenth-century Europe, is striking and instructive, as is also the difference in his reactions to portraits and tapestries. Oil paintings hanging on the wall were new and alien, entirely outside his experience. Tapestries (which he calls *kilim*) were related to a familiar form of art and there-fore more readily intelligible. The contrast can be seen in his uninterested dismissal of the one and his enthusiastic response to the other.

European painting, and in particular European portraiture, were not, however, entirely unknown to the Muslim east. There is evidence that Sultan Bayezid II paid some attention to the work of Leonardo da Vinci. It seems, though, to have been the engineer rather than the artist who interested him—and then only in conjunction with a project to build a bridge across the Golden Horn. That project came to nothing, but in Ottoman times increasing numbers of European artists visited Istanbul and other cities.

In the days before photography, European ambassadors and other travelers enjoying sufficient wealth often added an artist to their suites to serve the same purpose as the modern camera. There seemed to be a substantial market in Europe for wall paintings and, more particularly, for prints and book illustrations depicting the wonders of the East.

The presence of these Western artists in their midst did not go wholly unnoticed by the Turks. The Italian painter Gentile Bellini visited Istanbul after the conquest and even painted a portrait of the conqueror. The painter was selected and sent by the Signoria of Venice, allegedly at the request of the sultan. After Mehmed II's death, his very pious son and successor, Bayezid II, disapproving of painting and of portraiture in particular, broke up his father's collection and had the pictures sold in the bazaar. The portrait was acquired by a Venetian merchant and eventually found its way to the National Gallery in London.[9]

A portrait was indeed something new in the Islamic world. The holy law of Islam has been interpreted as banning the representation of the human image. This ban was totally effective against sculpture, which did not begin to penetrate the Islamic world until the late nineteenth century and is still viewed with strong disapproval by purists. Two-dimensional painting was, however, widely practised, especially in the Persian and Turkish lands. It differed from Western painting in two important respects. One was that it was limited in the main to book illustration and miniature, occasionally also to mural painting. The practice of hanging paintings on the wall was Western and was not adopted by Muslims until the late nineteenth century. The other was that the figures depicted in these paintings were mostly literary and historical. Portraiture does occur in classical Islamic art, but it is exceedingly rare and subject to strong disapproval.

The adoption of portrait painting by the Ottoman sultans and their artists is a significant early sign of European influence. The example set by Mehmed the Conqueror was not followed by his immediate successors, but by the sixteenth century the practice became general. A work completed in 1579 even includes an album of portraits of Ottoman sultans. The compiler of the book was the court historian Seyyid Lokman, the artist was the Ottoman court painter Nakkaş Osman; he provided portraits of the twelve sultans who had ruled the Ottomans up to his day. Lokman's introduction indicates that there had been some difficulty in finding portraits of the earlier sultans, and that he and his colleague had had recourse to the work of "Frankish masters." The reference is probably to the engraved portraits—mostly imaginary—which adorned contemporary European books about the Ottoman Empire. The same influence may perhaps be discerned in the care taken to ensure accuracy of portraiture and even in depicting the correct attire for each sultan.[10] The popularity of this book is attested by the large number of copies which survive, and by the appearance of later albums of royal portraits of similar type.

By the seventeenth and early eighteenth centuries, the sultans and even other dignitaries seem to have been ready to pose for portraits. An outstanding European artist of the time was Jean-Baptiste Vanmour (1671–1737) who spent some thirty years in Turkey. Another was Antoine de Favray (1706–1792?), a knight of Malta, who stayed a while in Istanbul as guest of the French ambassador. Many of these artists depict the audiences given by the sultan or grand vizier to the foreign ambassadors, presumably commissioned by the latter. Vanmour also produced prints, for the European market, of the sultan, the grand vizier, and numerous other dignitaries, but it is not clear whether these were posed or not. That some of these paintings by Western artists were in fact commissioned is clear from the collections in the Topkapı Palace.[11]

Of far greater interest, however, than the work of Western artists in the Islamic world is the change discernible in the Islamic artists themselves. Two portraits of Mehmed the Conqueror, still preserved in the palace at Istanbul, seem to be the work of Turkish artists inspired by Italian prototypes. Their style is still Islamic but with clear Western influences, notably in the use of shadow. One of them has been attributed to the first notable Ottoman painter, Sinan, said to have been the pupil of a Venetian master called Paoli.

In the eighteenth century, particularly towards the end of the century, Western influence on Turkish art becomes clear. One reason is certainly the foreign artists employed in and near the Ottoman court. One of them, a Pole called Mecti, was converted to Islam. Several pictures by an Armenian painter called Raphael were seen in the palace by a European visitor between 1781 and 1785. By the end of the eighteenth century, the old artistic tradition was virtually dead, and even book illustrations to Turkish literary works are predominantly \ Jestern in style. The westernization of Turkish art long preceded any Western influences on literature and by even longer those on music.[12]

Western artistic influence was not limited to Turkey but can also be seen in Iran and even further east. One of the outstanding figures in Islamic art is the painter Behzād, who flourished in the late fifteenth and early sixteenth centuries. He formed many pupils who followed his style and together constitute what is known as the School of Herat. There are many paintings of this School, including some portraits of royal persons attributed, on uncertain authority, to Behzād himself. There are very few such portraits in earlier times and the practice of commissioning portraits and sitting for artists is undoubtedly due to the influence of both the manner and organization of European painting. This influence seems to have spread from Turkey to Iran, where, already at the beginning of the sixteenth century, we find a copy made by a Persian artist of a picture by Bellini. This work has been attributed to Behzād, though this attribution is not generally accepted. The significant point is that one of Bellini's Turkish pictures was not only known but copied by a Persian artist.

After the accession of the Safavid dynasty in Iran in 1502, that country developed closer contacts both with the Ottoman Empire and with western Europe, from which many visitors began to arrive in Iranian ports and other cities.[13] One of the early shahs of the line, Ṭahmāsp, was specially interested in painting, and invited the great Behzād to take charge of the royal workshops in Tabriz, a position which he held until his death in 1537. By this time, the export of silks and brocades to Europe was an important source of revenue to the Persian state, and the shahs did what they could to encourage and develop this trade. ʿAbbās I transferred the capital to Isfahan, authorized the establishment of Catholic communities there, and encouraged both diplomatic and commercial relations with Europe. ʿAbbās was also much concerned to beautify and improve his city. An Italian visitor, Pietro della Valle, visited Isfahan and met the shah. Pietro was not impressed by Persian miniature painting, of which he speaks with contempt. He notes, however, that Italian pictures were on sale in Isfahan at the shop kept by a Venetian merchant, one of the most active in the city. The shah himself visited this shop "which was full of pictures, of mirrors and other Italian curiosities." The shah treated Scudendoli [the Venetian merchant] with great cordiality and showed the Indian ambassador [who was with him] these paintings—for the most part portraits of princes similar to those sold for one crown in the Piazza Navona in Rome "but which are bought here for ten sequins" —and invited him to choose any that he pleased.[14] Additional historical evidence of the influence of European art comes from a Spanish ambassador, Don Garcia de Silva Figueroa, sent by Philip III of Spain to the shah in 1617. Describing a small royal pavilion which he visited, he notes that "there were fine pictures incomparably better made than those which one usually sees in Persia . . . we learned that the painter . . . was called Jules, that he was born in Greece and brought up in Italy where he had learned his art. . . . It was quite easy to see that this was the work of a European, because one recognized the Italian manner. . . ."[15]

Shah ʿAbbās died in 1629 but his successors continued a certain interest in Western art. One of them in particular, ʿAbbās II, was especially interested in Western art. He invited Italian and Dutch painters to Isfahan where, thanks to royal favor, they greatly influenced the further development of the art of the miniature. The shah himself is said to have taken lessons in painting from two Dutch artists.

Increasing contacts with Europe, and especially with Venice and the Netherlands, favored the extension of European artistic influence. The presence of significant resident communities of Europeans in Iran and the establishment of regular communications between that country and Europe, made it possible for numbers of Western artists to visit and, for a time, reside in Iran and, therefore, for Iranian artists to see and appreciate their work. The influence can be seen in the numerous mural paintings in the royal palaces of Isfahan depicting court scenes and personages and even in miniatures.

The influence of Western models, and perhaps even training, soon becomes apparent in the development of the Persian miniature. The decor pales and dwindles into a background. The figurants retreat and disappear. The central figure becomes at once more dominant and more relaxed, his rigidly idealized and stereotyped features softening into human lineaments. The artist was discovering the rewards of portraiture, the opportunities of light and shade, and the touch of reality. This new realism grows in Persian art during the seventeenth and still more the eighteenth centuries, and becomes dominant in the early nineteenth.

As in Turkey, several European painters whose names are known

8. *Fatḥ ʿAlī Shāh receiving a foreign delegation*

9. A Muslim warrior fighting Crusaders

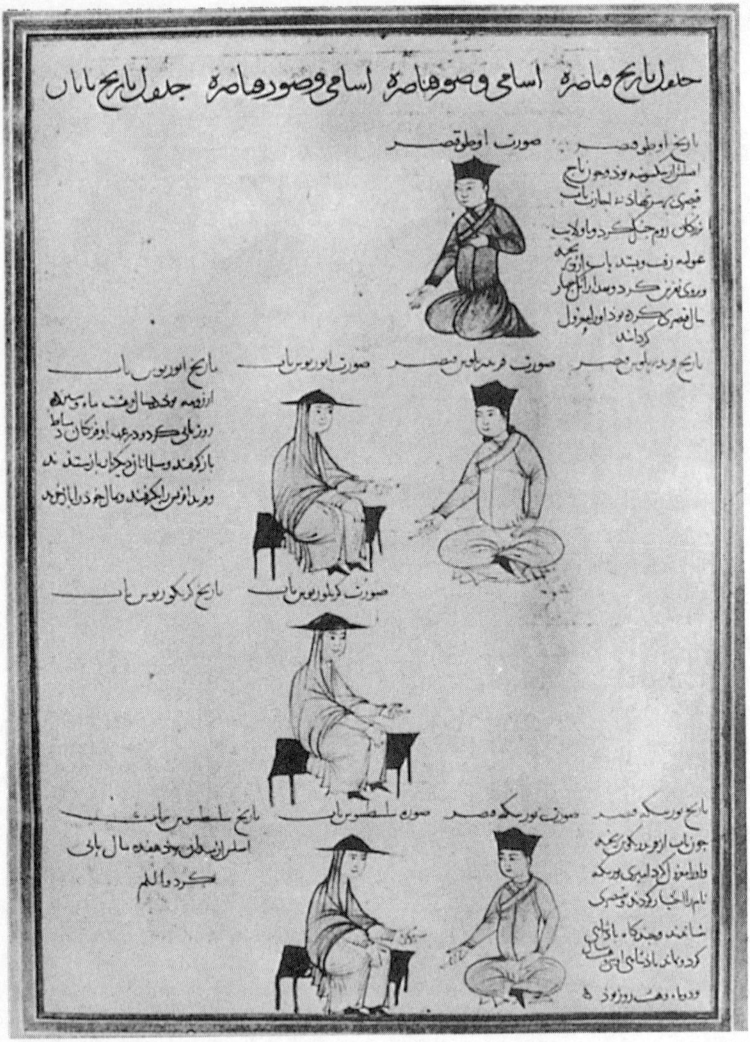

10. and 11. Popes and Emperors

وطرفند و وطرف الحاجم بود و مجتبی علیه السلام قسم ذکری کرد الاسراب ساختار انواع الوان میرو قرار و خراب
شاید و سی بریسید و سر سر و سر سرداد او موعود کرد و زساید و مود و نظاری حاسنت د لکن لکسار ند و رحی ضراب
شاید و درایده بر سنو بند و کایج رکت و دعای جود ضدو در هس ضر مکده و رویو نعش میرو روی بذ حایکه محنه نعلقا
رسید ایقا نرساید و اسند و اهر عقب قوتا بباید اورا وکسی بداید بداید و سلع و مقداسید و سلع و ساسی و سیم ام
جود از اسک که مرا د د رارسید هر ارهار جفنت کد رازاندای طوراید او د مقداعضراید و صدوزند ز نبای بود اینداز
اماک سرو نوارع لساک که خلا رمسع الند و مایع قاهر مسی و مغول و موسم و سرسع سلع علارص ار روا ولی و جد هم ا و ردیسم

دکر

نولدیه قاهر دیماک و سعی احوالی
که در دیمان اسناثر عقاست

سع اسناسلو من بهر اورا کماس و سرکفد از سنع علاد من جل و وسال عباطی کد و بود و اوادی کسی اسک
داد قیمر خوادز ذ رو بعاشناز ارکای و بخباع بود و ساع یا د سار رضای جودر ارمع اکش سطی رمسع علیه السلم
د سطاین خوا د هادجود مود مجوره تلوکده جره از از هطاری داراو راسلای سار سی و ضدو مضان و سام ازنازدن سطان او من برد و سکو کزیده
وارد داریا شی یوشت اسع طاری من قیصر طاریوس سر راسطلوس سرد و داما و دا رادیار و قیصر ضدو کده و حد سش
اندشا هیوکه کشرد سع علیه السلم سکه خده از سلطان ارمع جل د دونای سالطانی روسن اد اساب فرنسلا اوجاره کز رایکت
و مسع یاد مشع او د کشب شده ارمع یا در جون طاری رو سخو اورا کنف یا کایس من بعض قصری شبی شساد سال رو دانش
بابا در روز و واسلو اکودای ده سربا او د ماخواهر و در خرود ارباکد اکال کشرد ارمع یا در قصری ضدو و وریا سف فاحر بود و بعد او
سدان کما سوی قصر اکشرد فلو دونع المقاسی با سار بدایتا سار مضر و مضع یا سسو و ری سینا و ند
در مصر سمع یاد رعد و عزای ارمن اید یدی مک دد یعطی رب حوا کرد ارمع یا کرد مضرعبال مطربان بود و مسع
عضف خوش کرد د اند و بدار و هست سالم ارعد عوای ناطقت باب د کرسی جاعاد رویت فروی او و سلدان رویت فروی
مورد او من قیصر سنع حوکده د و دیسالم ارخین ار رو رای من و سند و اسر کم روبه ند و واهل دیا اورا سکسند

حد د ولی سدر لساب و کل سور اکاکشره یاد مک دد لساب و وعا هرم یان قاسر باشد و ایا مطر رب د را د الی عهد
مورد او من قیصر سنع حوکده د و دیسالم ارخین ار رو رای من و سند و اسر کم روبه ند و واهل دیا اورا سکسند
جماره ... ارتسنا شی جود د دیمال ارخین ارجندن جود رو رای من و سند مدار عوز د و سال و د من و مصر قیصرست و دوت

12. and 13. Wall paintings in Isfahan showing European visitors to Iran

14. *A court page in European dress*

15. *A youth with a lady in European costume*

16. *A European page holding a wine cup*

17. A Persian Prince with attendants including a European and a Mughal Indian courtier

to us resided in Iran and some of them worked for the shahs. Even more remarkable is the action of ʿAbbās II in sending a Persian artist to Italy for further training. He is known as Muḥammad Zamān and stayed in Rome, where he studied modern techniques. He is said to have adopted the Catholic religion and is sometimes mentioned as Muḥammad Paolo Zamān. Several other Persian painters of the time show evidence of European influence and perhaps even training—if not in Europe then at least by European artists in Iran.[16]

The same processes can be seen in India, where the Mogul emperors were great patrons of the arts and showed considerable interest in the new styles brought by visitors from Europe who were then beginning to penetrate their country. As early as 1588, an Indian painter prepared an album of copies of paintings on Christian themes for the Emperor Akbar. His successor Jahāngīr is said by European visitors to have had European paintings hanging on the walls of his palace. The impact of European influence is even clearer on Indian than on Persian painting. Unlike Iran, the cultural traditions of which had been exclusively Islamic for many centuries, India was a country of religious and cultural pluralism. Indian artists were familiar with Hindu as well as Islamic artistic traditions and had, moreover, an acquaintance, lacking in other Muslim countries, with statuary. All this made the acceptance and assimilation of European art far easier for them. Curiously enough, neither in Iran nor in India does there seem to have been much inclination to adopt the material techniques of Western painting. The oil painting, for example, so central to the development of European art, was not adopted by Persian or Indian painters, who preferred to preserve the implements and materials of the old tradition.

An interesting feature is the depiction, by Islamic artists, of Western men and women. This is a late development. From the entire period of the Crusades, for example, only a single picture has survived in which Crusaders are shown. It is a painting on paper coming from Fusṭāṭ in Egypt and made during the twelfth century. It depicts a battle under the walls of a town and shows one warrior with a round shield, therefore presumably Muslim, fighting against several others, at least four, with kite-shaped shields and therefore presumably Norman.[17]

The interlude of Mongol-European contacts during the thirteenth and fourteenth centuries left some artistic as well as literary records. Some manuscripts of Rashīd al-Dīn's history of the Franks are copiously illustrated with portraits of emperors and popes. These are, of course, entirely imaginary, and the portraiture shows clear signs of Sino-Mongol influence in the costume, posture, and even the features of the persons portrayed. There are, however, enough recognizably authentic elements of medieval European dress, especially of clerical dress, to show that the Persian artist had seen European visitors or perhaps pictures.[18] Similar evidence of European iconographic influence can be seen in some illustrated manuscripts produced in Iraq and western Iran in the thirteenth and fourteenth centuries.

The activities of Europeans in the Levant and in Northern Africa received even less attention from Muslim artists than from Muslim writers. The next attempts to portray European visitors come from the late sixteenth and early seventeenth centuries, and are found in Iran. Two palaces, the Chihil Sutūn (Forty columns) of the late sixteenth century and ʿAlī Qāpū of the early seventeenth century, both in Isfahan, were used by the shahs of Iran as audience halls within which to receive foreign and other visitors. The paintings, with which the walls of both buildings are decorated, include a number of pictures of the various types of visitors who came there. As well as Indians, they include several Europeans, mostly in Spanish and Portuguese dress. Similar representations are found in Persian miniatures of the same period.

The Western presence in Mogul India also left some impact on Indian and Muslim art. A number of miniatures have survived depicting European men and occasionally women. There are even what purport to be portraits of named persons—the English envoy, Sir Thomas Roe, appearing before the Emperor Jahāngīr (1605–1627), as well as portraits of two functionaries of the British East India Company, the famous Warren Hastings, depicted in European court dress, and Richard Johnson, wearing a red coat uniform, holding a three-cornered hat, and sitting on a chair. He is accompanied by a servant holding a parasol.

Some of the most interesting, from the artistic point of view, are the paintings of the Turkish artist Abdüljelil Çelebi, known as Levni. A native of Edirne, he became an apprentice at the "painting office" (Nakişhane) at Istanbul. He began as an illuminator, and even in this traditional area his surviving work reveals Western rococo influences. He later began to paint and was appointed court painter to Mustafa II (1695–1703) and to Ahmed III (1703–1730).[19] Levni produced albums, illustrated manuscripts, and a number of individual paintings. As well as portraits, he painted pictures of palace celebrations. Some of these show foreign ambassadors, easily recognizable by their European dress and by the fact that, unlike the other persons present, they sit on chairs. They are discreetly escorted by dragomans and guards. There are, in particular, two charming pictures of young European gentlemen. A Turkish manuscript, probably dating from some time after 1793 and containing portraits of European ladies and gentlemen

18. *Warren Hastings in European court dress*

19. *Richard Johnson in redcoat uniform*

20. *Three men in early 17th century dress, possibly Portuguese at the Mughal court*

21. Arrival of the Castilian envoy Don Clavijo at the court of Tīmūr

of various nationalities, shows much stronger European influences, and may in part be adapted from European plates. The costume depicted, however—apart from the tricolor cap warn by the French woman—is that of the previous century.[20]

European artistic influences are to be seen, not only in painting, but also, perhaps to an even greater extent, in architectural decoration. In both Turkey and Iran, wall paintings appear with increasing frequency in place of the painted floral decoration which was more common in traditional style. These are painted directly on plaster, often surrounded by a framework of baroque motifs. In Iran, they frequently depict court scenes and personages. In Turkey, they are mostly landscapes, often scenes from the city of Istanbul but including views of other places and of a variety of mosques. Both portraiture and scenic art are new to the Islamic tradition and illustrate an important inroad of European style and taste. For Ottoman artists, westernization was easier in landscape painting than in portraiture. Ottoman art had its own tradition of "topographical" painting. The depiction of scenes and buildings did not raise the difficult moral and religious problems posed by the representation of the human figure.[21] For the same reason, even at a time when the influence of European architecture and painting became not only powerful but dominant, there was still virtually total resistance to sculpture and even to reliefs.

The new trends in the art of painting in Turkey, Iran, and Muslim India found no parallel in the Arab countries, where the art of miniature painting had virtually died out in the Middle Ages and where architecture, except in the far western lands of North Africa, had become no more than a provincial copy of Ottoman styles. It is not until the second half of the nineteenth century that Western art and architecture can be seen to have any influence in Egypt and even later in other Arab lands.

The music of an alien culture, it would seem, is more difficult to penetrate than its art. Western interest in the arts of Asia and Africa is far greater than in the music of these continents. Similarly, Muslims appreciated and even produced Western art long before they were able to listen to Western music. Indeed, until comparatively recent times, both interest and influence were virtually nil. The earlier travelers to Europe make very few references to any music they might have heard. Ibrāhīm ibn Yaʿqūb, speaking of Schleswig, notes that:

> I have never heard worse singing than that of the people of Schleswig. It is a humming that comes out of their throats, like the barking of dogs, but more beastlike.[22]

22. *Foreign ambassadors at Ottoman palace festivities*

23. and 24. Young European gentlemen in Istanbul

25. *Frankish woman of Istanbul*

دخی آنکله صدرنک ویرر | دخنی بلبله آهنگ دیرر

جدوسی پاک طبیعتدر کر | خائل زیور وزینتدر لر

مزراول طنطنه آراسته خص | سرلرنده مذداول لاشی

طعنم یتنجه نها فی یوزیلید | اکه اله یوروه دفن اول چوخیود

26. *Englishwoman*

27. *Frenchwoman*

28. *Austrian woman*

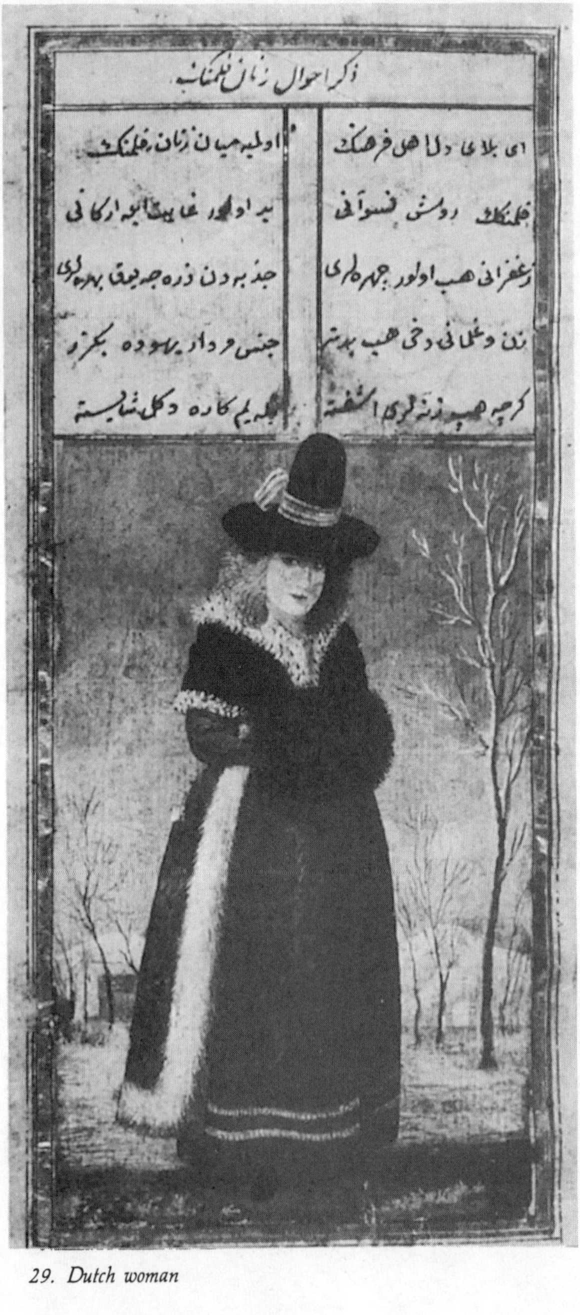

29. Dutch woman

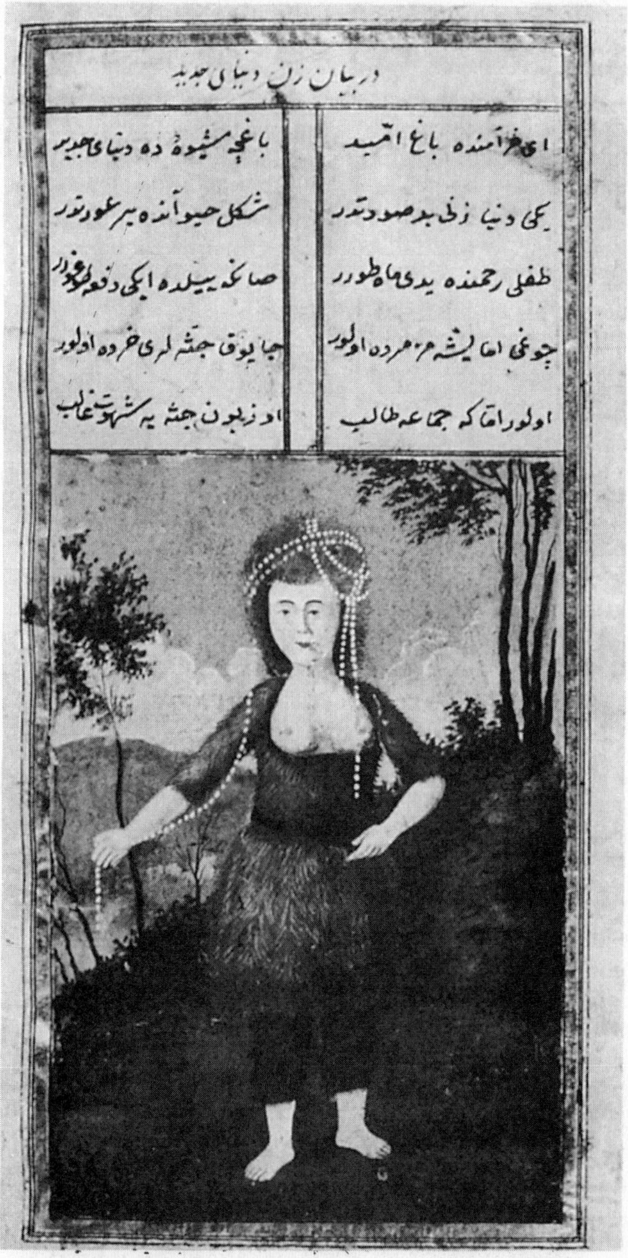

30. *American woman*

Centuries later, the Ottoman Evliya Çelebi, in Vienna, is slightly more tolerant. Among the things he describes is an orchestra of infidel musicians of whose music he remarks that it sounds quite different from the musical instruments of Turkey, but has "an exceedingly attractive, warm, and melting sound."[23] He also has high praise both for the performance and the appearance of the Vienna Boys Choir. This incidentally, apart from a brief account of a library, is his nearest approach to any recognition of European cultural life. Mehmed Efendi, during his stay in Paris, conscientiously went to the opera but clearly saw this more as a spectacle than as a musical performance:

> There is in Paris a special kind of entertainment called opera, where wonders are shown. There was always a great crowd of people, for all the great lords go there. The regent goes often, and the king from time to time, so I decided to go too. . . . Each is seated according to his rank, and I was seated next to the king's seat, which was covered with red velvet. The regent came that day. I cannot say how many men and women there were. . . .
>
> The place was superb; the staircases, the columns, the ceilings, and the walls were all gilded. This gilding, and the brilliance of the cloth of gold that the ladies were wearing, as well as of the jewels with which they were covered, all in the light of hundreds of candles, created the most beautiful effect.
>
> Opposite the spectators, in the place of the musicians, hung a brocaded curtain. When everyone was seated, the curtain was raised, and a palace appeared, with actors in theatrical costumes and about twenty angel-faced girls, with gold-laced dresses and skirts, that cast new radiance on the assembly. Then there was music, then a moment of dancing, and then the opera began. . . .[24]

The ambassador then narrates the plot of the opera and describes the scenery and costumes. He notes that the director of the opera is an important personage and that it is a very expensive art.

The Moroccan Wazīr al-Ghassānī had something to say about music in Spain. He names three musical instruments used in that country. The most popular is the harp (arba), of which he remarks that "it produces pleasant sounds for one who knows how to play it," and that it is to be found in churches, at festivals, and in most Spanish homes. There is no lute, but the Spaniards have an instrument which resembles it and is called "guitar.'" A little later, speaking of churches and church services, he mentions a third instrument, the organ—"a very large instrument with bellows and large pipes of gilded lead which produces remarkable sounds." Visiting Spain in 1690, this was apparently all the Wazīr discovered about Spanish music.[25] The Ottoman envoy Vasif, who was in Spain some ninety years later, has even less to say. The Spaniards, he remarks, greatly admired the musicians and singers whom he had brought with him from Turkey. He did not admire theirs: "All the great men, by order of the king, invited us to meals, and we suffered the tedium of their kind of music."[26]

Since classical Islamic music is transmitted almost entirely by oral tradition, there is no record of the music of the seventeenth and eighteenth centuries and therefore no way of judging whether, if at all, it was influenced by the sound of European music. The first official move in favor of Western music came after the destruction of the Janissaries in 1826. The sultan, as part of the modernization of his armed forces, decided to replace the famous Janissary *mehter* of reed pipes, trumpets, cymbals, and kettledrums with a Western-style band.

In 1827, the Serasker, or military commander, Mehmed Hosrev Pasha asked the Sardinian minister in Istanbul to help him obtain a number of musical instruments of the kind used in Sardinian army bands. He also asked for the loan of a bandmaster to train a first group of musicians. Agreement was reached between the Ottoman and Sardinian authorities and, in due course, Giuseppe Donizetti, a brother of the composer Gaetano Donizetti, was sent to Istanbul, where he conducted or rather commanded the imperial band and later was placed in charge of the Imperial Ottoman School of Music, created to provide the new style army with drummers and trumpeters. These efforts are described by contemporary European visitors. An Italian compatriot noted: "In less than a year many young people who had never before heard European music were instructed by Signor Donizetti, a professor from Bergamo, to the point when they could be grouped in fairly complete military bands, in which each individual player could read well enough and perform well enough."[27]

In a book published in 1832, an English visitor gives an impression of this band:

> Presently the songs of a party of Greek boatmen, which had enlivened our dessert, gave way to the strains of a military band, and, unexpected treat to me on the banks of the Bosporus, we heard Rossini's music, executed in a manner very creditable to the Professor, Signor Donizetti (Piedmontese). We rose, and went down to the palace quay, on which the band was playing. I was surprised at the youth of the performers . . . and still more surprised on finding that they were the royal pages, thus instructed for the sultan's amusement. Their aptitude in learning, which Donizetti informed me would have been remarkable even in Italy, shows that the Turks are naturally musical; but these young gentlemen have not time to acquire proficiency, for their destinies call them to other pursuits. As the embryo grandees of the empire, after

having finished their probationary studies of the manege, the Koran, and music, they were intended to be placed in important situations; and thus, I thought, looking at them, we may in a month see the flute, captain of a frigate; the big drum, governor of a fortress; the bugle, colonel of a regiment of cavalry. . . .

Donizetti was promoted to the rank of *miralay* and made a pasha. It is said that in later years he trained and conducted an orchestra of harem ladies for the entertainment of Sultan Abd al-Hamid II.[28]

In spite of this and of a series of further later measures, the acceptance of Western music in the Islamic world has gone very slowly. Though some talented composers and performers from Muslim countries, especially from Turkey, have been very successful in the Western world, the response to their kind of music at home is still relatively slight. Music, like science, is part of the inner citadel of Western culture, one of the final secrets to which the newcomer must penetrate.

There was one spectacle which definitely failed to amuse—the Spanish bullfight. Ghassānī, the Moroccan ambassador, has this description of one, obviously at a time when the bullfighter was still a noble amateur and had not yet become a professional:

> It is one of their customs that in the middle of May they choose strong, brave bulls and bring them to this plaza which they adorn with all kinds of silk and brocades. They sit on balconies overlooking the plaza and release the bulls one by one into the middle of the plaza. Then whoever claims courage and wishes to display it enters the plaza on horseback to fight the bull with his sword. Some die and some kill the bull. The king has a set place at the plaza. He attends accompanied by his wife and all his suite. The people, of all kinds, are at the windows, the rent for which, on that day or during a festival, is as much as for a whole year. . . .[29]

Al-Ghazzāl, a later Moroccan ambassador in Spain, disapproved strongly:

> When we were asked about it we replied perforce, out of courtesy, that we had liked their games, but we really believed the exact opposite, for the torture of animals is not permitted either by the law of God or by the law of nature. . . .[30]

Other forms of spectacle had somewhat greater success. Hatti Efendi, for example, who visited Vienna in 1748, notes:

> They have in Vienna a playhouse, four or five storys high, to present their plays, which they call comedy and opera. There men and women foregather every day, except the days when they assemble in church,

and most frequently the emperor and empress themselves come to their reserved boxes. The prettiest German girls and the finest young men, in golden garments, perform various dances and wonderful acts; beating the stage with their feet, they present a rare spectacle. Sometimes they represent stories from the Book of Alexander, sometimes stories of love, whose devastating lightnings set fire to the sheds of patience and serenity.[31]

A more direct influence than such casual visits was exercised by Jewish immigrants from Europe, who presented dramatic spectacles in Turkey as early as the sixteenth and seventeenth centuries. They were followed by Greek, Armenian, and even gypsy theatrical troupes. The Jews, in particular, newly arrived from Europe, seem to have played an important part in introducing the notion of the theatrical spectacle to Turkey, and in arranging the first performance. It was they who trained the first Muslim performers, mostly gypsies. By the time of Sultan Murad IV (1623–1640) performances of young gypsies were held in the palace every Thursday. These influences helped greatly in the development of a characteristic Turkish art, the *orta oyunu*, a kind of popular, largely impromptu, dramatic performance not unlike the Italian *Commedia dell'Arte*. An example of such a performance is depicted in a miniature preserved in an album of Sultan Ahmed I (1595–1603). The Turkish *orta oyunu* draws on several sources—the surviving tradition of the antique mime, the new type of performance introduced by the Spanish Jews, and increasingly, the example of the Italian theater itself, becoming known through European residents in Istanbul and through contact with Europe, especially Italy. It is even possible that some European plays may have become known in this form. The theme of Othello, for example, readily understandable by Muslim audiences, forms the basis of a popular and widespread *orta oyunu*.[32]

From Turkey, the example of popular, dramatic performances spread further east to Iran, where the passion play, commemorating the martyrdom of Husayn and his kin, first appeared at the end of the eighteenth and beginning of the nineteenth centuries.

In general, however, the barrier against Western literature was almost complete. For the visual and musical arts, all that was needed was to see and to hear and to achieve the measure of understanding necessary to follow the one or the other. Difficult as this might be, it was less so than the problem of mastering a foreign language or even of acquiring the desire to do so.

It is noteworthy, for example, that even educated Muslim visitors to Europe, such as the Ottoman and Moroccan ambassadors, show virtually no interest in European writings. They were, of course, inter-

ested in the products of their own civilization. Thus Muslim envoys
to Spain speak of the great collection of Arabic manuscripts in the
library of the Escurial. Far, however, from expressing any satisfaction
at this extension of Muslim cultural influence, they seem to regard
these books as captives in infidel hands, to be redeemed if at all
possible, rather than as carriers of the Muslim message to the West.
The Ottoman ambassador Vasif, who was shown the library at the
Escurial and given a copy of the catalogue of Arabic books, is quite
explicit: "When we found that the library included about ten early
manuscripts of the Noble Qur'ān and numberless works of Holy Law,
Theology, and Tradition, we were deeply moved and grieved."[33]
Moroccan envoys even went so far as to try to include the Arabic
manuscripts in this collection in their arrangements for ransoming
Muslim prisoners. Prisoners were valuable and fetched high prices
when ransomed. This high rating accorded to Arabic manuscripts may
be seen not so much as an indication of esteem for literature but rather
as a desire to rescue Muslim Arabic writings from exile and defilement.
In the same spirit, the eighteenth-century Moroccan ambassador al-
Miknāsī even wanted to "redeem" a few Muslim coins because they
bore the names of God and the Prophet and some verses from the Qur'
ān which he did not want to leave in infidel hands.[34] The Moroccan
envoys seem to show no interest in European books, while among the
Ottomans only Evliya records a visit to a Christian library, that of the
cathedral of St. Stephen in Vienna.

He was impressed by the size of the library—bigger than the great
mosque libraries of Istanbul and Cairo, and including "many books in
all the scripts and languages of the infidels"—and also by the care
devoted to their conservation: "The unbelievers, for all their unbelief,
venerate what they regard as the word of God. They dust and wipe
all their books once a week, and have seventy or eighty servants
assigned to this task." This must be one of the earliest examples of a
comparison in which Europeans do better than Muslims, and—by
implication—deserve to be imitated. There are few other examples
before the age of the reforms. Another comparison is somewhat more
equivocal. The Vienna library, Evliya notes, contained a great number
of illustrated books: "But among us pictures are forbidden and there
are therefore no illustrated books. That is why there are so many books
in these monasteries of Vienna." Of the actual books, he mentions by
name only the *Atlas Minor* and a *mappemonde,* and refers more generally
to "works on geography and astronomy"—in other words the practical
sciences, where Europe might have something useful to teach. Of the
arts and letters of the West Evliya has nothing to say.[35]

Much the same attitude was maintained by the Ottomans towards Frankish Europe as by the classical caliphate towards Byzantium. Political and military intelligence was necessary, science and weaponry could be useful. The rest was without interest. While, by the eighteenth century, a considerable body of Arabic and, to a lesser extent, Persian and Turkish poetry and other literature was available in translation in most of the languages of Europe, not a single work of literature had been translated into any Islamic language from any European language. The first Turkish work based on a Western source is, as has been noted, Ali Aziz's Turkish adaptation of the *Mille et un jours* of Pétis de la Croix. The latter, however, is itself a pastiche of *A Thousand and One Nights,* not long previously translated for the first time into French, and hardly constitutes a discovery of Western literature.

The next book to be translated is *Télémaque* by Fenelon, an Arabic version of which was prepared in Istanbul in 1812, by a Christian Arab from Aleppo. It was never printed but is preserved in a manuscript in the Bibliothèque Nationale in Paris.[36] *Télémaque* seems to have exercised a special fascination for Middle Eastern Muslim readers. Half a century later it was the first Western book translated and published in both Turkish and Arabic.

Another early translation was an Arabic version of *Robinson Crusoe,* printed in Malta in the early years of the nineteenth century. It was not until several decades later that the first versions of French and, later, English works of literature were made in Arabic and Turkish. Meanwhile *Robinson Crusoe* and *Télémaque* served as not unworthy guides to the treasures of European literature.

XI

Social and Personal

The great English orientalist Sir William Jones (1746–1794), lamenting the backward state of Ottoman studies in Europe, observed:

It has generally happened, that the persons who have resided among the Turks, and who, from their skill in the Eastern dialects, have been best qualified to present us with an exact account of that nation, were either confined to a low sphere of life, or engaged in views of interest and but little addicted to polite letters or philosophies; while they, who from their exalted stations and refined taste for literature, have had both the opportunity and inclination of penetrating into the secrets of Turkish policy, were totally ignorant of the language used at Constantinople, and consequently were destitute of the sole means by which they might learn, with any degree of certainty, the sentiments and prejudices of so singular a people. As to the generality of interpreters, we cannot expect from men of their condition any depth of reasoning, or acuteness of observation; if mere words are all they profess, mere words must be all they can pretend to know.[1]

Sir William's well-grounded explanation of the poor state of Ottoman studies in Europe applies with still greater force to the even poorer state of Western studies in Turkey. The total number of Muslim visitors who traveled in Christian Europe between the advent of Islam and the French Revolution was exceedingly small. Of even these few, the great majority will have had no inkling of a European language and felt no desire or need to learn one. Their contacts will have been limited to the political or commercial purposes for which they traveled and their communications filtered through translators and interpreters. Their opportunities, therefore, to observe and comment on the European scene were severely restricted. This limitation troubled them the less as neither they nor their readers saw anything of interest or value in the infidel lands beyond the frontier.

If Muslim writers on Europe were moved neither by anthropological nor by historical curiosity, there is, however, another motive which sometimes gave rise to interesting comments—an interest in the strange and the wonderful. The civilization which produced such masterpieces as *The Thousand and One Nights* had a great appetite for wonders and marvels and an extensive literature came into being to gratify it.

Europe was not lacking in suitable raw material and Muslim visitors found much which struck them as least odd and often extraordinary. An example is the European habit of shaving. For Muslims, as for many other peoples, the beard was the pride and glory of manhood, and later the visible sign of wisdom and experience. Hārūn ibn Yaḥyā, the Arab who was a prisoner in Rome in about 886, found an explanation of this curious practice.

> The inhabitants of Rome, young and old, shave off their beards entirely, not leaving a single hair. I asked them as to the cause of their shaving their beards, and I said to them: "The beauty of men lies in their beards; what is your purpose in doing this to yourselves?" They answered: "Whoever does not shave his beard is not a true Christian. For when Simon and the Apostles came to us, they had neither staff nor scrip [cf. Matthew X:10], but were poor and weak while we were then kings robed in brocade and seated on golden seats. They summoned us to the Christian religion, but we did not answer them; we seized them and tortured them and shaved their crowns and beards. And then when the truth of their words appeared to us, we began to shave our beards in expiation of our sin in shaving their beards.[2]

A later writer, possibly Ibrāhīm ibn Yaʿqūb, also comments on the Frankish practice of shaving as well as on other dirty habits.

> You shall see none more filthy than they. They are a people of perfidy and mean character. They do not cleanse or bathe themselves more than once or twice a year, and then in cold water, and they do not wash their garments from the time they put them on until they fall to pieces. They shave their beards, and after shaving they sprout only a

revolting stubble. One of them was asked as to the shaving of the beard, and he said: "Hair is a superfluity. You remove it from your private parts, so why should we leave it on our faces?"[3]

The dirty habits of Westerners continued to arouse Muslim disgust. As late as the end of the eighteenth century, the Indian Muslim visitor Abū Ṭālib Khan notes that in Dublin there were only two bathhouses, both of them small and poorly equipped. Of necessity he went to one of them, but did not enjoy the experience. In summer, he notes, the people of Dublin wash their bodies in the sea; in winter they do not wash at all. The two bathhouses are intended for the sick and are only used by those who are very sick indeed. When Abū Ṭālib went to the bath he found no cupper or barber or attendant of any kind. In place of a masseur he was offered a horsehair brush of the kind used for cleaning shoes or boots. "Everybody removes his own dirt with his own hand."[4]

European clothes receive an occasional comment from Muslim visitors. Evliya has something to say about the ladies and other women of Vienna:

> Like the men, the women wear as outer garments sleeveless quilted coats made of black cloth of various kinds. Under these, however, they wear gowns of brocade and silk and cloth-of-gold and diverse other precious and gold stuffs; these are not short and scanty as are women's gowns in the other lands of the infidels, but rich and copious, so that they drag yards of cloth on the ground behind them like the trailing skirts of the Mevlevi [whirling] dervishes. They never wear drawers. They wear shoes of all colours, and their belts are usually studded with gems. Unlike the young maidens, married ladies there go about with their bosoms uncovered, gleaming as white as snow. They do not catch their dresses around the waist with belts, like the women of Hungary, Wallachia, and Moldavia, but put sashes round their midriffs, as broad as the rim of a sieve. This is an ugly garb, which makes them look like hunchbacks. On their heads they wear white muslin caps adorned with fine lace and embroidery, and over them hoods with gems and pearls and bands. By God's providence, the breasts of the women of this country are not, like those of the women of Turkey, as big as waterskins, but are as small as oranges. Nevertheless, they mostly suckle their children with their own milk.[5]

Sheikh Rifāʿa noted another surprising feature of European clothing—the odd trick of changing its style from time to time:

> One of the characteristics of the French is their avid curiosity for everything that is new and their love of change and variety in all things and especially in the matter of dress. This is never fixed with them and

no fashion or adornment has remained with them until now. This does not mean that they change their dress entirely; it means that they vary it. Thus, for example, they would not stop wearing a hat and replace it by a turban, but they sometimes wear a hat of one kind and then after a while replace it with a hat of another kind, whether in shape or color, and the like.[6]

Abū Ṭālib regarded the complicated clothing of the European as a ridiculous waste of time. In a lengthy discussion of the weaknesses and defects of the English he lists in sixth place "their wasting much time on sleeping and dressing and arranging their hair and shaving their beards and such like. . . ."[7] In order to follow the fashion they wear from hat to shoes not less than twenty-five pieces of clothing. They have, moreover, different garments for morning and evening, so that the entire business of dressing and undressing is gone through twice a day. They spend two hours dressing, arranging their hair and shaving, at least one hour on breakfast, three hours on dinner, three hours in the company of the ladies or listening to music or gambling, and nine hours sleeping, so that not more than six hours remain for the conduct of business and among the great not more than four. The cold weather, says Abū Ṭālib, is no excuse for so great a number of garments. They could halve the number of garments and still keep warm and could save much time by cutting down on shaving, hairdressing, and the like.

Some of these Muslim visitors were sufficiently imaginative to realize that they presented as odd a spectacle to the Westerners as the Westerners did to them.

Like other Ottoman visitors to Europe, Vasif comments, not without satisfaction, on the impression which he made and the crowds that came to stare at him. It began even in quarantine, when people from the neighborhood came to stare at him from the other side of the fence.

Later, when he made his ceremonial entry into Madrid, "the number of spectators was beyond description. On the balconies of the houses overlooking the street the spectators were jammed five or six deep. Though the street was wide enough for five carriages abreast, it was so crowded that even a rider on horseback could only pass with difficulty. We were told that windows were let at 100 piastres each."[8]

A Persian dignitary who attended the opening of the London and Croydon railway in 1839 comments on the crowd of thirty or forty thousand people assembled there:

As soon as they perceived us they began to shout and to cry out in astonishment and derision. But the Ājūdān-Bāshi took the lead in greeting them politely, and they responded by taking off their hats, so all went well. But with even a little carelessness it could have gone badly. In fact, they had some justification, since our external appearance, in clothing and otherwise, must have seemed very strange to their eyes— especially my beard, the like of which, in all of Frangistan, is of rare occurrence."[9]

It is in clothing and in the vestimentary revolution which began in the early nineteenth century that one can see most clearly the change in the perception by Muslim rulers of the condition of the Islamic world and its relations with the outside world of European Christendom. The change begins with the adoption of certain European garments by the sovereign and the military elite, then by an increasing section of the bureaucracy and, finally, by the population at large.

It had happened once before. In the thirteenth century, the Islamic caliphate had been overthrown and a large part of the Muslim world conquered by the pagan Mongols from the Far East. The Muslims, overwhelmed and bewildered, had, at least at the higher military levels, abandoned their traditional style of dress and adopted that of the new masters of the world. Even in Egypt, never conquered by the Mongols, at the end of the century the Mamluk Sultan Qalā'ūn introduced a new set of regulations governing the clothes worn by the Emirs of the inner circle. They were to wear Mongol-style accoutrements and, instead of cropping their hair short in the Muslim style, were to allow their locks to grow and flow freely. In the same spirit, the Ottoman reforming Sultan Mahmud II appeared before his people in 1826 wearing trousers and a tunic and saw to it that an increasing part of his army was similarly attired. Tunics in the army, frock coats in the bureaucracy, and trousers in both were introduced by order. From these, they spread more generally among the urban, literate classes. First in Turkey, then in some of the Arab countries, finally in Iran, European dress became general. For a long time the Westernization of clothing was limited to the males and even for these only from the neck downwards. Headgear, which had always had a considerable symbolic importance in the Islamic world and which was, moreover, directly related to the performance of the Muslim prayers, remained distinctive. In the twentieth century, even this point was conceded, at least by the military, and the peaked and visored caps and kepis of Europe were generally adopted by the officers of even the mostly militantly Islamic states.

At the beginning of the fourteenth century, when the Mongols themselves were becoming Muslims and assimilated to Middle Eastern society, the Mongol style was officially abandoned and another Mamluk sultan of Egypt, Muhammad the son of Qalā'ūn, returning from the pilgrimage to Mecca, resolved to revert to the Muslim style. He and all his emirs and Mamluks cast off their Mongol coats and cut their flowing locks. The hats, coats, and pants of Europe still remain but are increasingly challenged, for both social and religious reasons, on both aristocratic and populist grounds.

The westernization of female clothing came much later and did not go nearly so far. The contrast may be related to certain basic cultural differences.

The Muslim visitors who have left records of their travels to Europe were, until the nineteenth century, without exception, males. Most of them, however, have something to say on the subject of women and their place in society. For seekers after strange and wonderful stories, there were few more fruitful topics. The Christian institution of monogamous marriage, the relative freedom of women from social restrictions, and the respect accorded to them by even exalted personages never failed to strike visitors from the lands of Islam with wonderment though rarely with admiration.

One of the earliest impressions of European sexual mores is given by the Arab ambassador al-Ghazāl, who visited a Viking court in about 845 A.D. According to his own testimony, during his stay among the Vikings he enjoyed a light flirtation with the Viking queen.

> Now when the wife of the Viking king heard of al-Ghazāl, she sent for him so that she might see him. When he entered her presence, he greeted her, then he stared at her for a long time, gazing at her as one that is struck with wonderment. She said to her interpreter: "Ask him why he stares at me so. Is it because he finds me very beautiful or the reverse?"
>
> He answered: "It is indeed because I did not imagine that there was so beautiful a spectacle in the world. I have seen in the palaces of our king women chosen for him from among all the nations, but never have I seen among them beauty such as this."
>
> She said to her interpreter, "Ask him; is he serious, or does he jest?" And he answered: "Serious indeed." And she said to him: "Are there then no beautiful women in your country?" And al-Ghazāl replied: "Show me some of your women, so that I can compare them with ours."
>
> So the queen sent for women famed for beauty, and they came. Then he looked them up and down, and he said: "They have beauty, but it is not like the beauty of the queen, for her beauty and her qualities cannot be appreciated by everyone and can only be expressed by poets. If the queen wishes me to describe her beauty, her quality, and her wisdom in a poem which will be declaimed in all our land, I shall do this."
>
> The queen was greatly pleased and elated with this, and ordered him

a gift. Al-Ghazāl refused to accept it, saying "I will not." Then she said to the interpreter: "Ask him why he does not accept my gift. Does he dislike my gift, or me?"

He asked him—and al-Ghazāl replied: "Indeed, her gift is magnificent, and to receive it from her is a great honour, for she is a queen and the daughter of a king. But it is gift enough for me to see her and to be received by her. This is the only gift I want. I desire only that she continue to receive me."

And when the interpreter explained his words to her, her joy and her admiration for him grew even greater, and she said: "Let his gift be carried to his dwelling; and whenever he wishes to pay me a visit, let not the door be closed to him, for with me he is always assured of an honorable welcome." Al-Ghazāl thanked her, wished her well and departed.

At this point the narrator of the story, Tammām ibn ʿAlqama, interjects a remark:

I heard al-Ghazāl tell this story, and I asked him: "And did she really approach that degree of beauty which you ascribed to her?" And he answered: "By your father, she had some charm; but by talking in this way I won her good graces and obtained from her more than I desired."

Tammām ibn ʿAlqama also said:

One of his companions said to me: "The wife of the king of the Vikings was infatuated with al-Ghazāl and could not let a day pass without her sending for him and his staying with her and telling her about the life of the Muslims, of their history, their countries and the nations that adjoin them. Rarely did he leave her without her sending after him a gift to express her goodwill to him—garments or food or perfume, till her dealings with him became notorious, and his companions disapproved of it. Al-Ghazāl was warned of this, and became more careful, and called on her only every other day. She asked him the reason for this, and he told her of the warning he had received.

Then she laughed, and said to him: "We do not have such things in our religion, nor do we have jealousy. Our women are with our men only of their own choice. A woman stays with her husband as long as it pleases her to do so, and leaves him if it no longer pleases her." It was the custom of the Vikings before the religion of Rome reached them that no woman refused any man, except that if a noblewoman accepted a man of humble status, she was blamed for this, and her family kept them apart.

When al-Ghazāl heard her say this, he was reassured, and returned to his previous familiarity.[10]

The narrator goes on to describe al-Ghazāl's dealings with the Viking queen, for whom he extemporized Arabic verses that were duly explained to her by the interpreter. This last detail adds a touch of improbability to the whole story.

The independence of Western women arouses frequent comment; Ibrāhīm ibn Yaʿqūb, for example, speaking of the people of Schleswig notes that:

> Among them women have the right to divorce. A woman can herself initiate divorce whenever she pleases.

The same author tells an even stranger story of an island in the western sea known as The City of Women:

> Its inhabitants are women, over whom men have no sway. They ride horses and themselves wage war, and have great courage in combat. They have men slaves, and each slave in turn goes to his mistress by night. He stays with her all night, and rises at dawn, and goes forth secretly at daybreak. If one of them bears a male child, she kills it at once, but if she bears a female child, she suffers it to live.

Realizing no doubt that his version of the ancient story of the Amazons might not convince his reader, Ibrāhīm ibn Yaʿqūb adds:

> The City of Women is an assured fact concerning which there is no doubt . . . Otto, the King of the Romans, told me about it.[11]

A point which could not fail to strike the Muslim observer in medieval as in more modern times was what seemed to him the licentious freedom of the women and the extraordinary lack of manly jealousy in the men. Usāma, a Syrian neighbor of the Crusaders, has several stories illustrating this point:

> The Franks have no trace of jealousy or feeling for the point of honor. One of them may be walking along with his wife, and he meets another man, and this man takes his wife aside and chats with her privately, while the husband stands apart for her to finish her conversation; and if she takes too long he leaves her alone with her companion and goes away.
>
> This is an example which I saw myself. When I visited Nabulus, I used to stay in the house of a man called Muʿizz. His place was a lodging house for Muslims, with windows opening onto the road. Opposite it, on the other side of the road, was the house of a Frankish man who used to sell wine for the merchants. He used to take a bottle of wine and go around crying: "So-and-so, the merchant, had just opened a cask of this wine. If anyone wants some, it is in such and such a place." His payment for acting as crier was the wine in that bottle.
>
> One day he came home and found a man in bed with his wife, and he asked him: "What brings you here to my wife?" The man replied: "I was tired so I came in to rest."

"And how did you get into my bed?"

"I found the bed made, so I lay down on it."

"But the woman was sleeping with you."

"It was her bed. Could I have kept her out of her own bed?"

"By my faith," said the husband. "If you do this again you and I will quarrel."

This was the whole of his disapproval and of his jealousy.[12]

Usāma's story has all the characteristics of an ethnic anecdote, but nevertheless illustrates vividly how Christian marriage customs must have seemed to contemporary Muslim observers.

The appearance of these Christian ladies was not, however, displeasing. Ibn Jubayr, a Spanish Muslim who visited Syria and Palestine under Crusader rule, had the good fortune to attend a Christian wedding.

> Among the most beautiful spectacles of this world was a bridal procession which we saw one day in Tyre, near the port. All the Christians, men and women, had assembled on this occasion, and formed themselves into two rows before the door of the house of the bride that was to be given away. They played flutes and horns and all kinds of musical instruments, until she came out, led by two men who held her hands on the left and the right, and seemed to be close relatives. She was beautifully dressed and splendidly adorned, wearing a dress of gold-braided silk, and drawing a train behind her as is their manner. On her head she had a gold band, around which was a net of spun gold, and on her breast a similar ornament tastefully arranged. . . . Behind her walked Christian men, the most important of her family, wearing the most splendid of their magnificent costumes and trailing their cloaks behind them, and after them her equals and companions among the Christian women, in the finest of clothes, and adorned with jewels, while the music played. . . .[13]

Centuries later, Evliya Çelebi was delighted with the aspects of the ladies of Vienna.

> Because the water and air in that country are so good, all the women are beautiful, of good height and fine figure and fairylike features. And everywhere there are girls without number as sweet, graceful, and beautiful as the gleaming golden sun, who enchant a man with every gesture and every movement, every word and every act. . . .

One feature of Christian society never failed to startle Muslim visitors—the public deference shown to women. Evliya comments:

> I saw a most extraordinary thing in this country. If the emperor encounters a woman in the street, then if he is on horseback he halts his

horse and lets the woman pass. If the emperor is on foot and meets a woman, then he remains standing, in a polite posture. Then the woman greets the emperor, and he takes his hat off his head and shows deference to the woman, and only when she has passed does he continue on his way. This is a most extraordinary spectacle. In this country, and elsewhere in the lands of the infidels, women have the chief say, and they are honored and respected for the sake of mother Mary.[14]

Small wonder that Evliya was regarded in Turkey as a liar, when he told such extraordinary tales.

Even in Spain, al-Ghazāl, a Moroccan ambassador traveling in 1766, was shocked by the freedom of women. Like other Muslim visitors, he is appalled by what strikes him as the sexual liberty of European— even Spanish—women. His shock began when he crossed the border to Ceuta, a Spanish-held port on the north Moroccan coast.

> Their dwellings have windows overlooking the street, where the women sit all the time, greeting the passersby. Their husbands treat them with the greatest courtesy. The women are very much addicted to conversation and conviviality with men other than their husbands, in company or in private. They are not restrained from going wherever they think fit. It often happens that a Christian returns to his home and finds his wife or his daughter or his sister in the company of another Christian, a stranger, drinking together and leaning against one another. He is delighted with this and, according to what I am told, he esteems it as a favor from the Christian who is in the company of his wife or whichever other woman of his household it may be. . . .

Al-Ghazāl's reports of what he saw in Ceuta and the interpretation which he placed on it seemed a little fevered. It is hardly surprising that he was deeply shocked—like other Muslim visitors before him— by the dancing couples at the balls and receptions given in his honor. Equally shocking to him were the shameless garb and self-display of girls of good family and the acquiescence, or even approval, of the men who should have been the guardians of their honor. After returning from one of these receptions, al-Ghazāl remarks:

> When the party dispersed we returned to our lodgings and we prayed to God to save us from the wretched state of these infidels who are devoid of manly jealousy and are sunk in unbelief and we implored the Almighty not to hold us accountable for our offense in conversing with them as the circumstances required. . . .[15]

Mehmed Efendi was similarly impressed by the independence and power of women in France:

In France women are of higher station than men, so that they do what they wish and go where they please; and the greatest lord shows respect and courtesy beyond all limits to the humblest of women. In that country their commands prevail. It is said that France is the paradise of women, where they have no cares or troubles, and where whatever they desire is theirs without effort.[16]

Abū Ṭālib Khan, however, visiting England at the end of the eighteenth century, observed another side of the story which previous visitors had overlooked, and on the whole finds English women worse off than their Muslim sisters. They are kept busy with a variety of employments in shops and elsewhere—a situation which Abū Ṭālib attributes to the wisdom of English legislators and philosophers in finding the best way to keep women out of mischief—and are further subject to a number of restrictions. For example, they do not go out after dark and do not spend the night in any house other than their own unless accompanied by their husbands. Once married, they have no property rights and are completely at the mercy of their husbands, who may despoil them at will. Muslim women in contrast are far better off. Their legal position and property rights, even against their husbands, are established and defended by law. And they have other advantages, too. Hidden behind the veil, he notes with some distress, they can indulge in all kinds of mischief and wickedness, the scope for which is very great. They can go out of doors as they choose and go to visit their fathers or their relations or even women friends, and stay away for several days and nights at a time. Abū Ṭālib has obvious misgivings about the opportunities which these liberties offer.[17]

From England Abū Ṭālib went to France where, in striking contradiction to commonly accepted ideas, he found neither the cooking nor the women as much to his taste as in England. Abū Ṭālib preferred plain English fare to made-up French dishes and has similar views about the ladies of the two countries. "The French women," he says, "are taller, plumper, and rounder than the English, but are far less beautiful, perhaps because they lack the maidenly simplicity and modesty and the graceful deportment of the English girls." Abū Ṭālib was much put off by the French style of hairdressing, which he found unpleasantly reminiscent of the appearance of common prostitutes in India. He found the French women, with their paint and jewels and almost bare bosoms, wanton in appearance. To make matters worse, they were "forward, talkative, loud voiced, and quick to retort." Their high-waisted gowns were comic rather than attractive. In conclusion, Abū Ṭālib notes that although by temperament readily affected by the sight of beauty, as he had occasion to observe while visiting various spectacles in London, nothing of the kind happened to him in Paris. At the Palais Royal, by day and by night, he found himself face to face with thousands, but was not to the slightest degree aroused by any of them.[18]

French peasant women, and indeed everything else in the villages, were even worse. The villages were very unpleasant, and quite unlike the towns. The women were so coarse that the sight of them merely aroused disgust, and their garments were such that village girls in India seemed like the inhabitants of paradise by comparison.[19]

A Turkish poet of the period is more explicitly sexual. Fazil Bey, also known as Fazil-i Enderuni (1757–1810) was the grandson of a famous Palestinian Arab leader who rebelled against the Ottomans in the 70s of the eighteenth century. Brought up in Istanbul he became famous for his erotic poems and, in particular, two lengthy poems, one on girls and the other on boys, describing them by nationality with an enumeration of the good and bad qualities, for the purposes Fazil Bey had in mind, of the various national groups. They include, in addition to the different ethnic groups in and near the Ottoman Empire, the Franks of Istanbul, the Danubians, the French, the Poles, the Germans, the Spaniards, the English, the Russians, the Dutch, and even the Americans, by which term Fazil Bey clearly means the Red Indians. There is no evidence that Fazil Bey ever traveled abroad but, as one who was brought up and lived in the Imperial Palace in Istanbul, he would have had ample opportunity to meet young women and young men of many nationalities. His descriptions of boys tend to be rather vague and reticent. His treatment of girls is much more explicit, filled with a mass of sometimes clinical detail. He does, however, give occasional importance to cultural context. French women are reproached with following the, for Fazil Bey, disgusting custom of cherishing small dogs and hugging them to their bosoms. He is also aware that Spanish ladies sing and play the guitar and notes that they arrive by way of Morocco. English women are chaste and rosy-cheeked and are part owners of India. Dutch women speak a difficult language—one wonders how Fazil Bey was able to reach this conclusion—but fail to arouse sexual desire.[20]

Halet Efendi, who stayed in Paris from 1803 to 1806, and is in general concerned to paint as negative a picture as he can, describes another aspect of European sexual mores. He begins by indignantly citing an accusation made against the Muslims by their detractors:

> They say: know that as a general rule, however many Armenians and Greeks there may be in the world, the Muslims are homosexuals. This

is a scandalous thing. In Frangistan, God forfend, such a thing cannot happen, and if it does happen they punish it severely and it makes a great scandal and so forth—so that, listening, one would think that all of us are of that persuasion, as if we had no other concern.

In Paris there is a kind of market place called Palais Royal, where there are shops for various kinds of goods on all four sides, and above them rooms containing 1500 women and 1500 boys exclusively occupied in sodomy. To go to that place by night is shameful, but since there is no harm in going there by day, I went to see this special spectacle. As soon as one enters, from all four sides males and females hand out printed cards to anyone who comes, inscribed: "I have so many women, my room is in such and such a place, the price is so much" or "I have so many boys, their ages are such and such, the official price is so much," all on specially printed cards. And if any boy or woman among them contracts syphilis, there are doctors appointed by the government to attend to them. The women and boys surround a man from every side, parade around and ask "which of us do you like?" What is more, the great people here ask proudly "Have you visited our Palais Royal? And did you like the women and the boys?"

Thank God, in the lands of Islam, there are not that many boys and catamites.[21]

A later visitor to Paris, the Egyptian Sheikh Rifāʿa, presents a somewhat different perspective on the question of homosexuality. He notes, with interest and approval, that in France homosexuality is regarded with horror and disgust, to such a degree that when French scholars translate homosexual love poems from the Arabic they change the masculine to the feminine form.

He was less favorably impressed by the ladies of France. He found the Parisian woman lacking in modesty, the men in manliness:

> Men among them are the slaves of women and subject to their commands whether they be beautiful or not. One of them said . . . women among the people of the East are like household possessions while among the Franks they are like spoiled children. The Franks harbour no evil thoughts about their women, even though the transgressions of these women are very numerous.

Rifāʿa goes on to explain that even if a wife's misconduct is made clear to a man, attested and proved by witnesses and he drives her from his house and they are separated for a while, it is still necessary for him to go to court and bring convincing proofs of her misconduct in order to obtain a divorce.

> Among their bad qualities is the lack of virtue of many of their women as above stated and the lack of manly jealousy of their men on

occasions which would arouse manly jealousy among the Muslims as, for example, in association and intimacy and dalliance. . . . Fornication among them is a secondary rather than a major sin, especially in the case of the unmarried.

The Sheikh does, however, admit to being impressed by the appearance, style, and even the conversation of French women:

> The French women excel in beauty and grace and conversation and courtesy. They always display themselves in their adornments and mingle with men at places of entertainment.

The sheikh, like other Muslim visitors, attended a ball and was duly struck by the odd ways of the Western world. Like his predecessors, he found much that was strange and wonderful but was less shocked than they had been. "A ball," he explains, "always includes both men and women, and there are great lights and chairs on which to sit. These are mostly for women to sit and no man may sit until all the women are seated. If a woman comes in and there is no vacant chair then one of the men stands up and seats her. No woman stands up to seat her." "Women," he notes with astonishment, "are always treated at these gatherings with more consideration than men."

There was another strange feature of these Western balls. "Dancing among them is considered an art . . . and is practised by everyone . . . as pertaining to the man of elegance and the gentleman and is not immoral in that it never goes beyond the bounds of decency."

The sheikh frequently makes comparisons between Western phenomena and their Egyptian equivalents, often favorable to the former. He compares the actresses of the French stage to the dancing girls of Egypt, and the theatre to the Muslim shadow play, though he notes in both cases that the Western form is superior. His comments on the dance are enlightening.

> In Egypt, the dance is practised only by women in order to excite desire. In Paris, on the contrary, the dance is simply a kind of jumping around without even a whiff of immorality.

This observation is the more remarkable in that Sheikh Rifāʿa, like earlier Muslim explorers of European ballrooms, was struck by the curious practise of changing partners.

> Each man invites a woman so that he may dance with her, and when the dance is finished another man invites her for a second dance, and so on. There is a special kind of dance in which the man puts his arm around the waist of the person with whom he is dancing and usually grasps her with his hand. In general to touch a woman anywhere in the

upper part of the body is not considered an offense among these Christians. The more a man excels in speaking to women and flattering them, the more he is regarded as well-bred.[22]

One final comment from a Persian, sailing from Izmir in 1838, about some fellow passengers.

> Four English girls came on board, very accomplished and intelligent, but ugly and ill-countenanced. Since they had apparently been unable to find suitable customers in their own country, they had been constrained to go abroad, and had been traveling around for some time in the hope of finding husbands. But they had failed in their purpose and were now returning home.
>
> On Sunday about noon we landed at the Island of Pire [? Sira], the first Greek territory we reached. We were kept there for twenty days in their quarantine, which could serve as a sample of hell. The four virgins (so they claimed) were our companions in the quarantine buildings, where the Ājūdān-Bāshī paid their living expenses. One of them was lucky and found a lusty young Greek who was our fellow-passenger on board ship and with whom she had been exchanging secret signs and signals. They now became intimate and shared a dwelling."[23]

Several of the diplomatic visitors have something to say about the cities which they visited and, occasionally, make comparisons with their own. Mehmed Efendi observes:

> Paris is not as big as Istanbul, but the buildings are of three, four, or as many as seven storeys, and a whole family lives on each storey. Great numbers of people are seen in the streets because the women are always in the streets going from one house to another, and never stay at home. Because of this mixture of men and women, the inner city looks more populous than it really is. The women sit in the shops and conduct business.[24]

Muslim visitors from North Africa and India as well as from the Middle East comment on the role of women as shopkeepers in Western cities and on their universal presence.

All in all these Muslim travelers, even in the late eighteenth and early nineteenth century, show no great interest in the internal affairs of Europe. Even Azmi, who visited Prussia in 1790, had little curiosity about matters outside his mission and comments with irritation about "one of the extraordinary practices of Europe," to try and show visitors from other countries the noteworthy sights of their cities, thereby distracting and delaying them and causing them to waste money on a useless extension of their stay. Of the Muslim visitors who traveled in the West until the early nineteenth century, only one, Mīrzā

Abū Ṭālib Khan, went into these matters in any detail.[25] Significantly, he came from a country which had undergone the direct impact of the West. In the course of the nineteenth century, Muslim visitors from Middle Eastern countries also found reason to extend their stay and expand their range of interest.

XII
Conclusions

During the French occupation of Egypt at the end of the eighteenth century, the Egyptian historian Jabartī visited the library and research center which the French had established in an abandoned Mamluk palace in Cairo. He noted that they had assembled a large and well-stocked library, in which even common French soldiers came to read, and—still more noteworthy—to which Muslims were readily, even eagerly, welcomed:

> The French were particularly happy if a Muslim visitor showed interest in the sciences. They immediately began to talk to him and showed him all kinds of printed books with pictures of parts of the terrestrial globe and of animals and plants. They also had books on ancient history . . .[1]

Jabartī visited the library a number of times. He was shown books on Islamic history and on Islamic learning in general, and was astonished to find that the French had a collection of Arabic texts, as well as many Muslim books translated from Arabic into French. He observed that the French "make great efforts to learn the Arabic language and the colloquial. In this they strive day and night. And they have books especially devoted to all types of languages, their declensions and conjugations as well as their etymologies." These works, Jabartī remarks, "make it easy for them to translate whatever they wish from any language into their own language very quickly."[2]

Jabartī had made a discovery, the existence of European orientalism. His surprise is understandable. By the end of the eighteenth century, when the first modern European incursion into the Arab east took place, the European student of the Middle East already had an extensive literature at his disposal. Some seventy books on Arabic grammar had been printed in Europe, about ten for Persian, about fifteen for Turkish. Of dictionaries there were ten for Arabic, four for Persian, and seven for Turkish. Many of these were not merely manuals and teaching aids based on indigenous works, but represented original and significant contributions to scholarship.

There was nothing comparable on the other side. For an Arab, a Persian, or a Turk, not a single grammar or dictionary of any Western language existed either in manuscript or in print. It was not until well into the nineteenth century that we find any attempt to produce grammars and dictionaries of Western languages for Middle Eastern users. When they do appear, the earliest examples are due largely to imperialist and missionary initiatives. The first bilingual dictionary of Arabic and a European language by a native Arabic speaker was published in 1828. It was the work of a Christian—an Egyptian Copt—"revised and augmented" by a French orientalist and, according to the author's preface, was designed for the use of Westerners rather than that of Arabs.[3] The thought that Arabs might need such dictionaries does not seem to have occurred to anyone until much later.

The European student of the Middle East was better placed than his Middle Eastern opposite number in more respects than in the availability of language aids. By the end of the eighteenth century, he already had at his disposal an extensive literature on the history, religion, and culture of the Muslim peoples, including editions and translations of texts and serious scholarly studies. In many ways, indeed, Western scholarship on the Middle East was already more advanced than that of the Middle Easterners themselves. European travelers and archeologists had begun the process which was to lead to the recovery and decipherment of the monuments of the ancient Middle East, and the restoration, to the peoples of the region, of the great, glorious, and long forgotten past. The first chair of Arabic in England was founded by Sir Thomas Adams at Cambridge University in 1633. There, and in similar centers in other west European countries, a great effort of creative scholarship was devoted to the ancient and medieval languages, literatures, and cultures of the region; very much less to recent and contemporary matters. All this is in striking contrast to the almost total lack of interest displayed by Middle Easterners in the languages, cultures, and religions of Europe. Only the Ottoman state, responsible for defense and diplomacy, and thus for dealings with the states of Europe, found it necessary from time to time to collect and compile some information about them. The record of their findings shows that, until the latter part of the eighteenth century, their information was usually superficial, often inaccurate, and almost always out of date.

The feeling of timelessness, that nothing really changes, is a characteristic feature of Muslim writing about Europe—as, indeed, it is of their writings about other times and places. A physician or scientist is content to translate a book on medicine or science written 50 or 100 years earlier. Kâtib Çelebi, writing on the Christian religion in 1655, draws on medieval polemics, without worrying about any changes which might have occurred in the Christian religion during the intervening half millennium, and without reference to the Reformation, the wars of religion, or even to the schism between Rome and Constantinople. In the same spirit, an early-eighteenth-century Ottoman historian, Naima, equates the European states of his time with the medieval Crusaders and disclaims any need to discuss them in detail, and a late-eighteenth-century Turkish artist, seeking to portray the costume of European women, draws on seventeenth-century models.

Why this difference in the attitudes of the two societies towards one another? Certainly it cannot be ascribed to any greater religious tolerance on the side of the Europeans. On the contrary, the Christian attitude towards Islam was far more bigoted and intolerant than that of the Muslims to Christianity. The reasons for this greater Muslim tolerance are in part theological and historical, and in part practical. The Prophet Muḥammad lived some six centuries after Jesus Christ. For Christians and Muslims alike, their own religion and their own revelation represented God's final word to mankind. But chronology imposed a difference in their mutual perceptions. For the Muslim, Christ was a precursor; for the Christian, Muḥammad was an impostor. For the Muslim, Christianity was an early, incomplete, and obsolete form of the one true religion, and did, therefore, contain elements of truth based on an authentic revelation. Christians, like Jews, were consequently entitled to the toleration of the Muslim state. For the Christian, dealing with a subsequent religion, no such position was theologically possible. Christians found it difficult enough to tolerate Judaism, at which they might have looked in the same way as Muslims looked at Christianity. For them to tolerate Islam would have meant admitting a revelation after Christ and scriptures later than the gospels. This was an admission which they were not prepared to make.

There were also some practical considerations. Islam came into a predominantly Christian world, and for a long time the Muslims were a minority in the countries they ruled. Some measure of tolerance for the religions of the subject majority was therefore an administrative and economic necessity, and most Muslim rulers wisely recognized this fact. Europe, in general, was subject to no such constraints. In the one European country where a parallel problem arose, in Spain, there was a heavy price to pay for the intolerance of the Reconquest, in the impoverishment of the country through the expulsion of Moors and Jews.

An important difference also exists between the two civilizations in the interest which they offered and the curiosity which they aroused. Compared with the vast variety of peoples and cultures in the Islamic world, Frankish Europe in the Middle Ages must have seemed a very monotonous place. Substantially, it was a region of one religion, one race, and in most parts, one culture. There was one kind of dress for each of the few major social classes. All this is in striking contrast to the kaleidoscopic variety of races, creeds, costumes, and cultures in the Islamic world. Frankish Christendom even cherished its uniformity; at least it seems to have had difficulty in tolerating or accommodating any kind of deviation, and spent much energy in the pursuit of heretics, witches, Jews, and others that departed from the norm.

The one respect in which Europe offered greater variety was in language. In contrast to the Arabic-speaking world, where Arabic was the sole language of religion, commerce, and culture, the treasure-house of the learning of the past, and the instrument for the business of the present, Europe used a wide range of different languages, for religion and scholarship as well as for everyday purposes. The classics of Europe and the scriptures of Christianity were in three languages, Latin, Greek, and Hebrew, to which one may add a fourth, Aramaic, if one takes note of the Aramaic books of the Old Testament. Europeans were thus accustomed from an early stage to the necessity of studying and mastering difficult languages other than their own vernaculars and, more than that, of recognizing that there were external sources of wisdom written in foreign languages, access to which involved learning them. The situation was very different among the Arabs, for whom their own language was scriptural, classical, and practical at one and the same time, and no one therefore felt or conceived the need to learn any other.

There were many different languages spoken in Europe, and the range of usefulness of any one of them was limited. The European therefore knew from childhood that he had to learn languages to make himself understood to his neighbors, or to travel for study or business. Most important of all, he had to learn languages in order to obtain a serious understanding of religious or, indeed, any other kind of knowledge. Even today, while the southern shore of the Mediterranean owns only one written language, Arabic, the northern shore has almost a dozen.

In the Muslim, and particularly the Arab, lands, the cities offered an infinite variety of types, enriched by returning travelers, visitors, slaves, and merchants coming from the far lands of Asia, Africa, and even Europe. The appearance of men with outlandish costumes and unfamiliar features aroused no curiosity in the great metropolises of the Middle East, where such were commonplace. There was nothing to resemble the extraordinary curiosity exhibited by the inhabitants of the monochrome capitals of Europe at the spectacle of Moroccan, Ottoman, Persian, and other exotic visitors in their midst.

This eager, often ill-mannered, curiosity was noted by many Muslim visitors to Europe. Early in the eighteenth century the Ottoman Ambassador Mehmed Efendi was astonished at the strange behaviour of Europeans who traveled great distances, waited long hours, and endured considerable inconvenience, merely in order to gratify their curiosity with the sight of a Turk. The word translated as curiosity is *hirs,* the meaning of which could more accurately be rendered as eagerness, avidity, or covetousness.[4] Azmi Efendi, pausing in Cöpenick on his way to Berlin in 1790, observes: "Since no envoy has been sent from the side of our exalted Sultanate to Berlin for thirty years, the people of Berlin were unable to contain their impatience until our arrival in the city. Regardless of the winter and the snow, both men and women came in carriages, on horseback, and on foot, to look at us and contemplate us, and then they returned to Berlin."[5] Azmi notes that all the way from Cöpenick to Berlin there were crowds of spectators on both sides. The crowds in the capital were even greater. Vasif describes similar scenes at his entry into Madrid.[6] Most of the other visitors were impressed and not a little flattered at the interest which impelled people to go to much trouble and even pay substantial sums of money for no better reason than to stare at them. This kind of curiosity was obviously quite unfamiliar and difficult to convey.

In the earlier stages one might attribute the difference in attitude of the two cultures to the fact that one had more to learn, the other more to offer. But already by the close of the Crusades this explanation is no longer adequate, and by the end of the Middle Ages it is clear that we are dealing with one of the more fundamental differences between two societies.

To begin with, Europe shared the general lack of curiosity concerning strange peoples. There were, of course, exceptions. Herodotus, the putative Father of History, wrote of barbarians as well as Greeks, and of ancient as well as recent times. Unable to read eastern scripts, he sought his information by travel and inquiry in the East. Many centuries later, another European, William (d. 1190), Archbishop of Tyre in the Latin Kingdom of Jerusalem, wrote a history of the neighbouring Muslim monarchies. He, too, found his sources in the East, and knowing Arabic, was even able to read the original texts.

But such students of alien history were rare. Most European historians, both ancient and medieval, confined themselves to the men and events of their own countries and, usually, of their own times. This, it would seem, was what their readers wanted. Herodotus had few imitators in classical historiography and, on the whole, was derided more than he was admired. William of Tyre's history of the Crusaders in the east was widely read, and even translated into French; his history of the Muslims has not, as far as is known, survived in a single manuscript.

It may well seem strange that classical Islamic civilization which, in its earlier days, was so much affected by Greek and Asian influences should so decisively have rejected the West. But a possible explanation may be suggested. While Islam was still expanding and receptive, western Europe had little or nothing to offer but rather flattered Muslim pride with the spectacle of a culture that was visibly and palpably inferior. What is more, the very fact that it was Christian discredited it in advance. The Muslim doctrine of successive revelations culminating in the final mission of Muhammad led the Muslim to reject Christianity as an earlier and imperfect form of something which he, himself, possessed in its final, perfect form, and to discount Christian thought and Christian civilization accordingly. After the initial impact of eastern Christianity on Islam in its earliest period, Christian influences, even from the high civilization of Byzantium, were reduced to a minimum. Later, by the time that the advance of Christendom and the retreat of Islam had created a new relationship, Islam was crystallized in its ways of thought and behavior and had become impervious to external stimuli, especially those coming from the millennial adversary in the West. Walled off by the military might of the Ottoman Empire, still a formidable barrier even in its decline, the peoples of Islam continued until the dawn of the modern age to cherish—as some of us in the West still do today—the conviction of the immeasurable and immutable superiority of their own civilization to all others. For the medieval Muslim, from Andalusia to Persia, Christian Europe was a backward land of ignorant infidels. It was a point of view which might perhaps have been justified at one time; by the end of the Middle Ages it was becoming dangerously obsolete.

Meanwhile Europe itself had radically changed its own attitude to the outside world. The great efflorescence of European intellectual curiosity and scientific inquiry was due in no small measure to the fortunate though not fortuitous coincidence of three major developments. One was the discovery of a whole new world, with strange peoples, both barbarous and civilized, and with cultures unknown to the scriptures, classics, and memories of Europe. Such a marvelous phenomenon could hardly fail to arouse at least some stirrings of curiosity. Another was the Renaissance, the rediscovery of classical antiquity, which provided both an example of such curiosity and a method for satisfying it. The third was the beginning of the Reformation—the weakening of ecclesiastical authority over both thought and its expression, and the freeing of human minds in a manner without precedent since ancient Athens.

The Muslim world had its own discoveries, as the expansion of the Arab Muslim armies brought them to civilizations as remote and as diverse as Europe, India, and China. It had also had its renaissance, in the recovery of Greek and, to a lesser extent, Persian learning in the early Islamic centuries. But these events did not coincide, and they were not accompanied by any loosening of theological bonds. The Islamic renaissance came when the expansion of Islam had ceased and the counterattack of Christendom was beginning. The intellectual struggle of ancients and moderns, of theologians and philosophers, ended in an overwhelming and enduring victory of the first over the second. This confirmed the Muslim world in the belief in its own self-sufficiency and superiority as the one repository of the true faith and—which for Muslims meant the same thing—of the civilized way of life. It required centuries of defeat and retreat before Muslims were ready to modify this vision of the world and of their place in it, and to look to the Christian West with something other than contempt.

An important and relevant difference between Islam and the West was in the range and scale of commerce, and the impact of those engaged in it. European traders in the Middle East were numerous, often wealthy, and increasingly able to influence and sometimes even control both policy and education. Muslim traders in Europe were few and insignificant, and the Muslim merchant class failed to achieve and maintain a bourgeois society, or seriously to challenge the hold of the military, bureaucratic and religious elites on the state and the schools. It was a difference the consequences of which can be seen in every aspect of Muslim social and intellectual history.

The contrast has sometimes been drawn between the very different responses of the Islamic world and of Japan to the challenge of the West. Their situations were very different. Apart from the obvious advantage which the Japanese enjoyed in living on remote islands far from attack or interference by the Western powers, there was a further difference. Muslim perceptions of Europe were influenced, indeed dominated, by an element which had little or no effect on the Japanese —namely religion. Like the rest of the world, Europe was perceived by Muslims first and foremost in religious terms, i.e., not as Western or European or white but as Christian—and in the Middle East, unlike the Far East, Christianity was familiar and discounted. What lesson of value could be learned from the followers of a flawed and superseded religion?

To make matters worse, that religion was seen as not merely inferior but also hostile. Since its first emergence from Arabia in the seventh century, Islam had been in almost continuous conflict with Christendom, through the original Muslim conquests and the Christian reconquests, through jihād and crusade, the Turkish advance, and the European expansion. Though Islam had fought many wars on many frontiers, it was the wars against Christendom which were the longest and most devastating, and which came to loom in Muslim awareness as the great jihād par excellence. Certainly there were lessons to be learned from the enemy on the battlefield, but they were restricted in value and effect and their impact was deadened by the social and intellectual defenses of Islam.

Some Muslim visitors to Europe were concerned with collecting useful information. At first this consisted almost exclusively of military information likely to be of value in the event of a renewal of armed conflict. Thus, the Turkish and Moroccan embassy reports from Europe usually contained fairly detailed accounts of the envoys' travels to and from their destinations, with some description of the roads, the relay stations, and the defenses of the places through which they passed. In time, some political information, judged to be useful, was added. But this comes remarkably late. It is almost entirely missing during the Middle Ages, and, until the end of the eighteenth century, even Ottoman political reports from Europe are to an astonishing extent fragmentary, rudimentary, and naive.

Towards the end of the eighteenth century, Muslims began to look to Europe with mounting concern, and to show signs of awareness of a need to study this strange and now dangerous society. For the first time, Muslims were ready to travel in Christian Europe and even to stay there for a while. Permanent embassies were established and Ottoman officials of varying ranks remained in Europe, sometimes for years. These were followed by students, first a few and then an ever-growing flood, sent to Europe by Middle Eastern rulers to acquire the arts and skills necessary for the maintenance of their regimes and the defenses of their domains. Though their purpose was still primarily military, this time the effects went very much further and the lessons which these students learned in European universities, even in European military schools, extended beyond the desires or intentions of their imperial masters. By the second quarter of the nineteenth century, the number of Turks, Muslim Arabs, or Persians able to read a European language was still remarkably small, and many of them were converts or sons or grandsons of converts from Christianity or Judaism to Islam. But they were beginning to form an important group, reading other things besides their textbooks, and they had a significant effect as interpreters and, increasingly, as translators.

In the course of the nineteenth century, the pace, scale, and range of the Muslim discovery of Europe were radically transformed—earlier in some countries, later in others, according to the incidence and intensity of the European impact—and the discovery assumed an entirely new character.

The main impetus to change was the by now unmistakable dominance of Europe in the world. But the process of discovery was also vastly accelerated by the opening of new channels and, above all, by the introduction of the printing press and the establishment of newspapers, magazines, and book publishing, by means of which European realities and ideas could reach the Muslim reader.

One of the most effective of the new channels was the newspaper. This European innovation was not entirely unknown in the Islamic east. As early as 1690, the Moroccan ambassador, Ghassānī, reported on what he called the "writing mill," that is to say the printing press, and mentioned the newsletters which were current in Spain at the time.[7] Among other things, he observes that "they are full of sensational lies". Ottoman observers first show some awareness of the European press in the eighteenth century, and there is evidence that excerpts from European newspapers were translated into Turkish for the information of the Imperial Council. What began as an intermittent practice grew into a press bureau which was maintained by the Ottoman government throughout the nineteenth century and after. The archives of the Khedivial Palace in Cairo show a similar preoccupation

with the Western press among the successors of Muḥammad ʿAlī
Pasha.

The first newspapers published in the region were due not to local
but foreign initiative. They were published in French, under French
auspices, and formed part of the propaganda effort of the French
revolutionary government. In the 1790s, the French set up a printing
press in their embassy in Istanbul, from which they issued bulletins,
communiqués, and other announcements, and by 1795 the French
ambassador was printing a fortnightly news sheet of from six to eight
pages, ostensibly for the guidance of French nationals. This was distributed throughout the Ottoman dominions and, in the following
year, became a newspaper, *La Gazette Française de Constantinople,* the first
to appear in the Middle East.[8]

By invading Egypt, Bonaparte put an end to the publication of the
French newspaper in Istanbul, but he made a new start in Cairo, to
which he had brought two printing presses equipped with Arabic and
Greek as well as French type. On 12 Fructidor VI, corresponding to
29th August 1798, the French printed and published the first number
of the *Courier de l'Égypte* which was thereafter published every five days
and provided a coverage of local and sometimes European news. In all,
116 issues appeared.

This news sheet, together with a more ambitious review, *La Décade
d'Égypte,* was exclusively in French. But after the assassination of General Kléber on 16th June 1800, his successor, Abdullah Menou,
launched the first newspaper in the Arabic language. Entitled *Al-Tanbīh,* it was of brief duration.

The next phase in the creation of the Middle Eastern newspaper
press began in Izmir in 1824, with the foundation of a monthly.
Though written in French and addressed in the main to the foreign
community, this paper played a role of some importance in the affairs
of the time and, on occasion, involved its editor in trouble with the
powers, as for example when he defended the Ottoman cause against
the Greek insurgents. The episode illustrated two new points—the
power of the press and the danger of censorship. The Russians, an-
noyed by the editorial line of the paper, tried to persuade the Turkish
authorities to suppress it. The contemporary Ottoman historian Lûtfi
quotes the Russian ambassador as saying:

> Indeed, in France and England journalists can express themselves
> freely, even against their kings; so that on several occasions, in former
> times, wars broke out between France and England because of these
> journalists. Praise be to God, the divinely guarded [i.e., Ottoman] realms

were protected from such things, until a little while ago that man turned up in Izmir and began to publish his paper. It would be well to prevent him. . . .[9]

Despite this terrible warning, the paper continued to appear and was joined in the course of time by other newspapers.

The Egyptian Sheikh Rifāʿa, who went to Paris in 1826, was quick to recognize the value of the press:

> Men learn about what goes on in the minds of others from certain daily sheets called *Journal* and *Gazette*. From these, a man may learn of new events which occur both inside and outside the country. Though he may find in them more lies than can be counted, nevertheless they contain news by which men can acquire knowledge; they discuss newly examined scientific questions or interesting announcements or useful advice, whether coming from the great or the humble—for sometimes the humble have ideas which do not occur to the great. . . . Among the advantages of these sheets are: if a man does anything good or evil and it is important, the people of the *Journal* write about it so that it may become known to both the great and the common people, in order to win approbation for men of good deeds and condemnation for men of evil deeds. Likewise, if a man is wronged by another, he writes of his grievance in these sheets, and everyone, the great and the common people, become aware of it and know the story of the oppressed and his oppressor, exactly as it happened, withholding or changing nothing, so that the affair reaches the place of justice and is judged according to fixed laws, so that this may be a warning and an example to others.[10]

The first regular periodical publication in a Middle Eastern language was founded in Egypt by Muḥammad ʿAlī Pasha. It was the Egyptian official gazette, the first number of which appeared in Cairo on 20th November 1828. Its Ottoman equivalent followed a few years later, in 1832. A leading article explained that the official monitor was the natural development of the ancient Ottoman institution of imperial historiography, and served the same function of making known "the true nature of events and the real purport of the acts and commands of the government," so as to prevent misunderstanding and to forestall uninformed criticism. A further purpose, it was stated, was to provide useful knowledge on commerce, science, and the arts. The inauguration of the Ottoman postal service in 1834 greatly helped the circulation of this journal, which remained the only newspaper in the Turkish language until the first nonofficial paper, a weekly news sheet, was founded in 1840 by an Englishman named William Churchill. In Iran, a kind of official newsletter was started in 1835 by Mīrzā Muḥammad Ṣāliḥ, who had been one of the first Iranian students in England.

To the modern reader, these official gazettes, from Cairo, Istanbul and Tehran, seem poor and dry, of limited interest and appeal. Nevertheless, they must have played a role of some importance in familiarizing their Turkish, Egyptian and Persian readers with at least the broad configuration of the outside world, and also in the creating of a new journalistic vocabulary, to denote and discuss hitherto unknown institutions and ideas. The resulting lexical revolution inaugurated a major advance in the process of discovery. With later newspapers and periodicals, it also provided a vehicle and a medium for the steadily growing volume of translations which were bringing information about Europe, much of it written by Europeans, to Muslim readers.

In the early decades of the nineteenth century, there were two main centers of westernizing reform, in Turkey and Egypt. In both of them the preparation and publication of translations of Western books was given central importance. In Egypt, more particularly, there was an organized, state-sponsored program of translations, unparalleled since the days when the Abbasid Caliphs ordered the translation into Arabic of Greek works of philosophy and science. Between 1822 and 1842, 243 books were printed in Cairo, of which by far the greater part were translations. Though printed in Egypt, an Arabic speaking country, more than half of them were in Turkish. In Muḥammad ʿAlī Pasha's Egypt, Turkish was still the language of the ruling elite, and works on military and naval subjects, including pure and applied mathematics, were, therefore, almost all in Turkish. More than half of the students whom the pasha sent to Europe were Turkish-speaking Ottomans from outside Egypt. Works on medicine, veterinarian science, and agriculture, on the other hand, were mostly in Arabic, these being subjects which were not reserved to the Turkish-speaking ruling elite. History, given temporary accreditation as a useful science, also appears to have been a matter for the elite, since the few historical books printed at Muḥammad ʿAlī's press in the early period are all in Turkish. Between 1829 and 1834, four books of historical content were translated, one on Catherine the Great of Russia and the other three on Napoleon and his time. There followed an interval of several years before the next historical translation appeared—a version of Voltaire's *Histoire de Charles XII,* published in 1841. This time it was not in Turkish but in Arabic as were also subsequent translations of historical works published in Egypt.[11]

The Turkish translations published in Egypt were, of course, read in Turkey, and some were reprinted there. But the translation movement in Istanbul was for long limited to scientific works, and it is not until the mid-century that translations of European books on history begin to appear in Istanbul. A turning point was the publication, in 1866, of a Turkish version of an English compendium of universal history.

In Iran, interest in Western history seems to have disappeared after the great chronicle of Rashīd al-Dīn. His work found many imitators but the treatment of remoter areas became stylized, and nothing new of interest was added. It was not until the early years of the nineteenth century that we find a few works, most of them still in manuscript, dealing with Western history. To a remarkable extent, these derive from Turkish rather than direct Western sources of information. An undated manuscript, probably of the early nineteenth century, by an unknown author tells the history of England from Julius Caesar to Charles I in twenty-eight chapters.[12] Apart from this, histories of western Europe written in Persian do not appear until well into the second half of the nineteenth century. By that time, there was already a very extensive literature in both Turkish and Arabic, which, together with the rapidly growing newspaper and periodical press, must have transformed the world picture as it appeared to Muslim readers.

During the first half of the nineteenth century, the process of discovery grew to the dimensions of a flood. Europe was no longer waiting to be discovered by the Muslim explorer, but was itself invading the Muslim lands and imposing a fundamental new relationship, to which the Muslim world took long to adjust itself and which it never really accepted.

During the early nineteenth century, the change can be seen in a number of respects. One, already noted, is the attitude to foreign, that is to say European, languages. For the first time, a knowledge of a Western language is seen as something admissible, then desirable, finally necessary, and young Muslims were placed under foreign teachers, at first in their own countries and ultimately even in Europe. Not long before such action would have been regarded as grotesque and unspeakable. Now a knowledge of foreign languages became an important qualification, and the language school and translation office ranked with the army and the palace among the avenues to power. The same change in circumstances gave a new and important role to the Christian minorities, especially in the Arab countries where, far more than in Turkey or Persia, they shared the language and culture of the Muslim majority.

The flood of Muslim visitors to Europe was growing—first diplomats, then students, then many others, including after a while even political refugees. The movement of knowledge and ideas from Europe to the Middle East went through the same channels and others, now incomparably wider. In addition to the much larger movement of persons, there were many new areas of contact. The school and the regiment, the book and the newspaper, the government office and the counting-house were all helping to deepen and broaden Muslim awareness of Europe, now increasingly seen as an immensely powerful and rapidly expanding force, threatening the very existence of Islam, and requiring that it be understood and in some measure imitated.

The old attitude of disdain and lack of interest was, for a while, changing, at least among some elements of the ruling elites. At last Muslims were turning towards Europe, if not with admiration, then with respect, and perhaps fear, and paying it the supreme compliment of imitation. A new phase in the discovery was beginning; it has continued almost until our own time.

Notes

Preface to the 2001 Paperback Edition

1. James, Boswell, *The Life of Samuel Johnson L.L.D.* (New York, The Modern Library) pp. 45, 1039.
2. See below, p. 57.

Chapter I

1. Edward Gibbon, *The Decline and Fall of the Roman Empire,* ed. J.B. Bury (London, 1909/1914), vol. 6, chap. 52:16.
2. Zuhrī, *Kitāb al-Djuʿrāfiya.* Mappemonde du Calife al-Maʾmun réproduite par Fazàri (III/IX s.) rééditée et commentée par Zuhrī (VIᵉ/XIIᵉ s.), ed. M. Hadj-Sadok in *Bulletin d'études orientales* 21 (1968): 77/230; cf. French transl., p. 39.
3. Ibn ʿAbd al-Ḥakam, *Futūḥ Miṣr wa-akhbāruhā,* ed. C. C. Torrey (New Haven, 1922), pp. 216–217.
4. Ibn al-Qalānisī, *Dhayl taʾrīkh Dimashq (History of Damascus 365–555 A.H.),* ed. H. F. Amedroz (Beirut, 1908), p. 134; cf. English transl., H. A. R. Gibb, *The Damascus Chronicles of the Crusades,* (London, 1932), p. 41.
5. Ibn al-Athīr, *al-Kāmil fiʾl-taʾrīkh,* ed. C. J. Thornberg (Leiden, 1851–1876), 10:185, year 491.
6. *Ibid.,* 10: 192–193, year 492.
7. E. Ashtor, "The Social Isolation of the *Ahl adh-Dhimma,"* Pal Hirschler *Memorial Book* (Budapest, 1949), pp. 73–94.
8. Abū Shāma, *Kitāb al-Rawḍatayn fī akhbār al-dawlatayn,* 2nd edition, ed. M. Ḥilmī Aḥmad (Cairo, 1962), 1 pt. 2: 621–622.

9. Ahmedi in *Osmanli Tarihleri,* ed. N. Atsiz (Istanbul, 1949), p. 7; cf. Paul Wittek, *The Rise of the Ottoman Empire* (London, 1938), p. 14.

10. Oruç, *Die frühosmanischen Jahrbücher des Urudsch,* ed. F. C. H. Babinger (Hanover, 1925), p. 124; *Oruç Beğ Tarihi,* ed. N. Atsiz (Istanbul, 1972), pp. 108–9.

11. English transl., E. J. W. Gibb, *The Capture of Constantinople* (London, 1879) pp. 33–34 (slightly revised); cf. Sa'd al-Din, *Taj al-tavarih* (Istanbul, 1279 A.H.), 1:419ff.

12. Tursun, *The History of Mehmed the Conqueror,* ed. and trans. H. Inalcik and R. Murphy (Minneapolis and Chicago, 1978), fols. 156a–156b.

13. Neşri, *Gihännümä, die Altosmanische Chronik des Mevlänä Mehemmed Neschri,* ed. F. Taeschner (Leipzig, 1951), 2:307–8; *Kitab-i Cihan Nüma, Neşri Tarihi,* ed. F.R. Unat and M.A. Köymen (Ankara, 1949), 2: 838–39.

14. R. Knolles, *The generall historie of the Turkes, from the first beginning of that nation to the rising of the Othoman families* (London, 1603), p.1.

15. Eskandar Monshi, *History of Shah Abbas the Great,* trans. R. M. Savory, (Boulder, 1978), 2:1202–3.

16. *Tarih al-Hind al-Garbi* (Istanbul, 1729), fol. 6bff.

17. On this project, see the article of H. Inalcik, "Osmanli-Rus rekabetinin menşei ve Don Volga Kanali teşebbüsü (1569)," *Belleten* 46 (1948): 349–402; English version, "The Origins of the Ottoman-Russian Rivalry and the Don Volga Canal, 1569," *Annals of the University of Ankara* 1 (1946–47): 47–107.

18. Ogier Ghiselin de Busbecq, *The Turkish Letters* . . . , trans. C. T. Forster and F. H. B. Daniell (London, 1881), 1: 129–30; cf. *The Turkish Letters* . . . , trans. W. S. Forster (Oxford, 1927), pp. 40–41.

19. *Silihdar tarihi* (Istanbul, 1928), 2:80.

20. *Ibid.,* 2:87; cf. German transl., R. F. Kreutel, *Kara Mustafa vor Wien* (Graz, 1955), pp. 160 and 166.

21. Cited in Ahmet Refik, *Ahmet Refik hayati seçme şiir ve yazilari,* ed. R. E. Koçu (Istanbul, 1938), p. 101.

22. F. von Kraelitz-Greifenhorst, "Bericht über den Zug des Gross-Botschafters Ibrahim Pascha nach Wien im Jahre 1719," *Akademie der Wiss. Wien: Phil. Hist. Kl. Sitzungsberichte* 158 (1909): 26–77.

23. *Das Asafname des Lutfi Pascha,* ed. and trans. R. Tschudi (Berlin, 1910), p. 34.

24. *Mühimme defteri,* vol. 16, no. 139: "Donanma-i hümayun küffar-i haksar donanmasi ile mülaki olup iradet Allah nev'-i ahire müte-'allik oldu . . ." Cf. M. Lesure, *Lepante: la crise de l'empire Ottoman* (Paris, 1972), p. 180.

25. *Tarih-i Peçevi* (Istanbul, 1283 A.H.), 1: 498–99; cf. A. C. Hess, "The

Battle of Lepanto and its Place in Mediterranean History," *Past and Present* 57 (1972): 54.

26. Kemalpaşazade, *Histoire de la campagne de Mohacz* . . . , ed. and trans. M. Pavet de Courteille (Paris, 1859), pp. 24–27.

27. Qur'ān, 60.1; cf. Qur'ān 5.51.

28. *Tarih-i Cevdet* (Istanbul, 1301–1309 A.H.) 5:14.

29. Vasif in Cevdet, 4:357–58; cf. French transl., Barbier de Meynard, "Ambassade de l'historien Turc Vaçif-Efendi en Espagne (1787–1788)," *Journal Asiatique* 5 (1862): 521–23.

30. V. L. Ménage, "The English Capitulations of 1580: A Review Article," *International Journal of Middle Eastern Studies* 12 (1980): 375.

31. Ibrahim Müteferrika, *Uṣūl al-ḥikem fī niẓām al-umem* (Istanbul, 1144 A.H.); *idem,* French version, *Traité de la Tactique* (Vienna, 1769).

32. T. Öz, ed., "Selim III ün Sirkatibi tarafından tutulan Ruzname," *Tarih Vesikalari* 3 (May, 1949): 184; cf. Cevdet, 6:130; cf. B. Lewis, "The Impact of the French Revolution on Turkey," in *The New Asia: Readings in the History of Mankind,* ed. G.S. Metraux and F. Crouzet (1965), p. 119, n. 37.

33. Cevdet, 6: 118–19; see further B. Lewis, "The Impact of the French Revolution . . . ," p. 57, n. 12.

34. E. Z. Karal, "Yunan Adalarının Fransızlar tarafından işgali," *Tarih Semineri Dergisi,* (1937), p. 113 ff; Cevdet, 6: 280–81.

35. Cevdet, 6: 311; cf. Bernard Lewis, *The Emergence of Modern Turkey* (London, 1968), pp. 66–67.

36. Jabartī, *'Ajā'ib al-athār fī al-tarājim wa'l-akhbār* (Būlāq, 1297 A.H.), 3:2–3.

37. Nicola Turk, *Chronique d'Egypte 1798–1804,* ed. and trans. Gaston Wiet (Cairo, 1950), text pp. 2–3; cf. French transl., pp. 3–4. See also George M. Haddad, "The historical work of Niqula el-Turk, 1763–1828," *Journal of the American Oriental Society,* 81 (1961), pp. 247–51.

38. *Ibid.,* p. 173; cf. French translation, p. 223.

39. E. Ziya Karal, *Halet Efendinin Paris Büyük Elçiligi 1802–1806* (Istanbul, 1940), pp. 32–34, 35, and 62; cf. B. Lewis, "The Impact of the French Revolution . . . ," p. 54.

40. *Asim Tarihi* (Istanbul, n.d.), 1:374–76; cf. Cevdet, 8:147–48 and Bernard Lewis, *The Emergence of Modern Turkey,* p. 72.

Chapter II

1. H. R. Idris, "Commerce maritime et kirād en Berberie orientale," *JESHO,* 14 (1961), pp. 228–29.

2. W. Cantwell Smith, *The Meaning and End of Religion* (New York, 1964), pp. 58ff, 75ff; cf Marcel Simon, *Verus Israel* (Paris, 1948), p. 136 ff.

3. Qur'ān, 112.

4. *Ibid.,* 16.115.

5. *Ibid.,* 109.

6. See D. Santillana, *Instituzioni di Diritto Musulmano,* 1 (Rome, 1926): 69–71; L. P. Harvey, "Crypto-Islam in Sixteenth Century Spain," *Actas del Primer Congreso de Estudios Árabes e Islámicos* (Madrid, 1964), pp. 163–178; al-Wansharīshī, *Asnā al-matājir fī bayān aḥkām man ghalaba ̔ila waṭanihi al-naṣārā wa-lam yuhājir,* ed. Ḥusayn Mu'nis, in *Revista del Instituto Egipcio de Estudios Islámicos en Madrid* 5 (1957): 129–191.

7. Ṣā'id b. Aḥmad al-Andalūsī, *Kitāb Ṭabaqāt al-Umam,* (Cairo, n.d.), p. 11; cf. French transl., R. Blachère, *Livre des catégories des nations, Publications de l'Institut des Hautes Études Marocaines* 28 (Paris, 1935): 36–37.

Chapter III

1. Rashīd al-Dīn, *Histoire universelle . . . ,* I, *Histoire des Franks,* ed. and trans. K. Jahn (Leiden, 1951), text p. 11; cf. French transl., p. 24; cf. German transl., K. Jahn, *Die Frankengeschichte des Rašīd ad-Dīn* (Vienna, 1977), p. 54.

2. G.S. Colin, "Un petit glossaire hispanique arabo-allemand de début du XVIᵉ siècle," *al-Andalus* 11 (1946): 275–81.

3. On the translation movement and its accomplishments, see F. Rosenthal, *The Classical Heritage in Islam* (London, 1975).

4. On the Orosius version, see G. Levi Della Vida, "La traduzione araba delle storie di Orosio," *al-Andalus* 19 (1954): 257–93.

5. Awḥadī, ed. M. Hamidullah, "Embassy of Queen Bertha to Caliph al-Muktafi billah in Baghdad 293/906," *Journal of the Pakistan Historical Society* 1 (1953): 272–300. See further, G. Levi Della Vida, "La corrispondenza di Berta di Toscano col Califfo Muktafi," *Rivista Storica Italiana* 66 (1954): 21–38; C. Inostrancev, "Notes sur les rapports de Rome et du califat abbaside au commencement du Xᵉ siècle," *Rivista degli Studi Orientali* 6 (1911–1912): 81–86.

6. Ibn al-Nadīm, *Kitāb al-Fihrist,* ed. G. Flügel (Leipzig, 1871), 1: 15–16; cf. English transl., B. Dodge (New York, 1970), 1: 28–31.

7. Both volumes of Osman Ağa's memoirs were first published in German translation: see R. F. Kreutel and O. Spies, *Leben und Abenteuer des Dolmetschers ʿOsman Ağa* (Bonn, 1954), and R. F. Kreutel, *Zwischen Paschas und Generalen* (Graz, 1966). The Turkish text of one

volume has been edited by R. F. Kreutel, *Die Autobiographie des Dolmetschers ʿOsman Ağa aus Temeschwar* (Cambridge, 1980).

8. Ö. L. Barkan, *XV ve XVIinci asirlarda Osmanli Imparatorluğunda zirai ekonominin hukuki ve mali esaslari,* vol. 1, *Kanunlar* (Istanbul, 1943), p. 213.

9. See J. Wansbrough, "A Mamluk Ambassador to Venice in 913/ 1507," *Bulletin of the School of Oriental and African Studies* 26, pt. 3 (1963): 503–30.

10. F. Babinger, "Der Pfortendolmetscher Murad und seine Schriften," in *Literaturdenkmäler aus Ungarns Türkenzeit,* ed. F. Babinger et al. (Berlin and Leipzig, 1927) pp. 33–54.

11. Evliya, *Seyahatname* (Istanbul, 1314 A.H.), 7: 322; cf. German translation, R. F. Kreutel, *Im Reiche des Goldenen Apfels* (Graz, 1957), p. 199.

12. Evliya, 7: 323; cf. Kreutel, p. 200.

13. Evliya, 3: 120–21.

14. Muḥammad b. ʿAbd al-Wahhāb, al-Wazīr al-Ghassānī, *Riḥlat al-wazīr fī iftikāk al-asīr,* ed. Alfredo Bustānī (Tangier, 1940), p. 96; cf. French transl. by H. Sauvaire, *Voyage en Espagne d'un Ambassadeur Marocain* (Paris, 1884), pp. 225–26.

15. Kâtib Çelebi, *Irşad al-hayara ila tarih al-Yunan wa'l-Rum wa'l-Nasara,* manuscript in Türk Tarih Kurumu Library, no. 19 (no pagination). Kâtib Çelebi is also known as Hajji Khalifa, in Turkish orthography Haci Halife. The ms. is briefly described by V.L. Ménage in "Three Ottoman Treatises on Europe," *Iran and Islam,* ed. C.E. Bosworth (Edinburgh, 1971), pp. 421–23.

16. Arnold of Lübeck, *Chronicon Slavorum,* ed. W. Wattenbach, *Deutschlands Geschichtsquellen* (Stuttgart-Berlin, 1907) bk. vii, chap. 8.

17. A. Bombaci, "Nuovi firmani greci di Maometto II," *Byzantinische Zeitschrift* 47 (1954): 238–319; *idem,* "Il 'Liber Graecus,' un cartolario veneziano comprendente inediti documenti Ottomani in Greco (1481–1504)," *Westöstliche Abhandlungen,* ed. F. Meier, (Wiesbaden, 1954), pp. 288–303. See further Christos G. Patrinelis, "Mehmed II the Conqueror and his presumed knowledge of Greek and Latin," *Viator,* 2 (1971): 349–54.

18. See H. and R. Kahane and A. Tietze, *The Lingua Franca in the Levant* (Urbana, 1958).

19. L. Bonelli, "Elementi italiani nel turco ed elementi turchi nell italiano," *L'Oriente* 1 (1894): 178–96.

20. Şem'danizade, *Şem'dani-zade Findiklili Süleyman Efendi tarihi mür'it-tevarih,* ed. M. M. Aktepe (Istanbul, 1978), p. 107. See preface to *Relation de l'ambassade de Méhmet Effendi à la cour de France en 1721 écrite*

par lui même et traduite du turc par Julién Galland (Constantinople and Paris, 1757).

21. Cited in C. Issawi, "The Struggle for Linguistic Hegemony," *The American Scholar* (summer, 1981), pp. 382–87.

22. Seid Mustafa, *Diatribe de l'ingénieur sur l'état actuel de l'art militaire, du génie et des sciences à Constantinople* (Scutari, 1803; reprinted by L. Langlès, Paris, 1810), pp. 16–17. According to Langlès, Seid Mustafa was a graduate and later a teacher of engineering. Hammer-Purgstall, however, says that "Seid Mustafa" was a fiction and that the tract was written at the request of the Reis Efendi by the Greek dragoman Yakovaki Argyropoulo. On Y. Argyropoulo, a key figure in the early translation movement, see "Jacques Argyropoulos," *Magasin Pittoresque* (1865), pp. 127–28.

23. Şanizade, *Tarih* (Istanbul, 1290–1291 A.H.), 4: 33–35; cf. Cevdet, 11: 43 and [J. E. de Kay] *Sketches of Turkey in 1831 and 1832* (New York, 1833).

24. B. Lewis, *The Emergence of Modern Turkey*, pp. 88–89.

25. S. Ünver, *Tanzimat*, 1, Turkish Ministry of Education (Istanbul, 1940), pp. 940–41.

Chapter IV

1. For contrasting views on the significance of the Hellenistic element in Islamic civilization and of the resulting affinities with Christendom, see C.H. Becker, *Islamstudien*, vol. 1 (Leipzig, 1924), especially chapters 1, 2, 3, and 14; and also Jörg Kraemer, *Das Problem der Islamischen Kulturgeschichte* (Tübingen, 1959).

2. Ibn al-Faqīh, cited in Yāqūt, *Muʿjam al-buldān*, s.v. "Rūmiya."

3. Part of his account is preserved and quoted in Ibn Rusteh, *Kitāb al-Aʿlāq al-nafīsa*, ed. M. J. De Goeje (Leiden, 1892), pp. 119–130. See further, *Encyclopedia of Islam*, 2nd ed., s.v. 'Hārūn b. Yaḥyā' (M. Izzedin). The *Encyclopedia of Islam* will hereafter be cited as EI1. or EI2. .

4. The Kadi's memoirs were published by I. Parmaksizoğlu, "Bir Türk kadisinin esaret hatiralari," *Tarih Dergisi* 5 (1953): 77–84.

5. On Osman Ağa, see above Chap. 3, n. 7. On other prisoners, see O. Spies, "Schicksale Türkischer Kriegsgefangener in Deutschland nach den Türkenkrieg," *Festschrift Werner Caskel*, ed. E. Graf (Leiden, 1968), pp. 316–35.

6. Usāma, *Kitāb al-Iʿtibār*, ed. P.K. Hitti (Princeton, 1930), p. 132; cf. English transl., P.K. Hitti, *An Arab-Syrian Gentleman and Warrior in the Period of the Crusades* (New York, 1929), p. 161.

7. On this story, see V. Barthold, "Karl Veliki i Harun ar-Rashid," *Sočineniya* 6 (Moscow, 1966): 342–64; Arabic transl. in V. V. Barthold, *Dirāsāt fī ta'rīkh Filaṣtīn fī'l-ʿuṣūr al-wusṭā,* trans. A. Haddād (Baghdad, 1973): 53–103. Also see S. Runciman, "Charlemagne and Palestine," *English Historical Review* 50 (1935): 606–19.

8. See above, chap. 3, n. 5.

9. Arabic text, R. Dozy, ed., *Recherches sur l'histoire et la litterature de l'Espagne pendant le moyen âge,* 3rd ed. (Paris-Leiden, 1881), 2: 81–88; reprinted by A. Seippel, *Rerum Normannicarum Fontes Arabici* (Oslo, 1946), pp. 13–20. Cf. German translation, G. Jacob, *Arabische Berichte von Gesandten an germanische Fürstenhöfe aus dem 9. und 10. Jahrhundert* (Berlin-Leipzig, 1927), pp. 38–39; French transl. in R. Dozy, *Recherches,* 3rd ed., 2: 269–78. For discussions, see W. E. D. Allen, *The Poet and the Spae-Wife* (Dublin, 1960), and E. Lévi-Provençal, "Un échange d'ambassades entre Cordoue et Byzance au IXe siècle," *Byzantion* 12 (1937): 1–24, who dismisses the story as a literary fabrication based on a genuine embassy to Constantinople. See further, EI2. , s.v. "Ghazāl" (A. Huici Miranda). Also see A. A. el-Hajji, "The Andalusian Diplomatic Relations with the Vikings during the Umayyad Period," *Hesperis Tamuda,* 8 (1967): 67–110.

10. The surviving fragments of Ibrāhīm ibn Yaʿqūb's travels have formed the subject of an extensive literature. Both texts, the ʿUdhrī version as preserved by Qazvīnī and the Bakrī passages are available in print: Qazvīnī, in the *editio princeps* by F. Wüstenfeld, *Zakarija ben Muhammed ben Mahmud al-Cazwini's Kosmographie,* II, *Kitāb Athār al-bilād. Die Denkmäler der Länder* (Göttingen, 1848); the Bakrī excerpt was first edited by A. Kunik and V. Rosen, *Izvestiya al-Bekri i drugikh' autorov' o Rusi i Slavyanakh* (St. Petersburg, 1878–1903), reprinted with a critical commentary by T. Kowalski, *Relatio Ibrāhīm Ibn Jaʿḳūb de itinere slavico,* in *Monumenta Poloniae Historica* 1 (Cracow, 1946): 139ff., and now conveniently accessible in an edition of Bakrī's book by A.A. el-Hajji, ed., *Jughrāfiya al-Andalus wa-Urūba* (Beirut, 1968). Translations include G. Jacob in *Arabische Berichte . . . ,* pp. 11–33; and most recently, A. Miquel, "L'Europe occidentale dans la relation arabe de Ibrāhīm b. Yaʿqūb," *Annales ESC* 21 (1966): 1048–1064. Other studies include, B. Spuler, "Ibrāhīm ibn Jaʿqūb Orientalistische Bemerkungen," *Jahrbücher für Geschichte Osteuropas,* 3 (1938): 1–10; E. Ashtor, *The Jews of Moslem Spain,* vol. 1 (Philadelphia, 1973), pp. 344–49; A.A. el-Hajji, "Ibrāhīm ibn Yaʿqūb at-Tartūshī and his diplomatic activity," *The Islamic Quarterly* 14 (1970): 22–40. See further EI2. , s.v. "Ibrāhīm b. Yaʿqūb," (A. Miquel).

11. G. Jacob, *Arabische Berichte,* p. 31, n. 1: "Es ist charakteristisch, dass der arabische Diplomat den Kaiser als Gewährsmann nicht nennt,

wahrend der jüdische Handelsmann sich mit dieser Beziehung brüstet."

12. Mentioned in the biography of John of Gorze, see R. W. Southern, *The Making of the Middle Ages* (London, 1953), p. 36ff.

13. Ibn Wāṣil, *Mufarrij al-kurūb fī akhbār banī Ayyūb,* ed. H. M. Rabie (Cairo, 1979), 4: 248.

14. Ibn Khaldūn, *Al-Taʿrīf bi-ibn Khaldūn wa-riḥlatuh gharban wa-sharqan,* ed. Muḥammad ibn Taʾwīt al-Tanjī (Cairo 1951), pp. 84–85; cf. French transl. by A. Cheddadi, *Le Voyage d'Occident en Orient* (Paris, 1980), pp. 91–92.

15. Usāma, pp. 140–141; cf. Hitti, pp. 169–76.

16. *Abū Ḥāmid al Granadino y su relación de viaje por tierras eurasiáticas,* ed. and trans. C.E. Dubler (Madrid, 1953). See further, I. Hrbek, "Ein arabischer Bericht über Ungarn," *Acta Orientalia* 5 (1955): 205–30.

17. Ibn Jubayr, *Riḥla (The Travels of Ibn Jubayr)* ed. W. Wright (Leiden, 1907), p. 303; cf. English transl. R. C. J. Broadhurst, *The Travels of Ibn Jubayr* (London, 1953), p. 318.

18. Ibn Jubayr, pp. 305–6; cf. Broadhurst, p. 321.

19. *Ibid.,* p. 301; cf. Broadhurst, pp. 316–17. The concluding quotation is from Qur'ān, 7.154.

20. Ibn Shāhīn al-Ẓāhirī, *Zubdat kashf al-mamālik,* ed. P. Ravaisse (Paris, 1894) p. 41; cf. French translation, J. Gaulmier, *La zubda kachf al-mamālik* (Beirut, 1950), p. 60. Cf. M. A. Alarcón and R. Garcia, *Los documentos árabes diplomáticos del Archivo de la corona de Aragón* (Madrid and Granada, 1940).

21. See P. Pelliot, "Les Mongols et la Papauté," *Revue de l'Orient Chrétien* 3rd ser., 23 (1922–23): 3–30, 24 (1924): 225–335, and 28 (1931); V. Minorsky, "The Middle East in Western Politics in the thirteenth, fifteenth, and seventeenth Centuries," *Royal Central Asian Society Journal* 4 (1940): 427–61; J. A. Boyle, "The Il-Khans of Persia and the Princes of Europe," *Central Asian Journal* 20 (1976): 28–40; D. Sinor, "Les Relations entre les Mongols et l'Europe jusqu'à la Mort d'Arghoun et de Bela IV," *Cahiers d'Histoire Mondiale* 3 (1956): 37–92.

22. ʿUmarī, *al-Taʿrīf bil-muṣtalaḥt al-sharīf* (Cairo, 1312 A.H.).

23. Qalqashandī, *Ṣubḥ al-aʿshā fī ṣināʿat al-inshā'* (Cairo, 1913ff), 8: 25ff; cf. M. Amari, "Dei titoli che usava la cancelleria di Egitto," *Mem. del. R. Acc. Linc.* (1883–84): 507–34; H. Lammens, "Correspondence diplomatiques entre les sultans mamlouks d'Égypte et les puissances chrétiennes," *Revue de l'Orient Chrétien* 9 (1904): 151–87 and 10 (1905): 359–92.

24. Qalqashandī, 7: 42ff.

25. Juvaynī, *Ta'rīkh-i jihān gushā,* ed. M. M. Qazvīnī, vol. 1 (London, 1912), pp. 38–39. Cf. English transl., J. A. Boyle, *The History of the World Conqueror* (Manchester, 1958), 1: 53.

26. Nicholas de Nicolay, *Les navigations . . .* (Antwerp, 1576), p. 246.

27. B. Lewis, *Notes and Documents from the Turkish Archives* (Jerusalem, 1952), pp. 32 and 34.

28. A. Arce, "Espionaje y última aventura de Jose Nasi (1569–1574)" *Sefarad* 13 (1953): 257–86.

29. C.D. Rouillard, *The Turk in French History, Thought, and Literature 1520–1660* (Paris, 1938), pt. 1, chap. 2.

30. M. Herbette, *Une Ambassade Persane sous Louis XIV* (Paris, 1907).

31. A. A. De Groot, *The Ottoman Empire and the Dutch Republic: A History of the Earliest Diplomatic Relations 1610–1670* (Leiden, 1978), pp. 125–29.

32. On the reports of Ottoman embassies to Europe and elsewhere, see F. Babinger, *Die Geschichtsschreiber der Osmanen und ihre Werke* (Leipzig, 1927), pp. 322–37, hereafter cited as *GOW;* and for a much fuller account, F. R. Unat, *Osmanli Sefirleri ve Sefaretnameleri* (Ankara, 1968). A few of these texts have been translated (see Babinger, *loc. cit.*); the best and most recent are the annotated German versions published by R. F. Kreutel in his series, *Osmanische Geschichtsschreiber* (Graz, 1955ff). On European diplomacy in Istanbul, see B. Spuler, "Die europäische Diplomatie in Konstantinopel bis zum Frieden von Belgrad (1739)," *Jahrbücher für Kultur und Geschichte der Slaven,* 11 (1935): 53–115, 171–222, 313–366; idem, "Europäische Diplomaten in Konstantinopel bis zum Frieden von Belgrad (1739)," *Jahrbücher für Geschichte Osteuropas* 1 (1936): 229–62, 383–440.

33. See Babinger, *GOW,* p. 325.

34. See K. Teply, "Evliyā Çelebī in Wien," *Der Islam* 52 (1975): 125–31.

35. Evliya, 7: 398–99; cf. Kreutel, p. 160–61.

36. There are several editions of the embassy report of Mehmed Efendi with some variations in the text. The book was first published in Paris and Istanbul with a French translation as *Relation de l'embassade de Méhmet Effendi à la cour de France en 1721 écrite par lui même et traduit par Julién Galland* (Constantinople and Paris, 1757). I have used the Turkish edition of Ebuzziya, ed., *Paris Sefaretnamesi* (Istanbul, 1306). When this book was already in proof a new edition of Galland's version appeared—Mehmed Efendi, *Le paradis des infidèles,* ed. Gilles Veinstein, (Paris, 1981).

37. Mehmed Efendi, p. 345; cf. French transl., pp. 34ff.

38. *Ibid.,* p. 43; cf. French transl., p. 49.

39. *Ibid.,* p. 64; cf. French transl., pp. 62–63.

40. Duc de St. Simon, cited in N. Berkes, *The Development of Secularism in*

Turkey (Montreal, 1964), p. 35. For a brief but illuminating appreciation of Mehmed Efendi and his role see A. H. Tanpinar, *XIX Asir Türk edebiyati tarihi,* vol. 1 (Istanbul, 1956), pp. 9ff.

41. Resmi, *Viyana Sefaretnamesi* (Istanbul, 1304), p. 33.

42. Azmi, *Sefaretname 1205 senesinde Prusya Kirali Ikinci Fredrik Guillaum'in nezdine memur olan Ahmed Azmi Efendinin'dir* (Istanbul, 1303 A.H.), p. 52; Resmi, *Berlin Sefaretnamesi* (Istanbul, 1303), p. 47.

43. Vasif's report is printed in Cevdet, 4: 348–58.

44. Vasif in Cevdet, 4: 349–50.

45. On Ratib, see Cevdet, 5: 232ff; F. R. Unat, *Osmanli Sefirleri,* pp. 154–62; C. V. Findley, *Bureaucratic Reform in the Ottoman Empire: The Sublime Porte, 1789–1922* (Princeton, 1980), pp. 118 and 372; S. J. Shaw, *Between Old and New, The Ottoman Empire Under Sultan Selim III* (Cambridge, Mass., 1971), pp. 95–98.

46. On Moroccan ambassadors and other Muslim travelers to Spain, see H. Pérès, *L'Espagne vue par les Voyaguers Musulmans de 1610 a 1930* (Paris, 1937).

47. See above chapter 3, note 14.

48. S.C. Chew, *The Crescent and the Rose* (Oxford, 1937), pp. 327–33.

49. M. Herbette, *Une Ambassade Persane,* passim.

50. On Shirāzī, see C. A. Storey, *Persian Literature,* vol. 1, pt. 2 (London, 1953) pp. 1067–8.

51. Parts of this narrative were translated from a manuscript by A. Bausani, "Un manoscritto Persiano inedito sulla Ambasceria di Husein Hān Moqaddam Āgūdānbāsi̇̄ in Europa negli anni 1254–1255 H. (1838–39 A.D.)," *Oriente Moderno* 33 (1953). The original was published in Iran but from a different manuscript, *Sharh-i ma'mūriyat-i Ājūdān bāshi̇̄ (Husayn Khān Nizām ad-Dawla) dar Safārat-i Otrish, Farānsa, Inglistān* (Tehran (?), 1347 S.).

52. A. Bausani, "Un manoscritto Persiano . . . ," p. 488. This paragraph is missing from the Tehran edition.

53. Ilyās b. Hannā, *Le plus ancien voyage d'un Oriental en Amerique (1668–1683),* ed. A. Rabbath, S. J. (Beirut, 1906). This edition first appeared in the Beirut review *al-Mashriq,* nos. 18 (Sept. 1905) through 23 (Dec. 1905) as "Premier voyage d'un oriental en Amerique."

54. Azulay, *Ma'gal tōb ha-shalem,* ed. A. Freimann (Jerusalem, 1934); English transl. in E. Adler, *Jewish Travellers,* pp. 345–68.

55. P. Preto, *Venezia e i Turchi* (Padua, 1975), p. 128 citing P. Paruta, *Historia della güerra di Cipro* (Venice, 1615), p. 35. On the Turkish colony in Venice, see also A. Sagrado and F. Berchet, *Il Fondacho dei Turchi in Venezia* (Milan, 1860), pp. 23–28 and G. Verecellin, "Mercanti Turchi a Venezia alla fine del cinquecento," *Il Veltro:*

Rivista della Civiltà Italiana, 23, nos. 2–4 (Mar.–Aug., 1979): 243–75. On the role of Venice as intermediary between Turkey and Europe, see W. H. McNeill, *Venice, the Hinge of Europe 1081–1797* (Chicago, 1974).

56. Preto, p. 129.
57. *Ibid.,* p. 132.
58. *Ibid.,* p. 139.
59. Sir Joshua Hassan, *The Treaty of Utrecht and the Jews of Gibraltar* (London, 1970).
60. For an early example, see F. Babinger, " 'Bajezid Osman' (Calixtus Ottomanus), ein Vorläufer und Gegenspieler Dschem-Sultans," *La Nouvelle Clio* 3 (1951): 349–88.
61. There is a considerable literature on Jem and his adventures in Europe, notably L. Thuasne, *Djem-Sultan: Etude sur la question d'Orient a la fin du XVᵉ siècle* (Paris, 1892); and I.H. Ertaylan, *Sultan Cem* (Istanbul, 1951). The Turkish memoirs were published under the title, *Vakiat-i Sultan Cem* (Istanbul, 1330 A.H.). See further, *EI2.* , s.v. "Djem," (H. Inalcik). For a collection of letters addressed to the sultan on this subject, see J. Lefort, *Documents grecs dans les Archives de Topkapi Sarayi, Contribution à l'histoire de Cem Sultan* (Ankara, 1981).
62. *Vakiat,* pp. 10–11.
63. Ahmad ibn Muhammad al-Khālidī, *Lubnān fī ʿahd al-Amīr Fakhr al-Dīn al-Ma ʿnī al-Thānī,* eds. Asad Rustum and Fuʾād Bustānī (Beirut, 1936, reprinted 1969), pp. 208–41, Mr. Arnon Gross, to whose unpublished study of this text I am indebted, has shown that the text is not, as the editors suggest, a "fake" but is an interpolation based on an authentic narrative.
64. Şerafettin Turan, "Barak Reis'in, Şehzade Cem mes'elesiyle ilgili olarak Savoie 'ya gönderilmesi," *Belleten* 26, no. 103 (1962): 539–55; V.L. Ménage, "The Mission of an Ottoman Secret Agent in France in 1486," *Journal of the Royal Asiatic Society* (1965): 112–32.
65. S. Skilliter, "The Sultan's Messenger, Gabriel Defrens: An Ottoman Master-Spy of the Sixteenth Century," *Wiener Zeitschrift für die Kunde des Morgenlandes,* ed. A. Tietze, vol. 68 (Vienna, 1976), pp. 47–59.
66. ʿUmarī, ed. M. Amari, "Al-ʿUmarī, Condizioni degli stati Cristiani dell' Occidente secondo una relazione di Domenichino Doria da Genova", *Atti R. Acad. Linc. Mem.,* 11 (1883): text p. 15, trans. p. 87. Hereafter cited as ʿUmarī (Amari).
67. Mehmed Efendi, p. 25; French transl., pp. 34–35.
68. Vasif, in Cevdet, 4: 349.
69. Azmi, p. 12.

70. A.W. Kinglake, *Eothen* (London, n.d.), pp. 9–11.
71. I'tişām al-Dīn, see C. A. Storey, *Persian Literature,* vol. 1, pt. 2, p. 1142. Cf. English transl., J. E. Alexander, *Mirza Itesa Modeen* (London, 1827).
72. *Masir-i Ṭalibī ya Sefarnāma-i Mīrzā Abū Ṭalib Khān,* ed. H. Khadīv-Jam (Tehran, 1974); cf. English trans., C. Stewart, *Travels of Mirza Abu Talib Khan . . .* (London, 1814). Also see Storey, *Persian Literature,* 1, pt. 2, pp. 878–79.
73. Seyyid Ali's report was published by Ahmed Refik in *Tarih-i Osmani Encümeni Mecmuasi,* 4 (1329/1911): 1246ff, 1332ff, 1378ff, 1458ff, 1548ff. See further M. Herbette, *Une ambassade Turque sous le Directoire,* Paris, 1902.
74. On Ali Aziz, see A. Tietze, "'Azīz Efendis Muhayyelat," *Oriens* 1 (1948): 248–329; E. Kuran, "Osmanli daimi elçisi Ali Aziz Efendi'-nin Alman şarkiyatçisi Friedrich von Diez ile Berlin'de ilmi ve fel-sefi muhaberati (1797)" *Belleten* 27 (1963): 45–58; and *EI2.,* s.v. "'Ali 'Azīz" (A. Tietze).
75. On these embassies, see T. Naff "Reform and the conduct of Ottoman Diplomacy in the Reign of Selim III, 1789–1807," *Journal of the American Oriental Society* 83 (1963): 295–315; E. Kuran, *Avrupa'da Osmanli İkamet Elçiliklerinin Kuruluş ve İlk Elçilerin Siyasi Faaliyetleri 1793–1821* (Ankara, 1968); S. J. Shaw, *Between Old and New* pp. 180ff.
76. On Mehmed Raif see S. J. Shaw, *Between Old and New,* index.
77. On the Egyptian student missions, see J. Heyworth-Dunne, *An Introduction to the History of Education in Modern Egypt* (London, 1938), pp. 104ff, 221ff, and *passim.*

There is an extensive literature on Sheikh Rifā'a in Arabic and in Western languages. See *EI1.,* s.v. 'Rifā'a Bey' (Chemoul); further, J. Heyworth-Dunne, "Rifā'ah Badawī Rāfi' aṭ-Ṭahtāwī: The Egyptian Revivalist", *BSOAS* 9 (1937–39): 961–67, 10 (1940–42): 399–415. The fullest treatment is that of Gilbert Delanoue, *Moralistes et politiques musulmans dans l'Egypte du XIXème siècle (1798–1882)* (Service de reproduction des theses, Lille, 1980), 1, chap. 5. Sheikh Rifā'a's travels in France, entitled *Takhliṣ al-ibriz fi talkhiṣ Bariz* (usually known as *al-Rihla*) has been printed a number of times. References are to the (Cairo, 1958) edition.

78. Published in I. Ra'in, *Safarname-i Mīrzā Ṣāliḥ Shīrāzī,* (Tehran, 1347s). See further Storey, *Persian Literature,* I, pt 2, pp. 1148–50, and Hafez Farman Farmayan, "The Forces of modernization in nineteenth century Iran: a historical survey," in W. R. Polk and R. L. Chambers (editors), *Beginnings of Modernization in the Middle East* (Chicago 1968), pp. 122ff.

Chapter V

1. *Irṣad.* See above chapter 3, n. 15.
2. See C.A. Nallino, "al-Khuwarizmi e il suo rifacimento della Geografia di Tolomeo" in *Raccolta di Scritti,* vol. 5 (Rome, 1944), pp. 458–532; D. M. Dunlop, "Muḥammad b. Mūsā al-Khwārizmi," *Journal of the Royal Asiatic Society* (1943): 248–50; and R. Wieber, *Nordwesteuropa nach der arabischen Bearbeitung der Ptolemäischen Geographie von Muḥammad b. Mūsā al-Hwārizmī* (Walldorf-Hessen, 1974).
3. The Muslim geographical literature of the Middle Ages is examined in two major works, one by A. Miquel, *La géographie humaine du monde musulman jusqu'au milieu du IIe siècle,* 3 vols. (Paris, 1967–80), especially vol. 2, *Géographie arabe et représentation du monde: la terre et l'étranger,* chapters 6 and 7 on eastern and western Europe; the other by I.J. Kračkovsky, *Istoriya Arabskoy Geografičeskoy Literatury, Izbranniye Sočineniya,* vol. 5 (Moscow-Leningrad, 1957), Arabic transl. by S.U. Hāshim, *Ta'rikh al-adab al-djughrāfi al-'arabī* (Cairo, 1963). For a briefer survey, see *EI*2. , s.v. "Djughrāfiya," (S. Maqbul Aḥmad). On medieval Muslim geographers' knowledge of Europe, see I. Guidi, "L'Europa occidentale negli antichi geografi arabi," *Florilegium M. de Vogüe* (1909): 263–69; E. Ashtor, "Che cosa sapevano i geografi Arabi dell'Europa occidentale?," *Rivista Storica Italiana* 81 (1969): 453–79; K. Jahn, "Das Christliche Abendland in der islamischen *Geschichtsschreibung* des Mittelalters," *Anzeiger der phil.-hist. Klasse der Österreichischen Akademie der Wissenschaften* 113 (1976): 1–19; Y.Q. al-Khūrī, "al-Jughrāfiyūn al-ʿArab wa-Urūba," *al-Abḥāth* 20 (1967): 357–92.
4. Ibn Khurradādhbeh, *Kitāb al-masālik wa'l-mamālik,* ed. M. J. de Goeje (Leiden, 1889), p. 155.
5. *Ibid.,* pp. 92–93.
6. *Ibid.,* p. 153. For an important recent study see M. Gil., "The Rādhānite Merchants and the Land of Rādhān," JESHO 18 (1974): 299–328.
7. Ibn al-Faqīh, *Mukhtaṣar Kitāb al-Buldān,* ed. M. J. de Goeje (Leiden, 1885); cf. French transl., H. Massé, *Abrégé des Livre des Pays* (Damascus, 1973) p. 8.
8. Ibn Rusteh, *Kitāb al-aʿlāq al-nafīsa,* ed. M. J. de Goeje (Leiden, 1892), p. 85; cf. French transl., G. Wiet, *Les Atours Precieux* (Cairo, 1958), p. 94.
9. Masʿūdī, *Kitāb al-tanbīh wa'l-ishrāf* (Beirut, 1965), pp. 23–24; cf. French transl., Carra de Vaux, *Macoudi, le livre de l'avertissement et de la révision* (Paris, 1897), pp. 38–39.
10. Masʿūdī, *Murūj al-dhahab,* ed. and transl. F. Barbier de Meynard and

Pavet du Courteille (Paris, 1861–77) 3: 66–67; *ibid.,* 2nd ed., C. Pellat (Beirut, 1966–70) 2: 145–46; cf. revised French transl., C. Pellat (Paris, 1962–71) 2: 342.

11. On Arabic accounts of the Vikings, see A. Melvinger, *Les premières incursions des Vikings en Occident d'après les sources arabes* (Uppsala, 1955); A. A. el-Hajji, "The Andalusian diplomatic relations with the Vikings . . ." The sources were collected by A. Seippel, *Rerum Normannicarum,* and translated into Norwegian by H. Birkeland, *Nordens Historie i Middelalderen etter Arabiske Kilder* (Oslo, 1954).

12. See *EI*2. , s.v. *"Asfar,"* (I. Goldziher) and *idem, Muslim Studies* vol. 1, transl. C.R. Barber and S.M. Stern (London, 1967), pp. 268–69.

13. Masʿūdī, *Murūj,* ed. Barbier de Meynard, 3: 69–72; C. Pellat ed., 2: 147–48; cf. Pellat transl. 2: 344–45. For an English translation and discussion, see B. Lewis, "Masʿūdī on the Kings of the 'Franks,' " *Al-Masʿūdī Millenary Commemoration Volume* (Aligarh, 1960), pp. 7–10.

14. Ibn Rusteh, p. 130; cf. Wiet transl., p. 146.

15. Yāqūt, s.v. "Rūmiya." On the Arabic accounts of Rome, see I. Guidi, "La descrizione di Roma nei geografi arabi," *Archivio della Società Romana di Storia Patria* 1 (1877): 173–218.

16. *Ibid.*

17. Qazvīnī, pp. 388–89; cf. Jacob, pp. 26–27; cf. Miquel, pp. 1057–58. For a later account of catching a "large fish," probably a whale, see *Vakiat-i Sultan Cem,* pp. 9–10.

18. A. Kunik and V. Rosen, *Izvestiya al-Bekri,* pp. 34–35; T. Kowalski, *Relatio Ibrāhīm ibn Jaʿkūb,* pp. 2–3; Bakri, *Jughrāfiya,* ed. A. A. el-Hajji, pp. 160–63; G. Jacob, *Arabische Berichte,* pp. 12–13.

19. Qazvīnī, pp. 334–35; cf. Jacob, pp. 31–32; cf. Miquel, pp. 1052–53.

20. Zuhrī, pp. 229–30/77–78; cf. French transl., p. 93.

21. Idrīsī, *Opus Geographicum,* ed. A. Bombaci *et.al.,* fasc. 8 (Naples, 1978), p. 944; cf. A. F. L. Beeston, "Idrisi's Account of the British Isles," *BSOAS* 13 (1950): 267.

22. Idrīsī, *Opus,* fasc. 8, p. 946.

23. *Ibid.,* pp. 947–48.

24. Ibn Saʿīd, *Kitāb Basṭ al-arḍ fiʾl-ṭūl waʾl-ʿarḍ,* ed. J.V. Gines (Tetuan, 1958), p. 134. Cf. Abūʾl-Fida, *Taqwīm al-buldān,* ed. J.S. Reinaud and M. de Slane (Paris, 1840), p. 187; and Seippel, *Rerum Normannicarum,* p. 23.

25. Ibn Khaldūn, *al-Muqaddima,* ed. Quatremère (Paris, 1858) 3: 93; cf. French transl., M. de Slane, *Les Prolégomènes* (Paris, 1863–68) 3: 129; cf. English transl., F. Rosenthal, *The Muqaddima* (New York-London, 1958) 3: 117–18.

26. Ibn Khaldūn, *Kitāb al-ʿIbar* 6 (Cairo, 1867): 290–91.

27. See K. Jahn's partial edition with French translation of Rashīd al-

Dīn's section on Europe, *Histoire universelle de Rasīd ad-Dīn,* and his later German translation, *Die Frankengeschichte* . . . See further, K. Jahn, "Die Erweiterung unseres Geschichtbildes durch Rašīd al-Dīn," *Anzeiger der phil.-hist. Klasse der Österreichischen Akad. der Wiss.* (1970): 139–49 and J. A. Boyle, "Rashīd al-Dīn and the Franks," *Central Asian Journal* 14 (1970): 62–67.

28. Rashīd al-Dīn, *Histoire,* pp. 5–18; Frankengeschichte, p. 49.

29. On Piri Reis and his map, see P. Kahle, *Die verschollene Columbus-Karte von Amerika vom Jahre 1498 in einer türkischen Weltkarte von 1513* (Berlin-Leipzig, 1932); R. Almagia, "Il mappamondo di Piri Reis la carte di Colombo del 1498," *Societa Geografica Italiana, Bolletino* 17 (1934): 442–49; E. Braunlich, "Zwei türkische Weltkarten aus dem Zeitalter der grossen Entdeckungen," *Berichte . . . Verhandl. Sächs. Ak. Wiss. Leipzig, Phil. Hist. Kl.* 89, pt. 1 (1939); Afetinan, *Piri Reis'in Amerika haritasi 1513–1528* (Ankara, 1954). On Ottoman geographical literature in general, see *EI2.*, s.v. *"Djughrāfiyā,"* vi, the article by F. Taeschner; *idem,* "Die geographische Literatur der Osmanen," *Zeitschrift der Deutschen Morgenländischen Gesellschaft* 77 (1923): 31–80; A. Adnan-Adivar, *La science chez les Turcs Ottomans* (Paris, 1939); *idem, Osmanlı Turklerinde Ilim* (Istanbul, 1943)—a fuller Turkish version of *La science.*

30. *Tarih al-Hind al-Garbi.*

31. Adnan-Adivar, *Ilim,* p. 73, citing d'Avezac, "Mappemonde Turque de 1559," *Acad. Inscr. et Belles Lettres* (Paris, 1865).

32. Kâtib Çelebi, *Mīzān al-haqq fī ikhtiyār al-ahaqq* (Istanbul, 1268 A.H.), p. 136; cf. English translation, G. L. Lewis, *The Balance of Truth* (London, 1957), p. 136.

33. Adnan-Adivar, *Science,* p. 121; *Ilim,* p. 134.

34. *Ibid.,* p. 122; *Ilim,* p. 135.

35. *Ibid.,* p. 135; *Ilim,* p. 153.

36. Vasif, *Tarih,* 2: 70; cited in J. von Hammer, *Geschichte des Osmanischen Reiches,* 2nd. ed. (Pest, 1834–36) 4: 602 and *idem,* French transl. by J. J. Hellert, *Histoire de l'Empire Ottoman* (Paris, 1835ff) 16: 248–49.

37. Hammer, *Histoire,* 16: 249 note.

38. Âli, *Künh al-ahbar* (Istanbul, 1869) 5: 9–14; *idem, Meva'iddü'n-Nefa'is fi kava'idi'l-mecalis* (Istanbul, 1956) facs. 152–53.

39. Evliya, 7: 224–25; cf. Kreutel, p. 39.

40. Oruç, ed. Babinger, p. 67. On Mehmed's alleged interest in Western scholarship, see F. Babinger, *Mehmed the Conqueror and His Time,* transl. R. Mannheim (Princeton, 1978), pp. 494ff.

41. On these works, see B. Lewis, "The Use by Muslim Historians of Non-Muslim Sources" in *Islam in History* (London, 1973), pp. 101–14.

42. V. L. Ménage, "Three Ottoman Treatises . . ." p. 423.

43. On Huseyn Hezārfenn, see H. Wurm, *Der osmanische Historiker Hūseyn*

b. Ġaᶜfer, genannt Hezārfenn . . . (Freiburg im Breisgau, 1971), esp. pp. 122–49. The mss. of the *Tenkih* are listed in Babinger *GOW,* pp. 229–30. The ms. used here is in the Hunterian Museum in Glasgow (cf. JRAS, 1906, pp. 602ff).

44. Müneccimbaşi, *Saha'if al-ahbar* (Istanbul, 1285/1868–69) 2: 652.

45. Oruç, Kreutel transl., p. 95, (from ms.; the Turkish original of this section of Oruç's book is still unpublished).

46. Firdevsi-i Rumi, *Kutb-Name,* eds. I. Olgun and I. Parmaksizoğlu (Ankara, 1980), p. 74.

47. *Ibid.,* p. 93.

48. Selaniki, ms. Nuruosmaniye 184, cited by A. Refik, *Türkler ve Kraliçe Elizabet* (Istanbul, 1932), p. 9.

49. Kâtib Çelebi, *Fezleke* (Istanbul, 1276 A.H.), 2: 234, cf. Naima, *Tarih* (Istanbul, n.d.), 4: 94.

50. *Fezleke,* 2: 134–35; cf. Naima, 3: 69–70.

51. *Ibid.,* 1: 331–33; cf. Naima 2: 80–82.

52. *Ibid.,* 2: 382; cf. Naima 5: 267. For a detailed and documented life of Cappello, see G. Benzoni in *Dizionario Biografico degli Italiani,* XVIII (Rome, 1975), pp. 786-89.

53. Peçevi, 1: 106.

54. B. Lewis, "The Use by Muslim Historians. . . ." pp. 107–8, p. 314, n. 20, citing F. V. Kraelitz, "Der osmanische Historiker Ibrāhīm Pečewi" *Der Islam* 7 (1918): 252–60.

55. Peçevi, 1: 184 (on expedition in 1552); *idem,* 1: 255 (Morisco rising in 1568–70); *idem,* 1: 343–48 (expedition against Spain); *idem,* 1: 485 (the Moriscos); *idem,* 1: 106–8 (on gunpowder and printing).

56. Naima, 1: 40ff.

57. *Ibid.,* 1: 12.

58. Silihdar, *Nusretname,* fols. 257–58. I owe this reference to Dr. C. J. Heywood.

59. Şem'danizade, 3: 21–22.

60. *Ibid.,* 1: 42–43.

61. *Icmal-i ahval-i Avrupa.* Süleymaniye Library, Esat Efendi Kismi, no. 2062. See V. L. Ménage, "Three Ottoman Treatises. . . ." pp. 425ff.

62. V. L. Ménage, "Three Ottoman Treatises. . . ." p. 428.

63. For details, see B. Lewis, *Islam in History,* p. 314 n. 26.

Chapter VI

1. F. Kraelitz, "Bericht über den Zug . . . ," p. 17.

2. Thus, the Tatar may be rhymed as *ṣabā-raftâr aduw-shikâr,* "moving

like the east wind, hunting the enemy," or simply as *bad-raftâr,* "of bad demeanour."

3. E. Prokosch, *Molla und Diplomat* (Graz, 1972), p. 19, translated from an unpublished Turkish manuscript.

4. *Irşad.* See above chapt. 3, n. 15.

5. R. Kreutel, *Kara Mustafa vor Wien* (Graz, 1955), pp. 140–41, translated from an unpublished Turkish manuscript.

6. Evliya, 6:224–25; cf. Kreutel, p. 39.

7. A. Hess, "The Moriscos: An Ottoman Fifth Column in Sixteenth Century Spain," *American Historical Review* 74 (1968): 19, citing Feridun, *Münşa'at al-salatin,* 2nd ed., (Istanbul, 1275 A.H.), 2: 542; Feridun, *Münşa'āt,* 1st ed. (Istanbul, 1265), 2: 458. On Moriscos, see also above p. 180.

8. S. Skilliter, *William Harborne and the Trade with Turkey 1578–1582: A Documentary Study of the First Anglo-Ottoman Relations* (Oxford, 1977), p. 37, citing Feridun, *Münşa'at,* 2nd ed., 2: 543; Feridun, *Münşa'āt,* 1st ed., 2: 450.

9. Yāqūt, s.v. "Rūmiya."

10. N. V. Khanikov reads this as a reference to the anti-Pope, Cardinal Peter, who had adopted the style of Anacletus II; see Khanikov in *Journal Asiatique* 4 (1864): 152 and text p. 161 of commentary.

11. Ibn Wāṣil, 4: 249.

12. Qalqashandī, 8: 42ff. The odd title "protector of bridges" may be an echo of *Pontifex Maximus.*

13. *Irşād,* see above, chap. 3, n. 15.

14. Ghassānī, pp. 52ff, 67ff; cf. Sauvaire, pp. 152ff, 162ff. The editor of the Arabic text omits some of the anti-Christian comments.

15. Ibn Wāṣil, 4: 248–49.

16. Ghazzāl, p. 24; cf. H. Pérès, *L'Espagne revue par les voyageurs Musulmans de 1610 à 1930* (Paris, 1937), pp. 29–30.

17. Azmi, p. 16.

18. F. Kraelitz, "Bericht . . . ," pp. 26ff.

19. Resmi, *Sefaretname-i Ahmet Resmi Prusya Kirali Büyük Fredrik nezdine sefaretle giden Giridi Ahmet Resmi Efindi'nin takriridir* (Istanbul, 1303 A.H.), p. 18.

20. Miknāsī, *al-Iksīr fi fikāk al-asīr,* ed. M. al-Fāsī (Rabat, 1965), *passim.*

21. Cevdet, 6: 394ff.

22. Turkish text in E. Z. Karal, *Fransa-Misir ve Osmanli Imparatorlugu (1797–1802)* (Istanbul, 1938), p. 108; Arabic in Shihāb, *Ta'rīkh Ahmad Bāshā al-Jazzār,* ed. A. Chibli and J. A. Khalife (Beirut, 1955), p. 125.

Chapter VII

1. B. Lewis, *Islam: from the Prophet Muḥammad to the Capture of Constantinople* (New York, 1974), 2:154, citing Jāḥiẓ (attrib.), *Al-Tabaṣṣur bi'l-tijāra,* ed. H. H. 'Abd al-Wahhāb (Cairo, 1354/1935).
2. Qazvīnī, p. 388; cf. Jacob, pp. 25–26; cf. Miquel, pp. 1058–59.
3. Ibn Saʿīd, p. 134.
4. Rashīd al-Dīn, *Histoire,* pp. 4–5/17–18; *Frankengeschichte,* pp. 48–49.
5. Ibn Ḥawqal, *Kitāb Ṣūrat al-arḍ,* ed. J. H. Kraemer (Leiden, 1938), p. 110; cf. French translation, J. H. Kramers and G. Wiet, *Configuration de la terre* (Beirut and Paris, 1964), p. 109; cf. C. Verlinden, *L'Esclavage dans l'Europe médiévale,* I, *Péninsule Ibérique—France* (Bruges, 1955), p. 217; on the Ṣaqāliba, see R. Dozy, *Histoire des Musulmans d'Espagne,* 2nd ed., revised by E. Lévi-Provençal (Leiden, 1932), 2: 154, citing Liudprand, *Antapodosis,* bk. 6, chap. 6.
6. On the Slavs under the Fatimids, see I. Hrbek, "Die Slaven im Dienste der Fatimiden," *Archiv Orientalni* 21 (1953): 543–81.
7. W. Heyd, *Histoire du Commerce du Levant au Moyen-Age,* trans. F. Raynaud (Amsterdam, 1967) 1: 95; I. Hrbek, "Die Slaven . . . ," p. 548.
8. On the Tatars and their activities, see A. Fisher, *The Crimean Tatars* (Stanford, 1978); *idem,* "Muscovy and the Black Sea Slave Trade," *Canadian American Slavic Studies* 6 (1972):575–94; and *idem, The Russian Annexation of the Crimea 1772–1783* (Cambridge, 1970).
9. E. J. W. Gibb, *A History of Ottoman Poetry,* Vol. 3 (London, 1904), p. 217.
10. On these works, see H. Müller, *Die Kunst des Sklavenkaufs* (Freiburg, 1980).
11. On these and other stories, see A. D. Alderson, *The Structure of the Ottoman Dynasty* (Oxford, 1956), pp. 85ff; Çağatay Uluçay, *Harem* II (Ankara, 1971); *idem, Padişahlarin Kadinlari ve Kizlari* (Ankara, 1980); E. Rossi, "La Sultana Nūr Bānū (Cecilia Venier-Baffo) moglie di Selim II (1566–1574) e madre di Murad III (1574–1595)," *Oriente Moderno* 33 (1953): 433–41; S. A. Skilliter, "Three Letters from the Ottoman 'Sultana' Ṣāfiye to Queen Elizabeth I" in *Documents from Islamic Chanceries,* ed. S. M. Stern (Oxford, 1965), pp. 119–57.
12. Ibn al-Ṭuwayr, cited by al-Maqrīzī, *al-Mawāʿiz waʾl-iʿtibār bi-dhikr al-khiṭaṭ waʾl-āthār* (Būlāq, 1270/1853) 1: 444.
13. J. Richard, "An account of the Battle of Hattin," *Speculum,* 27 (1952): 168–77.
14. *Bulla in Cena Domini,* Clement VII *anno* 1527, Urban VIII *anno* 1627. Cited in K. Pfaff, "Beiträge zur Geschichte der Abendmahlsbulle vom 16. bis 18. Jahrhundert," *Römische Quartalschrift für christliche Altertumskunde* 38 (1930): 38–39.

15. *CSP* Spanish (1568–79) London 1894 (n. 609), p. 706, Spanish ambassador in London to Phillip II (28 Nov. 1579); *CSP* Venetian (1603–07), p. 326; letter dated 28 Feb. 1605 o.s. from Venetian consul in Melos to Bailo in Istanbul. I owe the references in this and the preceding note to the late V. J. Parry.
16. Qazvīnī, p. 362; cf. Jacob, p. 32.
17. Ibn Saʿīd, p. 134.
18. Rashīd al-Dīn, *Histoire,* pp. 4–5/18; *Frankengeschichte,* p. 49.
19. N. Beldiceanu, *Les actes des premiers Sultans* vol. 1 (Paris, 1960), p. 127.
20. Peçevi, 1:365; translated in B. Lewis, *Istanbul and the Civilization of the Ottoman Empire* (Norman, 1963), pp. 133–35.
21. Ghassānī, pp. 44–45; cf. Sauvaire, pp. 97–99.
22. Vasif, in Cevdet, 4:357; cf. Barbier de Meynard, pp. 520–21.
23. Mehmed Efendi, p. 109; cf. French transl., p. 163.
24. Resmi, *Sefaretname-i . . . Prusya . . . ,* pp. 27–28, 33, and 36.
25. Azmi, *passim.*
26. Hashmet, *Intisāb al-mulūk,* appended to *Dīvān* (Būlāq, 1842), pp. 8–9.
27. *Masīr-i Ṭālibī yā Safarnāma-i Mīrzā Abū Ṭalib Khān,* ed. H. Khadīv-Jam (Tehran, 1974), p. 201ff; cf. English transl., C. Stewart, *Travels of Mirza Abu Taleb Khan . . . ,* (London, 1814), vol. 2, chap. 13:1ff.
28. Karal, *Halet,* pp. 32–33.

Chapter VIII

1. Cited in *EI*2. , s.v. "Ḳaysar" (R. Paret and I. Shahid).
2. Ṭabarī, *Ta'rīkh al-rusul wa'l-mulūk,* ed. M. J. De Goeje (Leiden, 1879–1901), 3: 695. Hārūn may have been insulted because Nikephoras had previously addressed him as "King of the Arabs"—a demeaning title in Muslim terms.
3. Ghassānī, p. 41; cf. Sauvaire, pp. 90–91. *Vakiat-i Sultan Cem,* p. 21.
4. S. M. Stern, "An Embassy of the Byzantine Emperor to the Fatimid Caliph al-Muʿizz", *Byzantion* 20 (1950): 239–58.
5. Many examples are preserved in the Public Records Office in London. For further references, see *EI*2. , s.v. "Diplomatic."
6. F. Kraelitz, "Bericht . . . ," pp. 24–25. Kraelitz's German translation of this expression is based on a misunderstanding of the Turkish text.
7. Public Record Office SP 102/61/14.
8. Ghassānī, pp. 80ff.; cf. Sauvaire, pp. 181ff.
9. Mehmed Efendi, p. 65; cf. French transl. p. 97.

10. Azmī, pp. 46ff and *passim.*
11. Abū 'l-Faraj al-Iṣfahānī, *Kitāb al-Aghānī* (Bulāq, 1285) 17: 14; English translation in B. Lewis, *Islam,* 1: 27.
12. Qalqashandī, 8: 53.
13. Rashīd al-Dīn, *Histoire,* pp. 2–3/15–16; *Frankengeschichte,* pp. 46–47.
14. ʿUmarī, (Amari) text pp. 96–97; translation, p. 80.
15. Qalqashandī, 8: 46–48.
16. Rashīd al-Dīn, *Histoire,* pp. 7–8/21; *Frankengeschichte,* pp. 51–52.
17. *Irşād.* See above, chap. 3, n. 15.
18. *Icmāl-i ahval-i Avrupa.* See above, chap. 5, n. 59.
19. Mehmed Efendi, pp. 33–36.
20. Şem'danizade, 2: 22.
21. Karal, *Halet,* pp. 32–44, and 62. On Halet's audience with Napoleon, see B. Flemming "Ḥālet Efendis zweite Audienz bei Napoleon," *Rocznik Orientalistyczny* 37 (1976): 129–36.
22. Asim, 1: 62, 76, 78, 175, 265, and 374–376.
23. Abū Ṭālib, *Masir,* p. 242; cf. Stewart, 2:55.
24. *Ibid.,* pp. 250–51; cf. Stewart, 2:81.
25. Qazvinī, ed. Wüstenfeld, p. 410; cf. Jacob, pp. 21–22.
26. Usāma, pp. 138–39; cf. Hitti, pp. 167–68.
27. Jabartī, 3:117ff.
28. Abū Ṭālib, *Masir,* pp. 278–79; cf. Stewart, pp. 101–4.
29. Rifāʿa, pp. 120 and 148.

Chapter IX

1. B. Goldstein, "The Survival of Arabic Astronomy in Hebrew," *Journal for the History of Arab Science* 3 (Spring, 1979): 31–45.
2. Usāma, pp. 132–33; cf. Hitti, p. 162.
3. U. Heyd, "The Ottoman 'Ulema' and Westernization in the Time of Selim III and Mahmud II," *Scripta Hierosolymitana,* Vol. IX: *Studies in Islamic History and Civilization,* ed. U. Heyd (Jerusalem, 1961), pp. 74–77.
4. Qur'ān, 9.36.
5. On mining in the Ottoman Empire, see R. Anhegger, *Beitraege zur Geschichte des Bergbaus im Osmanischen Reich* (Istanbul, 1943).
6. On these matters I have profited from a paper by Dr. Rhoads Murphey, "The Ottomans and Technology," presented to the Second International Congress on the Social and Economic History of Turkey, Strasbourg, 1980. The Ottoman use of firearms was extensively discussed by V. J. Parry in *EI*2. , s.v. "Bārūd" and in "Materi-

als of War in the Ottoman Empire," *Studies in the Economic History of the Middle East,* ed. M. A. Cook (London, 1970), pp. 219–29.

7. U. Heyd, "Moses Hamon, Chief Jewish Physician to Sultan Suleyman the Magnificent," *Oriens* 16 (1963): 153, citing Nicholas de Nicolay, bk. 3, chap. 12.

8. *Ibid.,* Nicholas de Nicolay, *loc. cit.,* "bien sçavants en la Theórique et experimentez en pratique."

9. U. Heyd, "An Unknown Turkish Treatise by a Jewish Physician under Suleyman the Magnificent," *Eretz-Israel* 7 (1963): 48–53.

10. U. Heyd, "Moses Hamon . . . ," pp. 168–69.

11. Adnan-Adivar, *Science,* pp. 97–98; *Ilim,* pp. 112–13. A Persian physician called Bahā al-Dawla (d. ca. 1510), in a work entitled *Khulāsat al-Tajārib,* the quintessence of experience, wrote a few pages on syphilis, which he calls "the Armenian sore" or "the Frankish pox." According to this author, the disease originated in Europe, from which it was brought to Istanbul and the Near East. It appeared in Azerbayjan in 1498, and spread from thence to Iraq and Iran (Haskell Isaacs, "European influences in Islamic medicine," *Mashriq: Proceedings of the Eastern Mediterranean Seminar, University of Manchester 1977–1978* [Manchester, 1981, pp. 25–26]). The same article also discusses a work produced in the Ottoman lands in the second half of the seventeenth century, by the Syrian physician of Sultan Mehmed IV.

12. *Idem, Science,* pp. 128–29; *Ilim,* pp. 141–43.

13. Mehmed Efendi, pp. 26ff and 122; cf. French transl. pp. 36–40, 186–90.

14. *Tarih-i 'Izzi* (Istanbul, 1199 A.H.), pp. 190a–190b.

15. Busbecq, pp. 213–14; cf. E. G. Forster, p. 135; cf. Forster and Daniell, 1: 125.

16. O. Kurz, *European Clocks and Watches in the Near East* (London, 1975), pp. 70–71, citing Rousseau, *Confessions,* English transl. (1891), p. 3; Voltaire, *Correspondence,* ed. T. Bestermann, vol. 78 (Geneva 1962), p. 127; and S. Tekeli, *16'inci Asirda Osmanlilarda saat ve Takiyuddin'in "Mekanik saat konstruksuyonouna dair en parlak yildizlar" adli eseri* (Ankara, 1966).

17. Jāmī, *Salāmān va-Absāl* (Tehran, 1306s), p. 36; English translation by A. J. Arberry, *Fitzgerald's Salaman and Absal* (Cambridge, 1956), p. 146; cit. Lynn White Jr., *Medicine, Religion and Technology* (Berkeley and Los Angeles, 1978), p. 88.

18. Janikli Ali Pasha's memorandum survives in a ms. in the Upsala University Library.

19. Adnan-Adivar, *Science,* pp. 142ff; *Ilim,* pp. 161–63.

20. Baron F. de Tott, *Memoires* (Maestricht, 1785) 3: 149.

21. G. Toderini, *Letteratura turchesca* (Venice, 1787) 1: 177ff.

22. Aubert du Bayet (later Dubayet) was born in New Orleans and had fought in the American Revolution under Lafayette. He had been active in the French Revolution from the start and sat in the French legislative assembly as deputy for Grenoble.
23. B. Lewis, *Emergence,* pp. 85ff.

Chapter X

1. S.K. Yetkin, *L'Architecture Turque en Turquie* (Paris, 1962), pp. 133ff.
2. Mehmed Efendi, p. 199; cf. Kreutel and Spies (Bonn, 1954), p. 71, where the same saying is quoted.
3. A. Refik, *Hicri on ikinci asirda Istanbul hayati (1100–1200)* (Istanbul, 1930), p. 58; Adnan-Adivar, *Science,* pp. 125–26; idem, *Ilim,* p. 133; Berkes, *Secularism,* p. 27.
4. Karal, *Tanzimat,* p. 19; Berkes, *Secularism,* p. 33.
5. Mehmed Efendi, p. 91; cf. French transl., p. 137.
6. *Ibid.,* pp. 139–40; cf. French transl., p. 214.
7. *Ibid.,* p. 78; cf. French transl., p. 118.
8. *Ibid.,* p. 109; cf. French transl., p. 163. Behzad was a famous Persian painter; Mani, the founder of the Manichean religion, is famed in Muslim legend as a great artist.
9. F. Babinger, "Vier Bauvorschläge Leonardo da Vinci's an Sultan Bajezid II. (102/3)," *Nachrichten der Akad. der Wiss. in Göttingen, I. Phil.-Hist. Klasse,* no. 1 (1952): 1–20; idem, "Zwei Bildnisse Mehmed II von Gentile Bellini," *Zeitschrift für Kulturaustausch* 12 (1962): 178–82; J. von Karabacek, *Abendländische Künstler zu Konstantinopel im XV. und XVI. Jahrhundert:* I, *Italienische Künstler am Hofe Muhammads II. des Eroberers 1451–1481* (Vienna, 1918).
10. N. Atasoy, "Nakkaş Osman'in padişah portreleri albümü," *Türkiyemiz* 6 (1972): 2–14 where color prints of the twelve sultans, from Osman to Murad III, are given.
11. See A. Boppe, *Les peintres du Bosphore* (Paris, 1911); and R. van Luttervelt, *De "Turkse" Schilderijen van J.B. Vanmour en zijn School* (Istanbul, 1958).
12. On Turkish painting and decoration, see G. M. Meredith-Owens, *Turkish Miniatures* (London, 1963), p. 16; N. Atasoy and F. Çağman, *Turkish Miniature Painting* (Istanbul, 1974); G. Renda, *Batililaşma döneminde Türk resim sanati* (Ankara, 1977).
13. A. Destrée, "L'ouverture de la Perse à l'influence européenne sous les Rois Safavides et les incidences de cette influence sur l'évolution de l'art de la miniature," *Correspondence d'Orient* 13–14 (1968): 91–104.

14. Cited in W. Blunt, *Isfahan Pearl of Persia* (London and Toronto, 1966), p. 100.

15. Cited in A. Destrée, "L'ouverture . . . ," p. 97.

16. I. Stchoukine, *Les peintures des manuscrits de Shah 'Abbas I*ʳ (Paris, 1964).

17. B. Gray, "A Fatimid Drawing," *British Museum Quarterly* 12 (1938): 91–96.

18. See facsimiles in Jahn (ed.), Rashīd al-Dīn, *Frankengeschichte;* D. S. Rice, "The seasons and the labors of the months in Islamic art," *Ars Orientalis,* I (1954), pp. 1–39.

19. On Levni, see S. Ünver, *Levni* (Istanbul, 1957).

20. The date in the colophon (1190/1776) is certainly wrong, as the Frenchwoman is depicted wearing a Phrygian cap with tricolor. A similar but rather better ms. in the Istanbul University Library is dated 1206/1793. See Norah M. Titley, *Miniatures from Turkish Manuscripts* (London, 1981), n. 23. See further, G. Renda, *Batılılaşma . . . ,* pp. 220ff; E. Binney, *Turkish Miniature Paintings and Manuscripts* (New York, 1973) p. 102.

21. G. Renda, *Batılılaşma, passim.*

22. Qazvīnī, p. 404; cf. Jacob, p. 29; cf. Miquel, p. 1062.

23. Evliya, 7:312; cf. Kreutel, p. 185.

24. Mehmed Efendi, pp. 83ff; cf. French transl. pp. 127–31.

25. Ghassānī, p. 97ff.; cf. Sauvaire, p. 277ff; cf. Miknāsī, pp. 624–25.

26. Vasif, in Cevdet, 4:355; cf. Barbier de Meynard, p. 518.

27. E. de Leone, *L'Impero Ottomano nel primo periodo delle riforme (Tanzimat) secondo fonti italiani* (Milan, 1967), pp. 58–59, citing Cesare Vimercati, *Constantinople e l'Egitto* (Prato, 1849), p. 65.

28. A. Slade, *Records of Travel in Turkey, Greece . . .* (London, 1832) 1: 135–36. On the harem orchestra, see Princess Musbah Haidar, *Arabesque,* revised ed., (London, 1968), p. 61.

29. Ghassānī, p. 62; cf. Sauvaire p. 141.

30. Ghazāl, p. 20; cf. Miknāsī, pp. 107–9 and 139.

31. Hatti in *Tarih-i Izzi,* pp. 190ff.

32. On the theatre, see A. Bombaci, "Rappresentazioni drammatiche di Anatolia," *Oriens* 16 (1963): 171–93; *idem,* "Ortaoyunu," *Wiener Zeitschrift für die Kunde des Morgenlandes* 56 (1960): 285–97; M. And, *A History of Theatre and Popular Entertainment in Turkey* (Ankara, 1963–64); *idem, Karagöz, Turkish Shadow Theatre* (Ankara, 1975).

33. Vasif, in Cevdet, 4: 355; cf. Barbier de Meynard, p. 518.

34. Miknāsī, pp. 52 and 70.

35. Evliya, 7: 267; cf. Kreutel, p. 108.

36. Bibliotheque National, Arabe no. 6243. See Blochet, Catalogue, p. 219.

Chapter XI

1. Sir William Jones, "A Prefatory Discussion to an Essay on the History of the Turks," in *The Works of Sir William Jones,* vol. 2 (London, 1807), pp. 456–57.
2. Ibn Rusteh, pp. 129–30.
3. Qazvīnī, pp. 334–35; cf. Jacob, p. 32; cf. Miquel, p. 1053.
4. Abū Ṭālib, *Masir,* p. 74; cf. Stewart, pp. 135–37.
5. Evliya, 7: 318–19; cf. Kreutel, pp. 194–95.
6. Rifāʿa, pp. 119–20.
7. Abū Ṭālib, *Masir,* p. 268; cf. Stewart, pp. 135–37.
8. Vasif, pp. 349, 351; cf. Barbier de Meynard, pp. 508, 512.
9. *Sharḥ-i maʿmūriyat-i Ājūdān bāshī . . . ,* p. 385; Bausani, "Un manoscritto persiano . . . ," pp. 502–3.
10. On al-Ghazāl, see above, chap. 4, note 9.
11. Qazvīnī, pp. 404 and 408; cf. Jacob, pp. 29, 30–31; cf. Miquel, p. 1062. Also cf. Jacob p. 14 and Kunik-Rosen, p. 37.
12. Usāma, pp. 135–36; cf. Hitti, pp. 164–65.
13. Ibn Jubayr, pp. 305–6; cf. Broadhurst, pp. 320–21.
14. Evliya, 7: 318–19; cf. Kreutel, pp. 194–95.
15. Ghazāl, pp. 12 and 23.
16. Mehmed Efendi, p. 25; cf. French transl., pp. 34–35.
17. Abū Ṭālib, *Masir,* pp. 225–26; cf. Stewart, 2:27–31.
18. *Ibid.,* pp. 315–16; cf. Stewart, 2:254–55.
19. *Ibid.,* p. 305; cf. Stewart, 2:255.
20. On Fazil see E. J. W. Gibb, *Ottoman Poetry,* 4:220 ff. On illustrated mss. of his poem, see above Chapter X, n. 20.
21. Karal, *Halet,* pp. 33–34.
22. Rifāʿa, pp. 123ff.
23. Ājūdānbāshī, p. 281; Bausani, "Un manoscritto persiano . . . ," pp. 496–97.
24. Mehmed Efendi, p. 112; cf. French transl. p. 169.
25. The original Persian text was edited and published by his son and another person in Calcutta in 1812. An Urdu version appeared in Muradabad in India in 1904. A scholarly edition of the text—the first in Iran—was published in Tehran a few years ago. In contrast, an English version published in London in 1810 enjoyed considerable success. It was republished in a second edition, with some additional matter, in 1812. A French translation from the English appeared in Paris in 1811 and another in 1819. A German translation from the French was published in Vienna in 1813. The English version is, to put it charitably, remarkably free and is

probably the result of some form of oral translation through an intermediary.

Chapter XII

1. S. Moreh, ed. and trans., *Al-Jabartī's Chronicle of the First Seven Months of the French Occupation of Egypt* (Leiden, 1975), p. 117.
2. Jabartī, *ʿAjā'ib*, 3: 34–35.
3. *Dictionnaire français-arabe d'Ellious Bochtor Egyptien* . . . *revu et augmenté par Caussin de Perceval* (Paris, 1828–29).
4. Mehmed Efendi, p. 43.
5. Azmi, pp. 30–31.
6. See above ch. XI note 8.
7. Ghassānī, p. 67; cf. Sauvaire, p. 150.
8. On this and other publications, see L. Lagarde, "Note sur les journaux français de Constantinople à l'époque révolutionnaire," *Journal Asiatique* 236 (1948): 271–76; R. Clogg, "A Further Note on the French Newspapers of Istanbul during the Revolutionary Period," *Belleten* 39 (1975): 483–90; and *EI2.*, s.v. "Djarīda."
9. Lûtfi, *Tarih* 3: 100; cf. A. Emin, *The Development of Modern Turkey as Measured by its Press* (New York, 1914), p. 28.
10. Rifāʿa, p. 50.
11. On the first translation movement in Egypt, see Jamal al-Dīn al-Shayyāl, *Tarīkh al-tarjama wa 'l-ḥaraka al-thaqāfiyya fī ʿaṣr Muḥammad ʿAlī* (Cairo, 1951), and J. Heyworth-Dunne, "Printing and Translation under Muḥammad ʿAlī," *JRAS* (1940), pp. 325–49.
12. Details in the amplified Russian translation of Storey, *Persian Literature* by Y.E. Bregel, *Persidskaya Literatura* (Moscow, 1972), pt. 2, p. 1298, where other Persian works on American and European history are listed.

Sources of Illustrations

Three miniatures from the *Jarūn-nāma,* a Persian heroic poem by Qadrī on the recapture of Hormūz from the Portuguese. Dated 1697, Isfahan style (B. L. add 7801, Persian).

1) Portuguese repelling Imām Kuli Khān's army at Hormūz (Folio 43a).
2) Setting the fortress of Hormūz on fire (Folio 48a).
3) Imām Kuli Khān receiving deputation of two Portuguese (Folio 58).

From a seventeenth-century Turkish album, prepared by a Turkish artist for a European ambassador (published by F. Taeschner), *Alt-Stambuler Hof und Volksleben, Ein türkisches Miniaturalbum aus dem 17. Jahrhundert* Hanover, 1925, Plates 14, 51–53.

4) Venetians bombard Tenedos.
5) Procession of the Bailo to his audience.
6) The Bailo is perfumed during his audience with the grand vizier.
7) Audience of the Bailo with the grand vizier.

8) Lacquered book-cover of the time of Fatḥ ʿAlī Shah (B. L. Or. 5302). Fatḥ ʿAlī Shāh receiving a foreign deputation, probably at Nawrūz.

9) Fustāt—twelfth century. A battle under the walls of a town. On paper, showing a warrior with round (Muslim) shield fighting others with kite-shaped (Norman) shields—at least four with mail (B. L. O.R. 1938–3–12–01).

From illustrated Persian manuscripts of Rashīd al-Dīn, published in Karl Jahn, *Die Frankengeschichte des Rašīd ad-Dīn* (Vienna, 1977).

10) Popes Honorius III, Gregory IX, Celestinus IV, Emperors Otto IV, Frederick II, Henry of Thüringia (Topkapi Treasure, Number 1654, dated 717/1317, Folio 311r, Plate 33).
11) Pope and Emperor (Topkapi Treasure, Number 1653, early fifteenth century, Folio 416r, Plate 46).

12 and 13) Wall paintings from the Chihil Sutun pavilion in Isfahan (late sixteenth century, rebuilt 1706) showing European visitors.

Persian miniatures, sixteenth and seventeenth centuries (B. L.)

14) A court page in European dress (O. R. 1948–12–11–015).
15) A youth, and a lady in European costume. The signatures of Riẓā-i ʿAbbāsī are not genuine (O. R. 1920–9–17–0294).
16) A European page holding a wine cup, Persia, period of Shah ʿAbbās II (1642–66) (O. R. 1948–10–0–062).
17) A prince, possibly Shāh Sulaymān (1667–94) with attendants, including a European and Mughal courtier. Inscribed, atrributed to Muhammad (or Paolo) Zamān. Persia, about 1680 A. D. (O. R. 1948–12–11–019).

Miniatures from Muslim India (B. L.)

From a ms. of the divan of Mīr Qamar al-Dīn Minnat. Eighteenth century (before 1792). Indian. (B. L. Or. 6633).

18) Warren Hastings in European court dress (Folio 67a).
19) Richard Johnson in redcoat uniform, holding tricorne and sitting on a chair. Servant holding umbrella and chauri (Folio 68a).

20) Three men in early seventeenth-century European dress. Possibly Portuguese at Mughal Court. Indian Album (B. L. add. 7468) (Folio 9).
21) Arrival of the Castilian embassy led by Don Clavijo at the court

of Tīmūr. Dressed in the costume of English gentlemen of the time of George III. The leader of the deputation, hat in hand, holding out a letter to Tīmūr, who stands before his throne *(Malfūzāt-i Tīmūrī,* early nineteenth century, Indian) (B. L. Or. 158, Folio 322).

Miniatures by the Ottoman painter Levni.

22) Foreign ambassadors at palace festivities. Dragomans and guards behind them. From Süheyl Ünver, *Levni,* (Istanbul, 1951), Figure 10.
23) Young European gentlemen walking with stick in right hand and wearing purple coat. Signed Levni, early eighteenth century (B. L. O. R. 1960–11–12–01).
24) Young European gentlemen walking wearing red coat. Signed Levni, early eighteenth century. (B. L. O. R. 1960–11–12–02).

Illustrations to the *Book of Women* by Fazil Bey (B. L. Or. 7094, wrongly dated 1190/1776, probably 1793 or later).

25) Frank of Istanbul (Folio 29b).
26) Englishwoman (Folio 43b).
27) Frenchwoman (Folio 43a).
28) Austrian woman (Folio 41a).
29) Dutch woman (Folio 44a).
30) American woman (Folio 44b).

Index